Psychology for Speech Therapists

Psychology for Professional Groups

Series Editors: Antony J. Chapman and Anthony Gale

Psychology for Professional Groups is a new series of major textbooks published with the British Psychological Society. Each is edited by a teacher with expertise in the application of psychology to professional practice and covers the key topics in the training syllabus. The editors have drawn upon a series of specially commissioned topic chapters prepared by leading psychologists and have set them within the context of their various professions. A tutor manual is available for each text and includes practical exercises and projects, further reading and general guidance for the tutor. Each textbook shows in a fresh, original and authoritative way how psychology may be applied in a variety of professional settings, and how practitioners may improve their skills and gain a deeper understanding of themselves. There is also a general tutorial text incorporating the complete set of specialist chapters and their associated teaching materials.

Other titles

Psychology and Management. Cary L. Cooper
Psychology for Social Workers. Martin Herbert
Psychology for Teachers. David Fontana
Psychology for Physiotherapists. E. N. Dunkin
Psychology for Careers Counselling. Ruth Holdsworth
Psychology for Occupational Therapists. Fay Fransella
Psychology and Medicine. David Griffiths
Psychology for Nurses and Health Visitors. John Hall
Psychology and People: A tutorial text. Antony J. Chapman and Anthony Gale

Psychology for Speech Therapists

Harry Purser

First published 1982 by THE BRITISH PSYCHOLOGICAL SOCIET and THE MACMILLAN PRESS LTD.

Distributed by The Macmillan Press Ltd, London and Basingstoke. Associated companies and representatives throughout the world.

ISBN 0 333 31855 2 (hard cover)
ISBN 0 333 31885 4 (paper cover)

Printed in Great Britain by Wheatons of Exeter

Note: throughout these texts, the masculine pronouns have been used for succinctness and are intended to refer to both females and males.

The conclusions drawn and opinions expressed are those of the authors. They should not be taken to represent the views of the publishers.

Contents

Foreword

This book is one of a series, the principal aims of which are to illustrate how psychology can be applied in particular professional contexts, how it can improve the skills of practitioners, and how it can increase the practitioners' and students' understanding of themselves.

Psychology is taught to many groups of students and is now integrated within prescribed syllabuses for an increasing number of professions. The existing texts which teachers have been obliged to recommend are typically designed for broad and disparate purposes, and consequently they fail to reflect the special needs of students in professional training. The starting point for the series was the systematic distillation of views expressed in professional journals by those psychologists whose teaching specialisms relate to the applications of psychology. It soon became apparent that many fundamental topics were common to a number of syllabuses and courses; yet in general introductory textbooks these topics tend to be embedded amongst much superfluous material. Therefore, from within the British Psychological Society, we invited experienced teachers and authorities in their field to write review chapters on key topics. Forty-seven chapters covering 23 topics were then available for selection by the series' Volume Editors. The Volume Editors are also psychologists and they have had many years of involvement with their respective professions. In preparing their books, they have consulted formally with colleagues in those professions. Each of their books has its own combination of the specially-prepared chapters, set in the context of the specific professional practice.

Because psychology is only one component of the various training curricula, and because students generally have limited access to learned journals and specialist texts, our contributors to the series have restricted their use of references, while at the same time providing short lists of annotated readings. In addition, they have provided review questions to help students organize their learning and prepare for examinations. Further teaching materials, in the form of additional references, projects, exercises and class notes, are available in Tutor Manuals prepared for each book. A comprehensive tutorial text ('Psychology and People'), prepared by the Series Editors, combines in a single volume all the key topics, together with their associated teaching materials.

It is intended that new titles will be added to the series and that existing titles will be revised in the light of changing requirements. Evaluative and constructive comments, bearing on any aspect of the series, are most welcome and should be addressed to us at the BPS in Leicester.

In devising and developing the series we have had the good fortune to benefit from the advice and support of Dr Halla Beloff, Professor Philip Levy, Mr Allan Sakne and Mr John Winckler. A great burden has been borne by Mrs Gail Sheffield, who with skill, tact and courtesy, has managed the production of the series: to her and her colleagues at the BPS headquarters and at the Macmillan Press, we express our thanks.

Antony J. Chapman
UWIST, Cardiff

Anthony Gale
University of Southampton

May 1981

Introduction to Psychology and Speech Therapy

Harry Purser

Introduction

Sue W. is a speech therapist working from a city centre clinic. Each morning she sees four adult patients; some patients present a stutter, others have voice disorders and several are recovering from strokes. On two afternoons she runs groups for language delayed children and their parents. For the remainder of her time she carries out assessments on new patients, makes several home visits to follow-up recent cases and compiles reports on patients for GPs, consultants, educational psychologists, clinical psychologists and teachers.

Martin D. specializes in child language and travels between several locations conducting individual and group sessions with children ranging from 3.5 years to 11 years. Mornings may be spent at local schools, health centres and early care units. He may visit playgroups, infant schools, schools for physically handicapped and delicate children, or specialist child language clinics. Part of his time is devoted to the paediatric assessment unit of the local hospital where he conducts investigations on the language capacities of new patients and appraises the progress of current cases. On two half-days he supervises parent training schemes where the principles of language stimulation and behaviour modification are taught.

Liz B. is a member of the head injuries rehabilitation unit at her district hospital. As a member of a multi-disciplinary team she co-ordinates her work with a consultant neurologist and neurosurgeon, a senior registrar and registrar in neurology, two physiotherapists, two clinical psychologists, four occupational therapists, two social workers, a remedial gymnast and some 16 nurses. Together with her colleagues she is involved in the initial assessments of brain damage, the planning and formulation of treatment goals and the specific treatment programme of each patient. A proportion of her time is spent in multi-disciplinary meetings to discuss individual patients and their overall progress. A number of home visits are made, often in the company of team colleagues, to ascertain how well discharged patients and relatives are coping with the adjustment to normal living. Within the team Liz has the opportunity to be involved with the entire range of patient care provided.

These speech therapists practise in very different situations. The demands of generic speech therapy are considerable; therapists must be able to relate to both children and adults with equal ease. With both groups they must advise relatives and liaise with colleagues in various professions. In specialist work there may be more commitment to research through developing effective intervention schemes for specific types of difficulties. Each type of therapist has much in common; in addition to requiring specialist assessment and treatment skills they must be able to relate easily to their patients and command the respect of their colleagues in other branches of the health and education services. Most importantly, they share the status of independent clinical practitioners, thereby having full autonomy in their professional work.

In some professions (notably medicine) there is a lengthy period of supervised practice where, ultimately, decisions about an individual patient are taken by a more senior colleague. In speech therapy it is recognized that on completion of formal training a clinician is expected to operate independently when managing a particular case. This responsibility brings with it a very great emphasis on the quality of clinical training. Professionals must be equipped not simply with a catalogue of knowledge of their particular field, but with the intellectual equipment to appreciate new advances in research and to make an active contribution to the development of research. In addition, the therapeutic professions require the development of effective social and emotional capacities in their practitioners. The study of disorders of human communication is still in the early stages of development. Many more questions exist than reliable answers. It is against this background that training schemes have been designed which attempt to supply the range of academic, clinical, social and emotional experience necessary for the production of a professional speech therapist.

Training in speech therapy is entering a new era; following an enquiry into the organization of speech therapy services in 1972 (the Quirk Report) it was recommended that training in speech therapy be elevated from the Diploma in Speech Therapy to graduate status. The various Diploma training courses are gradually being upgraded to degree courses and are being joined by new degree courses in speech therapy. A further major advantage of this transition is the opportunity to offer considerable scope for specialization between courses. At some training centres there is a strong emphasis on developmental difficulties, whereas others offer opportunities to pursue brain function therapy. These unique characteristics of each course are balanced by a broad, common curriculum, which ensures that each student receives the basic intellectual and clinical skills necessary for professional practice.

Speech therapists share a common core curriculum of speech pathology and therapeutics, psychology, linguistics and medical sciences. Academic and practical knowledge from these four disciplines make up the skills needed by professional speech therapists. This book is an attempt to provide the basic knowledge in psychology that is taught on the various training courses up and down the country. Some courses will inevitably have their own areas of special interest to which this text can only serve as an introduction.

The book was compiled after consultation with each psychology course at every training centre and we are deeply indebted to colleagues on these courses who made helpful comments on the general plan of the book. A number of experts have contributed chapters on their specialist topics and we have tried to offer introductions to particular areas of clinical relevance.

The book is divided into six major parts; Part I provides an introduction to scientific psychology in order to map out the main areas of professional concern. Part II focusses on child psychology to introduce major findings and provide an opportunity to pursue this area of study in more depth. In Part III we concentrate on individual psychology both as a way of understanding the unique characteristics of others and in order to assist in the development of self-knowledge. Part IV examines the social systems within which we diagnose and treat patients: it provides an insight into human relationships and a means of facilitating such relationships. In Part V we turn our attention to abnormal psychology; both theoretical and practical developments have had a profound impact on human communication disorders. Finally, in Part VI, we outline the framework of an exciting new branch of psychology: neuropsychology. Of all the specialisms in health care it is perhaps here that there is the most need for development.

The book should be of interest to both students and trained practitioners alike and the contributions of David Legge, Brian Foss, Peter Robinson, Paul Kline, Don Bannister, Michael Argyle, Neil Frude and David Shapiro should ensure this.

Acknowledgements

We would like to acknowledge the advice and encouragement offered by colleagues in psychology and speech therapy in the writing of this book. In particular, we wish to thank Ruth Lesser, Margaret Edwards, Lena Rustin, Dave Muller and Dave Rowley for their comments and criticisms.

Part one

Introduction to Psychological Science

Speech therapy is a relatively new profession within the health services, emerging after the Second World War in response to a need which was not satisfied. Workers in education and medicine identified individuals who presented speech difficulties which could not simply be attributed to poor hearing. In schools children were seen who had a poverty of spoken language and/or difficulties in pronunciation of speech sounds. In hospital clinics adult patients were seen whose speech was dysfluent and hesitant or completely abolished through damage to the brain. A few doctors and child psychologists specialized in such cases, but there was little general provision for people with this communication handicap. A small group of enthusiastic workers addressed the shortfall in trained personnel by founding a college which was to study human communication disorders and to promote training for speech therapists.

Human communication disorders are seldom simple problems. In some cases the cause of the problem is fairly clear: for example, children born with structural abnormalities of the speech apparatus, adults who have suffered a 'stroke', and degenerative diseases of the central nervous system all have characteristic communication difficulties. Other communication problems, stuttering, voice disorders, language delay in children and disturbances of written language, are less clear-cut in terms of their cause. Even where the particular cause of the problem is understood it is seldom possible to reverse the physical damage that has occurred. 'Speech pathology' refers to the causes (or aetiology) of communication disorders and involves contributions from a variety of related disciplines: medicine, psychology, linguistics, phonetics and sociology. Speech therapeutics, which deals with problems faced by those suffering from communication difficulties, draws its techniques from a range of disciplines, but primarily from the field of clinical psychology.

Psychology is essentially the study of the human mind and behaviour. When we communicate with others we exhibit 'speech behaviour' which is easily observed and open to analysis. This communicative form of behaviour is, however, the product of unobservable mental processes - thinking, planning and setting goals - which are translated into

7

speech through the anatomical and physiological mechanisms of communication: larynx, lungs, tongue, lips, etc. Communication disorders can result from problems at any level in this system. If mental processes deviate from normal then some deviation in verbal behaviour is likely. However, if some structural abnormality exists in the speech mechanisms, a qualitatively different type of deviation in verbal behaviour results. The speech therapist's task is to differentiate at which level in the system a difficulty exists, and to design appropriate strategies for either circumventing, or re-organizing the verbal behaviour which it affects. In the case of anatomical and physiological abnormalities it may be the case that very little physical repair can be achieved and so the therapist needs to know how best to help individuals adapt to their handicap. Where mental processes are seen as the source of the problem a careful analysis of the factors which influence mental functioning is required. Neuropsychology - the study of the relationship between the brain and mental processes - is one possible source of information. In the absence of brain damage we must look to the ideas that individuals have about themselves, their emotional difficulties and their social awareness as potentially important factors in understanding their communication problems.

Psychology addresses these problems of individual learning and adaptation, of development, emotional functioning, social functioning and self-image, which may be crucial factors in both the aetiology and treatment of human communication disorders. Psychologists would be the first to point out that despite a century of scientific research there are no easy answers to these problems. At best psychology offers a number of tentative ideas about the causes and treatment of communication disorders. These ideas are the product of careful scientific enquiry, but require considerable development before they can be accepted as 'answers'. Speech therapists draw from such theories in psychology and apply them to individual cases of communication disorder in order to evaluate their usefulness as approaches to changing human behaviour. Thus speech therapy is closely related to applied psychology, which translates scientific theory into clinical practice and scientifically evaluates the utility of different theories.

The science of therapy
In treating individual patients there is a need to uphold the principles of scientific enquiry if reliable therapeutic techniques are to emerge. When a number of therapists treat a large number of cases from different theoretical standpoints it is obvious that valuable information is being created, information which, if systematically collected and distributed to other therapists, could lead to rapid advances in therapeutic practices. If technique X has been extensively applied to a particular patient population, with little tangible improvement, then there is a clear implication for the future practice of that particular therapy

technique. This information would, of course, call for the revision of the theoretical position which generated the technique. In time, the accumulation of such information leads to both theoretical and practical innovations which ensures that patients receive therapy for which there is clear evidence of efficacy. Scientific method is the common language of professional therapists. Such a common language allows for contact between various theories, so that new ideas may emerge to do with the treatment of communication disorders.

In chapter 1 we trace the development of psychological science and highlight the difficulties that have been encountered in the study of mental functioning. The various schools of thought in psychology are outlined and their relevance to communication disorders discussed. These schools of thought have generated the various approaches to therapy encountered in contemporary practice, and so form the basic training of speech pathologists and therapists. In chapter 2 David Legge describes the principles of scientific enquiry which have generated these various schools of thought, and which offer clinicians the tools to contribute to the continuing development of human understanding.

I

Modern Psychology
Harry Purser

Harry Purser

Introduction

Modern psychology is the product of a century of scientific debate in which a number of rival schools of thought have pursued the study of Man from different approaches. This picture, of competing approaches and viewpoints, is characteristic of the early stages of development in any science. Physics and chemistry passed through this stage before general agreement was reached on the relationships between different schools of thought. Beloff (1973), in a review of modern psychology, argued that there is no single science called 'psychology' but rather a number of independent 'psychological sciences' with their own areas of study. Some of these 'sciences' are interested in the relationship between the mind (consciousness) and the body (neurophysiological functioning), and others consider the differences between personality types and social functioning. It is this diversity of 'psychologies' that makes it difficult to define psychology. This task is further complicated by the fact that, since Beloff's review, psychology has begun to reach the point where the divisions between the 'psychological sciences' are receding.

In the first quarter of this century there were two major definitions of psychology: 'Psychology is the study of mind' and 'Psychology is the science of human behaviour'. These definitions reflect two opposing views of the proper topic of study in psychology. The first suggests psychology is about the mental aspects of life: our self-consciousness. The second definition introduces two related ideas; the use of scientific method as the particular form of study, and the consequent restriction of study to only those aspects of mental functioning which can be directly observed (actual behaviour such as walking, talking, learning and socializing). Psychology is therefore the study of the human mind, but differences exist in how that study should proceed. For those who argue that consciousness should be studied there is a major limitation. Our self-consciousness is a unique phenomenon; it is only available for study to one person, and as a consequence we can never know anything about the mind of another person. Scientific method is a way of reaching general conclusions about phenomena and thus a scientific approach to psychology would aim to tell us things about ourselves and others.

Leaving aside the problem of giving an acceptable definition of psychology we turn to the next question: what use is psychology? Psychology is about mental processes and human behaviour, but what is the product of this study and how can it be applied to human problems? Modern psychology studies infants, young children and adolescents in an attempt to find out how intelligence develops, how language is acquired and how social and emotional development proceed. These studies enable us to understand problems such as mental retardation, multiple handicap, specific language disorders and psychiatric disorders. Psychology studies how personality develops, the impact major life events such as bereavement, redundancy and marital problems have on people and the range of psychiatric disturbance that affects people. This knowledge is essential if we are to develop effective health care and offer practical solutions to the problems of living. The major schools of thought in psychology have often come to different conclusions about these problems and have thus suggested different treatment approaches. In recent years the interrelationships between these different schools have become apparent, with the result that a trend towards integration is emerging. Much of the disagreement between schools of thought was generated through debate on the usefulness of scientific method as a means of studying Man. The advocates of science pointed to the rapid development of the natural sciences such as physics and chemistry since they adopted the methods of scientific enquiry; the dissenters argued that scientific methods could only be applied indirectly to mental processes and thus could not answer the real questions of psychology.

Psychology and science

Science, or rather scientific method, changed alchemy into chemistry. From stewing rats' tails in order to combat fever to the development of sophisticated antibiotics would seem a staggering advance and it was made possible by adherence to a specific set of 'rules' for study. These 'rules of discovery' allow scientists to put forward explanations of events which differ from the common-sense explanations in terms of their predictive power. A scientific explanation is designed to give us general information about a particular phenomenon. This general knowledge allows us to predict what will happen in the future when a particular event takes place. Our scientific knowledge of how motor cars (in general) work allows us to predict what will happen if a particular component is damaged. In chemistry our knowledge of two elements and the nature of their interaction allows us to predict what will happen if we heat them in a particular solution. It was therefore argued that if psychology adopted the methods of science and could explain the nature of Man (in general) it would allow predictions to be made of how humans interact.

Science generates explanations by adherence to a systematic method of investigation. This investigation begins with a series of controlled observations where the topic of study is subjected to a number of different conditions. If we were interested in how metal fatigue develops we would assemble a number of identical metal bars and subject them to different stresses. We could then note the amount of stress each bar received and what fatigue resulted. By carefully measuring the stresses and the extent of the fatigue we might see a relationship between stress and fatigue. This early stage of enquiry, where a tentative relationship is suggested between two events, is the hypothesis stage. The hypothesis is really an informal guess about the relationship, but it allows us to make predictions about what would happen if we took a thicker metal bar and subjected it to a specific amount of pressure. This prediction is then tested by subjecting a thicker bar to those pressures and measuring whether the predicted outcome is the same as the actual outcome. If the prediction is confirmed by experimental test then we can offer an early explanation of metal fatigue. If the prediction is not confirmed by the test we must return to our original hypothesis and reconsider it. If we accurately predict the outcome our early explanation becomes a theory of metal fatigue. The term 'theory' implies a temporary explanation: one which may have to be revised if any future predictions are found to be inaccurate. Science, then, offers a cautious approach to the discovery of knowledge. In trying to formulate general explanations of events it must outline the general rules that are involved and how these rules may change in different conditions. For example, our general theory of how metal fatigue develops may not hold when we vary the temperature of the metal, so this effect of temperature variation may invalidate our early theory. The theory will therefore have to be revised to allow accurate predictions when temperature variations are involved.

Scientific theories are thus tentative explanations of events and they are subject to revision should they make inaccurate predictions. These theories allow models of events to be constructed. In chemistry the model of atomic structure with protons, neutrons and electrons interacting in specific ways allows us to predict what will happen when we combine, say, sodium and chlorine. This example makes a telling point: models are no more than crude representations of events. Chemists and physicists now realize that the atom is made up of a great many particles with very different properties, yet it is only under very special circumstances that the very simple model of atomic structure makes faulty predictions. Science is characterized by a number of stages and each stage is a further step towards more accurate predictions and therefore more certainty that we really understand a particular phenomenon. The success of this method of discovery is obvious in our current technology, but can this method be applied to people as well as objects?

Problems

The study of physical objects such as metals is possible because we can ensure that a number of identical samples are available for study. We can be sure that any differences between our samples are the result of our experimental tests. We can also measure very accurately the differences between our samples after the test. Human beings, however, are far from identical.

If we place two people in the same situation and apply some sort of influence we may see them respond in different ways. Psychology aims to explain these differences and build models of how such differences come about. This venture faces a number of difficult problems.

* Science is objective in its approach. Scientists do not simply rely on their own subjective experiences to describe events. They use measurement to gather reliable evidence about events, evidence which can also be gathered by other scientists. Measurement is therefore the common language of science which allows different scientists working in different areas to compare findings. As a consequence scientific method can only be applied to events which can be objectively described through measurement. A scientific psychology must limit itself to studying those aspects of the mind which can be objectively described through measurement.
* Science generates hypotheses which are subjected to experimental tests to estimate their predictive accuracy. Experiments require careful control over all the likely variables which may have an effect on the particular relationship that we are interested in. These controlled manipulations of the experimental environment raise serious ethical questions when we contemplate a scientific psychology. Should we subject human beings to experimental manipulation in order to verify our theories?
* A scientific theory is a temporary explanation which is modified and reformulated in the light of new evidence. If scientific explanations vary in their accuracy, have we the right to apply these explanations to real human problems?

These problems have been tackled in different ways by the psychological sciences; some have focussed on offering very general explanations of human behaviour, others have concentrated on specific mental processes in isolation from other events. The alternative to scientific methods is 'introspection', where an individual examines the content and processes of his own consciousness. Introspection had been the basis of philosophy for several centuries, but there was always the problem that no general conclusions could be reached about the nature of the human mind. Self-knowledge does not necessarily mean we have knowledge of the minds of others. It was against this background that the first steps towards a scientific psychology were taken. Wundt is credited with setting up the first psychological laboratory in 1879 where experimental methods were used to study general principles of mental functioning. This development took place at a time when rapid advances were being made in the biological sciences such as physiology. Science was beginning to offer a picture of life which emphasized the similarities between species and the relationship between Man and other creatures. The Darwinian view of evolution forced a radical rethink of Man's place in the world. Prior to Darwin it was thought that Man, as a special creation of God, was fundamentally different from other species of life: he had a non-physical soul. It was Man's soul which gave rise to his mental experience and this experience was unrelated to the physical body. This dualistic view - the separation of mental life and the physical body - suggested that no amount of knowledge of how the physical body works would ever answer the questions about mental life. The Darwinian theory of evolution gave cause to re-examine this belief and suggested that mental life was probably closely linked to the activity of the physiological processes of the human brain. Further, the theory of evolution suggested that by studying other species, especially Man's closest relatives, insight could be gained into the general structure and functioning of the mind.

By the beginning of the twentieth century the distinction between mental life and physical (physiological) functioning had been eroded and the time was right for a new approach to psychology. Scientific psychology was born in Europe and elaborated in the USA, but the crucial development occurred in Russia where a physiologist, Ivan Pavlov, discovered a phenomenon which resulted in the launch of 'modern' psychology.

Classical conditioning

Ivan Pavlov showed the way to modern psychology through a combination of rigorous physiological experimentation and luck! His early work as a physiologist concerned the function of the nerves of the heart but in the last decade of the nineteenth century he turned to the study of digestion. In this work Pavlov used dogs which had been operated on to reveal their digestive glands in order to observe their functioning under different conditions. He was unhappy with these surgical preparations because of the difficulty in separating the real glandular secretions from the effects of the surgery. Instead he decided to use chronic preparations where the animals were fitted with tubes which diverted their digestive secretions to collection vessels. In this way the animals could recover from the surgery and provide measurable samples of their secretions to various foods on a continuous basis. The results of these studies were published in 1897 and Pavlov noted that a number of irregularities were seen in the functioning of the salivary glands. He explained these anomalies as being due to 'psychic causes'. For example, it was noticed that on certain occasions the salivary glands would begin to function before food was

given to the animals. As soon as the assistant who regularly
fed the animals entered the laboratory the dogs would begin
to salivate. At first Pavlov did not pursue these findings,
but in 1902 he began a systematic investigation to discover
how these 'psychical' responses came about.

Briefly, Pavlov discovered that his experimental dogs
could learn to associate a wide variety of non-food stimuli
(lights, bells, buzzers) with the presentation of food. This
was a surprising finding since salivation is a naturally occurring reflex response when food (or any other object) is
actually placed in the mouth. Salivation serves to lubricate
the swallowing reflex and thus it should only occur when
some substance is actually placed in the mouth. A reflex is
the physiological term for an innate, physiological pathway
which is directly activated by a natural stimulus. Food is
the natural stimulus to activate the physiological reflex of
salivation. Lights, bells and buzzers are hardly 'natural
stimuli'. Pavlov argued that two processes were involved in
the formation of these associations. An innate, reflex pathway exists which is directly activated by natural stimuli,
and these reflex responses are termed 'unconditioned reflexes'. These innate reflexes can become associated with
other environmental stimuli to result in 'conditioned reflexes' and so salivating to the sound of a bell would be a
conditioned reflex, whereas salivation to food in the mouth
would be an unconditioned reflex.

In a typical conditioning experiment a bell (the conditioned stimulus, CS) is repeatedly sounded before food (the
unconditioned stimulus, UCS) is placed in the mouth. The UCS
of food activates the unconditioned response of salivation
(UCR). After a number of pairings of UCS and CS (food and
bell) the animal begins to show a salivation response to the
bell alone, before the food is presented. This response to
the bell alone is termed the conditioned response (CR). This
simple experiment demonstrates how new stimuli can become
associated with existing responses, but more importantly it
demonstrates how a scientific study can be conducted on the
relationship between physiological events and the environment. Pavlov went on to investigate further aspects of his
conditioning procedure. He found that once a CR was established it could be extinguished by the withdrawal of the
UCS. Thus if food is withdrawn the animal continued to
salivate to the sound of the bell for a number of trials,
but eventually the CR waned. This process of extinction may
not be permanent. After a time interval the CR may reappear
to the CS, although it may be much weaker. This reappearance
of the CR to the CS following extinction is termed 'spontaneous recovery'. Furthermore, once a CR is established to a
particular CS the CS can be gradually altered and this in
turn affects the strength of the CR. Thus if we condition an
animal to salivate to the sound of a particular bell it will
also salivate to the sound of a different bell, but the
strength of this response depends on the similarity between
the two bells. If the second bell is very different from the

CS bell only a small CR will result; if the bells are similar then the CRs will be similar. This phenomenon is known as stimulus generalization, and it was realized that here was a means of discovering how similar two stimuli appeared to an animal. Thus auditory and visual perception could be studied in animals without having to guess if the animal could discriminate between different stimuli.

Pavlov's studies of what has become known as 'classical conditioning' opened up new avenues in the study of living creatures. Whereas anatomists and physiologists had traditionally studied animals purely to investigate their internal processes, Pavlov had shown how it was possible to study the relationship between internal processes and external events. Pavlov then developed a theory, in physiological terms, which explained how external events and internal processes relate to each other. This model of internal functioning accounted for conditioning by postulating two kinds of physiological activity: excitation and inhibition. Excitation was a process that occurred when new physiological pathways became connected with existing innate reflex pathways, whereas inhibition was a process which shut down these new connections when the UCS was withdrawn (extinction). The degree of excitation determined the strength of the CR; if the CS was altered in some way from the original, less excitation would occur leading to a weaker CR as in stimulus generalization. If the UCS was withdrawn completely, then after a number of trials inhibition would build up to shut down the CR pathway, resulting in extinction of the CR. When the UCS is reintroduced the CR recovers to its previous strength since the actual pathway of the CR is not destroyed, but simply inhibited. Thus the excitation caused by the reintroduction of the UCS reactivates the CR pathway.

Pavlov saw conditioning as a physical change in the central nervous system (CNS) through the growth of new pathways and the action of excitatory and inhibitory processes. This model of CNS functioning was purely hypothetical since the actual excitatory and inhibitory processes could not be directly observed. What could be observed was the salivatory behaviour of the animal to measurable environmental stimuli. Through controlled experiments general features of the relationship between input (environmental stimuli) and output (actual behaviour) could be observed. This evidence was then used to speculate on the internal processes (physiological functioning) that were likely to occur between input and output. Pavlov's model of conditioning tried to relate environmental input (stimuli) to specific internal processes (physiology) which generated behavioural output (responses). This type of explanation is termed 'reductionist' because it tries to account for phenomena at one level by describing activity at a different level; for example, explaining a complex behavioural response in terms of underlying physiological events. Pavlov's reductionist psychology suggested that, just as a table can be described in terms of how it looks and feels, it can also be described as a mass of atoms bound in electrical relationships with each other; similarly, psychological descriptions of behaviour could be more fundamentally described in terms of physiological processes. Although this reductionism suggests that in the final analysis only a physiological explanation will be adequate to account for psychological events such as hearing, seeing, and learning, a number of scientists objected to the need for physiological speculation. A scientific psychology could restrict itself to observing environmental input and behavioural output and describing the observable relationships between them. These descriptions are known as explanations in breadth: where events at the same level of analysis are brought together in a systematic way. Such breadth explanations do not deny the importance of the physiological level of functioning but argue that, since this level of analysis cannot be directly observed, it is not a scientific endeavour but a speculative exercise without direct evidence.

Psychological explanations
Scientific psychology emerged from the physiological laboratory at the turn of the century and immediately developed two schools of thought: those who by observing input(S)-output(R) relationships tried to construct a model of the underlying physiological events that mediated these relationships (reductionists), and those who sought lawful relationships between input and output without speculating on underlying physiological functioning. Both schools were agreed on the need for hypotheses to guide study which made specific predictions and could be experimentally tested. In this way a theoretical system could be built up from experimental evidence which would account for both animal and human behaviour. This approach to psychology was by no means universal at the beginning of this century. The mental philosophers argued that introspection, despite its obvious limitations, was still the most realistic way to study mental life. By limiting study to only those observable aspects of mental life (behaviour), the essential point of being self-conscious was lost. It was further argued that a scientific psychology could never answer particular questions about human behaviour because of its form of reasoning. Biological systems differ from pieces of metal because their behaviour is not simply the result of external forces. Living behaviour is purposive; it is aimed at reaching some goal. How could we 'explain' a smile in terms of its underlying physiological components? If we ask how someone smiles a physiological account will do, but if we ask why someone smiles we must say what the purpose of the smile is. This distinction between a 'how' explanation and a 'why' explanation is a major objection to reductionism in the biological sciences, although in recent years the two positions have not been viewed as mutually exclusive. For example, if we understand the genetic principles behind evolution we have an explanation of how evolution occurs, but we cannot answer

the question why evolution occurs. Yet if we wished to predict what might happen if we manipulated genetic material in
a particular way we need only understand the genetic principles themselves; knowing why evolution occurs does not
necessarily enhance such a prediction.

This practical point emphasizes that under certain
circumstances knowing how things happen is sometimes more
useful than knowing why. This new form of scientific
psychology was termed 'behaviourism' and gave rise to the
definition of psychology as 'the science of behaviour'.
Pavlov's revolutionary application of scientific methodology
to 'psychic phenomena' paved the way for a number of behaviouristic psychologies, differing in the type of explanation they offered. However, this approach has encountered
opposition from both within the psychological sciences and
from related disciplines with an interest in the study of
Man. Introspection - the direct study of the mind through
self-conscious analysis - has led to the development of a
distinct school of psychology which pursues a meaningful
theory of mental experience without recourse to physiological or behavioural explanations. Humanistic psychologists emphasize that self-awareness and awareness of
others is still the central topic of psychology, and these
mental states cannot be fully understood purely in physiological terms. This latter school would prefer a definition
of psychology which indicates that it is the mind, rather
than 'behaviour', which is the proper object of study.

Psychology and human communication

When Man is compared to the other species which have been
produced by evolution one major feature sets him apart: his
capacity for language. All species have communication systems which allow individuals to interact in specific ways.
In some species these communication systems are chemical in
nature, in others visual and auditory. Further, the amount
of information that can be transmitted by these systems is
usually rather limited: they can warn of danger, delineate
territory and indicate sexual attraction; only in Man do we
see a communication system which is not simply limited to
making observations of the here-and-now, but can transmit
detailed information about past events, present events and
future events with apparently limitless capacity. Human
language allows individuals to function as social units, to
co-operate on common projects and to convey information
about their emotional and mental states. In short, the study
of human communication is a central feature of psychology.
Anatomy and physiology supply explanations of physical
mechanisms of speech and hearing and thus the physical
features of the input and output mechanisms are known.
The internal, psychological process of language is another
matter. Language can be defined as a system of symbols
which represent thoughts in time and space, and thus the
question of language is inextricably bound up with the
nature of mental processes: thinking, reasoning, perceiving,

remembering and learning. Further, language is a purposeful act: it conveys information for social reasons.

Human communication can be studied from a number of viewpoints, but what are the practical implications of study from these viewpoints? A physiological study could explain how certain kinds of physical damage result in specific communication deficits. But what implications would such an analysis have for remedial action? Would it really help to know that damage to a particular neurophysiological system results in the inability to communicate? Since damage has occurred it is damage that must be repaired. This may be fine for the neurosurgeon, but what value is it to the remedial therapist? A description of the neural substrate of language may tell us how language is stored and how damage therefore disrupts its functioning, but it may tell us very little about what to do about it. For professions which operate 'outside the skin', such as teachers and therapists, there is a need to know how such functioning can be influenced at the psychological level: how a mentally retarded child with diffuse brain damage can learn to read most effectively or how a deaf child may be taught to cope with his handicap. These questions are not tackled by a physiological explanation; they need knowledge of the psychological processes that operate in reading and learning. With this kind of knowledge specific programmes of psychological therapy can be designed that can enhance psychological development and help offset the effects of physical damage.

The development of speech therapy illustrates the ways in which our understanding of human communication has grown. Speech therapists draw on physiological and medical knowledge to understand how physical damage disrupts communication. They incorporate the objective techniques of phonetics and linguistics to describe language and draw on psychology for models of the processes of human communication and for the design of therapeutic intervention. Indeed, it remains the case that certain types of communication disorder do not seem to have any physical basis at all. Where no organic damage can be found there is no alternative to a psychological explanation.

The study of human communication is shared by a number of disciplines, but intervention in communication disorders is usually at the psychological level. Where physical damage is involved the aim of psychological therapy is to enhance recovery or circumvent the deficit. Where no physical aetiology is observed a psychological explanation is offered of the dysfunction which may refer to social, intellectual or emotional causes. These explanations should all have clear implications for intervention.

Psychological sciences

Beloff (1973) has pointed out the essential differences between the various schools of psychology. The first dimension of difference relates to the primary assumptions made about Man by each psychological science. For some, Man is primarily a product of evolution, a specific design of CNS engineering which gives rise to a wide variety of adaptive behaviour. This view attempts to study Man as a psycho-biological system, programmed with a set of neural mechanisms which process environmental input and can take autonomous action. For others, Man is essentially a social being whose behaviour is not heavily dependent on biological programming. This view would not deny the importance of physiological investigation, but would argue that since people are conscious of an inner 'self' and an outer 'world' largely made up of other people, it is at this level of analysis that study should be focussed. If we wish to understand such social and individual processes we must seek our explanations in ordinary human language rather than in terms of neuronal firing sequences.

These fundamental differences in assumptions about Man lead to very different methods of investigation. Every psychological science would claim to be scientific in creating a theoretical system, but their methods will be appropriate to the level of analysis suggested by the primary assumptions. For the physiological psychologist the direct study of the living central nervous system has been revolutionized by the development of new technology such as microelectrodes for recording cell firing and computer-enhanced measurement and visualization of the brain. These developments allow reliable experimental manipulation to be carried out for hypothesis testing. For the social psychologist, observation of social processes requires a different technology. A wide variety of social and individual processes occur in normal living, but in order to study such processes it is necessary to participate in them, a fact which can change the nature of the original process. Imagine having a normal conversation with a friend when a silent 'observer' is present; science at this level of analysis is a social venture by definition, and adopts methods of study which recognize the intrusive nature of study.

For convenience we consider five branches of psychology: behaviourism, cognitive psychology, individual psychology, social psychology and neuropsychology. It is to these areas that professional clinicians look for explanations of human functioning and for theories to guide therapeutic intervention when dysfunction arises.

Behaviourism

It was Pavlov's discovery of classical conditioning which launched behaviourism as the first scientific psychology. This view is reflected in the definition of psychology as the science of human behaviour. Since science can only be applied to observable (and measurable) events, psychology would have to limit its study to observable events in the environment (stimuli) and to behavioural responses. This kind of psychology would aim to predict, given a particular stimulus, what behavioural responses might occur. To achieve such a prediction required a theoretical account of how

environmental input is related to behavioural output. For
Pavlov the answers lay in neurophysiology: a reductionist
explanation. But a group of more extreme behaviourists
argued that to seek internal, physiological explanations of
overt behaviour without any direct means of studying these
underlying processes was as bad as introspection. If science
could only analyse the observable then hypotheses about
unobservable underlying processes were unscientific concepts. This group of 'Radical Behaviourists' was spearheaded
by B. F. Skinner in the 1930s and 1940s and advanced an
analysis of human behaviour which only included directly
observable and measurable events. Skinner had no interest in
the underlying physiological basis of behaviour, since he
argued that if we wish to predict and control behaviour we
must utilize a knowledge of the causes of behaviour which
are environmental as well as physiological events. If we
wish to change behaviour in a given direction there is
little we can do with a physiological explanation apart from
chemotherapy or neurosurgery. We can, however, make changes
in the physical environment which may have an effect on
behaviour. Skinner's science of behaviourism attracted many
capable researchers who studied animal and human behaviour
in a search for general laws which governed behaviour. This
approach to psychology emphasized rigorous hypothesis testing in highly controlled experimental environments (achieved
by studying non-human species) in order to produce a breadth
explanation of behaviour.

Behaviour therapy
These two forms of behaviourism are still central features
of modern psychology, together with neo-behaviourist theories which attempt to integrate both psychological (breadth)
explanations and physiological (reductionist) accounts of
human functioning. Behaviouristic theories have made an
enormous contribution to social care: in education, mental
health and the care of the handicapped. The main reason
for this diversity of application rests in the fact that behaviouristic accounts of human functioning are very general,
and consequently they generate simple but effective means
of intervening in behavioural problems. Amongst the first
examples of the application of behaviourist principles to
human problems is the classic study by J. B. Watson, the
father of American behaviourism, in 1920. Watson was quick
to grasp the significance of Pavlov's conditioning experiments and in 1916, as President of the American Psychological Association, he delivered a paper on the place of the
conditioned reflex in psychology. He interpreted the conditioning process as an explanation of how habits develop
in everyday life. Watson considered conditions such as
phobias (irrational fears about objects or situations) were
good examples of learned habits and set out with his co-
worker Rayner to demonstrate how phobias arise (Watson and
Rayner, 1920). A young child called 'little Albert' was
introduced to a white laboratory rat to which he showed no

fear; he would happily play with the creature as he would with a toy. Watson then introduced a powerful UCS (a very loud noise) each time Albert approached the rat. This UCS of noise directly elicited a UCR of fear and anxiety (an innate, reflexive response). Watson reasoned that continued pairings of the noise (UCS) with the sight of the rat (CS) would lead to the formation of a conditioned response (CR) of anxiety and fear. This prediction was confirmed: Albert became very frightened of the rat after a number of CS and UCS pairings. A number of further conditioning phenomena were also seen in Albert's behaviour; he became afraid not only of rats, but of other small furry creatures and toys (stimulus generalization).

Mary Cover-Jones (1924), under Watson's direction, took this research a stage further. She tested a sample of young children for the presence of fear towards a variety of objects and situations (being left alone, snakes, rats and frogs). Having identified those children with an obvious fear she set about testing six methods of reducing fear. She concluded that her 'direct conditioning' method, which consisted of pairing the CS (fear-arousing object leading to CR of fear) with a pleasant UCS, such as food, gave rise to a UCR of pleasure. By feeding the child with the fear-evoking object present, but at a safe distance, it was reasoned that the UCR of pleasure would outweigh the CR of fear, thus weakening the prior conditioned association. Although strictly speaking the child's fear is apparently unconditioned, it is assumed that previous conditioning has forged a CS-CR bond which occurs with the strength of an unconditioned response. This application of conditioning had profound implications for the field of mental health. It now looked as if conditioning theory offered an explanation for phobias and anxiety states, and a means of treating such conditions. At this point behaviour therapy was born, but it did not reach a peak of development until the 1950s.

Watson believed that at birth Man is equipped with a number of innate, reflex responses, which are directly elicited by natural, environmental stimuli. Thus sudden noises, sudden loss of support, etc., are natural stimuli which elicit defensive reflexes such as fear. Food is a natural stimulus which elicits a response of pleasure and thus stimuli associated with feeding (mother's face, or a particular mug) can become associated through classical conditioning with various innate, reflex responses. As we develop, a wider range of CSs are associated through stimulus generalization and some associations can decay through extinction. This account of emotional conditioning is, however, only part of the story.

Classical conditioning deals with the association of new stimuli with innate biological reflexes such as anxiety and salivation. The main feature of such reflex responses is that they are involuntary acts. We cannot control such responses consciously because they are mediated by automatic physiological pathways which are directly activated by a

range of natural stimuli. We are aware that in addition to
making emotional associations with new stimuli we 'behave'
constantly by learning new skills which are under voluntary
control. So in addition to forming new stimulus associations
we acquire new voluntary behavioural responses, and it was
for this range of behaviour - the non-reflex spontaneous
behaviour of animals and Man - that E. L. Thorndike
developed his theory of 'trial and error' learning, or
instrumental conditioning.

Thorndike (1932) outlined a series of experiments where
animals were placed in 'puzzle boxes' from which they tried
to escape. Cats were placed in special boxes fitted with
levers or dangling strings which, when touched, could open
the box and allow the animals to escape. By closely observing what these animals did in such situations Thorndike put
forward an explanation of how the animals learnt to press
the lever and pull the string without recourse to describing
any underlying physiological events. At first the trapped
animals would scratch, bite and move around the cage in a
random fashion. Eventually, by chance, the animal would paw
the lever or string with the result that freedom would be
achieved. Each time the animal was placed in the box it took
less time to escape, until whenever the animal was caged it
would make the appropriate response and gain its freedom.
These experiments demonstrate a decrease in unprofitable
behaviour (scratching and pawing away from the lever) and an
increase in behaviour which had preceded escape (pawing in
the area of the lever). From these experiments Thorndike
formulated the Law of Effect which states:

> Of several responses made to the same situation, those
> which are accompanied or closely followed by satis-
> faction to the animal will, other things being equal, be
> more firmly connected with the situation, so that when
> it (the situation) recurs they (the responses) will be
> more likely to recur (Thorndike, 1911).

Thorndike therefore offered an explanation of how new
behavioural responses are learnt in specific situations by
emphasizing the relationship between actual behaviour and
its environmental consequences. In 1938 Skinner took these
ideas and incorporated them in a new behaviouristic scheme
which he termed 'operant conditioning'. It was Skinner's
belief that general laws governed all behaviour from simple
organisms right up to Man. It was the task of psychology to
discover these laws and to use them to intervene in cases of
behavioural dysfunction. This assumption, that a common
learning mechanism governed the behaviour of all living
species, implied that differences between species were due
to variation in their storage capacity for associations. Man
was different from other species because of his greater
storage capacity for learned behavioural responses; but
through the experimental study of simpler species the general principles of behaviour learning would be illustrated
and applicable to Man.

Being a rigorous researcher, Skinner required full control over the experimental environment and thus avoided the possibility of random variables interfering with his experiments. To achieve this control the 'Skinner Box' was designed, which consisted of a small, empty chamber with a lever protruding from one wall. This set-up prevented extraneous auditory and visual stimuli from distracting the experimental animal and allowed a record to be made of the frequency with which the animal manipulated the lever. The lever was connected to a food pellet store, so that each time it was depressed a food morsel was delivered down a chute into the box.

When an animal is placed in this environment it gradually explores the box until, by chance, it operates the lever. A food reward is then delivered which the animal consumes. After a period of time the frequency of lever pushing increases until the animal has eaten enough. If the animal is reintroduced to the box on another occasion it quickly begins to push the lever for food reward. The animal has therefore learnt a behavioural response (lever pushing) which has become associated with receiving a food reward. Skinner explained this response acquisition as an example of Thorndike's Law of Effect. Because the response was followed by 'satisfaction', it had been learnt in preference to any other behaviour that had been produced in the experimental environment. Skinner argued, therefore, that the external environment can be viewed as a source of 'satisfaction', or reinforcement. Animals spontaneously 'emit' a variety of behavioural sequences in an environment, but those sequences which lead to some rewarding consequence (such as obtaining a food pellet) are reinforced and thus stored (learnt) for future use in a similar environment.

Skinner went on to demonstrate a number of features of this form of instrumental learning. Operant conditioning refers to the process where spontaneously emitted 'behaviours' which operate in a given environment (hence 'operants') will be increased in frequency by their reinforcing consequences. Reinforcement can be of two fundamental types: positive reinforcement occurs when a pleasant consequence happens and response rate increases; if an unpleasant consequence is contingent with a particular operant then response frequency rapidly decreases: an example of aversive reinforcement or punishment. Reinforcement can therefore increase or decrease response frequency, but it was found that the way in which reinforcement is applied also affects the rate of change in frequency. Skinner demonstrated that different schedules of reinforcement had a variety of effects on response acquisition and extinction. For example, if reinforcement is made available after every single 'correct' response this would be a continuous schedule. If reinforcement is only given after a certain number of correct responses this would be an intermittent schedule. When new responses are acquired and reinforcement is withdrawn the

response decays and becomes extinguished; when reinforcement
is reintroduced the response 'spontaneously recovers' to its
previous learnt frequency. The rate at which extinction
takes place is related to the particular schedule of reinforcement that was used to establish the original response. If a continuous schedule was used then extinction
takes place quickly; if an intermittent schedule was used,
then it occurs more slowly.

Operant conditioning offered an explanation of how new
responses are learnt rather than describing how new stimuli
could become associated with existing responses (classical
conditioning). Further, it concentrated on voluntary behaviour (lever pressing) rather than involuntary behaviour
(innate reflexes). Skinner's explanation of this learning
was in terms of environmental reinforcement either strengthening or weakening a given response frequency. He proceeded
to demonstrate that any kind of emitted behaviour could be
associated with environmental reinforcement and thus it was
possible to change these behaviours in any desired direction. Simple responses could be individually reinforced and
then 'shaped' into a more complex sequence by selective reinforcement. In a famous experiment Skinner taught a group
of pigeons to 'dance' by shaping simple responses into a
fluid sequence through systematic application of reinforcement in the form of food rewards.

Skinner's new behaviourism made more explicit the laws
which govern the acquisition of new behavioural responses.
Further, because these laws operate at the level of the
environment, it was possible to change behaviour without
probing the physiological substrate of the behaviour.
Operant conditioning was eagerly adopted in a variety of
settings where behavioural change was required. Apart from
circuses, Skinner's analysis of learning was applied to the
fields of education and health care. In education the most
significant development was the 'teaching machine' or programmed learning device. This consisted of a machine which
displayed information to be learnt and then posed a number
of questions. By operating a lever pupils could select a
particular answer which the machine would reward or punish
according to the accuracy of the answer. Rather than deliver
food rewards the machine would flash up reinforcing or
punishing messages such as: 'Correct!' 'Well done!' or
'Wrong! Please try again!' It was reasoned that students
would have correct responses strengthened and wrong responses weakened. In the field of health care operant conditioning offered a means of controlling undesirable behaviour
such as temper tantrums, aggressive behaviour and self-
injurious behaviour. These forms of behaviour could be seen
as being maintained because of their reinforcing consequences; children who have tantrums find the attention they
receive from others positively reinforcing and the answer
would be to remove attention (that is, punish the child),
ignoring the the wrong-doer when he misbehaves, and thus
extinguishing the problem behaviour.

The use of operant conditioning as a therapeutic procedure rapidly spread in the 1950s and 1960s and became known as 'behaviour modification'. The treatment of speech disorders in the 1950s and 1960s was almost wholly based on the operant procedures of Skinner. By 1957 Skinner turned his attention to the acquisition of that most human attribute, language. For Skinner speech and language were simply further examples of conditioned responses. He argued that the acquisition of words follows the same general rules as the acquisition of any motor behaviour. Initially the infant vocalizes spontaneously, but with increasing physical maturation he can bring vocalization under voluntary control and as a result it can be 'shaped' by the reinforcing consequences that follow. A child may, by accident, make a word-like sound 'Ma' which immediately receives reinforcement because of the attention parents lavish on this 'first word'. The response strength of 'Ma' is therefore increased. Words may also be established when in contact with a reinforcing object, such as milk. The child comes to associate the sound 'milk' with the appearance of real milk and consequently emits the sound 'milk' in order to bring about the availability of milk. After a number of words have been established the child further learns to produce sentences because of greater reinforcement consequences. This view of language acquisition as the learning of 'verbal behaviours' through the systematic application of environmental reinforcement had a tremendous impact on the clinical treatment of children with speech and communication problems. A number of different 'verbal behaviours' were categorized by Skinner which were reinforced in different ways and at different times during the course of development. Children who had some problem in developing language were seen as either suffering from a lack of environmental reinforcement for their verbal operants (e.g. a severely deprived environment with minimal interpersonal communication and little attention paid to the child) or as having poor learning capacities which could be enhanced by reinforcement of specific responses. So children with known brain damage resulting in poor discriminative abilities could have tasks simplified and reinforced for correct responses. In this way complex language operants could be built up through shaping techniques.

Skinner's 'Radical Behaviourism' provided a truly scientific analysis of human behaviour because it focussed on only objectively observable events. Rather than seek a speculative physiological explanation for these events Skinner emphasized the need to look to the environment for the causes of such behaviour. Such a view does not deny the existence of more fundamental analysis of behaviour in physiological terms; it simply acknowledges that a truly psychological explanation or model must analyse behaviour at the behavioural level. To speculate on the nature of unobservable physiological processes was not a scientific analysis: nor was any other unobservable concept such as 'innate' behaviours or the 'unconscious mind' open to the methods of psychological science. Radical behaviourism was therefore able to offer an account of the acquisition of new responses through reinforcement and of abnormal behaviour as 'shaped' through a faulty reinforcement schedule. This in turn led to the development of behaviour modification techniques which could be applied in educational and health settings to treat a range of disorders from spelling dysfunctions to hyperactivity.

Neo-behaviourism

Although Skinner's analysis of learning rapidly gained ground in practical treatment settings the theoretical adequacy of the system was constantly questioned. One simple prediction the theory makes is that learning (in the sense of some response strengthening) should not occur in the absence of positive reinforcement. Tolman (1932), in a classic experiment, demonstrated that learning does seem to take place in the absence of any environmental reinforcement. He compared the learning curves of two sets of rats in a simple maze learning experiment. The animals were introduced to a small maze in which there was a food reward. After a number of trials the rat learnt which responses (right/left turns) to make to reach the food reward directly. Tolman allowed one group of rats to have some time in the maze without any food reward being present. When both groups were then placed in the maze the group which had been allowed to 'explore' the maze prior to the introduction of a food reward were seen to reach a learning criterion before the unexposed group. This simple demonstration suggests that some kind of learning does take place in the absence of any obvious environmental reinforcement.

An experiment by Solomon and Wynne (1953) also throws conditioning theory into doubt. They administered very mild punishment (a tap on the rump with a newspaper) to a group of puppies each time they approached a food dish. Since the physical reinforcement is not great in this case we would predict that some mild inhibition about approaching the food dish would be the outcome. Instead, Solomon's puppies became very afraid of the food dish and their emotional reactions to this mild punishment seemed out of proportion to the possible pain. This kind of disconfirmatory evidence suggested that to view the environment as the sole mediator of learning was an oversimplification. The internal physiological state of the animal would have to be taken into account if a more accurate set of predictions were to be made. It was to this reductionist behaviourism that Hull (1943) made a landmark contribution with his neo-behaviouristic 'drive theory'. Hull recognized that a simple S-R analysis of behaviour could not explain every example of learning because of its reliance on a purely environmental view of reinforcement. What was required was a description or model of how intrinsic processes mediate stimulus-response associations. Although such processes were not

directly observable, a conceptual model of their likely
functioning could be inferred from observing how specific
environmental input (stimuli) could lead to operant output
(responses).

Hull postulated that every species is equipped with a
basic set of internal biological drives. These drives are
physiological energizers of behaviour which are experienced
as hunger, thirst and sexual needs. When an animal is in
some state of deprivation (e.g. hunger) a drive will energize behavioural sequences that are aimed at satisfying the
deprivation (catching food). These behaviours, which are
energized by drives and serve to reduce those drives, have
been learnt because they led to successful conclusions: they
reduce some drive state. Thus Hull redefined the concept of
'reinforcement' as anything which reduced a drive state.

A further postulate of drive theory was the concept of
habit. Each individual would have a stored habit hierarchy
of behaviours which had been learnt in previously successful
drive reduction outcomes. At low drive levels only the most
general of these behavioural habits would be activated. A
cat, therefore, could wake up, feel peckish and look around
for potential food sources. As drive level increases more
effective behavioural habits will be activated. The cat may
begin trying to scent a source of food and track it down. As
drive levels become very high more effective behavioural
habits will be activated. The cat may open a cupboard and
ransack the larder!

Hull argued that in Man one specific drive state - fear
(or, at lower levels, anxiety) - had a pervasive effect on
much of our social learning. Anxiety was the prime motivator
of most social and interpersonal behaviour; it energized
behaviours which led to drive reduction and so even hobbies
were seen as having drive-reducing properties. Drives were
therefore intervening variables between environmental stimuli and behavioural responses which could modify individual
responses according to previous learning history (habit
store) and actual level of drive. In order to predict accurately an animal's behaviour in a given situation we need to
know its previous learning history and its current drive
level. Hull actually tried to measure objectively the
strength of these internal drives using a variety of
methods: the amount of food consumed after three hours
of deprivation was used as a measure of hunger drive.

Hull's neo-behaviourism generated considerable clinical
interest because it emphasized the role of anxiety and other
internal emotional states in facilitating new learning. In a
classic experiment it was demonstrated that mild to moderate
levels of anxiety do enhance learning abilities, but when
anxiety reaches a certain level a performance decrement
results. This relationship seemed to account for a variety
of clinical anxiety problems such as phobias, obsessive-
compulsive disorders and the more common tics and nervous
habits. Clinicians such as Wolpe in South Africa and Eysenck
in the UK began to refine the Hullian neo-behaviouristic

theory through the systematic application of its principles to clinical treatment. Wolpe (1958) developed an anxiety management technique known as 'reciprocal inhibition' which owed much to Jones' counter-conditioning procedure. Briefly, Wolpe reasoned that if a patient were put in a bodily state that was incompatible with anxiety maladaptive responses could be extinguished. Anxiety responses had been conditioned to certain environmental stimuli which on subsequent occasions evoked an anxiety response: that is, a phobia. This explanation of the initial appearance of a phobia is simple classical conditioning. But conditioning theory would predict that this CR of anxiety would extinguish in the absence of the real UCS, such as some genuinely dangerous stimulus situation (in the case of a lift phobia the person may have had a fearful experience in a lift which has made him avoid them). But in phobias anxiety increases rather than decreases. This could be explained by the fact that individuals with phobias tend to avoid phobic objects in the environment and thus they learn these avoidance responses because they reduce phobic anxiety. Thus fears are acquired by classical conditioning and maintained by operant conditioning which leads to avoidance, and hence no further conditioning trials can take place to extinguish the fear. This two-factor view of anxiety states seemed to reconcile the radical and neo-behaviourist positions; but radical behaviourists could point out that since therapy must eventually be aimed at the avoidance response (the actual phobic behaviour), there was no need to postulate an underlying physiological dysfunction.

Psychopathology and personality

Neo-behaviourist clinicians such as Wolpe and Eysenck maintained that the primary problem was the internal anxiety state which resulted in the learning of avoidance and other responses which served to reduce anxiety. To focus on the behavioural symptoms of this anxiety was no solution. The anxiety had to be tackled directly through evoking incompatible responses which would extinguish the anxiety to feared stimuli. Reciprocal inhibition consists of teaching the patient some incompatible bodily response (such as muscle relaxation) and constructing a hierarchy of feared situations. For a spider phobic this may consist of imagining a real spider at the far side of an empty room, imagining a real spider two feet from the patient and finally imagining holding a spider in his hand. In practice several more intermediate steps would be inserted in the hierarchy progressing from low-anxiety to high-anxiety situations. By making the patient relax and imagine each situation in the hierarchy in turn (without experiencing any anxiety) the maladaptive fear response could be modified. This application of neo-behaviouristic learning theory to clinical problems is termed 'behaviour therapy' and consists of modifying internal anxiety states through systematic exposure to fear-arousing situations. Reciprocal inhibition is better known today as 'systematic desensitization' and is either carried out using imagined situations or by taking the patient out into the real world to confront his fears 'in vivo'.

Eysenck has been responsible for further theoretical developments in neo-behaviouristic theory. He has devoted a considerable research effort to specifying more precisely how internal variables modify input-output relationships, and has produced a theory of individual differences in personality and learning which argues that we inherit specific types of nervous system functioning which underlies psychological functioning. Briefly, Eysenck has (through mathematical techniques) identified three major dimensions of individual differences which he has called extraversion-introversion, neuroticism-stability and psychoticism. The first dimension refers to individual differences in preferred levels of stimulation. Each of us has an optimum level of stimulation which we try to maintain at a consistent level. When we feel understimulated we seek stimulating events and, if overstimulation is experienced, we withdraw to seek peace and quiet. The extravert individual is stimulus hungry and seeks out new social and emotional contacts as well as pursuing other interests. The introvert individual is in a higher state of internal stimulation than the extravert and thus avoids social and emotional contacts and additional sources of stimulation.

The second dimension refers to our emotional reactivity to events. Neurotic individuals have a highly labile emotional system which reacts strongly to even mild stimulation. The stable individual has a less active system which does not over-react to emotional events. The dimension of psychoticism has been added lately to the theory and represents a further independent continuum of individual differences. Individuals scoring high on this factor are usually solitary, cruel and inhumane. They lack sensitivity to social demands and may be aggressive to their own families. Psychoticism is believed to vary with certain hormonal balances in the body which may underlie antisocial behaviour.

Thus each individual (from normals to psychiatric patients) can be described in terms of these three major personality dimensions. The sources of these differences lie in the variations in the CNS, autonomic nervous system and endocrine functioning. The value of this system in accounting for neurotic illnesses has been acknowledged, for it predicts that certain personality types are prone to different kinds of disorder. Individuals high on neuroticism and low on extraversion will develop anxiety conditions and depressive illnesses whereas neurotic extraverts are more likely to develop hysterical conditions. These predictions are based on the ways in which learning is influenced by these biological differences in psychological functioning.

Behaviourism, as a scientific approach to psychology, has generated a number of theoretical viewpoints which have had direct implications for therapeutic intervention. The development of behaviour modification techniques and the neo-behaviouristic therapies has radically affected practices in diverse fields of care. For some it fails to capture the richness of human behaviour for it cannot analyse such capacities as creativity and free will. Behaviourism represents Man as buffeted by stimuli and emitting responses in accordance with internal anxieties. Its sheer objectivity restricts study to very general features of human interaction and thus does not tap the beliefs and ideas that are characteristic of mental life. Behaviourists would argue that at this stage only a general and crude model is possible. Future developments could enable a more detailed, objective analysis to be conducted.

In recent years behaviouristic psychology has had to cope with increasing evidence that many of its theoretical assumptions are incorrect. The power of behavioural treatments does, however, suggest that this level of analysis is a worth-while venture. Modern clinical therapy has responded to these theoretical shortcomings by designing new models of intervention which adhere to behaviouristic standards of objectivity and quantification, but which aim to modify conscious psychological processes as well as specific behavioural responses.

Cognitive psychology

The development of behaviourism in the USA was paralleled by the European development of cognitive psychology. This school of psychology came into being amongst the students of experimental introspective psychology which had been launched by Wundt (1907). During the 1920s and 1930s this movement became known as the Gestalt school of psychology, and held a fundamentally different set of assumptions about the nature of Man and of his psychological processes. These scientists wished to study conscious mental processes such as perceiving objects in the environment, thinking and remembering: the higher mental processes which are the basis of our self-awareness. These were termed cognitive processes after the Latin term for 'thinking'. Gestalt psychologists used experimental techniques to investigate these processes by means of manipulating perceptual input, and describing potential cognitive processes which analysed this input and controlled motor output. The term 'Gestalt' is the German word for 'form' or 'pattern' and refers to the theory put forward by this group of psychologists: that is, that the mind was designed to process complex patterns of stimulation rather than single, isolated stimulus events. They demonstrated how the mind seeks form in its perceptual processing and can process identical patterns in different ways in different situations.

The existence of visual illusions demonstrated a further argument of the Gestalt school. In the Müller-Lyer illusion (figure 1), two identical line stimuli are transmitted to the brain, yet we perceive one to be longer than the other.

This kind of evidence suggested that there was more to cognitive functioning than a simple physiological representation. If physical stimuli are literally translated by the brain why should we believe one line is longer than the other? Further studies of reasoning and remembering suggested that environmental input is not simply a selection of stimuli but a source of information, which is analysed by cognitive psychological processes. If incoming information is deficient in some fashion (e.g. a series of dots rather than lines) then stored information can supplement the incoming stimulation to achieve a more satisfactory analysis. It has been suggested that just such a phenomenon occurs in the Müller-Lyer illusion; that the mind, designed to process three-dimensional (3-D) input, is unable to process simple 2-D line drawings and analyses the illusion as if it were a 3-D object. One possible interpretation of the two lines would be the inside corner and outside edge of a building, and thus we perceive B to be longer than A because we allow for perspective by expanding the single line in B and contracting it in A.

Figure 1

Müller–Lyer illusion

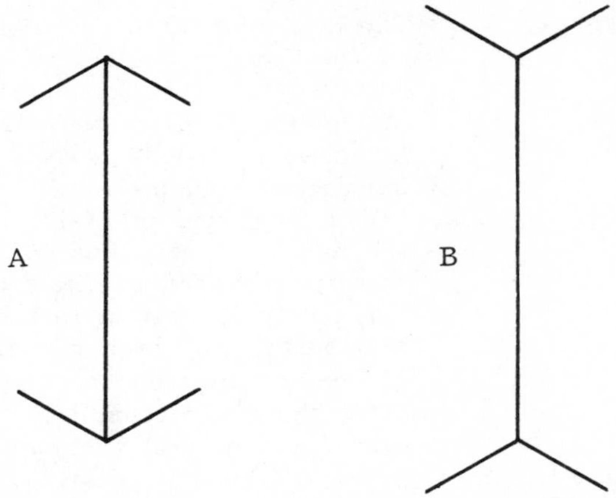

This shift in emphasis, from regarding the environment as a series of objective stimuli to a source of information, which is processed by cognitive capacities to yield meaning, is the hallmark of cognitive psychology. Köhler (1917) argued that similar cognitive processing capacities exist in other species and demonstrated that apes could reach solutions to problems through 'insight' rather than trial and error conditioning. This classic experiment set apes the problem of trying to reach bananas placed outside their cage by making use of wooden rods. The apes readily used such 'tools' and quickly learnt to retrieve the reward. The bananas were then placed further away, beyond the reach of the rod. The apes were supplied with two identical rods which fitted together. Köhler describes how he observed the apes look at the bananas and then the rods, and immediately join the two sticks together to reach the reward. This single trial 'insight' learning is most characteristic of human functioning. Although we may take several trials to learn to ride a bicycle (behavioural learning), we learn in one trial how to solve more complex intellectual problems.

Gestalt psychology proposed a model of these internal cognitive processes which did not attempt to speculate on the actual neurophysiology of psychological processes, but tried instead to describe such processing as being like an electromagnetic field. The mind was said to be made up of a number of interacting 'mental fields' which could generate different perceptual experiences and produce insightful and novel solutions to problems. This choice of analogy - the mind as a series of overlapping electromagnetic fields - was largely determined by the available concepts in the natural sciences and the desire to avoid the simple telephone exchange model of internal processing that Pavlov had postulated. But this analogy proved too inexact to generate any really testable hypotheses, and consequently Gestalt psychology did not advance as a psychological science.

This school of thought in psychology continued along diverse lines for a further two decades before a new development in the fields of mathematics and electrical engineering provided a more specific analogy for the modelling of cognitive processes: the computer. Computers are described as 'thinking machines' or, more appropriately, as 'counting machines', but it is difficult not to believe that they are capable of something approaching thought. Computers accept environmental input (data) and analyse this information according to an internal programme. They can then 'reply' to the questions or problems set. To all intents this process looks very like human cognitive functioning, and a new science of cognitive psychology came into being in the early 1960s which used computer analogies to describe cognitive processes and, further, used the computer to control highly complex cognitive processing experiments and to analyse these experimental data in highly sophisticated ways. Thus models of internal cognitive processes such as perception, thinking, memory and language were developed through highly controlled experimental research.

A crucial new concept in this psychology is the notion of feedback. Man is viewed as an active processor of environmental information, and on the basis of these analyses formulates plans of action which control further behavioural action. These internal plans are constantly subject to modification by a continuous analysis of the outcomes of behavioural action, that is, feedback on the relative success or failure of the strategy. Thus in reaching for a pencil we analyse incoming information about the position, weight and distance of the pencil from our hand. We plan a general reaching strategy which will involve a sequence of arm and finger movements. When we actually put this plan into operation we continuously utilize feedback information of where our hand is in relation to the pencil to modify our internal plan and guide our motor action more accurately. These models of internal psychological functioning give rise to predictions about the development of plans, and of how information is stored and accessed during problem-solving activities.

The cognitive solution to developing a scientific psychology is to devise a model of mental functioning which is inferred from observing input-output relationships, but with the fundamental difference of viewing Man as a much more active and selective processor of environmental information than has been the case in behaviouristic accounts. The advent of new technology in the natural sciences has provided more sophisticated models for psychological analogies than was available when Pavlov and Skinner presented their theories. Much more rigorous control is now available over the presentation of input, and recording of output, than was previously possible and thus the earlier objections to this type of psychology were no longer valid. However, cognitive psychologists emphasize that their models of 'cognitive functioning' are highly abstract and do not speculate on the actual nature of the underlying physiological processes which are assumed to be the mechanisms of cognition. This point is emphasized by the use of box diagrams (flow charts) to represent internal cognitive processing. This new approach allowed for the investigation of far more complex learning problems than had been the case with traditional behaviourism. Because scientific observations of input-output relationships could be made in great detail, higher mental functions such as perception, memory, thought and language became permissible topics of study. The main thrust of cognitive psychology is seen in the way it reinterprets 'learning'. Behaviourism suggested that external reinforcement 'stamps in' operant responses; cognitive psychology suggests that actions (responses) are the result of internal plans which arise to achieve some desired goal state. Goal states exist when there is some perceived discrepancy between internal and external knowledge. We process incoming information in order to generate internal models of the external environment. These models are used to represent the external environment within consciousness. Such representations free our awareness from the here-and-now and allow us to set up internal pictures of the external world in order to plan future courses of action in a particular situation.

By processing, analysing and storing past experience, we have a frame of reference to interpret the present and to plan for the future. Behaviourism emphasizes the importance of the past in determining the present, but cannot explain the obvious point that human consciousness can also anticipate the future. From an evolutionary perspective the development of the capacity to think in time and space would represent a major survival advantage over simply reacting to the here-and-now as many lower forms of life do. A further point is the flexibility with which we 'respond' in actual behaviour. Behaviourism of the Skinnerian school argued that when a response is learnt through reinforcement it is the actual muscular movements which are stored, so a fixed sequence of motor programming would be learned in a specific situation to reappear in a future situation. Cognitive psychology pointed out that detailed study of the acquisition of complex behavioural responses, such as skills, demonstrates that these sequences are not invariant but have tremendous flexibility in their performance. Skilled behaviour - such as tennis playing - is the result of intensive cognitive processing of the basic sequences which leads to the development of an internal model or plan of the 'ideal' strokes. These plans are then executed under careful feedback scrutiny which is compared with the internal model for any source of discrepancy. If a discrepancy exists between the internal model of the skill and the feedback performance, the action will be modified to reduce this discrepancy. Cognitive psychology reinterprets 'stimuli', 'reinforcement' and 'responses' as sources of information which are available for analysis.

Pre-programmed behaviour

One final implication emerges from cognitive psychology. Behaviourism regarded the notion of innate capacities for behaviour as an inappropriate topic for scientific study. It was argued that we must assume all behaviour is the result of environmental learning through the application of reinforcement. This assumption did not rule out the existence of simple Pavlovian reflexes, but it would not accept the notion that species may be genetically 'programmed' from birth to behave in complex sequences at some future point in development: a notion which resulted from the study of animals in their natural habitat (ethology). By non-experimental observation it had been established that many species demonstrate highly stereotyped patterns of behaviour in their natural habitat which emerge despite the lack of opportunity for learning. Ethologists attempted to specify the relative contributions of nature (genetic endowment) and nurture (learning) in a wide range of species. These studies strongly suggested that biologically significant behaviour such as hunting, shelter building and sexual behaviour was species-specific in the sense that a major genetic component was responsible for the existence of general behavioural sequences shared by every individual in the species. Although it seemed that species varied in the amount of 'innate behaviour' displayed, it was argued that Man may also have 'innate capacities' for specific kinds of behaviour. Clearly those aspects of human functioning which are of obvious biological significance are the most likely sources of innate, pre-programmed processing. Since Man is primarily a social animal who owes his survival as a species

to complex, co-operative activities, a likely area of innate
capacity would be social communication.

Cognitive psychologists have postulated that Man's
capacity for language may well be innately programmed to
process incoming auditory, visual and tactual information in
a highly specialized way to give rise to meaningful, internal symbolization. This symbolization can be externalized
through actual speech to act as a source of information for
another individual who has similar specialized processing
capacities. A major effort in cognitive psyhology and its
related fields of neuropsychology and psycholinguistics is
to create a model of these specialized internal processing
capacities which allow even very young children to extract
meaningful symbolic information from complex auditory and
visual input. This capacity may well be the very basis of
our ability to generate internal models (representations) of
the external world.

Cognitive therapy
To take a practical example of how cognitive psychology
approaches the problems of clinical practice, we can consider the treatment of articulation disorders in young
children. Suppose we have a child who substitutes a particular sound. For a behaviourist this would be an example of
faulty reinforcement shaping. Treatment would consist of
rewarding all correct sounds and ignoring (or withdrawing
positive reinforcement for) all incorrect sounds. Thus
therapy would consist of assembling a list of words (perhaps
with pictures) which contained opportunities for substitution and systematically reinforcing all correct responses.
It may be preceded by intensive conditioning of the correct
sounds alone before using whole words, but repetitive,
reinforced drilling would be the main therapeutic aim. A
cognitive approach would be to postulate the kinds of breakdown which could disrupt this articulatory skill. We could
postulate that peripheral information-processing channels
such as hearing may be damaged and thus the child is unable
to discriminate sound differences accurately. This would
lead to the development of a faulty internal model of these
speech sounds. Such damage may affect feedback channels,
with the result that the child is unable to perceive any
discrepancy between environmental input and his own output.
We could also hypothesize that internal cognitive processing
channels are not functioning efficiently for some reason,
leading to poor construction of internal models. The child
may have specific attentional deficits which make sustained
concentration difficult. In such a case hearing may be quite
normal, but detailed processing of input may not be possible
because of short attention span and distractability. It may
be that a problem exists in memory storage of incoming verbal information, where the child can only store beginnings
and endings of complex words because they are more prominent. Deficits in cognitive processing may also be general
rather than specific, and this knowledge would have valuable

therapeutic implications. This more complex analysis of articulation disorders is really a series of predictions (hypotheses) which can be systematically tested by investigating and assessing various aspects of cognitive functioning. Such an investigation is essentially diagnostic and thus has direct implications for treatment. If we find that a child is having difficulty utilizing all feedback channels in articulation (auditory, visual, motor) we may decide to enhance available information by supplying new sources of feedback (e.g. use of a mirror to train motor feedback awareness) and supplying continuous feedback on the child's performance.

A therapist may provide such feedback verbally by encouraging the child when he approximates the sound and being less enthusiastic when he is far from the target; here feedback information about the success of the child's internal model is given in the same way we guide someone through a hide-and-seek game. As the person gets near the hidden object we tell him he is getting 'warm' and when he is moving away we tell him he is 'cold'. We can therefore offer this feedback information to the child in the same way. In practice, cognitive therapy looks identical to behaviouristic therapy for both offer the child continuous encouragement; in behaviourism this is reinforcement, and in cognitive therapy it is feedback information.

This approach to psychology has found application in a wide range of fields. In education the work of Jean Piaget on the development of the intellect is a good example. Piaget (e.g. 1929) revolutionized our concepts of 'intelligence' by pursuing a developmental study of cognitive functioning. This analysis has subsequently offered educationists a more detailed model of learning than earlier behaviourist theories. In the field of mental health cognitive psychology has produced a variety of models of abnormal functioning; conditions such as the psychoses have been described as disruptions of basic cognitive processes which result in such symptoms as hallucinations and delusions. A number of cognitive therapies have emerged as treatments for anxiety states, depression and other neurotic disorders. Cognitive psychology has, like behaviourism, emphasized the point that all clinical applications of psychology are 'mini-experiments'; hypotheses generated by theory. The behaviour therapist attempts to discover which features of the environment typically reinforce a specific piece of behaviour and a number of experiments may be conducted before the correct source is identified. In cognitive psychology the clinician sets up hypotheses of the kinds of internal dysfunction that could account for the presenting problem. These hypotheses are then subjected to empirical test by investigating the suspect capacities through measurement devices. If these measurements confirm a particular hypothesis, then a therapy can be designed from the basic theory to enhance or circumvent an area of deficit. This therapy is, however, regarded as another hypothesis which predicts positive change in the target symptoms and it is the responsibility of the clinical scientist to collect evidence of the accuracy of the prediction; whether the therapy works or not!

Individual psychology

Both cognitive and behaviouristic psychology try to specify the general ways in which individuals differ in their functioning through attempting to identify the general properties of learning. Individual psychology is concerned with the unique functioning of individuals; it tries to identify the most important dimensions of difference between individuals and explain how such individual differences come about. This aim is stressed by the theory of evolution which predicts wide variations amongst individuals through selective survival and genetic recombination. Evolution proceeds by conducting a number of 'experiments' in design. An individual may arise in a species who displays a new characteristic which has high survival potential. This individual will survive, reproduce and create several new individuals who also display this characteristic. These individuals are more likely to survive and reproduce and thus more of the species features this new, adaptive characteristic. Such new characteristics can be the result of genetic mutation or of genetic recombination. Clearly, if we understood the reasons for individual variation at the psychological level we could infer what underlying processes might be involved. More practically, individual psychology also pursues an understanding of our conscious experience; of being a unique human being. We are self-aware; and we are aware of our self-awareness. We have no direct experience of the self-awareness of others and can only infer how it 'feels' to be someone else through interpersonal communication. Some individuals are highly concerned about their own self-awareness, particularly when they feel they cannot communicate their concern to anyone else. This negative self-awareness is a major feature of several types of mental illness and there is an urgent need for theories of individual functioning which have implications for the treatment of such conditions.

Two major areas of difference in psychological functioning have been identified. The most obvious is temperament, or personality. People do seem to differ in the extent to which they display emotion and in the frequency of emotional display. This basic dimension of difference was recognized by the ancient Greeks who claimed they arose from the configuration of the planets at the time of birth, or that temperament differences were due to the excess supply of certain basic bodily fluids such as black and yellow bile, phlegm and blood! The second dimension of difference is of more recent origin although it has existed as a vague notion from the beginning of history: intelligence. Perhaps psychology and psychologists are most widely known through their work on intellectual functioning and the IQ test in particular. The development of the IQ Test by Binet was a

landmark achievement in psychology (Binet and Simon, 1905).
For many years measurements of intelligence have assisted
educational decision making and helped to control experimental variables in research. Yet the IQ test is a paradoxical concept; if we design a test of a particular ability
we need to be able to define very accurately exactly what
that ability is. Once we understand what processes are
involved in the ability, we can set about designing a test
which will tap those processes. But the IQ test has evolved
from a very simple definition given by Binet and Simon: To
judge well, to reason well, to comprehend well, these are
the essential activities of the intelligence'.

It was on the basis of such general definitions that
much of the test construction was carried out. IQ tests
tend to be designed in order to resemble other tests of IQ
and as a consequence the tests themselves provide an operational definition of intelligence. Operational definitions
apply to situations where a researcher asserts that a given
concept – say, extraversion – can be defined as that property which is measured by a test of 'extraversion'. This
has resulted in a definition of intelligence which states
'intelligence' is that which is measured by IQ tests!

Both these areas of study have received a great deal of
attention from poets and dramatists over the centuries, but
it took the advent of modern mathematics, and of statistical
inference, to begin to investigate these processes scientifically. A new science of psychological measurement has
developed in the past century with the emergence of psychometrics. However, measurement is after all only a way of
describing some phenomenon. We can measure the vital
statistics of virtually anything which exists without being
able to say exactly what that phenomenon is and how it
functions.

Theorizing on the causes of individual differences has
had a rather stormy history; two extreme views have emerged,
one emphasizing the biologically adaptive significance of
human variation, while the other holds that individual differences in personality and intelligence are the product
of life-long social learning. The biological theorists view
human beings as intricate evolutionary experiments in adaptation. Man is as much the product of evolution as any other
species and his evolution has been marked by the development
of several unique characteristics which have greatly increased his capacity for survival. In particular the use of
language which enables co-operation is one very distinctive
attribute. Variation within a given species is the fuel of
evolution, allowing new characteristics produced by genetic
recombination (mating) to be 'tested' in the natural environment. In general this will lead to several characteristics
being distributed along several dimensions in the total
population, with some individuals having more or less of
each characteristic leading to unique blends of linguistic,
cognitive, social and emotional capacities. The ultimate
'test' of each unique blend will be the extent to which it
survives to maturity and reproduces a new, equally adaptive

offspring. Two important points follow from this position. The first maintains that people differ from each other along specific and relatively independent dimensions. Because characteristics will tend to be distributed more or less normally in the human population we would predict that there will be extreme ends in each distribution. For example, intelligence is described in terms of a normal distribution with an extreme high-scoring group of a small number of individuals who may be classified as geniuses. Similarly there is a low-scoring sub-group who fall within our definition of mental retardation. This would suggest a similar distribution for other characteristics with extreme groups representing exaggeration of perfectly 'normal' characteristics. The second point is more intriguing. Some evolutionary theorists argue that the answer to the question 'What comes first: the chicken or the egg?' should be 'A hen is just an egg's way of making another egg.' This viewpoint is elaborated upon in Dawkins (1976).

Social learning theorists reply that although some very basic emotional differences may have a physiological basis, the vast majority of personality and intellectual differences are socially and culturally determined. Sex-differences are a good case in point; it has been maintained that women are poor drivers and excellent talkers because of a basic biological difference in the brains of males and females. Social learning theorists would argue that such differences are mainly the result of generally held social conventions about the differences between men and women. The traditionally dominant, technical and unemotional male has been contrasted with the submissive, romantic and emotional female. Such informal 'theories' of men and women lead to the specification of fixed 'roles' for men and women which further bolster the original 'theory'.

An obvious implication of the social/cultural view is that male-female differences may not be as great as has been thought. Before examining the various theories of individual functioning which have emerged, some consideration is required of how individual differences are measured.

Psychometrics

The earliest theorizing about the nature of individual differences was characterized by an appeal to subjective judgement. The Greek philosopher Galen arrived at four distinct personality types:

* SANGUINE individuals are hopeful, optimistic and confident;
* MELANCHOLIC types are depressive and prone to anxiety;
* PHLEGMATIC individuals are sluggish, lethargic and apathetic;
* CHOLERIC types are active, outgoing and quick tempered.

Galen further speculated on the causes of these personality types and concluded that each temperament cluster was the result of having some excess of a particular 'body

humour': either blood, black and yellow bile or phlegm.
Galen was therefore a 'reductionist'; before any serious
investigation of the causes of individual differences is
undertaken we need to develop more scientific methods of
personality description.

The endeavour to provide objective measurements
of variation in psychological functioning resulted in the
production of the 'mental test'. All mental tests have three
basic features in their design: (i) validity, (ii) standardization and (iii) reliability. These three criteria
for test construction are crucial if genuinely objective
measurement is to be achieved. Consider what we would need
to do if we tried to discover whether men are as aggressive
as women in verbal discussions. We would need to measure how
aggressive males and females really are in discussion and
thus we would need some measurement device of 'verbal aggression'. We would have to define 'verbal aggression'
operationally by describing specific examples of what is,
and is not, 'verbal aggression'. From these definitions we
could set about designing a simple questionnaire with some
arbitrary scale made up of items like: 'I always like to get
the last word in an argument ... YES ... NO ... SOMETIMES'.
This simple three-point scale for perhaps 20 or so items
would yield a wide variety of scores between 0 and 60. We
could simply claim that people who score high on this test
are more likely to be verbally aggressive in conversation;
but how could we confirm this hypothesis? We could administer the questionnaire to a sample of individuals and
also rate each individual as 'verbally aggressive' or 'non-
aggressive' after observing them in a group discussion. The
test score could then be compared with the actual observational ratings to see if the two agree on the majority of
classifications. But rating 'real' behaviour is clearly open
to subjective bias which can be offset by using a group of
independent raters whose judgements are then averaged and
compared with the test score. But in order to make rating a
more objective method of measurement we would need to describe, and have raters agree on, exactly what constitutes
'verbal aggression'; for example, interrupting frequently in
conversation, use of sarcasm, etc.

It is through this exercise of finding some other source
of measurement which can be compared with test data that
the criterion of 'validity' is reached for a mental test.
Traditionally there are two sources of validity evidence:
the first is the extent to which the new mental test of
characteristic 'A' correlates with a well-established test
of 'A'. Although this has tended to occur in the development
of IQ tests, it is usually the case that new tests are developed to measure new characteristics, so a second method
is to compare the test predictions with already identified
groups which display the particular characteristic the test
is designed to measure. If we design a test of depression
then groups of clinically depressed patients should score
significantly higher on this test than the general public or
other patient groups. Once we feel confident that our test

really is measuring the characteristic we are interested in
we have an operational definition of that characteristic
which can guide future research.

But often we need to say by how much a given individual
differs from people in general on a test. In order to answer
this kind of question the test must be standardized on a
large group of individuals to determine the average scores
and the shape of the dispersion of high and low scores. Only
when we have this information can we make judgements about
normal and abnormal scores. The test we have designed may be
of wide generality, such as a test of 'memory', or highly
specific, such as a test of problem-solving for low IQ children. The purpose of the test determines the kind of representative sample we need to draw in order to standardize the
test.

'Reliability' refers to the extent to which our test
always obtains the same score for the same individual at
different times. If a test is unreliable it will produce two
different scores when used on different occasions. (See Paul
Kline, chapter 6, for further discussions of reliability.)

These three principles of validity, reliability and
standardization guide the construction of all mental tests
from IQ to language capacities. Test construction is a
process of continuous refinement, since a test is always an
hypothesis about a particular ability or characteristic.
Such hypotheses should, of course, be modified as our understanding of these abilities and characteristics develops.
Modern psychometrics presents a landscape of bewildering
complexity with many tests purporting to measure a common
characteristic. Closer examination reveals how each test
defines that characteristic and it can be seen that some
tests use rather simple definitions of their topic, whereas
others may be based on a more complex theoretical account.
Although it is very important to be aware of the constructional features of tests and their methods of yielding
scores, there is no substitute for a careful appraisal of
the theoretical basis of a mental test if meaningful
interpretation of the test score is to be achieved.

Personality and individual differences: theory

Man is like: every man
               some men
               no other man.

This truism is traditionally used to introduce various
levels of analysis in individual psychology. Some workers
look for the common dimensions of individual differences
by studying groups of people using objective measurement
devices. This 'like every man' level of analysis is seen in
the study of intelligence. 'Like some men' relates to the
study of broad areas of individual differences such as
extraversion and introversion in Eysenck's analysis of
personality.

Eysenck's theory

Eysenck (1947) administered a large number of psychometric and behavioural scales to a sample of 10,000 normal and neurotic soldiers. By applying the statistical technique of factor analysis to these data he isolated two very broad dimensions of difference which he termed extraversion-introversion (E-I) and neuroticism-stability. A further psychometric test was developed which classifies individuals on these two unrelated dimensions. This questionnaire has been standardized and revised over the years and is currently available as the Eysenck Personality Inventory (EPI) and the Eysenck Personality Questionnaire (EPQ). This self-report questionnaire contains items such as:

* Do you enjoy meeting new people? (Yes: Extraversion)
* Do you like going out a lot? (Yes: Extraversion)
* Do you worry about your health? (Yes: Neuroticism)
* Do you worry about awful things that might happen? (Yes: Neuroticism)

In this way each individual obtains a score on both extraversion and neuroticism, pinpointing his place in two-dimensional space.

Eysenck (1963) has compared his dimensional approach to personality description with the early categorical systems of the Greeks to illustrate the behavioural traits manifested by extraversion/neuroticism combinations. As mentioned earlier Eysenck sees these two dimensions of personality as having biological significance. Extraversion/introversion differences arise from variation in the CNS functioning which is determined by genetic recombination. Neuroticism/stability reflects differences in the reactivity of the autonomic nervous system; again, the product of genetic recombination. This is not to say that 'personality' at the psychological level is the sole product of genetics, but rather that what is inherited is a general tendency to behave in certain cognitive and emotional ways. The interests and activities of similar individuals may be radically different, but their general tendency to react in the same way will be common.

In more detail Eysenck sees extraversion-introversion as the result of specific kinds of physiological functioning. He adopted the notions of 'excitation' and 'inhibition' in neural functioning as a model of how E-I differences arise. It is assumed that a balance of excitation/inhibition is typical of neurophysiological functioning. Extraverts have low excitation/high inhibition balances. This results in the extravert conditioning slowly because with low excitation it takes longer to form new neural associations and the high inhibition will tend to dampen activation quickly. Introverts have a high excitation/low inhibition balance resulting in rapid conditioning. Using simple eyeblink conditioning experiments it has been found that extraverts and introverts do differ in the predicted direction in their conditionability. Neuroticism-stability was seen as the general reactivity of the autonomic nervous system to stress. This again is a fundamental biological dimension: an extension of the fight-flight system in other species which prepares the body for some strenuous activity. These two mechanisms of emotional and cognitive processing interact to result in a wide variety of individual differences in functioning at the physiological, psychological and social levels.

Evidence of Eysenck's claim that extraversion and neuroticism have a biological basis is found in numerous twin studies where it has been shown that identical twins are much more alike on these two dimensions than fraternal twins. Further evidence comes from the study of other species where 'emotional reactivity' and 'conditionability' have, through selective breeding, been shown to have a strong genetic basis. This biological theory of personality types can form the basis of an explanation of psychopathological behaviour. Neurotic disorders can be viewed as instances of faulty learning through (i) excessive emotional reaction to reinforcement and (ii) cortical excitation/inhibition balances. Thus the anxiety neurotic may have high N (emotional reactivity) and low E (excitation/inhibition balance) whereas hysterics will have high N and high E, resulting in inhibited cortical activity leading to sensory and motor disturbances. Behaviour therapy is a way of tackling these anxiety conditions by designing highly structured conditioning experiences which loosen anxiety associations. More recently Eysenck has identified a third dimension of personality termed 'psychoticism', which is unrelated (orthogonal) to E and N, and which may shed light on the psychotic illnesses.

The work of R. B. Cattell (1965) is closely associated with Eysenck's reasoning. Cattell has conducted a similar analysis using a less rigorous form of factor analysis which identifies some 16 primary personality traits that are said to make up the common core of human personality. What is important, however, is the profile an individual obtains on this test which may have significant clinical implications. This study has led to the development of the 16PF questionnaire (Cattell, 1963) and the child/adolescent form (the High School Personality Questionnaire). These devices have been extensively used in research into various disorders to describe individual differences in personality. Cattell's 16 factors, when further factor analysed using Eysenck's techniques, reduce to two broad factors which seem virtually identical to Eysenck's extraversion and neuroticism. The difference between the two systems is technical; Eysenck is interested in describing types of personality, Cattell offers a range of trait descriptions.

Freudian theory
If the previous approach to personality has made a significant contribution to theory and therapy in abnormal psychology, it is limited in comparison to the impact made by the

father of clinical psychology, Sigmund Freud. Freud's theory of personality not only offers universal dimensions of personality description but further stresses the uniqueness (like no other) of each individual personality. The comprehensiveness of Freudian theory to account for behaviour as diverse as mental illness and art has never been equalled in psychology, partly because there are serious doubts that such inclusiveness is feasible. Freud, trained as a physician and specializing in neurology, realized that a description of psychological functioning could not be given in purely physiological terms. As a neurologist Freud came into contact with patients who were assumed to have brain damage but on investigation were found to be perfectly normal apart from their often bizarre symptoms. These cases were examples of hysteria where it seemed that mental events were disrupting physical functioning. Blindness, deafness, paralyses and analgesias are all seen in cases of hysteria. Sensory functioning of this kind has a clear organic basis which can be directly inspected for damage, and any damage has a typical sequence of dysfunction. In hysteria no damage was apparent and the presenting symptoms often did not follow typical sequences of dysfunction. This kind of clinical phenomenon led Freud to develop a theory of mental functioning in purely psychological terms.

At the turn of the century Freud was influenced by the prevailing energy models in the physical sciences. He saw the mind as being an energy system divided into three distinct parts: the ID, EGO and SUPER-EGO. The id, the most primitive component, comes into being at birth and is the storehouse of basic biological drives such as hunger, thirst and sex. These primitive survival instincts demand immediate gratification or they increase and result in some emotional output. The id is joined later in development (around six months) by a second kind of mental energy: the ego, which is our conscious, cognitive capacity. The ego exerts a controlling function over the id and can thus control gratification of these instincts if it perceives that the external environment does not contain suitable conditions for gratification. By the age of four the super-ego emerges, which can be viewed as the 'conscience' for it serves to censure thoughts and behaviour which do not conform to the values of society acquired through growing up. Freud postulated that the most significant point about these energy relationships lay in the fact that we are only aware of ego processes. The ego is our conscious and self-conscious awareness whereas the id and the super-ego are unconscious entities which process incoming information at levels above and below our awareness. Freud saw the causes of psychopathology in these unconscious areas and set out to describe how these three kinds of mental energy interact in both normal and abnormal development.

Although the mind is therefore a biologically determined phenomenon the content was the product of a mental-environmental interaction. Freud argued that the mind develops through negotiating four states of psychosexual development. This aspect of the theory - the importance of sexual drives in young children - caused outrage in Victorian times, but Freud was convinced that of all the instinctual drives in the id, sexuality was the most important. He described the first stage in this development as the oral stage, where id impulses are optimally gratified by sucking and placing objects in the mouth. In the next anal stage (two years) the focus of gratification shifts to the anus, through the retention and expulsion of faeces. Between three years and six years the child reaches the phallic stage where genital manipulation is preferred and subsequently a universal crisis occurs in development known as the Oedipal conflict. During the phallic stage the child is attracted towards the parent of the opposite sex. But the child may experience threat from the parent of the same sex during this infatuation and tries to resolve this conflict by repressing its desires through increased identification with the parent of the same sex (little boys act as 'tough men' and have no time for cissy pastimes or too much affection from mother). This first awareness of environmental censure gives rise to the development of the super-ego. Following the Oedipal conflict is a period of asexual development known as the latency period which lasts until the age of 12 years when the final, adult, genital stage is reached and heterosexual interest in peers develops.

Freud moved from this psychological description of mental development to postulate a number of personality types that could occur if a particular stage of psychosexual development was not negotiated successfully. Successful development occurs when an optimum level of stimulation and gratification is achieved at each stage of development, and if the Oedipal conflict is resolved satisfactorily. If too much, or insufficient, gratification is achieved in any stage this could lead to fixation (arrestment of development) at that stage. For those who had not negotiated the anal stage successfully two types of personality resulted: the anal retentive was mean, moody and obsessive; the anal expulsive carefree and happy go lucky. Either personality could result if under- or over-stimulation was encountered. This arrestment of development was characterized by the use of ego defence mechanisms which blocked further id impulses from seeking expression and thus forcing these impulses to remain at an unconscious level. When forbidden id impulses seek gratification via the ego they cause the ego to experience anxiety. This uncomfortable sensation can be removed by using ego defence mechanisms to block the impulses and force them to exist at an unconscious level. In the case of hysteria it is these emotional impulses seeking gratification that results in the sensory disturbances as the ego defence mechanism of conversion comes into play. Conversion serves to express mental dysfunction in a physical form. A number of defence mechanisms exist to cope with anxiety-provoking impulses which may have been kept dormant in the unconscious for many years through the simple mechanism of repression.

But if a situation or relationship develops in adult life which resembles these earlier childhood conflicts then the dormant impulses may be strengthened and seek expression. A new, more effective defence mechanism comes into play which results in some form of psychiatric symptom. Freud argued the need to reach down into the unconscious mind and come to terms with the specific repressed impulse. He reasoned that these immature impulses could be resolved in the light of adult reality if the individual could be made aware of, and gain insight into, the nature of the conflict. Once this conflict had been resolved the need for the particular cluster of defence mechanisms would disappear and function would return to normal.

Assessment in this psychoanalytic account of personality has traditionally been viewed as a continuous process in which a clinician is constantly building a picture of his patient's personality from a variety of sources. Two formal techniques have become established as ways of gaining access to the unconscious mind. Both are based on the existence of the ego defence mechanisms known as projection. In projection the ego externalizes anxiety on to objects and people in the social world. In the Rorschach (inkblot) Test individuals are asked to examine several symmetrical inkblots. These unstructured stimuli provide a 'blank screen' on to which the patient projects his unconscious worries and fears. Thus in looking at an inkblot a person may say he sees two men carrying an animal and in another he might see a butterfly, or two elephant heads. These responses are analysed for pathological significance. In the Thematic Apperception Test (TAT) the patient is asked to tell a story about what is portrayed in a picture. The content of this story is assumed to reveal important features of the individual's unconscious life.

Freud's approach to personality theory horrified behaviouristic scientists who argued that his clinical methodology of obtaining case history information and building general theories from his subjective analysis of this information was a mockery of scientific method. Freud did not study the predictions of his theory in any experimental way, but preferred to infer early causal processes of psychopathology from mature, adult neurotics. This retrospective analysis was also condemned as unscientific. Despite these objections psychoanalytic theory has been refined and developed in modern times and remains a widespread and popular method of psychotherapy. The emphasis on the uniqueness of each individual personality has been an obvious reason for this central position in understanding people's problems.

Conclusion

Further discussion of psychometrics and theories of personality is given in chapter 6 by Paul Kline. In the field of human communication the application of psychometric devices is steadily growing. Techniques for the diagnosis of learning difficulties in children, emotional disturbance in adolescents and the description of cognitive functioning in adults are commonly encountered in speech therapy practice. These devices allow detailed description of cases for further investigation and allow research in human communication disorders to proceed in a systematic fashion. Tests are operational definitions of functioning and only by using common definitions can scientists hope to ensure that they are all studying the same problems. The importance of individual differences is also a central interest in disorders of human communication. Therapy is usually tailored to suit the cognitive and emotional levels of each patient and it is often the case that what appears to be a cognitive problem (cannot talk) can be due to an emotional cause (do not want to talk). The investigation of individual functioning in cognitive and emotional processing is therefore of vital importance if we seek explanations of the individual case. In the field of brain damage the need for a coherent theory of individual reactions to brain damage is an urgent priority. Our present broad descriptions of the cognitive, emotional and social consequences of neural lesions have only broad implications for treatment. When a more detailed analysis is produced there will be a wider range of options open to the therapist.

Individual psychology is conducted at several levels of analysis. The importance of theories of individual differences for the explanation of mental and physical dysfunction cannot be overstated. In recent years this area of study has received additional attention with the realization that an individual's 'frame of mind' plays a significant part in recovery from physical illness; it is even suggested that psychological factors may precipitate certain kinds of physical illness by altering the efficiency of bodily defence mechanisms. This new link between mental and physical events is a complete reversal of earlier views of the mind-body relationship. Individual psychology contains within its boundaries a number of distinct approaches to the study of personality function but all are agreed on the importance of this topic in the solution of clinical problems.

Social psychology

Social psychology begins with the premise that Man is first and foremost a social creature. It would seem that social co-operation, rather than brute strength, has been the secret of Man's survival and proliferation as a species. This level of analysis has traditionally focussed on the social phenomena involved in co-operative or confrontational situations, such as group dynamics and highly structured social interaction. Social psychology interfaces with two other disciplines: sociology and social anthropology. The former studies the institutions, political structures and philosophy which predominate in societies in order to infer general principles of social life, whereas the latter studies the social order in different societies from the technological western nations to the agricultural communities of Africa and South America. By examining these products of social co-operation it is hoped a greater understanding will be gained of the social nature of Man. Social psychology operates at a lower level of analysis in order to generate more limited, but more specific, theories of how social behaviour and social perception function.

Modern social psychology began in the 1920s and 1930s with the application of experimental methods to the study of social functioning. Much of this early work was carried out in order to investigate and improve work performance in industry. Very basic questions were asked: does work performance increase or decrease when individuals are working on their own or as part of a group? This kind of question is amenable to experimental investigation because there is a ready measurement available of overt behaviour in the shape of work output. Further, experimental manipulation of environmental variables is possible by designing a number of work environments which differ in the number of people involved, the physical surroundings, etc. Finally, the effects of different kinds of reinforcements could be measured in productivity as different means exist to pay workers: piece rate, flat rate, group piece rates, and bonus systems. This experimental, behaviouristic investigation of work performance generated a number of interesting hypotheses about group processes which soon began to attract academic psychologists. The social psychology of 1940-1960 was largely laboratory-based experimental studies of small group and interpersonal processes. Asch (1952) offers a classic example of this approach in his study of social conformity. One finding which emerged from industrial research was the phenomenon of group conformity among individuals. It seemed individual group members would, under social pressure, change their values in the direction of the group norm. To study this phenomenon Asch asked for volunteers to take part in an experiment on 'visual perception'. These subjects arrived at the psychology laboratory to meet three other 'subjects' and formed groups of four which were asked to judge the length of various lines by comparing them with a standard line. Three of the 'subjects' in each group were actually confederates of the experimenter and were instructed to make incorrect judgements from the half-way point in the experiment. What was really being studied in this experiment was whether the real subject would tend to agree or disagree with the other three when they began to make incorrect judgements. Asch discovered that 75 per cent of the real subjects who took part in these experiments did go along with the erroneous group judgements and this was seen as an example of group conformity. But were the subjects really doubting their own judgement as a result of group pressure or were they simply embarrassed by having to disagree with three other people?

The last question is extremely difficult to test in social psychology because the very act of asking the question would mean a departure from strict, objective analysis. Indeed, it has been argued that the cost of objectivity in studying social phenomena results in the study of highly artificial social situations where deception must be employed in order to study these situations in secret. This use of deception has been a particular worry in social psychology. Some argue that it is unethical to subject people to any form of treatment without their full consent. On the other hand this would mean fully explaining the purpose of the experiment, which would result in a different form of social behaviour arising. Where deception was employed in an experiment the subjects were always 'debriefed' by the experimenter - told the real aims of the study - before leaving the laboratory. This in turn generated considerable public interest and after a while 'psychology experiments' became notorious. Such notoriety leads to future experimental subjects approaching tasks with apprehension and suspicion. The need for deception in social psychology was lessened by the introduction of non-obtrusive methods of study, such as using hidden cameras and microphones to investigate real-life situations. It is common practice to 'bug' buildings where sieges are taking place in order to study the social and emotional dynamics of the occupants. These more naturalistic investigations have given us considerable insight into very specific social situations, but the most provocative findings in social psychology have come from research which has employed deception.

Obedience to authority

Milgram (1963) conducted a study which sent a chill down the spine of society when he investigated how people tend to show obedience to authority. He devised an ingenious experimental set-up where subjects were told they were taking part in an experiment about 'learning'. They played the role of 'teachers' who had to read out simple, paired-associate words from a list which were relayed to a 'learner' in another room by a microphone. The 'learner' was to memorize the paired words and respond to the 'teacher's' questions correctly. If the 'learner' made a mistake in recalling the words the 'teacher' was told to press a switch and deliver an electric shock to the 'learner'. The 'teacher' sat at a console which contained microphone and speaker with an array of switches marked in volts which began at 'Mild Shock: 15 volts' to 'Danger: Severe Shock: 450 volts'. The 'teacher' was to begin adminstering the lowest shock at the first mistake by the 'learner' and to increase the voltage at each subsequent mistake all the way to 'Severe Shock'. In reality there was no 'learner' and no electric shock, only another confederate of Milgram's who was instructed to make deliberate errors and to cry out in pain when the 'shock' reached a particular level. These cries of 'pain' would accompany each increasing 'shock' until at around 400 volts there would be complete silence from the 'learner'. The question was: how far would people be prepared to go when they actually believed that they were causing increasing pain to another person? It was found subjects would argue with the experimenter about continuing the 'experiment' and, each time, they were simply told by the experimenter to continue with the test and complete the experiment. It was predicted that most subjects would go as far as 'Strong Shock: 150 volts' but only a few would reach the severe shock. In fact, 65 per cent of those tested (40 subjects) went all the way to 450 volts and not one stopped before 300 volts. Milgram went on to study how different variations would affect the outcome of this experiment, such as giving the 'teacher' visual contact with his 'learner' or moving the entire experiment to less prestigious surroundings than the University Psychology Department. These differences did have a small effect on the outcome, but in general the finding that people are highly obedient to authority was confirmed.

Experiments such as Milgram's have been designed in order to investigate real life social phenomena like conformity and obedience. Social psychology has also been investigated from purely theoretical viewpoints when, for example, behaviourism makes predictions about 'social behaviour'. Cognitive psychology has stimulated social psychologists to study how individuals and groups make social perceptions and how beliefs and attitudes develop. This finer level of social analysis is represented by the work of Festinger (1957). From studying how individuals process social information, Festinger arrived at his theory of 'cognitive dissonance'. This theory states that when individuals are confronted with new information which runs contrary to their held beliefs there are three ways of dealing with it.

* The new information can be accepted and the belief discarded.
* The meaning of this new information can be reinterpreted in order to make it conform more to existing beliefs.
* The new information can be ignored or further supporting evidence sought for the held belief.

These processes occur when new information is processed through an existing belief system which will differ between individuals. Thus, if the new information runs up against a particular belief system, the extent to which it will be incorporated into that belief system will vary from one individual to another. In general, Festinger found that complete acceptance of such information is the exception rather than the rule. Most people tend to distort or reinterpret new information in such a fashion that dissonance is reduced. Festinger suggested that this state of 'cognitive dissonance' had motivational properties for the individual to seek reduction and so dissonance can be regarded as a 'cognitive drive'. A non-seatbelt wearing driver may be faced with mounting evidence of their effectiveness in crashes yet continue not to use his belt. He may argue that in some accidents seatbelts are dangerous because they can trap a driver inside a flaming car. He may ignore the fact that such accidents are a tiny proportion of all car accidents. He may reinterpret this evidence in a particular way by arguing that belts are most effective at slow speeds and since he is a high-speed driver he is safer without. Finally, he could seek out specific examples of drivers who have not worn belts yet have survived major crashes. Such 'real life' evidence seems to carry more weight than statistical inferences. This shift in emphasis from group study to the study of individuals in social groups gave rise to a new generation of theory in social psychology.

Attribution theory

Attribution theories emphasize the individual's capacity for self-observation in social situations and, by studying how the individual perceives his circumstances through examining the causes that are advanced for his own behaviour and the behaviour of others, it is possible to advance predictive theories of how social influence operates. Schachter and Singer (1962) studied how individuals perceive their own emotional and motivational states. In one study subjects were told they were participating in the evaluation of a 'new drug' which was said to have 'behavioral side effects'. The injected subjects were then placed in a room with another 'subject' who was also testing the drug. In reality the injection was a general stimulant and the other 'subject' was a confederate of the experimenter who was asked to display different moods and 'symptoms' to the real subject. It was found that real subjects always reacted to the general stimulant in the same way as the phoney 'subject'. If anger, excitation, laughing, or crying was projected by the confederate, the same states would be displayed in the real subject. This was even the case when the confederate displayed sleepiness despite the stimulant nature of the drug! Schachter interpreted these findings in attributional terms. The real subjects reasoned that the drug produced side effects, the other 'subject' had taken the drug, and therefore the reactions he was displaying would also occur in him. This study showed how internal states are interpreted using social information.

Interpersonal attraction

The discovery of how people develop bonds of attraction to others has enormous practical implications. Byrne (1972) demonstrated that people develop likings for others when they perceive the other person to be similar to themselves. This finding can be interpreted from a behaviouristic viewpoint; it is reinforcing to perceive such similarity and so we develop a stronger attachment. A cognitive interpretation would argue that in perceiving similarity in another person we build up an internal model of that individual which allows us to make predictions of how they will behave (like us) in given situations. The need to make social predictions about others can be seen as an extension of our general tendency to make predictions about the future. Such predictions are made on the basis of past experience and thus we cannot always predict accurately how others will behave in the future. We often do not have sufficient information about what 'makes a person tick' to construct accurate internal models of them. But in the case of someone whom we perceive to be similar to us we can make confident predictions about them by asking ourselves what we would do in a given situation. This accuracy of prediction is a goal we strive towards which in turn leads to greater attraction to certain people.

Both accounts of attraction emphasize the need to understand how individuals make interpersonal judgements about others. Modern social psychology has approached this question in a number of ways. The field of interpersonal perception has begun to offer answers to the question of attraction and is reviewed in a book by Cook (1979). This area of research is of vital clinical significance when faced with problems of relations between individuals and within families. On a more specific level interest has focussed on the nature of patient-therapist relationships, and the social psychology of therapy. A number of special social pressures are evident in the conduct of health care. Individual patients may feel they have to conform to a particular role, that their consultant is of very high status and that a need exists to communicate accurately with professional consultants. A related area of research investigates the personal qualities of professional therapists. Truax and Carkhuff (1967) have outlined a number of dimensions which distinguish effective from less effective therapists engaged in individual counselling. The cognitive view of social interaction emphasizes the need to gain access to the individual's cognitive and emotional processing of social situations and this aim has been pursued by George Kelly (1955).

Personal construct theory
Kelly, an American clinical psychologist, hit on the analogy that people can be viewed as 'mini scientists' who are engaged in the business of making predictions about the future. Man is seen as being at his most adaptive when he is actively making predictions about how the future will be, and how he will behave in these future situations, rather than simply reacting to the here-and-now. Kelly further stressed the uniqueness of individuals. All of us have things in common, but these are far outweighed by the more relevant and subtle differences in the way we process information and the conclusions we reach. It was dissatisfaction with existing psychological theories of individual functioning, which could only make crude predictions about individuals, that led Kelly to develop the idea of 'man as scientist'. According to Kelly each of us is a scientist who

develops hypotheses and tests these hypotheses in everyday
living. Man actively seeks out information (evidence) which
generates predictive hypotheses about the future. We may
gather information on a certain individual in a variety of
situations and create an internal 'scientific model' or
'theory' about how that individual will behave in some
future situation. These 'models' will make more or less
accurate predictions and real-life 'evidence' allows us to
modify our original hypothesis (model) in the direction of
achieving more accurate predictions in the future.

How are these 'models' created? Kelly postulated a
common means of classifying incoming information which
he termed 'personal constructs'. A construct is a bipolar
concept which provides a dimension of classification for
incoming information. Constructs are therefore ways of
representing the similarities and differences which we
perceive in our environment. Black-white is a construct
because it suggests a continuum of colour along which
objects could be represented. We can therefore make comparisons between objects in terms of their 'blackness' or
'whiteness'. But constructs do not always have two exactly
opposite poles. Kelly argues that an individual's constructs
are personal, implying that they have meaning only to the
individual who uses them. For example, 'kind-cold' could be
a personal construct which does not have semantically opposite poles, but nevertheless may have personal meaning for
an individual. He may classify people along a personal continuum from 'kind' to 'cold' implying emotional differences,
so personal constructs are not objective definitions with a
single semantic interpretation. They are unique ways, employed by unique individuals, to view their world and are not
therefore comparable between individuals. Individuals will
have their own unique construct system consisting of a
number of dimensions which enable them to represent the
external world. An individual may represent an item like a
needle on the following constructs

* bright-dull
* thin-thick
* sharp-blunt
* hollow-solid
* painful-no pain
* masculine-feminine

In this way Kelly argued that people classify the world
around them and these classifications allow predictions to
be made of the future. A number of fundamental postulates
were made by Kelly about the nature of Man's interaction
with his environment.

1. A PERSON'S PROCESSES ARE PSYCHOLOGICALLY
CHANNELIZED BY THE WAYS IN WHICH HE ANTICIPATES
EVENTS. Just as Festinger demonstrated that we distort in-
coming information which is contrary to our beliefs, Kelly

postulates that our personal construct system is a dynamic entity which is continually processing new information, and making constant adjustments, to enable more accurate predictions in the future. When radically new information reaches our construct system we may not immediately change the organization of the system. We may process that new information through another construct system that specializes in the credibility of different sources of information. If this system predicts that it is likely the information is biassed or misleading, we may continue to hold our existing beliefs (constructs) and reinterpret the new information differently. People will, of course, differ in the actual constructs that make up their systems and in the type of system they employ. Some individuals may have a 'tight' system which is made up of a few constructs and leads to unvarying predictions of future events. This type of system leads to very specific predictions (all young people are rebellious) but is open to many instances of invalidation. A 'loose' construct system may be more elaborated and lead to much less rigid predictions (she may either like me or hate me) which can tolerate instances of poor prediction much more easily. People also differ in the extent to which they are prepared to modify their construct system in response to such examples of poor prediction. A healthy construct system is constantly in the process of evaluating, sifting and storing new evidence in order to make future predictions as accurate as possible. An unhealthy construct system makes poor predictions and cannot respond to the challenge of change.

In addition to possessing our own unique set of personal constructs which allows us to view the world differently from each other we also possess a set of core role constructs which enable us to make predictions of how we, ourselves, will behave in some future situation. These core constructs build up an internal representation of self-consciousness and allow us to predict what we will like and dislike about future events. These predictions may, however, from time to time be invalidated by our actual behaviour. We may behave 'out of character' by enjoying something we did not predict we would enjoy. In these instances an effort is made to adjust these core role constructs by healthy individuals. If adjustment is not made then we continue to make predictions about future events which may not be borne out in practice. Often, having made some negative prediction of how we will feel in a future situation, we avoid such a situation. But if our construct system is poor, and we make faulty predictions, we never know if our core constructs are accurate because we avoid putting them to the test.

2. EMOTION IS THE AWARENESS OF THE FACT THAT OUR CONSTRUCT SYSTEM IS IN A STATE OF CHANGE OR TRANSITION. This postulate refers to any situation where powerful new information demands revision in our personal construct system. Kelly sees emotional experience

as arising when our construct system makes faulty predictions, and thus we must either make extensive readjustments, or in some way reinterpret the new information to deny its disconfirmatory nature. He sees different emotions resulting from specific instances of construct system failure.

3. ANXIETY IS THE AWARENESS THAT THE EVENTS WITH WHICH ONE IS CONFRONTED LIE MOSTLY OUTSIDE THE RANGE OF CONVENIENCE OF ONE'S CONSTRUCT SYSTEM. Construct systems are built up to allow predictions of specific situations. These systems can extend to take in a wider range of situations if they are sufficiently similar to the specific situation that generated the system. For example, if we have experienced a few interactions with the police we will develop a construct system which makes predictions about the likely outcome of dealing with authority figures. If we then find ourselves in a situation where we have to deal with customs officers, we may use the system developed through our experience with police in order to predict the likely outcome. If we find ourselves facing a magistrate we may (i) have no construct system which allows us to make predictions about magistrates (our 'authority figure' system may be obviously deficient by the fact that it failed to predict the outcome of dealing with customs officers!) or (ii) experience anxiety because we are aware we have no system to enable predictions to be made.

4. GUILT IS THE AWARENESS OF DISLODGEMENT OF THE SELF FROM ONE'S CORE ROLE STRUCTURE. Core role structure refers to the system of constructs which allows us to represent 'self' and anticipate our own actions and emotions in future situations. If we behave 'out of character' these core constructs are invalidated, and this awareness can result in the feeling of guilt. It would seem this is a very threatening experience as it suggests that we may become unpredictable to ourselves.

5. HOSTILITY IS THE CONTINUED EFFORT TO EXTORT VALIDATIONAL EVIDENCE IN FAVOUR OF A TYPE OF SOCIAL PREDICTION WHICH HAS ALREADY BEEN RECOGNIZED AS A FAILURE. When we cannot accept incoming information which has invalidated some aspect of our construct system we continue to strive for confirmatory evidence. This effort is characterized by hostility where one person, having made a prediction about another which has been completely disconfirmed by his actual actions, becomes hostile and attempts to get the other person to admit he has really made a mistake in his actions.

Personal construct systems allow individuals to give meaning to their world in terms of defining self and building up internal models of the social environment. By anticipating future events, rather than reacting to the present, Man becomes more adaptive; he can plan his future responses by considering alternatives. If an individual's construct system suffers considerable invalidation a variety of emotional responses will ensue. The way in which an individual deals with such evidence may range from denial and rationalization to re-organization of the construct system. Kelly considered that psychiatric problems resulted when individuals were unable to maintain a stable, accurate construct system and thus the therapeutic task would be to explore an individual's construct system and assist him in making readjustments to the system. Two problems arise with this analysis. Since construct systems are personal they have meaning only for the individual who uses them. This phenomenological theory - that individuals will always have a unique view of the world which is not open to objective definition - raises the question of how another can assist an individual to make changes in his personal system. The second problem concerns how access can be gained to a personal construct system. A method is required to elicit an individual's construct system in order to examine it for predictive accuracy.

Both these problems are resolved by the use of repertory grid technique. A grid is generated by asking an individual to examine areas of similarity and difference between several 'elements' which may be people, places or institutions; in fact, anything which may have a construct system related to it. We could ask someone to consider their mother, father and girl friend and say how two of them differ from the third. A person may respond that father and girl friend are more tolerant than mother, who is intolerant. Thus we have elicited a personal construct of tolerance-intolerance with which an individual classifies three important people in his life. Continued enquiry using these elements (mother, father and girl friend) and other elements (boss, best friend, worst enemy) will generate a further sequence of constructs which can be displayed along a vertical axis with elements along a horizontal axis. The person can then work along his element axis classifying each individual on the constructs he has provided. The resulting matrix of classification can be analysed statistically to reveal how many constructs a person is actually employing when representing people in his immediate social environment.

Some constructs are superordinate to others; the construct good-bad may be superordinate to a number of other constructs, such as intelligent-dull, outgoing-reserved, since classifying someone as 'GOOD' may imply that they are also intelligent and outgoing. Statistical analysis determines how many superordinate constructs are being employed, and thus we can see how 'tight' or 'loose' an individual's system really is. We can also examine the resulting system for consistency in the way it classifies elements. An inconsistent system would demonstrate a number of instances where individuals classified along positive constructs would be assigned to some negative constructs which are incompatible with the positive ones. In these cases we would expect the construct system to make varying and possibly inaccurate predictions.

Repertory grid technique is not an objective 'test' in the traditional sense of the term; rather it is a way of describing the topography of an individual's construct system without attempting to assign any meaning to the actual constructs. By examining the pattern of interrelationships between constructs we do not violate the phenomenological nature of a person's constructs. But we can objectively demonstrate where inconsistency and lack of predictive power lies in a construct system and, by asking the individual to consider these sources of inaccuracy, we can assist him to make the necessary changes in the way he views his world.

6. TO THE EXTENT THAT ONE PERSON CONSTRUES THE CONSTRUCTION PROCESSES OF ANOTHER HE MAY PLAY A ROLE IN A SOCIAL PROCESS INVOLVING THE OTHER PERSON. Kelly indicates in this postulate that it is possible for two people to determine accurately each other's construct system, and when this occurs their psychological processes will be similar. By using the grid techniques to explore an individual's system a therapist can begin to appreciate how that individual views his world, and thus the therapist builds up a construct system about that individual. Kelly developed fixed role therapy as a means of aiding individuals to alter their existing construct system, particularly in respect of their core role constructs. In fixed role therapy the patient is asked to behave in a different role from usual. For example, a person may construe himself as slow, ineffective and unattractive. In fixed role therapy he is encouraged to think of himself as quick witted, effective and attractive and asked to behave for, say, a week as if he had this view of himself. This experience may result in the patient questioning some of his previous constructs about himself and lead to a change in his core role system.

Personal construct theory (PCT) is a very significant contribution to clinical practice because it acknowledges the interaction between individuals and their social world and emphasizes the unique nature of that interaction. As a consequence of this unique view we must use introspection as a means of access to the individual's phenomenological experience. But, by describing the content of an individual's construct system and its organization in objective terms, we do not resort to interpretation of what an individual's constructs actually mean. This view of 'man as scientist' stresses the dynamic nature of personal constructs and the importance of change in people's lives. Individuals who cannot contemplate change in their construct systems will fail to make accurate predictions and this results in emotional disturbance and may in turn lead to maladaptive behaviour. PCT attempts to encourage individuals to change their views and ideas about themselves and others towards a more realistic and predictive construct system. In speech therapy this approach is gaining ground in both the understanding of stuttering (Fransella, 1972) and in the care of brain-damaged patients (Brumfitt and Clarke, 1982).

Recent developments

Social psychology has undergone a series of changes in both its methods of investigating social phenomena and in the theoretical assumptions that have guided research. Considerable attention has been devoted to group processes which have had practical implications for the use of group therapy in health care. By identifying how groups of individuals conform to social pressure and produce 'group identities' and 'group cohesion' it has been possible to harness these effects in the treatment of individuals. The emergence of 'therapeutic communities' in the 1960s in the mental health field owed much to social psychological research. In recent years there has been an explosion in the numbers of 'self-help' groups in health care. Alcoholics Anonymous was one of the first examples of individuals joining together to offer mutual support and strength to combat a problem which the lone individual may find impossible to control. In the field of human communication, 'stroke clubs' and groups for the parents of children with language problems are attempts to harness the power of groups to resolve individual problems collectively. The use of group training techniques for health professionals has also been a direct consequence of social psychological research. Qualities such as accuracy of interpersonal perception and genuine self-revelation have been shown to be enhanced through group training techniques. Excellent reviews of these areas can be found in Tajfel and Fraser (1978), Armistead (1974), Blumberg and Golembiewski (1976) and Laver and Hutcheson (1972).

PCT has bridged the conceptual gap between individual psychology and social psychology and emphasized the importance of mutual interaction between the two levels. This approach, together with recent work on the processes of interpersonal perception, finds ready application in the field of human communication because it offers psychological accounts of a range of disorders from stammering to aphasia. The contribution by Fransella (1972, 1975) to research into stuttering has now become a major treatment option for therapists; PCT is also valuable as a general way of understanding the difficulties of the handicapped. Essential reading in this field includes Bannister and Fransella (1971), Bannister and Mair (1968) and Fransella (1975).

Interest in interactional models of individual-social processes is rapidly growing in modern social psychology. Two main positions are represented: the 'situational' theories of Mischel (1977) and Harré (1979) - who argue the need to explore the 'social rules' which are perceived to govern social action by individual agents - and Trower, Bryant and Argyle (1978) who have highlighted the need to investigate what constitutes 'skilled' social performance. Christie and Geis (1970) investigated the personal characteristics of individuals who were considered very effective social communicators. They discovered a type of social negotiator who was characterized by having Machiavellian attitudes to social interaction. The typical high Mach-type favoured the use of manipulation of other people to achieve results and felt that 'no holds were barred' in order to achieve one's goals. Argyle has analysed the behavioural components of effective social performers and highlighted how eye contact, questioning, smiling and body posture all serve to lubricate the process of social interaction. This approach has assumed that these 'skills' can be 'taught' to individuals who do not possess them just like any other behavioural response. The development of 'social skills training' for a wide range of psychological problems has accelerated in the past five years. These training programmes have ranged from the rehabilitation of psychiatric patients (Argyle, Bryant and Trower, 1974) to disturbed children and adolescents (Spence, 1980). An introduction to this field is given by Michael Argyle in chapter 8.

Social psychology began as an experimental science of social behaviour and has developed to include an exploration of the phenomenological perception of social action. In addition to offering valuable theories of the causation of psychological dysfunction, social psychology offers much practical insight into the nature of patient-therapist relationships; therapy is, after all, a social event.

Neuropsychology

Neuropsychology takes as its object of study the 'conceptual nervous system'. The goal of neuropsychology is to infer, from studies of brain damage, how the CNS functions to create consciousness and psychological processes. This relationship between brain and behaviour is represented by the kind of conceptual models found in cognitive psychology. Neuropsychologists are theoreticians who use experimental and quasi-experimental techniques to investigate psychological processes in normal and abnormal CNS functioning. Neurophysiology, in contrast, attempts to study the CNS directly through the use of surgical intervention and a variety of techniques to record and measure neurophysiological processes 'in vivo'. As a result, neurophysiology mainly confines its investigation to non-human species whereas the observation of input-output relationships in brain-damaged and normal individuals and the creation of abstract, conceptual models of the processing flow is exclusively the province of neuropsychology.

The studies of Hubel and Wiesel (1962) on visual information processing in the cat demonstrate neurophysiological investigation. By inserting very fine recording electrodes into the visual cortex of anaesthetized cats it was possible to record the activity of individual neurons when the retina was stimulated with a spot of light, or an illuminated pattern. This technique revealed that individual neurons could be activated by stimulation in a circumscribed area of the retina, known as the receptive field of the neuron. Areas of this receptive field activate the neuron when light is switched on or off. The result of this arrangement is the creation of 'feature detectors': neurons which specialize in firing to different kinds of contour information. When a stimulus is presented in a particular configuration it will selectively fire a range of 'feature detectors' which are sensitive to this perceptual form. If the stimulus is slowly rotated, new 'feature detectors' come into play whilst the previous cells are inhibited.

This research led to the development of a model of visual processing which emphasized the way retinal information passes through several stages of analysis before cortical representation (the highest level of processing) occurs. Yet this account can only tell us how these physiological processes take place. Rather than speculate on the organic basis of psychological functioning neuropsychology tries to investigate the end point in visual processing: the awareness of the visual world. Neuropsychologists had independently arrived at a model of contour coding processes which was capable of programming a computer to carry out simple visual searches (via a television camera) and recognizing various shapes in the outside world.

In contrast to these physiological and psychological models of information processing, which suggest considerable specialization in the CNS, came the 'holistic' theorists. This group saw higher mental functioning as a more complex activity mediated by neural activity throughout the brain. Lashley (1937) spearheaded this movement in his studies of memory in sub-human species. Despite the removal of the majority of cortical tissue his experimental animals were still able to make pre-surgically learnt discriminations amongst spatial stimuli. Lashley concluded that memory was diffusely stored throughout neural tissue such that damage does not interfere with recall. These holistic theories of brain function seemed to offer an explanation for recovery after irreversible brain damage. They postulated that a number of diffuse centres participated in mediating different psychological processes. When damage occurs to this system these centres can continue to function despite the loss of one of their number.

This theory, however, did not square with the clinical evidence of brain damage. Individuals who had suffered strokes resulting in the loss of communicative ability often showed wide variation in the specific form of handicap and an equal variation in their recovery from such damage. This evidence, together with more accurate ways of detecting and localizing organic brain damage, led theorists back to the notion of some localization of function which is represented by the views of Geschwind (1970) and Luria (1973). Further development has also been achieved in the use of psychometric methods of localizing brain damage. Clinical experience of different dysfunctions caused by specific types of organic damage has led to the development of objective and standardized mental tests of neuropsychological functioning. Tests are available which measure the severity of memory loss, detect damage to verbal and spatial processing skills, and describe patterns of dysfunction in a range of cognitive skills. The development of these instruments has enabled research to be carried out using common operational definitions of damage and dysfunction as well as tracing the patterns of recovery from brain damage. Such instruments are also employed in the initial investigation of neuropsychological damage to make predictions of where organic damage is likely to have occurred.

Continuing technological developments such as the EMI brain scanner have further refined our ability to localize organic damage which, together with new surgical techniques for the relief of intractable epilepsy, have led to new insights into the brain-behaviour relationship. The work of Sperry (1968) and Gazzaniga (1970) in their use of 'split brain' surgery to relieve epilepsy has offered evidence in favour of localization of function and yet demonstrated that the relationships between functions are very much more complex than was previously thought. Sperry introduced the split brain procedure where the corpus callosum (the fibres connecting the two cortical hemispheres) was cut, thus preventing epileptic discharges travelling through to the opposite hemisphere and causing a fit. In carrying out this procedure the most important fibres carrying information between the two hemispheres are cut, virtually isolating one hemisphere from the other. With such patients Sperry could study the abilities of the hemispheres in isolation from each other. It was found that in general the left hemisphere plays the largest part in mediating verbal information, whereas the right hemisphere specializes in processing spatial and temporal information. This general finding, however, had to be revised after a more detailed analysis of hemispheric functioning was carried out.

Modern neuropsychology employs information processing models of the brain which are based on the computer analogy. The brain is likened to an information processing system which has its own 'language', allowing cortical representation of the inner and outer world. This computer analogy has been referred to as 'boxology' because of the abstract flow diagrams and probabilistic models which represent neural functioning. But such models can often be formulated with sufficient precision to allow computer programmes to be written to determine whether perceptual and cognitive processes can be mimicked by the machine. The highly experimental area of 'artificial intelligence' tries to generate such models which are then used to create 'intelligent' machines. The engineering science of cybernetics (robots) has employed many neuropsychological concepts in the design of highly sophisticated information processing machines which can 'recognize' and categorize different objects and take pre-programmed action appropriately. Although these are exciting developments, we are still a very long way from even beginning to understand how more complex cognitive tasks are carried out by the brain.

Clinical neuropsychology

Clinical neuropsychology has been the applied arm of theoretical neuroscience. The study of wartime head injury made a great contribution to clinical neuropsychology as wounds often resulted in psychological rather than physical handicap. Neuropsychology also investigates the effects of degenerative CNS damage, vascular accidents, space-occupying lesions and the various forms of epileptic disorder. Clinical neuropsychology has sought to predict the kinds of psychological dysfunction likely to arise from local organic damage and has developed a series of mental tests which exploit the known facts of brain function to measure dysfunction accurately. Although this study has resulted in the development of sensitive psychological measures of dysfunction, there has been remarkably little effort devoted to studying what can be done in a practical sense for the brain-damaged person.

It is a fact that neuropsychologists, with a few exceptions, have failed to offer any concrete guidelines for tackling psychological dysfunction. Further, clinical assessment may provide sensitive and highly controlled measurements of dysfunction, but these assessments may ignore the practical difficulties of the brain-damaged in everyday life. Speech therapists have stood out as the only group of professionals involved in the care of brain-damaged persons who have had an optimistic and vigorous approach to brain function therapy. Difficult problems exist in evaluating the effects such therapy has in assisting recovery from dysphasia. To begin with, there are a number of taxonomies of aphasia which lead to different classification systems of dysfunction. This makes the comparison of research a very problematic area since different investigators classify patients in different ways. A further area of concern is separating natural recovery from the effects of therapeutic intervention: the so-called 'spontaneous recovery' factor. But the most glaring deficit lies in the lack of theory concerning recovery of psychological functioning after brain damage. What theory there is makes very general predictions which are often difficult to test. Recently neuropsychologists have begun to put this position on a more scientific footing by attempting to reach a consensus on classification through analysing patterns of deficit using the statistical techniques of factor analysis and cluster analysis. More carefully controlled studies of recovery of function have been planned which attempt to control for pre-morbid variables, spontaneous recovery, and non-specific treatment effects through the use of matched control groups. This increasing rigour will lead to less ambiguous conclusions on the process of recovery and the specific effects of intervention. Powell (1981) has introduced the notion of a systematic science of 'brain function therapy' which approaches each patient as an individual experiment and attempts to specify therapy goals in a clear and measurable form. Further consideration of human clinical neuropsychology is given in chapter 12.

Clinical science

Reference has been made to the clinical relevance of psychology, and it will be seen in subsequent chapters how psychological theories offer an understanding of cognitive, social and emotional processes. These theoretical positions have emerged from careful academic research and the value of clinical studies as the empirical test of theory will become apparent. Professional psychology consists of two related branches: educational psychology and clinical psychology. Educational psychologists investigate cognitive functioning in normal and handicapped children in order to provide the optimum learning environment for each child. Clinical psychologists deal with a very broad range of psychological problems from specific developmental disorders, such as language delay and emotional disturbance in children, to adult neurosis. Both these applied branches of psychology draw on existing psychological theory to guide their intervention in a particular case and contribute to theory by describing clinical dysfunctions and reporting on the effects of intervention based on a particular theory.

It is amongst these applied branches of psychology that a quiet revolution has been taking place. Clinicians are faced with highly complex human problems which may display a number of facets. The behaviourally disturbed child with specific language problems, poor vision and emotional lability is a far cry from the highly controlled academic investigation of language development amongst normal children. The clinician needs a theory of language acquisition, a theory of behavioural disturbance and a theory of emotional development if the individual child is to be treated comprehensively. These clinical needs have led to the development of multi-model therapies where theory from several areas is gathered and woven into a comprehensive treatment strategy. Similar needs are being acknowledged by speech therapists who must manage the social and emotional adjustments to communication handicap as well as working specifically on the identified problem.

If psychology has evolved in the past century to a position where there is close agreement on the important questions, and progress towards integrated theories, then clinicians are providing additional evidence through their own scientific approach to human problems. Clinicians have put theory to the test and have conducted comparative research of different treatment methods. This research has led to the use of multi-model therapy design which has, in turn, enriched academic theories. The traditional distinction between individual psychology and social psychology is a case in point; researchers have realized the most appropriate focus of study is the interaction between individual and environment. The distinction between behaviourist and cognitive psychology has also become eroded with the appearance of the new 'cognitive behaviour therapies' which attempt to modify cognitions as well as overt behaviour (Meichenbaum, 1977). In conclusion, modern psychology is entering a new era of scientific sophistication where the full complexity of human thought, speech and behaviour is being recognized. The contribution that clinical scientists such as psychologists and speech therapists can make to this development is inestimable. The demands of clinical science have already led to the use of multi-model treatment methods; experience, and careful research using these techniques, may generate new theoretical formulations of the science of mental life.

References

Argyle, M., Bryant, B.M. and Trower, P.E. (1974)
Social skills training and psychotherapy: a comparative study. Psychological Medicine, 4, 435-443.
Armistead, N. (1974)
Reconstructing Social Psychology. Harmondsworth: Penguin.
Asch, S. (1952)
Social Psychology. Englewood Cliffs, NJ: Prentice-Hall.
Bannister, D. and Fransella, F. (1980)
Inquiring Man (2nd edn). Harmondsworth: Penguin.
Bannister, D. and Mair, J.M.M. (1968)
The Evaluation of Personal Constructs. London: Academic Press.
Beloff, J. (1973)
Psychological Sciences: A review of modern psychology. St Albans: Crosby, Lockwood, Staples.
Binet, A. and Simon, T. (1905)
Méthodes nouvelles pour le diagnostic du niveau intellectuel des anormeaux. L'Année Psychologique, 11, 191-244.
Blumberg, A. and Golembiewski, B. (1976)
Learning and Change in Groups. Harmondsworth: Penguin.
Brumfitt, S. and Clarke, P. (1982).
An application of psychotherapeutic techniques to the management of aphasia. In C. Code and D.J. Müller (eds), Aphasia Therapy. London: Arnold.
Byrne, O. (1972)
The Attraction Paradigm. New York: Academic Press.
Cattell, R.B. (1963)
The Sixteen Personality Factor Questionnaire (The 16 PF). Champaign, Ill.: Institute for Personality and Ability Testing.
Cattell, R.B. (1965)
The Scientific Analysis of Personality. Harmondsworth: Penguin.
Christie, R. and Geis, F. (1970)
Studies in Machiavellianism. New York: Academic Press.
Cook, M. (1979)
Perceiving Others - The psychology of interpersonal perception. London: Methuen.
Cover-Jones, M. (1924)
The elimination of children's fears. Journal of Experimental Psychology, 7, 382-390.
Dawkins, R. (1976)
The Selfish Gene. Oxford: Oxford University Press.

Eysenck, H.J. (1947)
Dimensions of Personality. London: Routledge & Kegan Paul.

Eysenck, H.J. (1963)
Biological basis of personality. Nature, 199, 1031-4.

Festinger, L. (1957)
A Theory of Cognitive Dissonance. Evanston, Ill.: Row Peterson.

Fransella, F. (1972)
Personal Change and Reconstruction: Research on a treatment of stuttering. London: Academic Press.

Fransella, F. (1975)
Need to Change? London: Methuen.

Gazzaniga, M.S. (1970)
The Bisected Brain. New York: Appleton-Century-Crofts.

Geschwind, N. (1970)
The organisation of language in the brain. Science, 170, 940-944.

Harré, R. (1979)
Social Being. Oxford: Blackwell.

Hubel, D.H. and Wiesel, T.N. (1962)
Receptive fields, binocular interaction and functional architecture in the cat's visual cortex. Journal of Physiology, 160, 106-154.

Hull, C. (1943)
Principles of Behaviour. New York: Appleton-Century-Crofts.

Kelly, G. (1955)
The Psychology of Personal Constructs, Volumes 1 and 2. New York: Norton.

Köhler, W. (1917)
The Mentality of Apes (translated 1957). Harmondsworth: Penguin.

Lashley, K. (1937)
Functional determinant of cerebral localization. Archives of Neurology and Psychiatry, 38, 371-387.

Laver, J. and Hutcheson, S. (1972)
Communication in Face to Face Interaction. Harmondsworth: Penguin.

Luria, A.R. (1973)
The Working Brain. Harmondsworth: Penguin.

Meichenbaum,D. (1977)
Cognitive-Behaviour Modification: An integrative approach. New York: Plenum.

Milgram, S. (1963)
Behavioural study of obedience. Journal of Abnormal and Social Psychology, 67, 371-78.

Mischel, T. (1977)
The Self. Oxford: Blackwell.

Piaget, J. (1929)
The Child's Conception of the World. London: Routledge & Kegan Paul.

Powell, G.E. (1981)
Brain Function Therapy. Farnborough, Hants.: Gower.

Schachter, S. and Singer, J.E. (1962)
Cognitive, social and physiological determinants of
emotional state. Psychological Review, 69, 379-399.
Skinner, B.F. (1938)
The Behavior of Organisms. New York: Appleton-Century-
Crofts.
Skinner, B.F. (1957)
Verbal Behavior. New York: Appleton-Century-Crofts.
Solomon, R.L. and Wynne, L.C. (1953)
Traumatic avoidance learning: acquisition in normal
dogs. Psychological Monographs, 67, No.354.
Spence, S. (1980)
Social Skills Training with Children and Adolescents.
Windsor: NFER.
Sperry, R.W. (1968)
Hemisphere deconnection and unity in conscious
awareness. American Psychologist, 23, 723-733.
Tajfel, H. and Fraser, C. (1978)
Introducing Social Psychology. Harmondsworth: Penguin.
Thorndike, E.L. (1911) Animal Intelligence. New York:
Macmillan.
Thorndike, E.L. (1932)
The Fundamentals of Learning. Columbia University, New
York: Teachers College Bureau of Publications.
Tolman, E.C. (1932)
Purposive Behavior in Animals and Men. New York:
Appleton-Century-Crofts.
Trower, P.E., Bryant, B.M. and Argyle, M. (1978)
Social Skills and Mental Health. London: Methuen.
Truax, C.B. and Carkhuff, R. (1967)
Towards Effective Counselling and Psychotherapy:
Training and practice. Chicago: Aldine.
Watson, J.B. and Rayner, R. (1920)
Conditioned emotional reactions. Journal of Experimental
Psychology, 3, 1-14.
Wolpe, J. (1958)
Psychotherapy by Reciprocal Inhibition. Stanford, Ca:
Stanford University Press.
Wundt, W. (1907)
Outlines of Psychology. Leipzig: Engelmann.

Questions

1. What are the distinctive characteristics of scientific
   psychology?
2. Compare and contrast the behaviouristic and cognitive
   models of human functioning.
3. Outline the features of a psychological explanation.
   Show how such an explanation differs from physiological
   explanations.
4. Why are theories of individual differences important to
   clinical therapists?
5. What principles have emerged from the study of social
   psychology which have direct relevance to patient
   treatment?

6. What are the aims of clinical neuropsychology?
7. Contrast the models of man implicit in Kelly's and Eysenck's approaches to personality.
8. Outline the value of psychometrics as a clinical tool.
9. To what extent are speech therapists 'applied scientists'?
10. Summarize the clinical developments that have accrued since the birth of modern psychology.

Annotated reading

Beloff, J. (1973) Psychological Sciences. St Albans: Crosby, Lockwood, Staples.
   An advanced account of the development of modern psychology and a critical evaluation of the major schools of psychology. Highly recommended for final year students.

Chapman, A.J. and Jones, D.M. (1980) Models of Man. Leicester: The British Psychological Society.
   Again, an advanced collection of papers which resulted from an important conference. Every major model in psychology is analysed and discussed by a group of leading psychologists.

Fransella, F. (1981) Personality. London: Methuen.
   A clear and concise account of personality theories from a highly respected clinical practitioner.

Kristal, L. (1979) Understanding Psychology. London: Harper & Row.
   A very readable introduction to psychology which covers basic issues and demonstrates the relevance of contemporary work.

Medcof, J. and Roth, J. (1979) Approaches to Psychology. Milton Keynes: Open University Press.
   A clear and thoughtful review of the main schools of thought in psychology. This intermediate text provides a comprehensive account of modern psychology.

Pyle, D.W. (1979) Intelligence. London: Routledge & Kegan Paul.
   A lucid discussion of practical and theoretical issues in intelligence.

2

How Do You Know?
Psychology and Scientific Method
D. Legge

Of all the lessons that one might learn at school, probably
the most important is how to find out. Systematic changes
in the school curriculum and in methods of teaching have
given pupils today arguably the soundest preparation they
have ever had and the best foundation for intellectual
independence.

There is a basic dilemma in education: on the one hand
there is the plethora of facts unearthed and polished by our
predecessors, and on the other is the need to prepare pupils
to find out for themselves and to develop sufficient confidence to question academic authority. It would be a denial
of the principal benefits of a literate culture to withhold
the hard-won knowledge received from earlier generations: we
have the advantage of standing on the shoulders of those who
have gone before. But too great a dependence on received
wisdom could over-emphasize the value of current knowledge,
hiding the real possibility that it is wrong, misunderstood
or out of its relevant context.

The introduction of discovery learning methods in
schools has tended to strike a better balance between these
two sources of knowledge than faced earlier generations of
pupils. In a previous time 'experiment' was used loosely as
a label to refer to a wide variety of practical demonstra-
tions and enquiries. At the worst it was used about practical work that was designed to bring about a particular
specified outcome. If that outcome was not achieved the
'experiment' might even be said to have failed. This is a
travesty. An experiment cannot fail. It may give rise to
unexpected results, it may be poorly designed and the
desired experimental conditions may not be achieved, but it
cannot fail. In contrast, an attempt to demonstrate a
phenomenon can fail. The difference is that the experiment
is a special procedure for finding out. It gives rise to
knowledge. What the knowledge is about depends upon the
design of the experiment.

Discovery learning is a rather slow way of becoming
better informed. It would be many thousands of times quicker
to learn chemistry from text-books than by repeating centuries of experimentation and building up the same body
of knowledge from one's own painstaking experimentation.
Didactic instruction is undoubtedly quicker, but knowledge

acquired from an authority may be received as if impressed on tablets of stone. It may be depended upon as if it were inviolable and unquestionably reliable. Few scientists have such a view about the original knowledge that they have personally discovered. Truth is a relative concept and the 'facts' of today may be exploded as myths tomorrow. It is important to be just a little sceptical of received wisdom lest it be elevated to the status of dogma. It is important to find out, and it is important to know how you know.

Making a mental model of the world

Few of our school experiences prepare us for a view of science that identifies a reality outside ourselves which we seek to describe by our scientific theories. That reality is not open to us. We have to build a model of it for ourselves, and that model is our scientific knowledge. In general, the model is simpler than reality, and it has the massive advantage that since we have built the model, we can understand it. Reality is a different order of problem. If the model is a sufficiently good one, it will behave like reality. It will give us a way of understanding reality because we understand our model.

For example, Newton developed his celebrated laws of motion. They describe how bodies move in space as a function of the forces bearing upon them. They are precisely formulated as mathematical equations and offer a basis for predicting the movements of physical bodies. They are not, however, correct under all circumstances. In particular they break down at extremes of velocity and distance. But on an earthly and human scale Newton's model is immensely valuable because it works. The model describes closely enough how certain aspects of the world work.

Acquiring knowledge

How do you know? The simplest way is by deduction from a set of assumptions or premises. Provided the assumptions are true and the logic is sound, knowledge flows unremittingly. This is knowledge that depends upon the existence of a developed model that is relevant to the issue. Sometimes such models relate to only part of the real world and we then extend them beyond their domain of relevance and validity at our peril. Scale models offer some assistance to design engineers but only as analogies. It could be disastrous to assume that the load-bearing characteristics of a model bridge would be reflected in comparable scale in the full-grown version.

Another way of finding out is to ask. Asking another person, or his writings, is a way of seeking human authority. The success of this approach depends upon the question being well phrased so that it is understood; and likewise the answer. It also depends upon the questioner choosing an authority who knows the answer! The main problem with this approach is that a critical evaluation of answers can only be attempted where several authorities can be approached. Several versions of the same basic authority should not mislead us into believing that such consensus guarantees truth. Reference to an authority does have one cardinal virtue, however, and that is its convenience and speed. No other way of getting answers can be accomplished so quickly.

Empirical enquiries

The best way of finding out about the real world, however, is to ask a question directly of that world rather than of its interpreters. If you have a question about the motion of moving bodies (like billiard balls) the best way of finding an answer is to study the motion of, say, billiard balls. It is more direct and less likely to be distorted than asking a snooker-player his opinion. It may even be better than asking a physicist. This reference of questions to the world to which they refer is the essence of empiricism. It is the foundation upon which all science is based. Science has as its principal aim the description of the world in sufficient detail that at least it will be possible to predict its behaviour.

The physical sciences were the first to break away from natural philosophy as a methodology developed that allowed these empirical questions to be posed. Chemistry and physics were born. Somewhat later biology established itself as well. At the same time it became clear that there were relatively good ways of asking empirical questions that led to unambiguous answers, and there were also less satisfactory ways.

Causal explanations

A prominent feature of the physical sciences was the success of explanations couched in causal terms. The concept was that a particular act or condition would unerringly be followed by another, much as a billiard ball will move predictably (by Newton's Laws more or less!) when struck by another. The causational concept is a very attractive one because it offers a very compact basis for description, but even more so because it provides an obvious basis for prediction. It also identifies strongly the sort of observation that should be made in order to test the prediction, and hence to test that particular model of the world.

Once a phenomenon of some kind has been identified an obvious first question is 'What causes it?' What set of conditions willl guarantee its occurrence? For example, what are the critical factors which determine photosynthesis? It is fairly obvious that one way of getting an answer to this sort of question is to vary conditions and observe what happens. It would quite quickly become clear that one of the main features of an efficient procedure is the unambiguous determination of the relation between the factor being manipulated (the independent variable) and the factor being observed (the dependent variable).

Attributing effects

Perhaps the strongest, and therefore most sought after, evidence in science is the kind that leads to 'unequivocal

71

attribution of effect': in simpler language, 'we know what caused it'. It establishes that two variables should be considered and connected, perhaps by a causal chain. It may also establish the nature of that connection, perhaps in sufficient detail to admit a mathematical definition of the relationship.

The simplest way of achieving this desirable unequivocal attribution is to demonstrate that introduction of a factor is associated with the appearance of a phenomenon and removal of that factor with its disappearance. If no other factor affects the phenomenon, one would be likely to feel confident in asserting that the factor caused the phenomenon. An investigation in which a factor is carefully manipulated and the effects of such manipulation are carefully monitored is an experiment. The key feature of the experiment is the manipulation of some factor, which must not be left to vary by chance or by association with some other uncontrolled factor. Sometimes the term controlled experiment is used to stress the fact that close control of the conditions of observation is essential. The controlled experiment produces the best evidence there can be leading to unequivocal attribution of effect.

The importance of the experiment as a method of finding out becomes more obvious when one compares it with other techniques that might be used instead. For example, let us consider the problem of isolating factors that lead to the development of lung cancer. A number of studies of the incidence of lung cancer (and also bronchitis and other chest diseases) revealed that cigarette smokers seemed to be more likely to develop lung cancer than non-smokers. The data were not absolute, of course, so that many smokers died of 'natural causes' without ever developing cancer and some lung cancer victims had never smoked. The next problem is to discover just what this statistical association between smoking and cancer means.

A number of substances are known to be carcinogenic. For example, certain coal tar compounds applied to the skin of mice have been shown to produce tumours. Though in much reduced concentrations, similar compounds are produced in burning tobacco, so the suggestion that tobacco smoke might produce tumours in the respiratory tract is not a far-fetched one. At least some of the intermediate links in a causal chain already exist. On the other hand, the fact that many smokers manage to avoid lung cancer shows that the story is not a very simple one. Smoking is clearly not the only factor and, indeed, it may very well not be the most significant one.

More sophisticated studies have contrasted the morbidity of smokers in rural and urban areas, of different ages and socio-economic groups. There have also been national comparisons. One of the most interesting findings is that smokers who give up the habit have a smaller chance of developing lung cancer than those who do not, though a higher chance than abstainers. This sort of study focusses

on smoking and cancer rather than on the general problem
of the aetiology of cancer. Decades of studies searching for
a single cause have left researchers sceptical of finding
such a solution and, instead, the prevailing expectation is
that a cluster of factors will together determine the onset
of the disease. At most, smoking could be identified as one
of those causal factors. Its status might be a major factor,
or subsidiary; it might have a primary or a contextual role
to play. Either way, if causal, its influence would be
relatively direct.

The principal limitation of the studies of associated
incidence such as that described above is that one cannot be
sure how whatever was observed happened. The effect cannot
be unequivocally attributed to particular prior events and
conditions. In the case of smoking and cancer the group of
smokers differs from the group of non-smokers by more than
just the breathing in of tobacco smoke. For instance, they
comprise different individuals. This might not be a serious
difficulty, provided that the people in one group do not
share a common feature other than smoking. Unfortunately,
they probably do. Why do the smokers smoke? Is it perhaps
because they have some characteristic, no matter whether it
be psychological (such as anxiety) or physiological (such as
nicotine dependence)? If so, then smokers differ from non-
smokers, not only in what they do (that is, smoke) but also
in their constitution. Logically we are now incapable of
separating two hypotheses about where the association
between smoking and cancer comes from. On the one hand
is the causal relationship, on the other the possibility
that a tendency to smoke is due to some internal
characteristic which is also a predetermining factor
influencing the development of cancer.

One might argue that this confusion would be removed
by observing that smokers who become abstainers have a
reduced morbidity. Unfortunately, and this is borne out by
the experiences of smokers who attempt to give up, some
smokers find it relatively easy to give up, some difficult,
and some try but never succeed. This variation between
individuals could reflect a variation in the power of the
internal factor. A weak factor would allow a smoker to give
up easily but would also mean a relatively weak tendency to
develop cancer. Studying the morbidity of smokers who become
non-smokers voluntarily would tell nothing about the direct-
ness of the link between smoking and cancer. Smoking might
still be no more than an index of an individual's morbidity.

The only way of settling this question is to gain
control of the main variable that has hitherto been left
uncontrolled: that is, the question of who smokes. If the
experimenter chooses who smokes, instead of allowing the
subjects to choose, he can effectively separate the act of
smoking from the predilection to smoke. In practice this
means either forcing non-smokers to smoke and smokers to
stop smoking or both. The decision of who is treated in this
way has to be unrelated to any other relevant factor and a

random decision is usually found to be the best way of achieving this.

Ethical considerations make it unthinkable to carry out this experiment on human beings. Clearly it would be unacceptable to force on people a treatment - smoking - that was thought might very well induce a fatal disease. Forcing people to give up a potentially dangerous habit is less of an ethical problem than a problem of practicability. It is doubtful whether sufficient control over other people's lives can be exerted outside a prison or similar institution. Animals have, however, been subjected to enforced smoking and a sufficient proportion have developed tumours to lend very powerful weight to the hypothesis that tobacco smoking is a primary causative agent in the development of lung cancer. It is not a necessary cause, since non-smokers may also develop cancer. Nor is it a sufficient cause because by no means all smokers will succumb. It is, however, a very significant factor, and a very substantial improvement in health could be achieved if tobacco smoking were to become an extinct behaviour pattern.

When experiments may not be used

The logical preference for using experiments to ask questions is, perhaps, an obvious one. The reasons for not using experiments are less obvious in the abstract, although when one is plunged into the actuality of doing research they become overwhelmingly real. We have mentioned one or two reasons in discussing the cancer example above. There are some things that it is generally agreed one should not do to one's fellow man. There are ethical constraints to our research. This difficulty is an intrinsic feature of social science or medical research, but it very seldom impinges upon research in the physical sciences. In general, we have little compunction about subjecting concrete beams to sufficient forces to destroy them, or stretching wires to the point that they cannot recover their previous form. Inanimate subject matter does not require much, if any, consideration. We see below that there are other advantages, too, that physical scientists enjoy and, perhaps, sometimes take for granted.

In the cancer example we saw how the ethical boundaries which would have prevented an experiment being carried out were circumvented by using animal subjects in place of the ethically unacceptable human ones. This is a partial solution in some instances. The limiting circumstances are, first, that there are ethical reservations about using animals (and there is increasing concern about the extent to which Man exploits sub-human species who have generally no way of lodging their objections) and, second, whether they really possess those essential characteristics which would permit the results of the experiment to be generalized to human beings. Animals may be invaluable in testing new drugs and pharmaceutical preparations that are intended for use with humans. The bulk of animal experiments are toxicity studies on new chemicals. It is reasonable to expect that substances which poison animals will probably poison Man, and vice versa. On the other hand, an experiment concerning feelings will inevitably have to be conducted on human subjects. Even if animals have feelings, they do not have the power to communicate them and this severely limits their usefulness. In consequence, it may be that no experiment could be done at all, in which case the only source of knowledge would be non-experimental.

In practice, surrendering the use of the experiment is seldom the result of ethical constraints. More often it is simply because the control necessary to do an experiment is not available. The resources required may exceed those that can be afforded. In some cases control is lacking on logical grounds. The missing resource may be knowledge rather than cash.

The classic example of resource limitations prohibiting experimentation is in astronomy. Observing the heavens from earth can lead to a plethora of hypotheses about the universe, its contents and how they relate to one another. Theories of planetary motion would be easiest to test if one could carry out experiments by, for example, moving planets about, extracting them from their orbits and so on. Failing the power to do that, astronomers have had to use other means of finding out. A considerable portion of social science research is like astronomy. The researcher lacks the power necessary to manipulate variables to the extent necessary to carry out an experiment.

The third main reason for not carrying out an experiment stems from the conclusions one would want to draw from its results. In order to effect the degree of control necessary to achieve experimental manipulations and make precise, preferably quantifiable, measurements, laboratory conditions are often preferred. In the physical sciences this is nothing but an advantage. It is of no concern to a concrete beam whether it is subjected to forces in a laboratory or in a tower block of flats. It is the forces, its composition and age, the prevailing temperature, humidity and to some extent, its past history that determines its behaviour.

Human subjects play a rather more active role in experiments than do concrete beams and they tend to be very well aware of the difference between the reality of their normal life and the unreality of the 'games' which they are invited to play in laboratories. Even without that awareness of context, it may be that the version of a task which is devised and enacted in the laboratory is critically different from the real-life situation it was designed to simulate. For example, one cannot be absolutely certain that the speed of reaction in a real-life emergency which arrives without warning will be accurately mimicked by a reaction-time experiment conducted in a laboratory where the 'unexpectedness' of the emergency is at best relative. The problem is to determine the 'ecological validity' of the simulation. It is really the old problem of what degree of

generalization is permissible from the observations that
have been made. Essentially the same questions have to be
asked about the concrete beam. Its characteristics in a
warm, dry laboratory might be radically different at the
bottom of the North Sea. But it is generally true that there
is more likely to be limited generalization in the social
sciences.

This problem has led many researchers to maximize the
reality value of their research situations and to minimize
the use of laboratory-based research. They feel that the
potentially misleading quality of laboratory research is so
serious a problem that they prefer to make their observations in more realistic circumstances, accepting the severe
restrictions placed on the manipulation and control of experimental variables. It is a dilemma. Should one conduct
relatively well-controlled experiments (which allow quite
precise attribution of experimental effects) but which have
limited relevance to natural behaviour, or use real-life
(ecologically valid) situations which frequently leave
considerable uncertainty about what induced whatever was
observed? There is likely to be room for both kinds of
research, and there are probably persisting differences in
preference between researchers. This underlines the importance of discovering the strengths and weaknesses of the
non-experimental and quasi-experimental methods that have
been devised as alternatives to experiments.

Alternatives to experimentation

One of the great advantages in doing experiments is that the
conditions under which the observations are made are very
carefully designed to provide information about particular
questions. In other circumstances one has to make the most
of whatever information is available. Returning for a moment
to the example of astronomy, the researcher has available to
him only the options of looking in different directions at
different times. His difficulty is to relate the information
he gathers to his developing model of the universe. In these
circumstances, since there is no way of knowing what particular aspects of what could be recorded might be relevant at
some time and from some particular perspective, there is
considerable pressure to record observations in as objective
a way as possible. There is also a premium on precise
description.

Non-experimental studies are usually either descriptive
or correlational. In the former an attempt is made to record
what is or what happens, without (necessarily) giving
reasons or accounts of what causes what. Studies of this
kind are potentially of immense value since they can define
the general arena in which detailed accounts of what leads
to what must be placed. They are also useful in relating the
development of theoretical models to the reality of a life-
situation. They are, however, very difficult to do because
of the virtually infinite variety of things that could be
relevant to record, so that even the most objective recorder

would find it necessary to make some selection. The appropriateness of that selection is what makes the results of such a study valuable or worthless.

Correlational studies come in various forms, varying as to the restrictiveness of the set of variables that can be intercorrelated after the data have been collected. In essence, correlation is a statistical technique which measures the closeness of an association between two or more variables. Associations may vary from perfect correlation in which any change in one variable is reflected by a change in the other, to a much looser relationship marked by a mere tendency for changes in the two variables to go together. Correlational studies may involve selecting what to observe, and that is certainly the case when specialized instruments are used to make the observations (mental tests, for example), but they do not intervene in ways that are necessary in an experiment which depends upon manipulating and controlling variables, as well as accurate observation and recording. Studies of this kind can reveal what variables tend to change together, but they cannot reveal why. As we saw above, statistical studies of the incidence of lung cancer and smoking reveal that the disease is significantly correlated with the behaviour. They cannot lead to the inescapable conclusion that the one causes the other. If two variables are causally related there must be a correlation between them, but the reverse is not true.

one-subject studies

A particularly difficult set of problems surrounds asking questions about a particular individual. For example, if a young man visits a hypnotist before taking a driving test and subseqently passes it, what can be said about the effect of the hypnotist's treatment on his success? The answer is very little, with confidence. Clearly the hypnotist may have helped: there are several reports available of people believing that their test anxiety was reduced in this way. But our particular young man may not be exactly the same as other people so grouping him together with them may not be appropriate. One basic difficulty is that we cannot set up a control. We cannot discover how our examinee would have fared without hypnotism. Once he has taken the test and passed it, no fair comparison could be made by subsequently testing him again without a visit to his hypnotist. Though in some studies it makes sense to use a subject as his own control, in many others it does not. The subject is likely to be affected to a significant extent by one experience, so that he is not going to behave in a comparable manner if that experience is repeated. From the research point of view this raises almost insurmountable problems. There is no way in which one can achieve an unequivocal picture of what causes a particular individual to behave in a particular way, without either assuming that his behaviour patterns will be very similar to those of other people, or that he will be unaffected by his experience. Neither assumption will ever be wholly true, and the advances that can be made in understanding him will depend upon how true these assumptions are for particular aspects of his behaviour.

On theories and data

One of the reasons why it is important to be careful about collecting data in attempting to find out why something happens is that of the difficulty in spotting when an answer is a true one.

Many people have been taught that one of the most important aspects of science is that its theories are disciplined by data. They are kept in touch with the real world they seek to describe. If the theory says one thing and the data say something else, then the theory must change to accommodate the data.

Two schemes of investigation have been described as representing two distinct ideals. Inductive research involves making unselected observations of phenomena followed by ordering and categorizing them, from which a theoretical structure may emerge. Linnaeus' development of a taxonomy of plants is often held up as an example of inductive research. The alternative scheme is hypothetico-deductive research which progresses by a series of two-phase investigations. The first step involves establishing an hypothesis. Following that, a prediction is derived which can be tested directly against data collected for the purpose.

It is most unlikely that either of these schemes is actually used in its pure form. It is inconceivable that Linnaeus never developed any ideas about relevant dimensions of this taxonomy until all the observations had been made, and that his later observations were uninfluenced by his earlier ones. Likewise, the hypothetico-deductive method cannot be used unless there is a pre-existing theory, which is likely to have benefitted at some stage from random, if not comprehensive, unselected observations of phenomenon under investigation.

This contrast focusses on the relative roles of theory and data. Ideally theory suggests relevant observations. Data indicate how satisfactory existing theories are and may point to how they should be modified to become more satisfactory. Having got an enquiry off the ground, progress ought to be orderly. In fact it very seldom is. The most basic problem is that human nature seems to abhor a theoretical vacuum. Almost any theory is better than none at all. Perhaps this explains why magical explanations are preferred to a simple state of ignorance. It is almost as if man needs to have the sense of power that 'knowing how it works' confers. Whatever the reason, however, an embarrassing piece of data is unlikely to result in the only available theory being jettisoned. If there are two or more competing theories, however, data appear to be more powerfu and the relative credibility of different theories may very well be adjusted accordingly.

The unexpected weakness of data is not completely accounted for by the need to maintain at least one theory. No theory is likely to survive when faced with strong data that are incompatible with it. The problem is that many data are just not that strong. There is residual doubt about just what the observations from a particular study really mean for that particular theory.

This undesirable state of affairs can arise most easily if the theory has been only poorly defined and, especially, if the rules of correspondence between the elements of the theory and observable aspects of the real world have been omitted or only ambiguously specified. But even when the rules of correspondence are clear, the status of data can be diminished if the data collection scheme has been a rather haphazard one, and particularly if the attribution of any effects observed remains equivocal. A fair conclusion is that a poorly defined theory that seems to explain phenomena which otherwise defy explanation, and an area of enquiry that precludes, or makes very difficult, experimental research, has a very good chance of surviving for a long time irrespective of its actual validity.

Progress without experiment

Much of the foregoing might seem to be pointing in a rather unpromising direction. In order to establish unambiguously that a particular variable reliably produces a particular effect, the experiment is not only the best available research design, it is also irreplaceable. As the advertisements used to say, 'accept no imitations'. However, it would be wrong to conclude that experiments are inevitably effective, as our brief consideration of the relationship between theory and data reveals.

Research is basically a slow business in which researchers inch towards some better appreciation of the world they study. They develop their models, making them increasingly sophisticated as they make progress. The barriers to progress are many and varied including their own mental limitations and the pressures upon them from the prevailing intellectual atmosphere. Experiments can be done which shed no light at all on the question at issue. Many experiments promise more than they deliver once the post mortem has been completed. In this climate of imperfection the fact that experiment may be precluded is disappointing but not, relatively speaking, a disaster.

The development of models of the world is not as neat and tidy a process as, perhaps, we should wish. The prevailing model is the one that seems best able to cope with all that is known (or, better, all that we believe) to be true about the phenomenon we seek to understand. Provided that enough different snapshots from different vantage points can be correlated it is quite possible that ultimately the same model will arise as would have come from direct experimentation. It will almost certainly take longer, but the same end-point may well be reached. This optimism is supported by the progress made in astronomy where experimentation is virtually prohibited. Since the system under investigation is in motion, successive observations provided different but complementary information. As a result Man has managed to navigate unmanned space ships to the outer parts of the solar system and successfully explored the moon.

In many areas of social science, experimentation is either very difficult or unlikely to provide what is needed. In such circumstances correlational studies and descriptive studies of one kind or another are the only sources of information available. Perhaps this will mean slow progress, but there is little doubt that our curiosity about ourselves will be a sufficient motive for the questions to be pressed, and eventually useful answers will emerge. It matters not at all that they should emerge untidily, only that they turn out to be effective aids to our understanding.

Research and common sense

Doing research is essentially detective work, but often with an all-important difference. Police detectives cannot ask questions in the same way that the experimental scientist can. Instead they have to hope that the (probably incomplete) set of data which they collect will distinguish between the competing theories they hold about the crime under investigation. Some science is also like that, and social science especially. Maybe scientists have one major advantage in that their antagonist is nature, which may not be co-operative but is most unlikely deliberately to confuse and deceive.

Just as police detective work has a list of dos and don'ts to guide it into a successful path, so there are good and bad ways of doing science. Most of this chapter is about using common sense in finding out. There are no magical methods and the main thing to remember is to avoid ambiguity. Before starting an investigation, be absolutely clear about what the question is. It will only get more confused later if it is not clear at the start. The study itself needs to yield data that can be interpreted. Ideally, any effect observed should be unequivocally attributable to a particular variable or set or variables. Whatever scheme seems likely to achieve these goals will be worth using. A scheme that will not may well not be worth the effort of putting into practice.

Unfortunately, while much of the physical sciences allow these guidelines to be followed closely, the social sciences are more difficult to tame. Unequivocal attribution is difficult to ensure, and easiest when dealing with laboratory behaviour: a version of behaviour which may not be identical with that in real life. Often compromise is necessary, and progress is painfully slow.

Statistics

There are relatively few special tools available to the

researcher corresponding to the finger-print kit of the detective. One of the principal ones, however, is statistics, a branch of mathematics concerned with the determination of the likelihood of events occurring. It is a particularly useful tool in those areas of study which are not very clearly determinate. It was originally developed to help analyse various questions in agriculture which are made difficult by the fact that plant growth is affected by a vast number of factors, some intrinsic to the plant, some extrinsic. This situation is not unlike that in human behaviour and it is no surprise that psychologists have taken up statistics enthusiastically and developed specialized procedures for their own use.

The main advantages that statistics confer are schemes for summarizing data and making them easier to remember and communicate, schemes for measuring the relatedness of two or more variables (correlation) and schemes for aiding decision making. They are important for deciding whether any effects have been netted in the data, and that is a precondition for determining what caused them. In conjunction with experiments, statistics make it possible to face psychological research with some confidence. However, the techniques, though not particularly difficulty to use, are specialist and study in some depth is recommended before trying to use them. It is best to practise under the guidance of an expert first, before launching oneself into research.

Further study

It has only been possible to mention a few basic ideas in this brief introduction to psychological discovery. The interested reader will, we hope, feel an urge to plunge deeper into the jungle. There are an ever-increasing number of texts to guide the way. The next stage in that journey may be aided by three slim volumes out of the Essential Psychology series published by Methuen. They are:

Gardiner, J.M. and Kaminska, K. (1975)
First Experiments in Psychology. London: Methuen.
Legge, D. (1975)
An Introduction to Psychological Science. London: Methuen.
Miller, S.H. (1976)
Experimental Design and Statistics. London: Methuen.

Questions

1. Discuss different ways of determining the age of a horse. Consider analogues in psychology.
2. Write a short essay on the function of theory in psychological research.
3. What are the principal advantages of experimental enquiries? Are there any disadvantages?
4. 'One can never step into the same stream twice.' Discuss in relation to the problems of conducting psychological research.

5. Statistics developed in order to clarify the results of agricultural research. Why should they have been applied so enthusiastically to psychological research?
6. Discuss how theoretical generalizations might inform enquiries about a particular individual.
7. The two main methods of obtaining data about the development of processes and behaviour are longitudinal and cross-sectional. Discuss the advantages and disadvantages of each.
8. 'Quasi-experiments are merely poor experiments.' Discuss.
9. 'There are lies, damn lies and statistics.' Are there?
10. Some researchers argue that if the research method and the task for the subject have been properly designed, statistics are redundant. What does that say for the widespread use of statistics in psychology?
11. What is meant by 'statistical control'?
12. Discuss, with particular reference to intelligence, the use of tests to explore personal psychological characteristics.
13. Laboratories permit more exact control over experiments but may condition the results that are obtained. Is there a resolution of this dilemma?
14. Discuss the limitations imposed on research by the exclusive use of correlational methods.

Annotated reading

Cook, T.D. and Campbell, D.T. (1979) Quasi-experimentation: Design and analysis issues for field settings. Chicago: Rand McNally.
    Describes techniques that may be available when experiments cannot be used.

Barber, T.X. (1977) Pitfalls in Human Research. Oxford: Pergamon Press.

Jung, J. (1971) The Experimenter's Dilemma. New York: Harper & Row.
    Some books have analysed the sources of difficulty in finding out; these are two useful ones.

Meddis, R. (1973) Elementary Analysis of Variance for the Behavioural Sciences. London: McGraw-Hill.
    The student can acquire more advanced treatments for complex experiments from this text.

Miller, S.H. (1976) Experimental Design and Statistics. London: Methuen.

Robson, C. (1973) Experiment, Design and Statistics in Psychology. Harmondsworth: Penguin.
    Two relatively simple and accessible paperback volumes which act as starter texts in psychological statistics.

Siegel, S. (1956) Non-parametric statistics for the Behavioural Sciences. New York: McGraw-Hill.
   The 'bible' of the non-parametric techniques that has proved indispensable to psychologists.

Snodgrass, J.G. (1977) The Numbers Game: Statistics for psychology. London: Oxford University Press.
   The student who masters the first two may want to go further. This should provide some help to that progress.

Acknowledgements

I am most grateful for the assistance I have received from Dr Hilary Klee who offered much constructive criticism and Ms Christine Harrison who painstakingly translated my manuscript into a readable form.

Part two
Child Psychology

Development, communication and dysfunction

Most workers in the therapeutic professions agree that children deserve maximum attention. As the birthrate has steadily grown over the past 30 years, so research into the problems of infancy and childhood has endeavoured to keep pace. One belief about childhood has survived for hundreds of years; that adult character and personality are laid down during the first seven years of life. This belief existed long before there were scientific studies of child development and it led to firm ideas about child-rearing and how to bring about a healthy adult personality. The supreme importance attached to early childhood experiences received strong support from the psychoanalyst Sigmund Freud at the turn of the century. He argued that parents were invariably responsible for the problems suffered by their offspring in later life, through their ignorance of the emotional needs of developing children. Freud's theories of child development were highly influential; and this was mainly because they could explain a wide range of both adult and child difficulties.

Young children have difficulty in communicating their problems and their ideas about the world they live in to adults. This is a major stumbling block for the study of childhood problems. However, Binet and Simon, who invented the modern intelligence test, showed that mental functioning could be explored by means of a standard set of tasks. Tasks were set which reflected the known abilities of children in particular age groups. If children were unable to do the tasks designed for their age, they could be identified as retarded. That meant that they would need special educational environments in order to make the most of their abilities. So a clear distinction could be drawn between children who suffered from intellectual handicap and those whose problems were largely emotional. The former group became the responsibility of doctors, teachers and psychologists, and the latter became the responsibility of child psychiatrists. As research continued, adolescence came under scrutiny. A number of specific learning deficits could be identified (reading, writing, etc.) and a broad range of social and emotional difficulties were recognized.

The measurement of mental abilities has developed in the past 30 years and has led to a finer analysis of childhood

difficulties. The identification of specific communication
disorders in children was now possible. It was found that a
number of young children did not begin to use language at
the appropriate stage of development. Investigation of these
children demonstrated that there were no hearing difficulties and no muscular problems which could account for the
abnormal development. Nor could these children be compared
to mentally retarded children, as their non-verbal abilities
were virtually age-appropriate. Speech therapists had been
interested in children with hearing impairment and children
with motor handicap and they had developed a range of
treatment techniques for them. The new group of language
impaired children opened up a new horizon for therapists.
While the children presenting articulation, voice and fluency disorders had readily identifiable physical problems,
this new population offered no overt reasons for their
condition. Two main theories emerged. Either such children
simply refused to use their inherent communicative capacities, perhaps because they were emotionally disturbed,
or they were suffering from a specific language-learning
difficulty which could be clearly distinguished from the
global difficulties of the mentally handicapped. In either
case there was a need to examine both psychological and
medical research in order to design a specific therapy.
　　Psychology offers theories of how childhood problems
arise and it also offers a number of intervention strategies
to combat the various difficulties which present in the
clinic. The success of psychological treatment methods is
indisputable in many childhood conditions. In the past few
years a new range of therapies has emerged which address the
difficulties of adolescence. In order to evaluate the appropriateness of various therapeutic strategies it is necessary
to understand the theoretical principles upon which many
treatments are based. In chapter 3 Brian Foss outlines the
main theoretical principles which characterize child psychology and which have led to particular therapeutic strategies. In chapter 4 we review the major types of childhood
disorders encountered in clinical practice and the various
explanations that have been advanced to account for these
conditions. In chapter 5 Peter Robinson offers a stimulating
psychological account of language development which challenges many previously held assumptions about the child's
language, and offers a framework for all therapists
interested in enhancing developmental progress.

3

Abilities and Behaviour in Childhood and Adolescence
B. M. Foss

Early development

Even at birth the differences between infants are very
great, and the range of abilities and behaviour which can be
called normal is large at all ages.

Apart from sleeping (80 per cent of the time), the
newborn seems to spend most of his time eating, excreting
or crying. There are several kinds of cry which most mothers
can distinguish from each other and which can be analysed
using spectographs (which break up the sound into its
frequency components). The birth cry appears to be unique.
Then there is a basic cry, sometimes called a hunger cry,
which is the common pattern. The pain cry, which may be
elicited on the first day (for instance, when a blood sample
is taken), is characterized by an initial yell followed by
several seconds of silence during which the baby maintains
expiration and which finally gives way to a gasp and loud
sobbing, which in its turn reverts to a basic cry. There is
also a frustration cry which is rather like a diminished
version of the pain cry. Many mothers have also recognized
a different kind of cry which starts at, say, the fourth
week. It seems to be a sham cry in the sense that it is
caused by no specific need, but seems simply to be a way of
calling for attention. Presumably this kind of cry develops
into the distress which older children show when separated
from their mothers.

What things does the infant attend to? Can it recognize
its mother's face and voice, or are these learnt gradually
over a period of time? Until recently it was believed that
recognition of faces and voices did not occur until the
infant was several months old, but it now looks as though
infants become competent in this way very much earlier, as
many mothers already suspected. At least, what they can do
is distinguish between different voices and faces probably
as early as the third week of life, and it is likely that
they can tell difference in smell between different people
as early as the second week of life, and there is some evidence that even at this age infants are particularly attracted to representations of the human face. This is a topic
on which there is a conflict of evidence. What is clear,
though, is that most babies have a great deal of opportunity
to get to know faces, in that mothers play face-to-face

games with their babies from the very first days of life;
indeed, where they are allowed to be with the baby from
birth they will tend to play these games immediately. By the
time the baby is three weeks old it gets 'turned off' if,
when face to face with an adult, the adult fails to react to
the baby's changes in facial expression.

Perception

What seems vital for later perceptual learning is some kind
of interaction between the child and the environment. In
describing what happens it is useful to think in terms of
perceptual categories. Probably from birth, infants are
able to categorize movements and discriminate them from lac
of movement and also to categorize various colours; so they
probably have a category for 'red moving objects'. If later
in life an infant reaches out to touch such objects a red
moving object which is a flame may be encountered, and as
a result of touching it the infant's behaviour will have
an outcome which is different from that when other kinds
of objects are touched. In such a way the infant's learn to
discriminate a special sub-category of red moving objects.
Movements of all kinds - eye movements, head movements,
body movements, and all kinds of interaction with the environment - seem to be important for the development of new
perceptions, and this leads to the possibility that perceptual development will be affected by the child's interests
(in the wider sense; that is, matters of concern): the child
is more likely to attend to and interact with those aspects
of the environment which are relevant to those interests.
One can see evidence for this kind of effect in the many
cross-cultural studies that show, for instance, that Eskimos
have many categories for snow. Similarly, small boys may
have many categories for motor cars. It will be seen that
the psychological idea of a percept is not very different
from a concept. One's perception of a dog is not only affected by the sight of the dog, but also knowing what it
sounds like, or what it feels like to be patted, or to be
bitten by, and what it smells like; and if one happens to be
a dog fancier one's perception of the dog will involve very
much finer discriminations than those made by other people.
Perception, then, is affected not only by the present state
of affairs - the stimuli from the environment, and the perceiver's attention, and motivation and emotional state - but
also by the perceiver's whole previous history, and this
leads to the possibility that different kinds of people have
rather different perceptions. The members of a gang will
perceive that gang's symbols (haircut and clothing, favourite music, favourite drink, etc.) quite differently from the
way they would be perceived by a member of an opposing
gang.

Skills

It is only about halfway through the first year of life that
a child begins to show good evidence for integrating its
movements with its perception by being able to get hold of

objects in an obviously intentional way. The gradual development from these early stages through walking and various kinds of play activity to complex skills involved in sports, for instance, are well documented. It may be useful to have a model of the way in which such skills are acquired, and one such model is to regard the skill as built up of a hierarchy of lower-order habits. For instance, a child learning to write must have first learnt to hold a pencil (there is an innate grasping reflex but the child will have to relinquish this method of grasping for one using finger and thumb opposition), will have had to learn to move the pencil across the paper hard enough to leave a mark but not break the paper, will have had to learn to match shapes, to move from left to right across the page, to distinguish between mirror image letters, and so on. Many of these habits can be learnt only in a fairly definite sequence because one will depend on the acquisition of previous habits. Eventually the child will have a whole hierarchy of writing and drawing habits, and at some stage these will have to be integrated with other hierarchies of talking and hearing habits if the child is to become an ordinary literate person. The establishment of these hierarchies depends obviously on having the necessary sensory and motor abilities. They also depend on practice (one cannot learn to drive a car just by reading a book), the knowledge of results (otherwise movements will not become perfected) and on having the motivation to continue learning. One of the characteristics of these skill hierarchies is that the lower-order habits become automatic, and the skilled person does not have to think about them at all but can concentrate on the 'higher' aspects of what is being done. Such a model helps to throw light on some of the reasons why children may fail to develop skills necessary for everyday life. For instance, some sensory or motor abilities may be deficient, an essential lower-order habit may be missing, there may have been difficulty in integrating one or more hierarchies, or there may have been inadequate motivation.

Solving problems

Investigation of problem-solving has been one of the main ways in which psychologists have studied thinking. A main impetus in the study of the development of this kind of ability has been the work of the Swiss psychologist Jean Piaget. He based an elaborate theory on the way in which children develop concepts of number, space, relationships, etc., and claimed that the thinking of a child develops through a series of definite stages, rather as in the development of a skill hierarchy. His results and his theory have been called into question, and although many psychologists do not agree with his theoretical formulation, many of his empirical results have been replicated in a variety of cultures. There has, though, been a tendency to show that some of the problems which Piaget posed can be solved by children at a slightly earlier age given a different method of presenting the problem, and it turns out that sometimes the child fails to solve a problem for reasons other than those given by Piaget. For instance, the child's short-term memory may be inadequate for the storage of information necessary to solve the problem. One of the most interesting class of problems used by Piaget is concerned with what he called conservation. For instance, in testing a child's ability to show conservation of volume, the child is faced with two identical beakers filled with equal amounts of, say, lemonade. If the child agrees that there is an equal amount in each beaker the lemonade from one is then poured into a tall thin glass. The child who has not acquired the concept of conservation will choose the lemonade in the tall thin glass in preference because it will appear greater in quantity. According to Piaget, it is only in middle childhood that children acquire conservation concepts, and it is only when they are, say, 11 or 12 that full logical thinking is possible.

One major concern of psychologists has been to determine how important language is in the development of a child's thinking abilities. Perhaps it is because educationists themselves are rather verbal people that many believe language to be the most important single thing. However, there is some contrary evidence. For instance, deaf mutes who have very little vocabulary or syntax may nevertheless be rather competent in dealing with a whole range of problems varying from those found in ordinary intelligence tests to complicated problems in logic. Of all the tests which have been tried, it happens to be that conservation problems are those which seem most affected by lack of adequate language. In dealing with questions of this kind it is important to realize that there are several kinds of thinking and of intelligence. For instance, when a very broad range of intelligence tests are analysed by a technique such as a factor analysis (which is essentially a way of classifying tests), it usually turns out that there are two broad groups of tests: those involving language and those which do not, but may depend more, for instance, on being able to manipulate space and pattern. There are also large individual differences between people in this matter. Some seem to use language very much more in ordinary thinking, and there is some evidence across cultures that on the whole girls are better at language skills and boys are better at spatial skills. There is one kind of problem whose solution seems to depend on developmental stages and which may hold the key to some of the changes which occur with age. If young children are given a series of objects varying in colour, size and shape, and asked to sort them, they may do so by their colour or their shape or their size, but having sorted by one method they will be unable to see that there is a second or third method of sorting them, and it is only when they are considerably older that they can see from the start that there is an ambiguity about how sorting should be done.

Play

Play in animals and humans is usually easy to recognize
but not so easy to define. Most play does have the property
of appearing to be 'not for real', but there are difficult
borderline cases. For instance, when children are playing
together with toys there may be frequent episodes where
there is competition for toys or for territory, and this may
involve aggression which certainly appears real. Play at
first tends to be solitary even when other children are
there. There may be 'parallel play' in which children pursue
the same tasks though with no obvious co-operation. Fully co-
operative play is not seen much before children are three or
four years old. In most cultures it seems that there are sex
differences in typical play. Boys tend to play more with
boys and girls with girls, and boys show much more of what
has come to be called 'rough and tumble play'. This is the
sort of play where there is a lot of wrestling and tumbling
about and rolling over, sometimes with open-handed arm
beating, often without contact, and rapid jumping up and
down sometimes with arm slapping, and the whole thing is
often accompanied by laughter. Where there is a largish
group of children, one variant is that there is a great deal
of group running, usually in a circle and often occurring
with a lot of laughter. Chasing is another very common
variant. Another sex difference is observed when children
play with their mothers, in that girls tend to have closer
proximity to the mother than boys do, at least on the
average. When play is solitary, dolls and other playthings
and pets are sometimes made to stand for parents and for
children. Such play is often taken to reveal a child's preoccupations, and play therapy is based on the notion that
emotional preoccupations can be acted out. In older children
a lot of play becomes competitive. The dominance fighting
to establish a 'pecking order', which can be seen in all
social animals, is very evident in children. Some of it may
be symbolic and indirect, especially in girls, where dominance fighting is more likely to be verbal than physical.

   Arguments about the functions of play are centuries old,
and the theories are on the whole untestable (as are most
functional theories). However, there is now a certain amount
of evidence from animals and from children regarding the
effects of deprivation of play. Harlow's experiments at
Wisconsin on the effects of various kinds of upbringing on
later behaviour in rhesus monkeys have shown that if small
monkeys are deprived of play, especially rough and tumble
play, they may become maladroit later at both sexual and
social behaviour. It is possible that play has this kind of
functional importance for humans also. A more popular theory
is that play in humans is essential for cognitive development. Many educationists believe this, and they get theoretical support from Piaget's notion that the growth of
understanding depends heavily on a child's actions with
respect to the environment. An intervention programme
has been reported in which children who appeared to be

intellectually backward as a result of malnutrition were given regular structured play sessions with toys, and as a result showed considerable development compared with children not given such a programme.

Reinforcement

This is the notion that behaviour is controlled by its consequences. In the sense in which 'reinforcement' is used by B. F. Skinner, a reinforcing state of affairs is one which, when it follows a response of an animal or human, will reinforce that response so that the probability of that response occurring in similar circumstances in the future will increase. Much of the fundamental work on reinforcement has been done on rats and pigeons but also on a very wide variety of other animals and on humans too, and it is the basis for many of the techniques used in behaviour modification. In a typical experiment a rat learns to press a lever which results in the delivery of a food pellet, and this is reinforcing to the hungry rat. Using such a simple set-up it is possible to investigate the effects of a wide variety of variables on the rate of learning. When the animal has learnt that food is no longer delivered when the lever is pressed (extinction trials) it will go on pressing for a while and then cease; but there may be spontaneous recovery. If the animal has been put on a schedule of reinforcement, in which reinforcement is not given for every response but only now and again, either regularly cr irregularly and unpredictably, then the animal tends to be much more persistent in pressing the lever and will go on doing so for much longer when food is no longer delivered at all. In other words, after a schedule of reinforcement, especially if the reinforcement has been irregular, the behaviour is much more 'resistant to extinction'. A rat can also be put very much under the control of the environment, in that if a light is always on during reinforced trials but never on during unreinforced trials the animal will learn quite rapidly to press the lever only when the light is on. The light is then described as a 'discriminative stimulus'. A wide variety of things may act as reinforcers. For instance, isolated monkeys will press a lever for a view of the monkey colony or for a tape-recording of other monkeys, and these stimuli act as reinforcers. These kinds of experimental results have to be applied to humans with a good deal of caution. It is not clear how human behaviour is modified if individuals knows that they are being subjected to a patterning of reinforcement; nor is it clear what the effects are of having language and being able to conceptualize the set-up.

Apart from behaviour modification techniques as used by therapists, the following are some applications which may be made. There is one kind of crying, which was mentioned earlier, whose function seems to be to get attention even though there is nothing physically wrong with the child. Such attention-getting crying may be very persistent, and attempts have been made to extinguish it by not attending to the child when he produces this kind of cry. There are several published papers indicating that this kind of procedure is effective. Getting attention, presumably benign attention, is an important reinforcer for many children. There are reports, for instance, of a child who spent most of his time in a horizontal position and crawling, and as a result obtained a lot of attention which presumably reinforced his crawling behaviour. The teachers were trained to attend to the child only when he approximated standing up and not to attend to him when he was crawling, and as a result the child learnt to produce more normal behaviour. One well-known experiment controlled the smiling of babies by reinforcing them with smiles and pleasant noises whenever they smiled. A comparison was made of babies who had been reinforced at every smile, and those who had been put on a schedule, that is, they had been reinforced only at every fourth smile. As predicted, the babies on the schedule smiled more and the smiling was more resistant to extinction. It is not known, though, how long this kind of learning persisted. One prediction of the theory would be that if a child produced a certain kind of behaviour to obtain affection, then that behaviour would be more persistent if the affection were given capriciously and, for the child, unpredictably. As Skinner himself pointed out, in everyday life most reinforcers are irregular rather than regular. This is particularly true in gambling and it is quite likely that one of the mechanisms at work in the persistent gambler is the direct result of unpredictable reinforcement. Bearing in mind the way in which an animal's behaviour can be controlled by a discriminative stimulus in the environment, one could argue that it would be much easier for a child to learn appropriate behaviour if it were made quite clear in the environment when that behaviour was appropriate and when not. To caricature the situation, if a father wore a tie whenever the child was expected to behave in a fairly orderly fashion, but not to wear a tie during playtime, then it should be much easier for the child to discriminate between those two situations. It must be very difficult for young children to know what is appropriate behaviour in a typical supermarket when everyone else is taking goods off the shelves but they themselves are not allowed to do so.

Imitation

There is some evidence that infants will imitate facial expressions when they are only a few weeks old. For instance, they will put out their tongue apparently imitatively at two or three weeks. However, it may not be true imitation since they will also put out their tongues at a pencil pointed at them at the same age. In the second half of the first year, though, a great deal of facial imitation does go on. Detailed analysis of videotape shows that in most cases it is the mother imitating the infant and not the

other way around. A lot of this imitative play seems to be
a precursor of language and conversation but it is not yet
known how important it is. In the second and third year and
later, there is a great deal of imitation, much of it important for 'sex typing'. For instance, a three-year-old girl
will spend a great deal of time imitating her mother's activities about the house. There have now been many studies
of the extent to which imitation or copying occurs in middle
childhood from adults or television. Boys in particular tend
to copy aggressive movement, especially if the person they
are imitating is a man and more especially if the man appears to be rewarded for what he is doing. It is still very
unclear to what extent this sort of behaviour persists as a
result of such imitation. It is still also not known in
general which people children imitate most.

Freud

Many present-day theories of child development are more
or less based on classical psychoanalytic theory, and many
people would consider that Freud's main contribution was to
focus attention on the first five years of life as being of
paramount importance in determining later personality. For
Freud the central concept in child development is identification, and he believed that imitation was one of the best
behavioural signs that identification existed. He believed
that identification with the mother figure occurred very
early in life and that later, at about the time the super-
ego develops, identification with the aggressor (the aggressive aspects of either mother or father figure) took
place. Freud also suggested that the child passes through
stages related to the way in which the libido (instinctual
energy) operates. The first stage is the oral stage, in
which the child's erotic life (in Freud's rather special
meaning) centres on the mouth; this is followed by the anal
stage, when life centres on excretion; then the phallic
stage in which sexual (but of course pre-pubertal) interests
centre on the genitals and the body surface as a whole.
There then follows a latent period during which there is
little development until the genital period is reached at
adolescence. Mental illness in later life was seen as originating from traumatic experiences occurring during these
periods. The situation is complicated for boys by the
Oedipus situation in which the five year old sees himself as
competing with his father for the love of the mother. Some
of these ideas were elaborated by other psychoanalysts by
devising personality typologies which were based on infantile experience. For instance, an orally-accepting type of
person would be a lover of food and drink, a smoker, fond of
words; the phallic type might be a lover of the body beautiful, perhaps an exhibitionist or an admirer of sculpture.
Needless to say, it is extremely difficult to test the
validity of such speculations.

Adolescence

In the first half of this century adolescence was treated as a period of 'storm and stress', of rebellion, of altruism, and searching for an identity. Some of these characteristics of adolescence now seem to be specific to the cultures in which the originators of the ideas lived, and this is particularly true for the notion that adolescence is a period of storm and stress. From anthropological and other studies, it is clear that in some cultures such a period does not exist. The last few decades have seen major changes occurring in the adolescent world so that many of the old generalizations no longer apply. A few decades ago the situation could be stated in fairly black and white terms: young adolescents were economically dependent; they were sexually capable but not expected to have, or were even legally forbidden from having, intercourse; and their social roles were essentially non-adult. In the course of a decade they were expected to go through a fairly clear series of transitional stages until they inevitably reached the de- sired position in an adult society in which their economic, sexual and social roles would all have changed utterly. At the present day sexual intercourse is often practised soon after the onset of puberty; many children, including working- class children, have considerably more spending money than their parents had at the same age; and there are now so many sub-cultures all the way from pre-adolescence to adulthood that at any age children can find themselves fully accepted within a culture, as a full member of society.

Biological factors

It is now generally accepted that the onset of puberty occurs earlier as time passes. The results of the onset of puberty on individual children seem to depend very much on what they and their peers expect those effects to be. For instance, there are large differences in the extent of men- strual pain, and those differences vary somewhat between cultures and seem to reflect the expectations within those cultures. Some studies suggest that menarche affects per- formance at school, whereas there are other studies giving contrary evidence. Here again much may depend on expecta- tions. It is likely that if an individual reaches puberty long before or long after other children in the peer group, this may have considerable effect on behaviour and atti- tudes. It may be that ignorance of biological factors is detrimental in individual cases, but no one has yet shown what is the best way to carry out sex education, or indeed yet shown that sex education is a good thing (and it would be extremely difficult to show, since the investigator would have the problem of deciding what sex education is good for).

Social factors

Not many generations ago a person was unlikely to survive if not attached physically to a group of people. The need to belong to a group is still as great, though little is known about the psychological mechanisms involved. Avoidance of loneliness is one powerful drive. In modern Man this need may be satisfied by simply identifying with the group and not necessarily belonging to it physically. A century ago a person's choice of group was limited usually to the family, the immediate neighbourhood, work, church, and perhaps hobbies and sport. Now, especially in cities or where people are mobile, groups are based more on common interests. It is very easy these days for a person to find other people who want to behave in the same way or have common goals. There is a tendency for members of a group to come to look alike, talk alike, make the same choices in food, music, beliefs, etc.; and these tendencies are often seen in an exaggerated form in adolescent groups, especially where the identification with the group is so complete that members see themselves as belonging to that group only and to no other. One very noticeable thing about human groups of all kinds (and this applies to groups at all levels of sophistication) is that they are not only bound together by common likes but also by common dislikes. All groups are against something. Anything which lessens old group allegiances will also make new groupings easier so that one would expect gangs to be especially prevalent in new high-rise housing estates, or with people who have just left school. One idea about adolescence, which seems not to have changed over the centuries, is that there is something called 'adolescent revolt'. It has been observed in many cultures (though not in all) that soon after puberty there tends to be a reaction against the parental ways of life. The idea that there is something primitive and possibly biological about this has been reinforced by many observations of primate societies which show that young males tend to form breakaway groups and also start fighting for dominance within the old group.

Dominance fighting is well accepted as an explanatory concept applied to social animals of all kinds, and some biologists and psychologists see it as a main source of competitiveness in human behaviour. Besides the pressures to belong to a group and to conform to it, there are still these largely competitive tendencies which may take the form of wanting to be unique, and to have a role of one's own within the group. Very often such a role involves being best at something. Being best may involve owning things, being most daring, or beautiful, or cleverest. With small boys, competitiveness may show itself in actual dominance fighting. Psychologists of various kinds have talked a lot about the adolescent need for having an identity. It is possible that that need may be partly and perhaps completely satisfied once the person finds a role within a group, especially if the role and the group are of high esteem.

Attitudes and beliefs
Sociologists and social psychologists use the concept 'reference groups'. Market researchers may want to know how to advertise a certain kind of cosmetic product. If it is intended to be attractive to adolescent girls, they may

well use the technique of finding out which reference group is relevant. For instance, they may, using questionnaire techniques, ask questions of the kind designed to find out with whom adolescent girls identify when buying cosmetics. In general, one's reference group is the group of people with whom one identifies with respect to one's attitudes, beliefs and values. Developmental studies show that for young children the home provides the main reference group, but in middle childhood already there is a tendency to adopt values of heroes from stories or from television and this becomes very marked in pre-adolescence. In adolescence there may be a complete change of reference groups as has already been suggested, and if this change is very radical then it may be a source of conflict. The way in which the conflict expresses itself will, of course, vary between individuals, and any of the usual clinical manifestations are possible, such as anxiety, depression, hysterical reactions, aggression, and in some cases an attempt at a rational solution of the conflict. Attitudes towards choice of work will be affected by group pressures in just the same way as all other attitudes. The situation is affected by the fact that in many adolescent sub-cultures all the heroes and heroines are roughly of the same age as members of the sub-culture, and there is no need to look ahead to what is going to happen when one belongs to an older age group. In such cases attitudes towards work are likely to be unrealistic in terms of planning ahead.

Questions

1. Write short notes on: crying; the development of perception and attention; the development of movement.
2. How do skills develop? Illustrate with examples of your own choosing from early and later childhood.
3. What is reinforcement? How may it operate in controlling behaviour?
4. In what ways does a child's ability to solve problems vary with age?
5. How would you classify different kinds of play? What functions may they have?
6. What are the main developmental stages a child passes through according to (i) Piaget, (ii) Freud?
7. Discuss the extent to which development during adolescence is determined by social factors.
8. How do attitudes and beliefs change during childhood and adolescence?
9. How do children learn to categorize things and people in their environment?
10. What part may imitation play in the development of personality?

Annotated reading

Hadfield, J.A. (1979) Childhood and Adolescence. Harmondsworth: Penguin.

Sandstrom, C.I. (1968) Psychology of Childhood and Adolescence. Harmondsworth: Penguin.
> These cover both childhood and adolescence. The book by Hadfield is particularly useful for parents. The one by Sandstrom is a little dated though there is a revised edition from 1979.

Bower, T. (1977) Perceptual World of the Child. London: Fontana.

Garvey, C. (1977) Play. London: Fontana.

Donaldson, M. (1978) Children's Minds. London: Fontana.
> These belong to a series of short books on children called The Developing Child and edited by Jerome Bruner, Michael Cole and Barbara Lloyd. The last of these three references is particularly good on cognitive growth and its relevance to education.

Turner, J. (1975) Cognitive Development. London: Methuen.

Green, J. (1974) Thinking and Language. London: Methuen.
> These are part of a series called Essential Psychology, and are particularly relevant.

Watson, R.I. and Lindgren, H.C. (1979) Psychology of the Child and the Adolescent (4th edn). New York: Collier Macmillan.
> This is an American book, but covers the non-American work well, and is slightly more advanced than the other suggested readings.

4

Clinical Child Psychology
Harry Purser

Introduction

The development of psychological services for children began
in 1909 when William Healy, a psychiatrist, set up the
Juvenile Psychopathic Institute in Chicago. This agency
dealt primarily with the problem of delinquency and was
staffed by a team of psychiatrists, social workers and
psychologists. By the 1920s the multi-disciplinary team
approach to the problems of childhood was further developed
through the establishment of 'child guidance clinics' in
America. These clinics expanded the range of interest to
include delinquency, mental retardation, neurological problems and personality disorders. At this time developmental
problems were seen as having either a physiological, medical
basis, or as the consequence of emotional disturbance. The
emergence of Freud's psychoanalytic model of child development offered clinicians an alternative to the medical
approach which gave rise to the specialism of child
psychotherapy.

These developments were soon influenced by the work of
Binet and Simon (1905) who had developed objective methods
of measuring intellectual development. In his work for the
French government, Binet designed the first intelligence
test and described 'mental growth curves' which could discriminate the mentally retarded from normal children. This
work paved the way for a new clinical psychological science
to build models of intellectual, social and emotional functioning in childhood and investigate the causes of abnormal
development. Further work on the notion of IQ measurement
was soon under way in both the USA and Europe. In the period
between 1920 and 1940 a number of longitudinal studies were
carried out at the Merrill Palmer Institute in the USA.
Children were investigated from physiological and psychological perspectives at different points in development. The
outcome of this research suggested a strong relationship
between physical (biological) maturation and psychological
development.

Behaviouristic psychology between 1920 and 1940 also
offered a very practical approach to behavioural disturbance
in childhood by emphasizing how environmental reinforcement
could maintain particular sequences of undesirable behaviour. This account led to the clinical application of behaviourism both as a way of analysing problems and as a
means of treating behavioural disorders such as aggression

or tantrum problems. By the 1950s Skinner's radical behaviourism had a firm base in clinical child psychology because of the range of problems it was capable of addressing.
Delinquency, self-injurious behaviour, temper outbursts,
self-help skills in the mentally retarded and even reading
and spelling difficulties could all be tackled from a
behaviourist standpoint.

During this period the team approach to developmental
disorders ranged from paediatric (medical) investigation of
physical disorders such as neurological damage, psychiatric
(psychoanalytic) assessment of emotional disturbance,
psychological (behaviouristic) treatment of maladaptive
behaviour and social work support for the families of problem children. Although this range of interdisciplinary expertise has continued to feature in child health care to
the present day, further theoretical advances in child
psychology have broadened the range of explanations of child
development and generated new approaches to intervention.
In particular the work of Jean Piaget (1929), the Swiss
psychologist, deserves special attention.

Piaget was interested in the development of intellectual
functioning in childhood but considered the IQ test no more
than a crude sample of cognitive functioning at a given age.
The psychometric approach to intelligence implied it was a
quantitative entity: that 'intelligence' simply accumulates
with increasing age. This additive model was in line with
the behaviouristic view of development where an increasing
number of learnt associations are built up through environmental reinforcement; it is these associations which are
measured by IQ tests. Piaget, however, conducted a detailed
study, first of his own children, then of other groups with
developmental problems, throughout the course of development. He concluded that intelligence is not simply an accumulation of learnt responses reinforced by the environment,
but can be represented more accurately by a stage model
where qualitatively different cognitive functioning is found
in each stage. Since IQ tests were not based on a qualitative model, they could offer little diagnostic information
in cases of abnormal development. Piaget's approach held the
promise of clinical intervention for the individual child
rather than simply comparing him with the general child
population.

Piaget's developmental psychology emphasized the inter-
play between biological maturation and environmental stimulation in the course of growing up, which results in
increasingly efficient ways of processing cognitive information. Although this work did not receive much attention
until the 1950s, it then generated a new wave of experimental research in cognitive psychology aimed at describing
the psychological functioning of both infants and young
children in order to build up a more detailed model of
cognitive development.

Models of development   For clinicians dealing with childhood problems three major models of development beckoned. These explanations differed in their implications for therapeutic intervention by virtue of the assumptions they made about the nature of development. Psychoanalytic theory emphasized the need to negotiate the various stages of psychosexual development postulated by Freud if healthy social and emotional development was to be attained. An emotionally reactive child who is unable to withstand periods of separation from his mother was seen as having an overdependent personality caused by fixation, and consequent emotional arrest, at a specific psychosexual stage. Treatment would consist of trying to create an emotional environment around the child which could enable him to progress to the next psychosexual stage. Evidence that such fixation had taken place would be found in the symbolic play of the child and in the account parents would give of their child's development. Psychoanalytic theory has little to say on the subject of intellectual development other than the general point that any fixation will lead to immaturity in ego (cognitive) functioning. The psychoanalytic view has found application in many developmental problems. It has been invoked in cases of delinquency, phobias, school refusal, speech disorders, depression, hyperactivity and psychosis.

Behaviouristic learning theory has applied both classical and operant conditioning procedures to a similar range of problems. Social, emotional and intellectual development were seen as regulated by environmental reinforcement. The highly emotional child may, through classical conditioning, have acquired a particular fear response to a specific stimulus. This fear may generalize to a wider range of stimuli and eventually the fear response may become primarily associated with attention from parents and comforting reinforcement. This results in a generally emotional child prone to sudden temper and crying tantrums. Intervention was a matter of changing reinforcement contingencies to extinguish the undesirable tantrums whilst encouraging the acquisition of new, more desirable behaviours. This view of development implies a continuous process controlled by environmental reinforcement alone, whereas the psychoanalytic model highlights the discontinuity (stages) in development.

In Piaget's cognitive theory of development it is intellectual functioning rather than emotional and social conditioning which is at the root of psychological disturbance. Piaget's stages of cognitive development are initially under maturational (biological) control, but require intensive interaction with the external environment for the characteristic forms of psychological functioning to be established. A child who was delayed in his use of symbolic functioning may be found to be operating at a lower stage of cognitive development than that necessary to progress to symbolic representation. The therapist's job is to design a suitable series of learning tasks to promote further cognitive development which would be carried out on an intensive basis. Once sufficient cognitive development had taken place symbolic functioning would emerge. These anomalies in development could be the result of individual differences in genetic programming, or of early environmental insult resulting in neurophysiological damage. Intensive and well-designed 'enriched environments' could facilitate further cognitive development. The child presenting social and emotional problems may have a primary cognitive dysfunction which results in deficient psychological functioning leading to frustration and misbehaviour.

For professional clinicians this range of models, together with a number of more specific hypotheses about different kinds of disorders (reading, writing, language acquisition, moral and social development), provided the bases of therapy. Reese and Overton (1970) review these models of development and list their points of divergence; the extent to which genetic programming controls psychological development rather than environmental stimulation is an obvious dimension of difference which has generated the great IQ debate. From the point of view suggested by the theory of evolution it is reasonable to expect wide individual differences in social, emotional and intellectual functioning which arise from specific genetic programming. The final form such functioning takes will be a result of the unique interactions the individual makes with his environment. But little evidence has been collected in any systematic way about the consequences of intensive, structured environmental input on the developing individual. This is exactly what any form of developmental therapy is trying to discover, but due to the fact that there has traditionally been a division between basic academic research and clinical practice it is only in relatively recent years that the scientific study of developmental therapy has been undertaken.

Modern clinical child psychology has developed in the spheres of education and health care. Educational psychologists are primarily concerned with cognitive development, and advise on the optimum educational provision for the individual child. Clinical psychologists investigate a broad range of developmental disorders and design intervention programmes for the individual case. This division between educational and clinical psychology is largely a result of administrative history, and in recent years it has been suggested there is little difference between the two sets of practitioners in what they actually do. Educational and clinical psychologists form part of the modern multidisciplinary team with psychiatrists, paediatricians, social workers, speech therapists, physiotherapists and nurses. Parents and teachers are advised of the needs of the individual child in carrying out intervention schemes, the outcome of which is carefully monitored by the team and supplemented, where appropriate, by intensive therapy.

Classification of childhood problems

A major stumbling block to the development of any systematic science is the lack of a generally agreed system of classifying the phenomena under study. Classification, as a simple descriptive venture, is a traditional prerequisite of all new sciences. A science of childhood needs to develop such a system if all workers are to agree on the range of conditions seen in clinic. Really a classification system provides a common language for researchers to discuss and investigate specific problems in a consistent way. Classification systems, however, differ in the assumptions they make about the phenomena under study. A categorical system offers definitions which can be differentially compared with each other. Two conditions, X and Y, may have very similar presentations but can be differentiated from each other by the presence or absence of particular components which would allow differential categorization. A dimensional system classifies dysfunction along various continua suggesting that 'normality' and 'abnormality' can be continuously represented. Thus the assignment of individuals to different categories is replaced by the identification of where the individual lies on several dimensions relative to the rest of the population. These two different systems represent the medical (categorical) and psychological (dimensional) approaches to classification.

The categorical system offers more than a simple description of a particular problem as it often incorporates assumptions about the causes of problems. These causes range from physiological damage to psychological trauma and so diagnosis is the process of correctly categorizing an individual and basing treatment on the implications of that categorization. Traditionally the medical categorical system has been applied to childhood disorders as an extension of the adult system. Many have become unhappy with this situation for two reasons: the reliability of the traditional medical system has come under suspicion and it is doubted whether the developmental disorders are sufficiently similar to adult problems to warrant a common categorical system. Classification is an essential ingredient in scientific research, although in the past it was regarded as a diagnostic exercise rather than an unambiguous description of a case. If an individual were diagnosed as suffering from 'separation anxiety', then this referred to an emotional disorder caused by early psychosexual trauma. Modern classification systems of childhood disorders have tried to remove this kind of theoretical bias and maximize the five essential ingredients of a good classification system.

* DEFINITIVE: in defining various phenomena clear, unambiguous and objective criteria should be employed.
* RELIABILITY: in order to ensure reliability, clinicians using the system must make identical allocations of cases.
* VALIDITY: there should be as little overlap as possible between conditions.
* COMPREHENSIVE: the system should be sufficiently

comprehensive to ensure clearly disturbed individuals
are invariably identified.
* SIMPLICITY: the system should be as simple as possible
to avoid errors which are inevitable in complex systems.

Given that children change rapidly, an acceptable system
should be able to classify and reclassify the individual
child in order to indicate progress in development. In the
United States a system known as DSM III (Diagnostic and
Statistical Manual, 3rd edition) was published by the
American Psychiatric Association in 1980. This system,
together with the World Health Organization (WHO) ICD 9
(International Classification of Diseases, 9th revision)
published in 1978, forms the basis of international research
into childhood disorders. The WHO system is notable for its
multi-axial approach to classification of childhood disorders developed by Rutter, Shaffer and Shepherd (1975).
In this approach the individual case is rated along several
dimensions for the presence or absence of abnormality which
can then form the treatment targets for intervention.
Further discussion of classification systems for childhood
disorders is provided by Quay (1979).
The development of rigorous classification systems has
greatly contributed in recent years to a scientific child
psychology; the impact of new explanations will continue to
influence classification systems and generate new methods of
intervention. The scientific evaluation of these treatment
methods is the major task of all clinicians.
In the current WHO ICD 9 system, five main dimensions
of childhood problems are identified:

* clinical psychiatric syndrome (emotional disturbance,
psychosis);
* specific delays in development (speech, language,
reading, etc.);
* intellectual level (mild, moderate and severe mental
retardation);
* medical conditions (cerebral palsy, etc.);
* psychosocial disturbance (family discord, etc.).

A given individual may manifest problems in one or several
of these dimensions and would be treated simultaneously for
each problem area. Treatment methods would be contributed by
each discipline in the team and so a child with mild neurological damage (medical condition) with a resultant cognitive impairment (intellectual) may display emotional
disturbance which adversely affects family life, leading to
even more emotional problems (psychosocial). Such a formulation emphasizes the interaction of several factors in
an individual case and the importance of identifying these
interactions for treatment. For convenience, four major
areas of childhood disorders will be described: childhood
psychoses, mental retardation, social and emotional problems
and specific developmental disorders.

Childhood psychoses

The term 'childhood psychoses' is a rather general description of severe and extensive disturbance in intellectual, social and emotional functioning in children between birth and puberty. Two major categories of psychosis are generally recognized: childhood schizophrenia and autism.

Childhood schizophrenia

Historically, childhood schizophrenia was simply seen as a very early form of later adult schizophrenia and implied that the same disease entity was at work. This diagnosis was given to children over the age of five years who had clearly suffered a regression in their behavioural and mental capacities. Bender (1955) has been an energetic worker in this field and has put forward a number of criteria which define the clinical syndrome of childhood schizophrenia. Briefly, these criteria include atypical and withdrawn behaviour, gross immaturity and general inadequacy of development. Often certain physiological rhythms such as sleep and eating cycles are disturbed. These children may develop uneventfully in families for several years before becoming socially withdrawn, uncommunicative and emotionally labile. Sudden panic anxiety attacks may occur, resulting in hyperactive behavioural episodes. The child may exhibit delusions, hallucinations and distractability whilst engaging in often bizarre behavioural rituals.

Early infantile autism

Autism, in contrast to childhood schizophrenia, is said to be apparent shortly after birth. The child appears detached and unresponsive to his environment in the absence of any discernible physical damage to the CNS. Rutter (1974) offers the following three criteria as indicative of the autistic child.

* ALONENESS: autistic children are often described as 'good babies' since they seldom engage in attention-seeking crying or tantrums. They do not babble, reach out for objects or smile at their caretakers and are usually aversive to physical comforting. At later stages of development they occupy themselves in solitary play, seemingly oblivious to their surroundings. Normal emotional attachments to parents and other children do not develop, although the child may become very attached to inanimate objects. This picture of 'aloneness' and social aversion is characteristic of the autistic child.

* PRESERVATION OF SAMENESS: autistic children can become disturbed if some aspect of their physical environment is altered, such as rearranging the furniture in a room or introducing some new items. In the daily routine of the child any deviation from the set pattern can result in an emotional outburst. This need for preservation of sameness can extend to eating preferences and their main caretakers, making the introduction of new adults a difficult task. Autistic children engage in

a variety of self-stimulatory behaviours (such as rock-
ing and swaying) which may be related to this need for
consistency and predictability in the environment.
* COMMUNICATION PROBLEMS: perhaps the most pervasive feature of autism is the lack of communicative
skills which has led some to conclude that the syndrome
is primarily the result of extensive damage to the
language capacity. From infancy the autistic child
deviates from normal in the failure to babble and experiment with sound. Experimental studies have confirmed
that qualitative differences can be found between the
pre-linguistic development of autistic, normal and other
groups of handicapped children. Bartak, Rutter and Cox
(1975) have also highlighted the inability to use non-
verbal communication systems amongst autistic children,
which suggests that the problem is not simply confined
to verbal communication. In later life these deficits
become more pronounced and Rutter (1966) has claimed
that about 50 per cent of autistic children never develop verbal communication. Those who do develop some
language capacity also display a number of abnormal
features such as echolalia and pronoun reversals, which
represent a more severe impairment than is found amongst
even the severely mentally retarded.

Despite this rather gloomy picture a number of special
skills can be found in autistic children, which seem inconsistent with the often global impairments they display.
Some researchers have emphasized the good general health of
autistic children and their very attractive physical appearance. Wing (1970) described the 'idiot savant' performances
often found in autistic children in which complex non-verbal
tasks such as jigsaws are rapidly and efficently solved, or
large passages of prose are committed to memory and recited
without error. Some children are particularly fond of music
or any other rhythmic activity, often sitting for hours
immersed in listening.

Theories of child psychosis

Because of the early onset of childhood psychoses, many
investigators have sought an explanation for the condition
in some deficiency in physiological functioning. Neurological damage through infections can also result in bizarre
behaviour which suggests that damage to the developing CNS
could result in psychosis. This organic account of the
psychoses is joined by purely psychological theories which
stress the importance of early social stimulation for normal
development, and thus sees autism as due to some inadequacy
in early social interaction.

Organic theories

Both autistic and schizophrenic children have been investigated intensively over the past 20 years in an attempt to
identify general differences in biological maturation.

Several workers have claimed psychotic children present either retarded or precocious physical growth and maturation. Werry (1979) concludes that the weight of evidence in these studies favours the position that physical abnormalities are more common amongst psychotic children, but the inadequacy of much of the research leaves room for doubt. Recent neurological studies using the EEG (electroencephalogram) also suggest that anomalies can be found in the brain waves of autistic children and, to a lesser degree, in the schizophrenic group. Ornitz and Ritvo (1976) have confirmed that such abnormalities can also be seen in other neurophysiological functions such as REM sleep.

A further source of evidence for the organic hypothesis comes from twin-study research where Kallman and Roth (1956) demonstrated that of 17 monozygotic twins, where one twin was diagnosed as suffering from schizophrenia before adolescence, a similar diagnosis was made for 12 of the co-twins. A further three co-twins received this diagnosis after adolescence, and thus 15 of the 17 pairs were classified as schizophrenic. In contrast, from a sample of 35 dizygotic twins, where one twin was diagnosed as schizophrenic, only six co-twins received the same diagnosis before adolescence and a further two after. This study estimates the concordance rates at 88 per cent for monozygotic twins and 22 per cent for dizygotic twins. Such evidence strongly suggests that childhood schizophrenia may have a genetic aetiology.

Autism
A number of researchers have concluded that a considerable proportion of the children diagnosed as autistic, who have manifested primary symptoms from birth, suffer from a serious congenital, or perinatally acquired, defect in their CNS functioning. Kanner (1971), Rutter (1971), Rimland (1974), and Ornitz and Ritvo (1976) have speculated on the nature of this deficit. Both Kanner (1943) and Rimland (1964) see the problem as the inability to form basic learning associations. The child's inability to form attachments to its caretakers is seen as an example of this learning deficit with the resultant solitary play and aloneness characteristic of the autistic child. The learning deficit means the child is unable to profit from past experience and thus behaviour is simply reactive to the here and now. This general theory of the autistic deficit cannot fully account for all the features of autism; the special skills found in some children and the need for sameness suggest that some learning capacity remains intact.

Rutter (1972) and Ornitz and Ritvo (1976) adopt a more specific, cognitive account of autism in which major disruption affects higher mental functioning such as perception, thought, and language processes. Bartak et al (1975) have suggested that autistic children seem most severely impaired in their capacity for language, even when compared with aphasic children. They propose that in autism language

is severely impaired through inadequate cognitive processing; storage capacities may not be affected, thus accounting
for the special skills possessed by some. Folstein and
Rutter (1977) have recently produced twin-study evidence
which now points to a genetic hypothesis of autism as an
inherited cognitive defect in symbolic processing.

Perhaps the most startling account of autism is given by
Moore and Shiek (1971) who propose that autistic children
may in fact have been destined to become gifted children.
This view of autism had already been put forward by Rimland
(1964), who noted that the parents of autistic children had,
on average, higher educational achievement than those of
normal children. They suggested that the offspring of such
parents could be particularly vulnerable to brain damage in
the womb. Moore and Shiek propose that massive, early sensory deprivation could account for the autistic syndrome.
Such deprivation could occur if the rate of physical maturation was faster in autistic children than normals. The
fast developer, destined for high IQ, may be ready for birth
several weeks before birth takes place and so experience a
profound deprivation which completely alters their cognitive
development. Evidence for this phenomenon of accelerated
physical development in children has not been found to date,
but further investigation is warranted.

Childhood schizophrenia
Childhood schizophrenia has been investigated along the same
lines as adult schizophrenia, by trying to isolate some biochemical dysfunction which disrupts normal CNS processing.
Particular attention has been paid to the role of neurotransmitters in schizophrenia. One hypothesis states that
the neurotransmitter dopamine is involved in the generation
of hallucinations and delusions. Either excessive dopamine
is available at synapses or the dopaminergic systems become
hypersensitive, resulting in a variety of cognitive and
emotional disturbances. Much of the evidence for this view
has come from the effects of anti-psychotic drugs such as
the phenothiazines which, in addition to alleviating psychotic symptoms, also have pronounced side effects which include a physical tremor very like that seen in Parkinson's
disease. This latter condition is believed to be caused by
low levels of the neurotransmitter dopamine in specific
brain regions, resulting in the characteristic tremor and
lack of muscular co-ordination. It has therefore been suggested that the phenothiazines interfere with dopamine
activity because of the chemical similarity between the
two molecules. This similarity results in the phenothiazine
occupying post-synaptic sites which would normally be filled
by dopamine and so reduces the amount of dopamine at the
synapse. By this reasoning it is proposed that schizophrenia
is caused by excessive dopamine activity, but no reason has,
as yet, been discovered for why the dopamine activity becomes disrupted. Genetic studies seem to indicate some in-
born anomaly which may be triggered during the course of
development.

Psychological theories

Psychological theories of childhood psychoses do not make any clear distinction between schizophrenia and autism. Both conditions are seen as resulting from early social and emotional interactions, particularly with parents. Two major models have been put forward to account for these conditions: psychoanalysis and behaviourism.

* PSYCHOANALYSIS: Freud saw psychotic states as the result of regression to an early stage of development where only the id functions. The id contains the basic biological drives and so the behaviour of the regressed individual is egocentric and detached from the external environment (see Paul Kline, chapter 6). This regression is caused by the need to defend the ego from the very strong sexual and aggressive impulses generated by the id which are punished by parents. The child is therefore unable to cope with his internal urges and this external censure and so employs regression to a more basic and more secure stage of development. Modern ego analysts see psychosis resulting from a poorly developed ego which is unable to distinguish its identity from that of the mother. This comes about when the mother is unable to offer a normal loving relationship or is very over-protective to her child and so prevents a separate identity from being formed. A further possibility is that the child identifies with parents who are either psychotic themselves, or behave towards their children in a psychotic manner.

Bettelheim (1967) proposes that the child is aware of the brutal danger which exists in his environment. Rejected and traumatized by his parents, the child becomes aware that he cannot influence this situation and so withdraws within himself to create an internal fantasy world as a means of coping with the negative, hostile environment that surrounds him. These theories place the causes of childhood psychosis within the family, and early research seemed to confirm that the parents of such children did exhibit unusual personality features. Kanner and Eisenberg (1955) described the parents of autistic children as cold, insensitive, meticulous and highly intellectual, their children growing up in 'emotional refrigeration'. More recent studies (Cox, Rutter, Newman and Bartak, 1975) have failed to confirm this picture when autistic children are compared with other handicapped groups. Parents seem to distance themselves from handicap at first and it is perhaps this reaction which was highlighted by earlier researchers. Certainly there is little evidence that psychotic children come from particularly brutal families as suggested by Bettelheim. A final point is that the families which produce disturbed children also produce perfectly normal children, and so a purely environmental account of the condition is difficult to justify.

* BEHAVIOURISM: Ferster and De Meyer (1961) saw the clinical features of autism as an impoverished repertoire of behaviours resulting from the failure to reinforce early, adult directed behaviours. This failure to reinforce the developing child could arise from depression or physical illness in the parents and be further compounded through active dislike of the child. Normal social behaviours during development (smiling, sharing, joint looking, etc.) had become extinguished through non-reinforcement, and in their place unpleasant behaviours had been established because they brought adult attention. This approach to the problem of psychosis has immediate practical implications for intervention, but it seems difficult to conceive of such an early environment so impoverished of adult attention; even in cases where such an environment has been found the children quickly adjust to normal levels of functioning. The behaviouristic account of psychotic behaviour may well offer powerful tools for intervention at the social and individual level, but a purely environmental account of the disorders seems difficult to substantiate.

Treatment

Intervention in childhood psychoses has been derived from the available theoretical models ranging from psychopharmacology (drug treatment) to psychotherapy. The organic theories suggest that irreversible brain damage has occurred which may be congenital or perinatal. Intervention consists of modifying the child's behaviour chemically and providing a suitable residential environment for him. Psychological theories offer a more optimistic outlook by emphasizing how maladaptive behaviours can be extinguished and desirable behaviour established through systematic, intensive reinforcement.

Mental retardation

Heber (1961) offered an operational definition of mental retardation which forms the basis of modern classification systems. He wrote that 'Mental retardation refers to sub-average general intellectual functioning which originates during the developmental period and is associated with impairment in adaptive behavior.' The sub-average intellectual functioning is measured by standardized tests of IQ as illustrated in table 1, taken from ICD 9. The impairment in adaptive behaviour refers to the degree to which individuals are able to function and maintain themselves independently. Naturally this capacity varies with age, but can be objectively described in relation to 'normal' progress through the use of social adjustment scales, such as the Vineland Social Maturity Scale (Doll, 1953) and the Bristol Social Adjustment Guides (Stott, 1974).

These indices are, however, very general descriptions of the abilities of the individual. 'Mental retardation' is

Table 1

Classification of mental retardation according to WHO International Classification of Diseases (ICD 9)
From: World Health Organization (1978), chapter 5.
Reproduced by permission.

Mental Retardation (317-319)

A condition of arrested or incomplete development of mind which is especially characterized by subnormality of intelligence. The coding should be made on the individual's CURRENT level of functioning WITHOUT REGARD TO ITS NATURE or causation - such as psychosis, cultural deprivation, Down's syndrome, etc. Where there is a specific cognitive handicap - such as speech - the four-digit coding should be based on assessments of cognition OUTSIDE THE AREA OF SPECIFIC HANDICAP. The assessment of intellectual level should be based on whatever information is available, including clinical evidence, adaptive behaviour and psychometric findings. The IQ levels given are based on a test with a mean of 100 and a standard deviation of 15 - such as the Wechsler scales. They are provided only as a guide and should not be applied rigidly. Mental retardation often involves psychiatric disturbances and may often develop as a result of some physical disease or injury. In these cases, an additional code or codes should be used to identify any associated condition, psychiatric or physical. The Impairment and Handicap codes should also be consulted.

317 Mild mental retardation

Feeble-minded   Moron
High-grade defect   IQ 50-70
Mild mental subnormality

318 Other specified mental retardation

318.0 Moderate mental retardation
Imbecile   Moderate mental subnormality
IQ 35-49

318.1 Severe mental retardation
IQ 20-34   Severe mental subnormality

318.2 Profound mental retardation
Idiocy   Profound mental subnormality
IQ under 20

319 Unspecified mental retardation
Mental deficiency NOS   Mental subnormality NOS

inevitably a blanket term which covers a great number of conditions caused by developmental damage. This may result in physical, intellectual, social and emotional problems in the same individual, creating a unique profile of disability. Mildly retarded children may experience considerable difficulties with schoolwork, yet progress through the system without any special provision. Moderate and severely retarded children have more obvious need of special provision. Such children place a very considerable strain on the emotional resources of their caretakers, since their basic self-help skills may be absent and communication skills rudimentary. The profoundly retarded child will display minimal development of sensori-motor functioning and require continuous care and supervision. Mild retardation does not prevent an individual from taking up routine employment or becoming self-supporting given adequate back-up.

Two broad populations can be seen among the mentally retarded. The mildly retarded make up around 75 per cent of the total population: the moderate, severe and profoundly retarded make up the remaining 25 per cent. The prevalence rate is around two to three per cent, and those children classified as severely and profoundly retarded are invariably associated with known organic conditions such as Down's syndrome, Phenylketonuria (PKU) and Rubella (German measles) infection.

Genetic causes of retardation
A number of syndromes of mental retardation have been identified which demonstrate a clear organic aetiology. Two conditions are briefly described: Down's syndrome and PKU.

*   DOWN'S SYNDROME: Angeli and Kirman (1971) estimate that Down's syndrome accounts for around 16 per cent of all children in hospital with a marked degree of retardation. In addition to mental deficiency, a number of characteristic physical symptoms are found; the presence of a vestigial third eyelid in the corner of the eye and the upward slant of the eyes results in a distinct, oriental appearance.

    The condition is due to a chromosomal abnormality known as 'trisomy of chromosome 21' in which the pair fail to separate during the early stages of egg development. When fertilization takes place, three rather than two chromosomes are found on pair 21. Thus the child with Down's syndrome has a total chromosomal complement of 47, rather than 46. It is not known why pair 21 fails to divide, but the risk of this happening increases dramatically with the age of the mother.

*   PKU (Phenylketonuria): PKU is a distinct metabolic disorder caused by the presence of a pair of recessive genes which interferes with the manufacture of the enzyme phenylalanine hydroxylase. This liver enzyme converts phenylalanine (an amino-acid found in high protein food) into tyrosine. In the absence of this enzyme a toxic build-up of phenylalanine occurs which

interferes with the process of neural myelinization. The result of this chemical sequence is a severe mental retardation due to a failure of myelinization. PKU children appear normal at birth, but after several months it becomes clear that general responsiveness and motor development are retarded. Fits can develop in such children and, unless intervention takes place, the child becomes severely mentally retarded with minimal language development and poor motor co-ordination.

PKU can be effectively controlled by strict dietary regimes. The diets ensure phenylalanine intake is kept to a minimum until the majority of CNS development has taken place. PKU is a relatively rare developmental disorder, but is only one of hundreds of recessive gene conditions which result in mental retardation. These conditions disrupt neural metabolic functioning which seriously affects CNS development.

Infections

Awareness of the relationship between the German measles virus - Rubella - and abnormal foetal development was discovered in the 1940s, but it was only when the infection reached epidemic proportions in the 1960s that general concern was aroused. An infected mother passes the virus, via the bloodstream, to the placenta of the developing foetus. The extent of damage is dependent on the amount of foetal development that has occurred. At early stages the cells are rapidly multiplying to form the various organs of the body. The virus slows this multiplication, resulting in malformation and atrophy. Microcephaly (small head and brain size) is a common outcome. At later stages the virus cannot cause such extensive damage, but mental retardation may still occur.

Infections contracted after birth - such as meningitis - can also result in profound retardation, particularly if contracted in the first 18 months. During this period of development very rapid growth takes place in the brain which is easily disrupted by virus infection. This irreversible early CNS damage invariably results in degrees of mental retardation.

Trauma

Mental retardation also results from a wide range of physical and chemical trauma during development. Evidence now suggests a strong correlation between the intake of certain chemical substances by the mother and developmental abnormalities. Alcohol and nicotine have been implicated in cases of prematurity and retardation; recent studies suggest that high lead levels in the bloodstream may also cause retardation.

Physical trauma at birth itself also contributes to retardation; any interruption of the blood supply to the infant brain results in anoxia (lack of oxygen) which can cause widespread neural damage.

Brain damage and development

The conditions outlined above lead to varying degrees of brain damage. The resulting handicap may be manifest on several dimensions of development.

* MOTOR PROBLEMS: brain damage can result in hyper-kinesis (inability to sit still), poor locomotor and fine motor control, and speech disturbances such as dyspraxia.
* SENSORY PROBLEMS: visual, auditory and tactile diffi-culties may occur which, together with attentional prob-lems, lead to poor concentration and distractability.
* COGNITIVE PROBLEMS: general mental deficiency to-gether with more specific learning disabilities (read-ing, writing, spelling and language skills) can result from CNS damage.
* EMOTIONAL PROBLEMS: brain damage can produce a low tolerance for frustration which leads to temper tantrums, emotional lability and self-injurious behaviour.
* SOCIAL PROBLEMS: brain-damaged individuals may be relatively insensitive to social demands which can manifest in antisocial behaviour such as lying, cruelty and stealing.

Treatment

Although it is widely accepted that early damage to the brain is the primary cause of mental retardation, a number of interesting studies have argued the importance of envi-ronmental factors in mild retardation. Koluchova (1972) cites a case study of five-year-old twins who were reared in extreme isolation, neglect and cruelty. They presented severe cognitive and emotional retardation in the absence of any obvious brain damage. These children quickly improved with transfer to a normal environment and were able to at-tend normal school within 18 months of being discovered. This study suggests that adverse environmental conditions have a profound effect on development: a thesis put forward by Bowlby (1951) to account for certain instances of mild mental retardation. In particular, Bowlby emphasized the mother's role in the child's developmental progress; the concept of 'maternal deprivation' as a source of develop-mental disturbance became popular in the 1960s but after a searching critique by Rutter (1972, 1979) the status of the concept is in doubt.

Apart from Bowlby's psychoanalytic perspective on mental retardation the only practical advances that have been made in caring for such children have come from behaviouristic psychologists. By applying the principles of reinforcement to maladaptive behaviour it is possible to extinguish un-desirable responses and promote self-help skills such as feeding and dressing in the severely handicapped and de-signing more efficient learning environments for the mildly retarded. A comprehensive guide to the application of be-haviour modification principles with the retarded is given by Gelfand and Hartmann (1975), and more detailed discussion of techniques can be found in Kiernan and Woodford (1975) and Yule and Carr (1980).

Within this broad dimension of development two major types of disturbance have emerged: conduct disorders and anxiety withdrawal disorders. Conduct disorders refer to instances where apparently inadequate social functioning results in delinquency and aggressiveness towards others. Children with anxiety disorders may display specific fears or phobias to environmental objects, or present very withdrawn, self-conscious behaviour.

Social problems: conduct disorders

Juvenile delinquency and antisocial aggressive behaviour in children have been shown to be predictive of later adult problems and consequently have received considerable re-search attention. The main defining characteristics of conduct disorders are aggressive and violent behaviour, temper tantrums, disobedience, destructiveness, unco-operativeness, attention-seeking behaviour and hyper-activity. Organic theorists see conduct disorders as the result of minimal brain damage (MBD) which leads to higher levels of behavioural activity together with general cog-nitive and affective impairment. This term, MBD, became rather fashionable between 1960 and 1970 to account for children who presented hyperactivity, impulsivity and specific learning problems in the absence of any 'hard' neurological symptoms. Wender (1971) has been an earnest advocate of this view of conduct disorders where minimal brain damage leads to decreased responsiveness to reward and punishment with an increase in behavioural activity levels. He speculates that some subtle dysfunction of transmitter substances in the child's brain could lead to these symptoms.

Psychological theories of conduct disorders have fo-cussed on the quality of parental management of such child-ren. Becker, Peterson, Hellmer, Shoemaker and Quay (1959) pointed out that the parents of these children are also maladjusted, given to dramatic outbursts of anger and inconsistent child-rearing practices. Bandura and Walters (1963) have argued that the development of aggressive behaviour requires a suitable model for imitation, which implies that conduct disorders may be 'learned' from par-ents. Rutter, Quinton and Yule (1977) have produced evidence relating quality of marriage to delinquency, where high-conflict marriages characterized by indifference and active dislike produce more delinquent children. In addition to these intra-familial factors Martin (1975) has given exam-ples of specific parental styles which are associated with antisocial behaviour. Extremes of authoritarian and permis-sive child-rearing practices have been found to correlate with highly antisocial and impulsive behaviour in children. This kind of research makes an important point; restriction of treatment to the individual child may not address all the causes of such behaviour. Intervention programmes which have aimed at improving the relationships between parents and children have enjoyed a high degree of success and have also resulted in improvements in the behaviour of other 'untreated' brothers and sisters (Arnold, Levine and Patterson, 1975).

Vulnerability hypothesis

Many clinical workers are now adopting the view that conduct disorders and related syndromes may result from the inter-action of specific physiological dysfunction with a parti-cular social environment. An inherited defect in the CNS functioning could give rise to higher levels of behavioural activation which may be further compounded by an inconsis-tent social environment. In this way developmental immatu-rity in cognitive and/or emotional functioning leads to poor social adjustment in a difficult family situation. This viewpoint has recently been advanced by Davison and Neale (1978) to account for many forms of human psychopathology under the term diathesis-stress. 'Diathesis' refers to some constitutional predisposition to a particular defect whilst 'stress' involves any adverse environmental circumstances which exacerbate the inherited defect. This position has generated a great deal of interest in clinical child psycho-logy which is summarized by Anthony, Koupernik and Chiland (1978).

Treatment

When behavioural disturbances such as hyperactivity, aggres-sion and delinquency are seen as having a physiological basis, then pharmacological treatments are pursued. Drug treatments for developmental disorders have been around since the 1930s when Bradley investigated the effects of the stimulant amphetamine on conduct disordered children between the ages of five and fourteen years. He concluded that the drug had a marked effect on the children towards more posi-tive behaviour and attitudes. Some of the children became calmer and felt mildly euphoric; others became more active and irritable, and one child became quite severely dis-turbed. Despite these equivocal findings stimulant drugs were used extensively in the USA as a means of controlling impulsive and aggressive children. Behaviour therapy has enjoyed as long a history as psychopharmacology but has not provoked the same public reaction to its methods of treat-ment. A radical behaviourist 'functional analysis' is brought to bear on the various 'problem behaviours' to de-termine the sources of maintaining environmental reinforce-ment. Once the reinforcement contingencies have been iden-tified techniques are applied which decrease maladaptive and undesirable behaviour whilst promoting new, adaptive behaviour. A child who becomes disruptive at school and exhibits other forms of attention-seeking behaviour may therefore be receiving reinforcement from his schoolmates

and his teachers for his tantrums. By removing these sources
of reinforcement and systematically reinforcing the child
for individual study and consistent work a new behavioural
repertoire is established. Again, detailed discussion of
these techniques will be found in Gelfand and Hartmann
(1975).

Increasingly it is being realized that treatment of the
individual child, in isolation from the full range of social
and interpersonal contexts in which he operates, is inadequate. The family is, without doubt, the most significant
source of influence on the problem child and has become the
prime focus for intervention in recent years. Patterson
(1974) has argued and demonstrated the value of parental
training programmes in the management of conduct disorders.
A more general 'family therapy' approach has evolved in
recent years which involves all members of the multi-
disciplinary clinical team. Family therapy contains a number
of distinct theoretical positions from behaviourism to
psychoanalysis, but recognizes the need to take context into
account when defining psychopathology.

Emotional problems: anxiety disorders

Children display a range of emotional disturbance from
anxiety, fearfulness, tension and shyness to depression,
hypersensitivity and psychosomatic complaints. In contrast
to the 'excessive behaviour' of conduct-disordered children,
the emotionally disturbed child may 'underbehave' by exhibi-
ting withdrawn and fearful behaviour towards the world outside the immediate family. Although anxiety-withdrawal
states can be further subdivided into relatively distinct
categories (anxiety states, phobic states, depressive disorders, hysterical and obsessive disorders, etc.), little of
significance is contributed to actual intervention. Anxiety
disorders are not related to any specific social or educational group although Rutter (1980) has identified birth
order as a significant variable where first born are most
often affected. The sexes seem equally represented in childhood but by middle adolescence girls are more prone to
anxiety and depressive disorders.

Organic theories of these conditions have been based on
the observation that they occur in the offspring of parents
displaying 'neurotic' symptoms. Shields and Slater (1961)
and Rutter (1980) stress that inheritance of 'emotionality'
can explain the general vulnerability of certain individuals
to anxiety disorders. Both behaviourism and psychoanalysis
have offered accounts of these conditions which stress the
importance of early child rearing as a potential cause of
later disorder; whilst Becker et al (1959) have identified
maladjusted fathers and Kagan and Moss (1962) argue that
over-protection by non-assertive parents in infancy and
early childhood can result in childhood anxiety disorders.
These findings suggest parental style is an important
priority for clinical attention whilst simultaneously
tackling the child's immediate problems. Psychoanalytic

views of anxiety disorders range from failure to develop independent ego functioning to castration anxiety. The anxious child is insecure because of some failure to negotiate the psychosexual stages of development. Treatment involves getting the child to resolve these conflicts through imaginative play and the formation of new attachments.

Again the relevance of the diathesis-stress paradigm can be appreciated in this group of disorders. Evidence of a biological basis to these disorders can be incorporated into a programme of family and school-based treatment designed to allow the child to overcome specific fears. This view is offered by Seligman (1974) in his account of depression as 'learned helplessness'. Experimental studies of learning situations in which no individual control could be attained led Seligman to postulate a model of depression as a state of 'helplessness'. This state represents the awareness that events are outside one's control and thus no coping, behavioural action is possible. Initially, when faced with uncontrollable situations, we become anxious but after considerable exposure we become depressed. The withdrawn child may well have inherited a particularly labile emotional system which is powerfully evoked by such situations as bullying by other children. The child becomes anxious or depressed and is treated by graded exposure to threatening events in which control is possible whilst strengthening the child's self-assertiveness.

Specific developmental disorders

Both ICD 9 and DSM III list a number of specific developmental disorders which can be distinguished from the more general problems of retardation or social and emotional disorders. The major categories employed in ICD 9 are given in table 2.

Speech therapists, together with clinical and educational psychologists, find themselves mainly dealing with the developmental speech and language disorders as well as cases of acquired aphasia, elective mutism, lisping and lalling and stuttering. The notion of 'specific language handicap' as opposed to a speech disorder only emerged in the late 1960s with the advent of psycholinguistics. Until that time theory and clinical practice often failed to make a distinction between the actual motor production of speech and the internal, psychological processes which generate human language. Developmental communication disorders were therefore tackled by clinicians from either a behaviouristic or a psychoanalytically-orientated stance.

Developmental speech and language disorders

Cooper, Moodley and Reynell (1978) offer three categories of language problems in childhood:

* environmental language delay;
* developmental language delay;
* developmental language disorder.

Table 2

Classification of specific developmental disorders according to WHO International Classification of Diseases (ICD 9)
From World Health Organization (1978), chapter 5. Reproduced by permission.

315 Specific delays in development

A group of disorders in which a specific delay in development is the main feature. In each case development is related to biological maturation but it is also influenced by nonbiological factors and the coding carries no aetiological implications.

Excludes: when due to a neurological disorder (320–389)

315.0 Specific reading retardation

Disorders in which the main feature is a serious impairment in the development of reading or spelling skills which is not explicable in terms of general intellectual retardation or of inadequate schooling. Speech or language difficulties, impaired right-left differentiation, perceptuo-motor problems, and coding difficulties are frequently associated. Similar problems are often present in other members of the family. Adverse psychosocial factors may be present.

Developmental dyslexia   Specific spelling difficulty

315.1 Specific arithmetical retardation

Disorders in which the main feature is a serious impairment in the development of arithmetical skills which is not explicable in terms of general intellectual retardation or of inadequate schooling.

Dyscalculia

315.2 Other specific learning difficulties

Disorders in which the main feature is a serious impairment in the development of other learning skills which are not explicable in terms of general intellectual retardation or of inadequate schooling.

Excludes: specific arithmetical retardation (315.1)
          specific reading retardation (315.0)

315.3 Developmental speech or language disorder

Disorders in which the main feature is a serious impairment in the development of speech or language (syntax or semantics) which is not explicable in terms of general intellectual retardation. Most commonly there is a delay in the development of normal word-sound production resulting in defects of articulation. Omissions or substitutions of consonants are most frequent. There may also be a delay in the production of spoken language. Rarely, there is also a developmental delay in the comprehension of sounds. Includes cases in which delay is largely due to environmental privation.

Developmental aphasia   Dyslalia
Excludes: acquired aphasia (784.3)
          elective mutism (309.8, 313.0 or 313.2)
          lisping and lalling (307.9)
          stammering and stuttering (307.0)

315.4 Specific motor retardation

Disorders in which the main feature is a serious impairment in the development of motor coordination which is not explicable in terms of general intellectual retardation. The clumsiness is commonly associated with perceptual difficulties.

Clumsiness syndrome   Dyspraxia syndrome

315.5 Mixed development disorder

A delay in the development of one specific skill (e.g. reading, arithmetic, speech or coordination) is frequently associated with lesser delays in other skills. When this occurs the coding should be made according to the skill most seriously impaired. The mixed category should be used only where the mixture of delayed skills is such that no one skill is preponderantly affected.

315.8 Other

315.9 unspecified

Developmental disorder NOS

Environmental language delay refers to otherwise normal children who experience difficulty in language specifically due to some known environmental inadequacy such as poor early language experience or when acquiring a second language (where only the first language is used at home).
Developmental language delay is seen as a constitutionally determined developmental handicap. It is further subdivided into mild and severe forms which may co-exist with other, more generally handicapping conditions such as mental retardation. This coding is given where:

receptive and/or expressive language development is not more than two thirds of non-verbal intellectual abilities in terms of age level. Although this is a serious and pathological delay, the language, when it appears, follows a fairly consistent developmental pattern, following the normal stages of early language development. The natural history of this type of delay is for verbal comprehension and expressive language to be approximately equally delayed at first, often with very immature attention control. Verbal comprehension recovers first, then the more central aspects of expressive language (words and sentences), and finally the more mature coding of sounds in words (intelligibility) (Cooper et al, 1978).

Developmental language disorder refers to a condition in which although language delay is severe it is also deviant. The individual child's progress reveals no clear pattern with highly uneven responses to treatment. The condition may be predominantly receptive or expressive and co-exist with obvious neurological problems.

Models of language

The publication of Skinner's 'Verbal Behaviour' in 1957 offered the first systematic explanation of child language. Behaviourism treated both 'speech' and 'language' as 'verbal behaviour' which was open to the same kind of functional analysis as any other operant responses. These verbal behaviours were shaped through the application of selective reinforcement in the child's environment. The infant associates his own babbling responses with parental attention which leads to shaping of simple sounds such as 'ma' and 'da' through eager parental reinforcement. Parents shape more complex sound sequences by corrective and selective reinforcement which builds up a repertoire of muscular sequences generating different phonological units. From this basic kit the child progresses to whole words, which are further reinforced through the effects they produce. Skinner identifies a number of categories of 'verbal behaviour' which are learned through environmental reinforcement.

The 'echoic' response refers to simple imitation of an adult utterance; the 'mand' corresponds to utterances which convey information to caretakers about the child's drive state; for example, 'milk' leads to the availability of milk, which is reinforcing. The 'tact' is a naming response which occurs whilst in physical contact with an object or person, such as 'nice dolly'. These classes of verbal behaviour are learnt because of their reinforcing consequences and thus any deviation or delay in this learning would be due to inadequate environmental input or inconsistent reinforcement.

The linguist Chomsky (1959), in a devastating critique of Skinner's theory, brought this view of language learning into disrepute. Chomsky argued that the behaviouristic analysis is unable to account for the creativity in children's utterances. Rather than simply 'emit' learnt sound sequences according to the rules of reinforcement, Chomsky saw the

child as actively engaged in deducing the rules which govern
the construction of language: the grammatical structure.
Clear anomalies in child language such as 'cutted' cannot be
explained in a purely behaviouristic fashion, since adults
seldom use this form. Chomsky saw such an utterance as the
application of a general rule about the formation of past
tenses (add 'ed' to word ending) being applied to an
irregular verb.

A distinction was made between language 'competence' and
'performance'. Behaviourists restrict study to performance:
the actual verbal output of the child. Linguists postulate
an internal state of knowledge about language referred to as
'competence' which results from the interaction between the
linguistic environment of the child and his innate Language
Acquisition Device (LAD). This device was seen as a uniquely
human neural organization which is capable of grasping symbolic meaning and deducing a set of rules which govern the
spoken structure of language. Chomsky argued that language
is a universal but uniquely human attribute which reflects
the actual structure of the human mind. All human infants
are therefore genetically programmed to perceive meaning in
language and deduce grammatical rules. This view of language
stresses the biological preparedness of the human brain to
generate language, a view also subscribed to by evolutionary
biologists such as Lenneberg (1967). This preparation led
to the use of the term 'language acquisition' rather than
'language learning', since the former implies the process
does not start from scratch.

These contrasting models of language led to two distinct
forms of treatment for communication-handicapped children.
Skinner's views offered clinicians a clear framework for
intervention. The child who did not follow the typical
developmental sequence was in need of a highly structured
and intensive language learning environment where total
control over input and output could be attained. The child
would have his articulatory skills shaped to form the
phonological features of speech through the application of
reinforcement which was then gradually faded to increase
frequency. Chomsky's psycholinguistic account of language
had less clear implications for clinicians. The language-
disordered child was seen as having suffered some damage to
the innate LAD. This impairment would make the acquisition
of syntactical rules a difficult, if not impossible, task.
To a large extent linguists have confined themselves to the
study of normal language development and describing the
syntactical structures which characterize early language
rather than advocating any specific form of active therapy.
By analysing samples of the child's linguistic performance
they deduce the internal state of language competence that
exists. But what clinical implications does such a description have? The notion of 'acquisition' rather than learning
makes the problem of intervention rather difficult. If the
child does not 'acquire' language given a perfectly adequate
input, then is linguistic bombardment likely to change the

situation? Often it seems that clinicians who adhere to this
view of language resort to 'teaching' certain syntactic
structures in the best behaviourist tradition, although a
remarkable paucity of evidence supports the value of such an
approach.

The work of cognitive psychologists such as Piaget did
much to reconcile the extreme nature-nurture positions of
Chomsky and Skinner. Piaget stressed the importance of
interaction in the development of children's thinking. To
attain the cognitive abilities necessary to employ symbolic
functioning the child has to pass through the sensori-motor
stage of development which culminates in language use. This
view of language acquisition stresses the importance of non-
verbal symbolic functioning as the foundation of later
language development. Clinicians faced with the language
handicapped child are urged to ascertain the particular sub-
stage of development that the child has reached and aim
therapy at a variety of pre-linguistic mental operations
considered necessary for language acquisition. Thus the non-
verbal treatment of language disorders was initiated with a
renewed attention on the stages of cognitive development
which precede language use.

These models of language acquisition have given rise to
several intervention schemes for language handicapped children. A selection of these programmes is briefly described.

Language therapies: behaviourism
The impact of Skinner's reasoning on language and speech
therapy was enormous. The framework offered highly specific
suggestions for the treatment of both the motor aspects of
speech and of verbal behaviour in a broad range of children.
Much of the pioneering work in this area was carried out on
mentally retarded and psychotic children who were trained to
speak for tangible rewards such as food and drink. In follow-
up studies of 13 autistic children it was found that four
children lost their treatment effects on transfer to a new
environment. A further nine children who were maintained on
a home programme of reinforcement by their parents showed
steady improvement. Many workers were not convinced that
these operant programmes really did improve spontaneous
language. Such children often utter specific phrases in a
rather robot-like fashion and only when some tangible reinforcer (like food) is available. Ferster (1974) argued
that to train children in language by using artificial
reinforcement such as rice pudding is a far cry from the
more subtle, interpersonal reinforcement envisaged by
Skinner. More sophisticated programmes for language training
have recently been described by Salinger (1978). Other developments have included the design of language assessment
techniques such as the Parsons Language Sample (Spradlin,
1963) which aids functional analysis. Several complete
language programmes have emerged which utilize behavioural
principles in the treatment of retarded children, the best
known of which are the Peabody Language Development Kits.

The use of token economies as a means of reinforcing interpersonal language use has also been undertaken, but with rather disappointing results. Although extensive verbal behaviour can be established through these systems there is often very little generalization to other contexts. Cullen, Hattersley and Tennant (1977) argued that these failures are due largely to confusion between institutional management and a genuinely rehabilitative scheme. Only by phasing out tangible token reinforcement can a truly general improvement in language use come about. Nordquist and Whaler (1973) have shown how parental training in behaviour modification techniques can avoid the limitations of institutionally-based or individual operant therapy.

Linguistics

Crystal, Fletcher and Garman (1976) have spearheaded the syntactical approach to developmental language disorders. By producing a standardized assessment device (LARSP) which pinpoints the stage of syntactical development reached by a given child, implications are generated about the forms of language which should be encouraged by therapists. Although this approach provides a rather detailed description of child language performance it offers no explanation as to why a particular child has deviated from the norm. Further, little specific information is given on how therapists should set about promoting further syntactical development other than by 'teaching' appropriate structures in a series of games and exercises.

Cognitive approaches

Cognitive or psycholinguistic approaches to child language emphasize the need for intact psychological processing of environmental input by the developing child. Piaget's framework stressed the need for central representation schemata during sub-stage VI of the sensori-motor period if the next, symbolic stage of development were to be attained. The clinical implications of this analysis would involve problem-solving therapy for the child which facilitates the formation of central, non-verbal schemata. Kirk and Kirk (1972) have advocated a psycholinguistic model of language processing represented in the Illinois Test of Psycholinguistic Abilities (ITPA). Basically they see the communication process involving auditory and visual input which is processed at two levels: the representational and automatic levels. This input then passes through three sequential processes: receptive, organizing and expressive.

Representational level processing involves the reception, analysis (organizing) and expression of symbolic input. Automatic level processing refers to more basic psychological processes such as memory and attention which are needed to ensure accurate processing at the representational level. Kirk and Kirk argue that language difficulties can result from inefficient processing which can then be treated by intensive training in order to improve overall functioning.

Two further programmes have been developed within this cognitive framework: the work of Fraser and Blockley (1973) and Cooper et al (1978).

Fraser and Blockley
Fraser and Blockley investigated both language-disordered children and deaf children using a wide range of non-verbal diagnostic tests to determine what cognitive processes exist in each group. Their research highlighted the fact that communication-handicapped children have a poor appreciation of relationships between stimuli distributed in time and space. Fraser and Blockley point out that speech is energy distributed in time and space and it requires a developmentally mature perceptual system to analyse this kind of input. Thus the primary deficit in language-handicapped children lies in their inability to process auditory and visual stimuli distributed in time and space.

This approach to communication handicap owes much to the Piagetian idea that language is not a highly specific area of learning controlled by some innate LAD but is rather an extension of the child's cognitive capacity to represent the external environment centrally. In order to reach this stage of cognitive processing the child must possess intact perceptual systems (visual, auditory, tactual, and attention) and have developed basic cognitive structures which are the prerequisites of symbolic processing. Fraser and Blockley see the deficit in temporal and spatial perception as the main focus for intervention before any attempt can be made to tackle verbal communication.

This hypothesis led to the construction of a totally non-verbal programme of therapy designed to accelerate the development of temporal and spatial processing. Five main features are characteristic of this approach.

* The therapy is non-verbal. Treatment does not proceed through the defective medium.
* The therapy is geared to the level where the child's perceptual abilities are most efficient.
* By designing individual programmes rather than group activities the child can progress in a virtually errorless fashion; thus the child's motivation is maximized by therapy.
* The therapy is designed to be carried out on an intensive basis rather than on a sessional basis. Intensive work is more effective than spaced practice.
* The treatment aim is the successful resolution of the child's perceptual disorder rather than bringing language up to an appropriate level.

Fraser and Blockley (1973) describe their position as 'Piagetian psycholinguistics', implying the limitations of confining attention to the actual linguistic performance of children. Performance may offer a detailed description of what the child can produce but it may not have diagnostic implications about why output is inadequate. By

investigating the basic cognitive processes thought to be
crucial for the development of communication, and focussing treatment at this level, it is hoped natural language
acquisition may proceed.

Cooper, Moodley and Reynell

These authors offer a more elaborate model of the cognitive
processes underlying the communicative process. Reynell
(1976) outlined a view of language development which emphasizes the need for a broad assessment of children's
cognitive processes.

This model lies behind a programme of assessment and
treatment for the language-delayed and the language-
disordered child; it is also applicable to the mentally
handicapped. Again, an intensive approach to therapy is
advocated for children between two and five years. The
programme can be carried out by parents or through conse-
cutive school-based sessions for two hours a day, five
days a week. A range of assessment procedures is used in
the programme varying from structured clinical observation
(attention control, intellectual use of language) to standardized psychometric instruments (Reynell Scales, symbolic
understanding, concept formation). An assessment yields a
profile of abilities which then forms the basis of
treatment.

The actual treatment programme consists of a range of
structured activities designed to improve various areas of
cognitive functioning. This method of clinical teaching
using enriched materials has recently been evaluated in a
five-year study reported by Cooper et al (1978). In this
study the progress of home-based programmes was contrasted
with the school-based version. Although both groups had made
good progress, the school-based programmes seemed most
effective. In follow-up studies of children discharged from
the programmes it was only possible to assess a small proportion of the original sample, but it would seem that good
maintenance was achieved by these children. Given the woe-
fully inadequate provision for handicapped pre-school children, the need to develop effective home-based language
programmes is paramount. Much of the success of such ventures lies in the extent to which parents can be trained as
effective therapists. This approach, described by Cooper et
al, deserves further research to establish the feasibility
of home-based programmes.

Sociolinguistics

The linguistic approach to human communication of the 1960s
concentrated on describing the formal structure of language
as a series of highly abstract transformations linking the
'deep structure' of language with the 'surface structure':
that is, language performance. For many this narrow preoccupation failed to capture the essential point about
language: it is a social phenomenon. Making inferences about
an individual's 'linguistic competence' from samples of his

'linguistic performance' could be a misleading venture. In-dividual children may not know what to say or they may decide not to say anything. In the latter case they may be afraid, confused or tired yet be perfectly capable of making an accurate observation if these states are resolved. Indeed Donaldson (1978) has argued that a great deal of research in cognitive development has been undermined through the fail-ure to make clear to children exactly what is required of them in experimental tests. Sociolinguistics has focussed on the social meaning conveyed through language and emphasized how factors such as dialect and stylistic variation contribute to meaning.

A shift in research emphasis in the 1970s has generated considerable evidence that this social dimension of communi-cation can be traced back to the earliest interchanges be-tween infant and adult. The work of Bower (1974) suggested that even very young infants possess a considerable range of perceptual and cognitive capacities which had previously been considered impossible. Further research by Condon and Sander (1974) and Schaffer (1974) demonstrated that even from a very early stage infants are capable of highly structured 'communicative sequences' with their caretakers. These sequences consist of synchronized arm and leg move-ments as well as babbling and paying attention to the care-taker. Newson and Newson (1975) describe the phenomena in the following way:

> Thus, when the adult talks to the infant, the infant displays all the complex gestural accompaniments that one normally expects of attentive listening; and when the adult pauses, the infant can reply with a fully articulated, gesturally animated, conversation-like response. Prolonged social interchanges comprising an alternative succession of passive and active role taking apparently occur with an effortless spontaneity; and this seems to 'come naturally' not only to mother who obviously has a long history of conversation experience but to her infant who in most other respects is conceptually and socially quite inexperienced.

This picture of some innate awareness of social interaction and social meaning has captured the imagination of many clinicians. Clearly such a capacity requires adequate adult-child interaction for further development and thus variation in infant-rearing styles may have implications for under-standing the non-communicative child. In particular, this radical new view of development has rekindled an interest in pragmatics: the approach to language which stresses the importance of language performance rather than the under-lying cognitive competence for communication.

Pragmatics
If we accept that language is primarily a social tool then a new emphasis on the social functions of communication

emerges. Pragmatics draws on models developed in various branches of research: psychology, psycholinguistics, anthropology, sociology, etc. A detailed review of the current state of pragmatics is given by Rees (1978). A rough definition of pragmatics would state that it is the study of language related to the context in which it occurs. As Ervin-Tripp (1971) puts it, language development, in pragmatic terms, is 'coming to say the right thing, in the right way, at the right time and place as defined by the social group'. Hart (1980) therefore offers a clinical definition of the language-handicapped child as 'one who has not come to use appropriate language in appropriate ways at the appropriate place and time (or for the delayed child - the appropriate age)'.

Hart (1980) offers several guidelines for clinicians who wish to adopt a pragmatic approach to treatment, and these are listed below.

* The training context should either be the context of use or it should be a replica. Bruner (1975) has emphasized the importance of mutual activity and attention between child and adult and this context must be replicated if the child is to begin actively to initiate such interactions.

* Training should focus on function. Sessions should create an environment where any kind of verbal or non-verbal communication by the child leads to control over aspects of the environment. The prime consequence of communication should be to effect some social change, but any change in the child's environment will reinforce communicative activity.

* Training should focus on rate of use. Nelson (1973) demonstrated how language acquisition improves with use and so pragmatics emphasizes the need to increase the rate of communication regardless of the 'correctness' of the performance through the provision of suitable functional consequences such as rewards, attention, social interaction, access to further activities and control over these activities.

* Assessment should be carried out in the context of use. Rather than measure what the child can make language do in the test situation we should describe what the child actually does in real contexts.

* Therapists are environmental engineers. Pragmatics is an exercise in environmental design which provides enriched situations for the encouragement of communicative skills through the provision of immediate, socially relevant reinforcements. In practice this approach draws heavily on behaviouristic contingency management, but rather than reinforce the child in an arbitrary context for the production of arbitrary language, the creation of socially meaningful contexts is a crucial ingredient.

Conclusion

These five major approaches to language intervention

illustrate differing theoretical perspectives on the nature
of language acquisition. The importance of language for
effective adaptation is self-evident: Man is primarily a
social being whose success in evolutionary terms owes much
to his ability to communicate complex symbolic information
about events in the here and now as well as events removed
in time and space. Although theorists differ in the extent
to which they see this capacity resulting from specific,
innate neural organizations or more general cognitive
abilities, there is little disagreement that the lack of
adequate language abilities is a profound handicap.

A major pitfall to the treatment of language-handicapped
children lies in the tendency to separate out specific areas
of disability and treat each in isolation. The individual
case seldom has problems confined to only one area of functioning. The language-handicapped child may exhibit social
and emotional disturbance as well as general intellectual
impairment and so treatment must address these problems
comprehensively. Clinicians therefore are faced with several
tasks:

* identifying the dimensions of handicap a particular
  child displays;
* investigating the inter-relationships between these
  areas;
* drawing on available theoretical models of development
  which offer practical implications for an intervention
  strategy;
* designing a comprehensive approach to treatment which
  may recognize the need to involve parents to the best of
  their abilities in carrying out home-based schemes;
* evaluating the outcome of these experimental treatments
  to gauge what progress has been made. This final step
  may form the basis of a statement about the adequacy
  of the particular theory under test and could lead on to
  further intervention schemes for the individual case.

**framework for child
sychology**

When we survey the childhood disorders and the theoretical
models offered for their explanation it is tempting to conclude that treatment is a matter of selecting an appropriate
theoretical model and designing a therapeutic regime based
on the model, and then awaiting positive results. A number
of limitations to treatment must be noted in clinical
practice.

Theoretical models vary in their range of convenience;
some focus on the development of specific cognitive skills
with little reference to social and emotional variables
which may influence skill acquisition. Other models are not
specific to childhood but have been developed in the field
of adult psychiatry. This makes selection of an appropriate
model a distinct clinical skill. Much depends on how the
clinician sees developmental problems. The traditional
classification categories imply specific aetiologies for
childhood difficulties and distinguish these conditions

qualitatively. Modern clinical child psychology suggests that such difficulties may often be no more than exaggerated reactions to very specific situations and so only differ quantitatively from 'normal' reactions. A case in point would be the child who presents school refusal. In child psychiatry it may be argued that this represents an 'emotional disorder' which may have been caused by over-identification with a parent during early childhood manifesting later as 'separation anxiety'. Clinical psychology would view school refusal as a particular behaviour which may have multiple 'aetiologies' and which is therefore an exaggeration of normal childhood reactions and should be understandable after a functional analysis of the behaviour has been conducted. We may find the child is socially isolated or being bullied at school. He may have specific academic difficulties that lead to constant failure in class and the ridicule of other children. An analysis of the home environment may reveal an over-concerned parent who in many ways is reinforcing the child's behaviour of not going to school. These findings would have multiple implications for intervention.

Having established a detailed description of the child's problem and gathered information on the child's developmental history, the family circumstances, social conditions and the environmental context of the difficulties, the clinician can move towards a formulation of the problem which recognizes these multiple determinants of development. This is essentially the approach of Rutter et al (1975) in their use of a multi-axial system of classification. Rather than selecting any one developmental model as the basis of treatment the clinician may require an explanation for a specific cognitive handicap, a theory of family processes and a theory of emotional development. Rather than aim intervention at a specific problem area it may be necessary to formulate a team approach in order to change a variety of aspects of the problem. This modern approach has already stimulated a great deal of new research. Turner (1980) offers a new account of the inter-relationship between cognitive and emotional development which will be of great value in contemporary clinical practice.

Careful psychological analysis of the problem will result in treatment goals being specified in advance of intervention. These aims require constant evaluation during the course of intervention since changing one aspect of a problem usually moves other aspects. These dynamic changes can be appreciated through systematic evaluation of the effects of treatment. The value of single case methodology cannot be over-emphasized in psychological treatment. Not only can the problem be tackled comprehensively but progress towards improvement can be reliably demonstrated. A further consequence of the scientific evaluation of intervention is the opportunity to conduct follow-up studies where treatment effects can be checked for generality and maintenance. By obtaining pre- and post-treatment baseline measures of a problem the clinician can evaluate the longer-term efficiency of intervention.

The psychological approach to childhood difficulties coincides with far-reaching changes in policy towards education, child health and social services. Clinicians are being encouraged to combat the traditional approach of individual treatment in specialist settings (e.g. large hospitals for the mentally handicapped) and promote a new 'community-orientated' approach to therapy. Essentially this approach highlights the need to treat children within the natural context of the problem. For the pre-school child this may indeed imply treatment within the home. This shift in emphasis gives parents a much more active role in the treatment of their children and is leading to the development of a number of 'parent training' groups. The clinician is therefore arriving at a treatment formulation which can be carried out at home and offers practical training for parents to create an intensive therapy environment within the context of the problem. Professional clinicians may effectively become 'research supervisors' for a child's parents rather than work directly with the individual child.

In conclusion, it must be mentioned that the ultimate goal of any enquiry into health and welfare is the development of adequate and effective preventitive services. The high correlation between birth complications and later maladjustment has clear preventitive implications. In other cases the implications for prevention may be less well defined. In the case of anxious and withdrawn children who cannot tolerate separation from their parents, we may be less able to arrange practical prevention measures save what can be done through better parental education. A major contribution has been made to the issue of preventitive services by a number of epidemiological studies of childhood difficulties. These studies measure the extent of difficulties in a defined population of children and try to identify other, associated factors, which may play a causal role. This type of research cannot be addressed by single case studies or group designs (see chapter 11 for further discussion of group designs); a valuable summary of two decades of epidemiological research into childhood problems is given by Graham (1979) together with a complementary review of follow-up studies by Robins (1979).

References

American Psychiatric Association (1980)
Diagnostic and Statistical Manual of Mental Disorders (DSM III). Washington, DC: American Psychological Association.

Angeli, E. and Kirman, B.H. (1971)
Genetic Counselling. Proceedings of the 2nd Congress of the International Association for the Scientific Study of Mental Deficiency; Warsaw, 1970. Warsaw: Polish Medical Publishers.

Anthony J., Koupernik, C. and Chiland, C. (1978)
The Child in His Family. Vulnerable Children, Volume 4.
New York: Wiley.

Arnold, J.E., Levine, A.G. and Patterson, G.R. (1975)
Changes in sibling behavior following family
intervention. Journal of Consulting and Clinical
Psychology, 43, 683-688.

Bandura, A. and Walters, R.H. (1963)
Social Learning and Personality Development. New York:
Holt, Rinehart & Winston.

Bartak, L., Rutter, M. and Cox, A. (1975)
A comparative study of infantile autism and specific
developmental receptive language disorder. I. The
children. British Journal of Psychiatry, 126, 127-145.

**Becker, W.C., Peterson, D.R., Hellmer, L.A., Shoemaker,
D.J. and Quay, H.C.** (1959)
Factors in parental behavior and personality as related
to problem behaviour in children. Journal of Consulting
Psychology, 23, 107-118.

Bender, L. (1955)
Twenty years of clinical research on schizophrenic
children with special reference to those under six years
of age. In G. Caplan (ed.), Emotional Problems of Early
Childhood. New York: Basic Books.

Bettelheim, B. (1967)
The Empty Fortress. New York: Free Press.

Binet, A. and Simon, T. (1905)
Méthodes Nouvelles pour le Diagnostic du Niveau
Intellectuel des Anormeaux. L'Année Psychologique, 11,
191-244.

Bower, T.G.R. (1974)
Development in Infancy. San Francisco: Freeman.

Bowlby, J. (1951)
Maternal Care and Mental Health. Geneva: WHO.

Bruner, J.S. (1975)
The ontogenesis of speech acts. Journal of Child
Language, 2, 1-19.

Chomsky, N. (1959)
Review of Verbal Behavior by B. F. Skinner. Language,
35, 26-58.

Condon, W.S. and Sander, L.W. (1974)
Neonate movement is synchronized with adult speech.
Science, 183, 99-101.

Cooper, J., Moodley, M. and Reynell, J. (1978)
Helping Language Development. London: Arnold.

Cox, A., Rutter, M., Newman, S. and Bartak, L. (1975)
A comparative study of infantile autism and specific
developmental receptive language disorder: II. Parental
characteristics. British Journal of Psychiatry, 126, 146-
159.

Crystal, D., Fletcher, P. and Garman, M. (1976)
The Grammatical Analysis of Language Disability. A
procedure in assessment and remediation. London:
Arnold.

Cullen, C., Hattersley, J. and Tennant, L. (1977)
Behaviour modification - some implications of a radical
behaviourist view. Bulletin of the British Psychological
Society, 30, 65-68.

Davison, G.C. and Neale, J.M. (1978)
Abnormal Psychology (2nd edn). New York: Wiley.

Doll, E. (1953)
Measurement of Social Competence: A manual for the
Vineland Social Maturity Scale. Circle Pines, Minn.:
American Guidance Service, Inc.

Donaldson, M. (1978)
Children's Minds. London: Fontana.

Ervin-Tripp, S. (1971)
Social backgrounds and verbal skills. In R. Huxley and
D. Ingram (eds), Language Acquisition: Models and
methods. New York: Academic Press.

Ferster, C.B. (1974)
The difference between behavioral and conventional
psychology. Journal of Nervous and Mental Disorders,
159, 153-157.

Ferster, C.B. and De Meyer, M.K. (1961)
The development of performances in autistic children in
an automatically controlled environment. Journal of
Chronic Disease, 13, 312-345.

Folstein, S. and Rutter, M. (1977)
Genetic influences and infantile autism. Nature, 265,
726.

Fraser, G.M. and Blockley, J. (1973)
The Language Disordered Child. Windsor: NFER.

Gelfand, D.M. and Hartmann, D.P. (1975)
Child Behaviour: Analysis and therapy. Oxford: Pergamon
Press.

Graham, P.J. (1979)
Epidemiological Studies. In H.C. Quay and J.S. Werry
(eds), Psychopathological Disorders of Childhood (2nd
edn). New York: Wiley.

Hart, B. (1980)
Pragmatics and language development. In B.B. Lahey
and A.E. Kazdin (eds), Advances in Clinical Child
Psychology, Volume 3. New York: Plenum.

Heber, R. (ed.) (1961)
A manual on the terminology and classification in mental
retardation (2nd edn). American Journal of Mental
Deficiency, Monograph Supplement.

Kagan, J. and Moss, H.A. (1962)
Birth to Maturity. New York: Wiley.

Kallman, F. and Roth, B. (1956)
Genetic aspects of preadolescent schizophrenia. American
Journal of Psychiatry, 112, 599-606.

Kanner, L. (1943)
Autistic disturbances of affective contact. Nervous
Child, 2, 217-250.

Kanner, L. (1971)
Follow up study of 11 autistic children originally

reported in 1943. Journal of Autism and Childhood
Schizophrenia, 1, 119-145.

Kanner, L. and Eisenberg, L. (1955)
Psychopathology of Childhood. New York: Grune &
Stratton.

Kiernan, C.C. and Woodford, F.P. (eds) (1975)
Behavior Modification with the Severely Retarded.
Amsterdam: Elsevier.

Kirk, A. and Kirk, W.D. (1972)
Psycholinguistic Learning Disabilities, Diagnosis and
Remediation. Ill.: University of Illinois Press.

Koluchova, J. (1972)
Severe deprivation in twins: a case study. Journal of
Child Psychology and Psychiatry, 13, 107-114.

Lenneberg, E. (1967)
Biological Foundations of Language. New York: Wiley.

Martin, B. (1975)
Parent child relations. In F.D. Horowitz, E.M.
Hetherington, S. Scarr-Salapatek and G.M. Siegel (eds),
Review of Child Development Research, Volume 4. Chicag
University of Chicago Press.

Moore, C. and Shiek, D. (1971)
Toward a theory of early infantile autism. Psychological
Review, 78, 451-456.

Nelson, K. (1973)
Structure and strategy in learning to talk. Monographs
of the Society for Research in Child Development, 38,
1-135.

Newson, J. and Newson, E. (1975)
Intersubjectivity and the transmission of culture: on
the social origins of symbolic functioning. Bulletin of
the British Psychological Society, 28, 437-446.

Nordquist, V.M. and Whaler, R.G. (1973)
Naturalistic treatment of an autistic child. Journal of
Applied Behavior Analysis, 61, 79-87.

Ornitz, E. and Ritvo, E. (1976)
The syndrome of autism: a critical review. American
Journal of Psychiatry, 2, 609-621.

Patterson, G.R. (1974)
Interventions for boys with conduct problems: multiple
settings, treatments and criteria. Journal of Consulting
and Clinical Psychology, 42, 471-481.

Piaget, J. (1929)
The Child's Conception of the World. London: Routledge
& Kegan Paul.

Quay, H.C. (1979)
Classification. In H.C. Quay and J.S. Werry (eds),
Psychopathological Disorders of Childhood (2nd edn). New
York: Wiley.

Rees, N.S. (1978)
Pragmatics of language: applications to normal and
disordered language development. In R.L. Schiefelbusch
(ed.), Bases of Language Intervention. Baltimore:
University Park Press.

Reese, H.W. and Overton, W.F. (1970)
Models of development and theories of development. In
L.R. Goulet and P.B. Baltes (eds), Life-span
Developmental Psychology. New York: Academic Press.

Reynell, J. (1976)
Assessment of language development. In B. Tanner (ed.),
Language and Communication in General Practice. London:
Hodder & Stoughton.

Rimland, B. (1964)
Infantile Autism. New York: Appleton-Century-Crofts.

Rimland, B. (1974)
Infantile autism: status and research. In A. Davids
(ed.), Child Personality and Psychopathology: Current
topics. Volume 1. New York: Wiley.

Robins, L.N. (1979)
Follow-up Studies. In H.C. Quay and J.S. Werry (eds),
Psychopathological Disorders of Childhood (2nd edn). New
York: Wiley.

Rutter, M. (1966)
Prognosis: psychotic children in adolescence and early
adult life. In L. Wing (ed.), Childhood Autism:
Clinical, educational and social aspects. Oxford:
Pergamon Press.

Rutter, M. (1971)
Infantile Autism: Concepts, characteristics and
treatment. Edinburgh: Churchill-Livingstone.

Rutter, M. (1972)
Maternal Deprivation Reassessed. Harmondsworth:
Penguin.

Rutter, M. (1974)
The development of infantile autism. Psychological
Medicine, 4, 147-163.

Rutter, M. (1979)
Maternal deprivation. New findings, new concepts and new
approaches. Child Development, 50, 283-305.

Rutter, M. (1980)
Emotional development. In M. Rutter (ed.), Scientific
Foundations of Developmental Psychiatry. London:
Heinemann Medical.

Rutter, M., Quinton, D. and Yule, W. (1977)
Family Pathology and Disorder in Children. Chichester:
Wiley.

Rutter, M., Shaffer, D. and Shepherd, M. (1975)
A Multi-axial Classification System of Childhood
Psychiatric Disorders. Geneva: WHO.

Salinger, K. (1978)
Language behaviour. In A.C. Catania and T.A. Brigham
(eds), Handbook of Applied Behavior Analysis: Social and
instructional processes. New York: Irvington.

Schaffer, H.R. (1974)
Behavioural synchrony in infancy. New Scientist, 62,
16-18.

Seligman, M.E.P. (1974)
Depression and learned helplessness. In R.J. Friedman

and H.H. Katz (eds), The Psychology of Depression:
Contemporary theory and research. Washington: Winston-
Wiley.

Shields, J. and Slater, E. (1961)
Heredity and psychological abnormality. In H.J. Eysenck
(ed.), Handbook of Abnormal Psychology. New York: Basic
Books.

Skinner, B.F. (1957)
Verbal Behavior. New York: Appleton-Century-Crofts.

Spradlin, J. (1963)
Assessment of speech and language in retarded children.
Journal of Speech and Hearing Disorders, Monograph
Supplement, 10.

Stott, D.H. (1974)
Bristol Social Adjustment Guides. London: University of
London Press.

Turner, J. (1980)
Made for Life. London: Methuen.

Wender, P. (1971)
Minimal Brain Dysfunction in Children. New York: Wiley.

Werry, J.S. (1979)
Organic factors. In H.C. Quay and J.S. Werry (eds),
Psychopathological Disorders of Childhood (2nd edn).
New York: Wiley.

Wing, L. (1970)
The syndrome of early childhood autism. British Journal
of Medicine, 3, 381-392.

World Health Organization (1978)
International Classification of Diseases (ICD 9).
Geneva: WHO.

Yule, W. and Carr, J. (1980)
Behaviour Modification for the Mentally Handicapped.
London: Croom-Helm.

Questions

1. Give an outline of the major developmental models
   available to the child therapist.
2. How could a satisfactory classification scheme be
   developed for childhood difficulties? Discuss the values
   of such a system.
3. What features distinguish autism from other childhood
   psychoses?
4. Describe the ways in which cognitive, social and
   emotional difficulties could result in behavioural
   disturbance. Illustrate your answer with a case-history
   account of behavioural disorder.
5. Which models of language acquisition offer the most
   clinically useful account of language disorders?
6. Outline the common features of the various approaches to
   language intervention.
7. What would be the advantages of creating a specialist
   'child language therapist'?
8. A ten-year-old boy is referred to you for assessment of
   a rapid onset stammer. He appears shy and withdrawn with

little eye-contact. On questioning he only replies with 'yes' and 'no' answers. Describe how you would set about investigating and treating such a case.

9. Sally is a five-year-old child with very immature phonology. When brought along for treatment by her mother she refuses to be separated and throws a violent tantrum when carried into the treatment room. When mother is asked to participate in the therapy sessions she constantly distracts the child who responds by seeking further attention. What can the clinician do to modify this behaviour?

10. Tom is a 16-year-old boy with a dramatic 'silent stammer'. He has a long record of disruptive and unruly behaviour at school. He frequently bullies younger children and is rather negative about attending a clinic. How would you set about specifying treatment goals for such a case?

Annotated reading

Furneaux, B. (1981) The Special Child (3rd edn). Harmondsworth: Penguin.
> A comprehensive account of the educational needs of special children (subnormal, slow learners, autistic and language-handicapped).

Miller, G.A. (1981) Language and Speech. Oxford: Freeman.
> A readable account of contemporary research on human communication.

Mittler, P. (1970) The Psychological Assessment of Mental and Physical Handicaps. London: Methuen.
> An excellent introduction to the areas of assessment and treatment for the entire range of clinical practice.

Müller, D.J., Munro, S. and Code, C. (1981) Language Assessment for Remediation. London: Croom Helm.
> An invaluable book for the speech therapist. A wide range of assessment techniques are discussed by the authors with an emphasis on practical applications.

Quay, H.C. and Werry, J.S. (1979) Psychopathological Disorders of Childhood (2nd edn). New York: Wiley.
> This text provides both an introduction and detailed reviews of major topics in clinical child psychology. Classification, psychoses, assessment, behaviour therapy, epidemiology and follow-up studies are treated in depth.

Rutter, M. and Hersov, L. (1977) Child Psychiatry. Modern approaches. Oxford: Blackwell.
> Perhaps the best modern text on child psychiatry from two leading practitioners. This comprehensive text covers all the major types of childhood difficulties and offers useful accounts of developmental theories and intervention strategies.

Yule, W. and Carr, J. (1980) Behaviour Modification for the Mentally Handicapped. London: Croom Helm.
This very readable account of behavioural intervention with the mentally handicapped is written by two practitioners with considerable experience in training parents and teachers in the principles of behaviour modification.

5

Language Development
in Early Childhood
W. P. Robinson

The practice of successful verbal communication requires
that the meanings intended by a speaker or writer are
expressed through combinations of sounds or marks that can
be received and interpreted by a listener or reader with
corresponding sense and significance. Most verbally proficient adults talk and act their way through each day without being unduly troubled by worries about failures in communication. We recognize that difficulties can arise, even
in conversation with those people we know best. We can mis-
hear words. We can fail to grasp the meanings of utterances.
We can misinterpret commands as questions. We can construe
polite inquiries as threats to privacy. However, we have
devices for dealing with these difficulties. We can suspend
and interrupt the conversation: we can ask for repetition,
reformulation, or clarification, or we can offer these if we
notice that our listeners look puzzled. The problems solved,
we can proceed with the flow of talk and action that make up
our daily lives. Most of us manage to cope to our satisfaction without recourse to detailed and systematic analyses
of what language is, how it works and how human beings
succeed in using it.

Nevertheless, all of us are less than perfect. Many of
us try to avoid interaction with particular other people
because we have difficulties communicating with them. Some
of us have difficulties with almost everybody. None of us
has learnt how to use language as easily and efficiently as
we might have done. This is hardly surprising since Man
remains relatively ignorant both about child development in
general and about language development in particular. What
we think we know is a blend of truth and falsity and a
mixture of over-estimation and under-estimation, while the
'knowledge' itself is not all controlled in the same way.
'Knowing how to' speak grammatically is not the same as
being able to write down the rules of grammar. Knowledge
realized through effective performance has to be distinguished from being able to talk or write systematically
about that knowledge. Because we know how to communicate

Note: some technical terms are marked with an asterisk (*).
Comments about their meanings are offered in the glossary at
the end of the chapter.

effectively does not guarantee that we can tell others how we manage to do so. And even the achievement of generally successful teaching or learning would not entail or presuppose understanding. Doctors were able to control malaria before they could describe and explain its character and transmission. Once these latter had been described and explained, however, new possibilities for control were opened up. And so it is with language development. Sound systematic description and explanation will greatly enhance the possibilities of our devising more efficient educational (and therapeutic) procedures.

For each of us who tries to achieve this greater understanding, we will have the advantages and disadvantages of great experience as participants in the use of language and the handicap of little experience as observers and students of its workings. Alas, there is no escape from the fact that one necessary condition of improving understanding is time for study and reflection. Perhaps a short prison sentence would afford an ideal opportunity for sorting out one's current state of knowledge, ignorance and false belief. Prompted by a friendly warder, well versed in linguistics, psycholinguistics* and sociolinguistics,* well trained in the art of guided discovery learning and well supported with suitable recording and displaying equipment, each of us would probably be amazed at the knowledge we could extract from our accumulated experience.

We could quickly come to see why linguistic experts in the sound system of English came to isolate about 45 distinctive features (phonemes)* to account for the range of variation in the units of sound in a given dialect of that language. We would, however, probably need training to appreciate the reasons for isolating five kinds of tone made up of variations in pitch and stress. We already know there are 26 letters (and a space) in the alphabet. Experiments to map the relations between phonemes and letters would show that these are not nearly as haphazard as some may believe. Duly encouraged, we might proceed to examine which sequence of sounds or letters can and do occur in English, thereby exposing our knowledge of morphophonemics and morphographemics (disciplines beyond our immediate concerns).

The friendly warder might point out that one or more phonemes make up a morpheme,* defined as the elementary unit of meaning. Hence 'cats' is made up of four phonemes /k//a//t//s/, but only two morphemes, 'cat' and 's'; the first functioning both as a word and as a morpheme, the second being one of the several forms that the plural morpheme can take. As far as I know, no estimates have been made of the number of the 100,000 or so morphemes of English that the average adult can use or understand.

In their turn, one or more morphemes may be used to make up a word. English currently boasts about 1,000,000 words, of which almost half are technical terms. The same word form may have many distinguishable linguistic meanings associated with it. The Shorter Oxford English Dictionary lists 13 meanings for 'about' and 23 for 'table', for example. The great majority of these words are content words (nouns, adjectives, verbs and adverbs); the so-called grammatical words are only about 150 in number in English but these occur with high frequency.

Estimates of the size of a person's vocabulary cannot be more than rough, partly because of the multiplicity of senses for many individual words and partly because there are differences in what we can recognize with varying degrees of contextual support and what we can produce when left to our own devices. Even at six years of age the hypothetical average child may well use over 2,000 words and understand some meanings of over 10,000. Either list for the average adult will run into many thousands. While the lists are long, the practice we have enjoyed and continue to experience is considerable: in an hour a lecturer may well utter about 5,000 words. Many of us utter and hear many thousands every day. Even with a reading rate as low as 250 words a minute, a 75,000-word novel could be skimmed, if not digested, in five hours.

Above the rank of word-guided discovery, procedures may well be needed again to bring into consciousness what you know about syntax:* the rules governing the sequences that can be used to form groups (phrases), clauses, and sentences. Linguistics usually treats English as though there are four types of sentence (declarative, interrogative, imperative and moodless or exclamatory) and three types of group: nominal (noun), verbal, and adjunctive (adverbial). The number of clause types proposed varies from one system to another, but is usually greater than 10 and less than 20. Free clauses can stand alone and can serve as sentences. Bound clauses are not free standing: they can be co-ordinate (linked by such conjunctions as 'and' or 'but') or subordinate (linked by such words as 'if', 'because', 'who' and 'although'). While these higher-rank structures are few in number, the large number of words in combination with the great variety of permissible sequences operative within any particular rank allow an infinite number of sentences to be constructed. It is these sentences, delivered with particular patterns of intonation* and stress, that we use to make our utterances.

Deciding how best to conceptualize grammar has proved to be a very difficult exercise in spite of our proficiency as users of it, and it is possible to write whole books on prepositions or the verb and still leave much unsaid. Although deciding how best to organize words in relation to their meanings was solved conveniently by dictionary makers with alphabetical listings, systems for organizing similarities and differences of meaning have not advanced importantly beyond Roget's Thesaurus. Discussion of the meanings of both words and sentences (semantics)* remains at what can best be described as an exploratory level and we are only at the beginning of thinking coherently about what we can do with utterances (pragmatics).* At least the last 20 years

have witnessed a revival of concern with how language
functions in context. We have been reminded that conversation succeeds only when certain social assumptions are met,
and what was once seen as an infinite number of possible
speech acts has been reduced to five by one philosopher.
Halliday (1975) has begun to illustrate how mastery of the
three components of sounds, lexico-grammar* and meaning can
be linked both with each other and with the significance of
language for action. It will probably be another ten years
before we are in a position to write both sensibly and
simply about the ways phonology, lexico-grammar, semantics
and pragmatics relate to each other in the developing
communicative competence of children.

Meanwhile, those who wish to facilitate such development in children will have to find out and rely upon what is
known and believed to date; and that could already occupy a
three-year degree course. For such a course to come alive it
would need a very strong practical component with two main
strands. One of these would concentrate upon a study of the
adult language, emphasizing the normally neglected areas of
pragmatics and the study of intonation and stress. Most of
us are conscious of our own deficiencies in coding capability. Adults normally code for meaning and significance for
action. What is one to do or say as a result of what you
have just said or done? We are less likely to notice or be
able to recall the precise wording. We are very unlikely to
be able to represent that wording phonetically, say in
International Phonetic Alphabet. Very few of us could write
the musical score of an utterance, and yet in spoken English
it is that score which will have signalled what is taken for
granted and what is offered as new, what is news and what is
taken to be already shared. Books still present 'The cat is
on the mat' as a single sentence that can be subjected to
linguistic analysis; to diagnose its significance in any
context would, however, require a specification of its
intonation and stress. What question was this utterance
answering? What is on the mat? Where is the cat? Was it
specifying where one of the household pets is? Is one of the
mats or cats known as 'the' mat or 'the' cat, just as some
household cupboards have that status? Had someone just
denied that the cat was on the mat? The crucial message
component remains unknown and unknowable in the version
cited. In practice we normally know how to respond, but we
do not know how to represent this knowledge in symbolic
form.

Practicals with adult speech alone would be dangerously
misleading if we are to work with children. Children constitute a double hazard. Not only do we need to know when
and how they can be helped to develop mastery over which
of the many units and structures of language, we need also
to be able to sense and interpret the world through their
minds. Halliday's (1975) analysis illustrates how Nigel not
only invented individual non-English sounds for his meanings, but devised special distinctions not actually made

in English. Young children can say the opposite of what they mean and then be confused as to whether they meant what they said or failed to say what they meant! They can say something and then genuinely believe it is true, while an adult accuses them of imagining or lying. As we see later, many five year olds do not know what either understanding or not understanding is; they have not isolated this dimension of experience, let alone discriminated which is which. Stripping away one's implicit adult assumptions when working with children is as difficult an exercise in taking the role of the other as can be imagined. Unfortunately, this important skill is not prominently practised in the professional training of those who are to work with young children.

The reading of books is no substitute for experience; just as experience is no substitute for academic knowledge. The learning problem is to advance both in harness, in dialectical support of each other. Here we have to concentrate on book learning, of which there is no dearth.

Introduction: a psychological frame of reference

For over 15 years a steady river of books about language development in children has flowed on to the market (see de Villiers and de Villiers, 1979, for a good introduction), while the journals have been flooded by research on the same topic. Much of this work has been clever and ingenious; not all of it has been sensible in its point of departure. It is encouraging that the more recent productions have begun at the starting point that common sense would have recommended; Halliday (1975) expresses the contrast between earlier work and some of the later work in terms of the questions asked by psycholinguists and sociolinguists. The former have tended to focus upon the child mastering the syntax of language (rules for combining words) at the expense of the other components of language: phonology* (sounds), lexis (words), semantics (meaning), and pragmatics (significance for action). They have asked: how does the child combine units into structures (combinations of units), particularly words into sentences? What do children's errors, in terms of what is acceptable in the adult language, tell us about the system their brains use for generating sentences? Are these errors common to all children learning any language? Are there fixed sequences of syntactic development within and across all languages? What are the characteristics of the language acquisition device that all children are born with? With the possible exception of the last, all these questions are proper in that evidence could be and has been collected to answer them.

Flow charts have been drawn up setting out stages in the development of negation and question formation, and these have been 'explained' by writing out rules that the child's mind appears to be following in producing these forms. The grammatical errors of children learning different languages have been examined for similarities and differences, and explanations have been offered for the patterns observed.

However, this emphasis upon syntactic structure and a corresponding neglect of function is alien to the sociolinguistic stance. From that perspective the questions are liable to be asked in terms of the ways in which units and structures develop to serve functions. Function is primary: children talk to communicate. Introductory questions would be: why do children talk? What kinds of meanings do they encode to what ends? We can proceed to ask how they code meanings; that is, which units and structures they use. How do the functions and their associated structures change in development and why?

The main reason for preferring the functional/structural to the purely structural approach might be summarized by stating that young children issue commands rather than utter imperative forms (Stand up!), they make requests and ask questions rather than form interrogatives, they comment about themselves, about others and about the world rather than utter declarative sentence forms; they achieve purposes by communicating meanings rather than constructing linguistic structures. In addition, and crucially, a functional/ structural approach obliges us to ask questions about the nature of children and their learning as well as about the language they are mastering.

That being so, if we wish to find out which units and structures are learned when and how, we have to turn to examine ways in which children can be encouraged to exercise functions requiring such units and structures. If we are to be able to specify what children can learn, what they do learn, and how, we have to look closely and attentively to theories of development, learning and instruction.

Three approaches have dominated thinking about the learning of children: associative principles, ideas of modelling, and the cognitive developmental. The first stresses that events occurring close to each other in terms of time and space are likely to become associated: the fact of their co-occurrence is likely to be learned. The work of Pavlov showed that new artificial stimuli could be substituted for the original stimuli to elicit responses already in the animal's repertoire, under certain conditions (classical conditioning). Thorndike, and latterly Skinner, have shown that new responses to stimuli can be learned if these are followed quickly by rewards or punishments (operant conditioning). What roles can classical conditioning and operant conditioning play for which aspects of language development? Have reward and punishment and their contingent use a significant part which they can and do play?

What determines when and how imitation can be important? Children can and do learn through observation as well as action; how might observational learning fit into the picture? Piaget (see Turner, 1975) offers a portrait of the child as an active organizer of experience, building up schemes* for action through processes of assimilation* and accommodation,* or adaptation.* These schemes grow in number. They become co-ordinated and differentiated. They become organized so far as to afford symbolic as well as physical solutions to problems. The symbolic systems themselves become qualitatively more powerful with growth, which is promoted through different interaction with a challenging environment. How is language development to be integrated into this approach and how do these developments relate to language mastery? The existence of each of these kinds of learning is thoroughly established. What we have yet to determine is whether they are relevant to language learning, and if so how, and under what conditions. Sadly, even recent texts are relatively reticent about these issues, but less so than those of earlier writers.

After closely observing the development of language in three children over a number of years, and particularly the syntax, Brown (1973) concluded: 'What impels the child to "improve" his speech at all remains something of a mystery'. At least two weaknesses in Brown's reasoning might be offered to explain this pessimism. First, the actual tests made of the possible relevance of principles of reinforcement (rewards and punishments) and confirmation/correction, or of observational learning examined only a very few linguistic features in very few children. We have, however, no reason to expect that identical processes will be of equal significance for all aspects of language learning in all children. Brown is not enthusiastic about common sense, but common sense easily observes that children learn the language and dialect of their caretakers rather than one of several thousand other languages in the world. That being so, modelling must have some potential role to play in part of the learning process, even if we cannot as yet be precise in saying how and when it occurs. While imitation and reinforcement principles of learning and performance may not be able to explain some features of language mastery, such as how adults become capable of generating an infinite number of novel sentences, it does not follow logically that these principles are irrelevant to everything else that is involved in learning to use language.

The second weakness in Brown's approach is revealed by the stripped-down characteristics of the data examined. Child speech was analysed as transcripted sequences of words. Prosodic features of intonation, pitch, and stress were not included. The caretaker's utterances and the non-verbal context in which utterances were made were generally, but not entirely, ignored. But the child's speech is only one component of the co-operative action involving conversation, and conversations are not about nothing. Imagine trying to describe and explain the learning of a trapeze artist's skills without mentioning the behaviour of a partner or of the trapeze! How can one expect to examine the role of the child's caretakers in the development of speech if their possible contribution to the interaction is not included in full measure? And how can one expect to study either without reference to the contextually embedded actions and interactions to which speech is directed? And if you have no theories of learning to test, then none will prove to be helpful in explaining the data.

The perspective adopted here will recognize that the growing child is an active self-organizing subject capable of building up action schemes, symbolic schemes, and sign systems through interaction with events, things and people (following Piaget), but we recognize that the child is at the same time an object whose behaviour can be shaped and developed through the contingent use of rewards and punishments (following Pavlov and Skinner). We also need to accept the idea that to produce and understand speech is to manifest a set of at least semi-automated skills (see claim 7 below), whose mastery will need repeated and varied practice in situations where others in the environment offer some corrective feedback. Accepting this eclectic view of children as growing persons who are both agents and victims allows us to conceive of them as inventing functions as well as units and structures to realize these, and as discovering these already available in the speech of others. We can also conceive of them as being responsive to direct instruction and training, both for learning new features and for deploying them more and more fluently in action.

What follows is a list of claims about children's mastery of language and the role of caretakers in this endless task. The claims may need amendment or partial abandonment in the light of advances in knowledge, but in 1981 they represent what is intended to be a balanced assessment of the evidence to hand.

Claims about language development

Claim 1. The use of language develops out of already established non-verbal means of communication

From birth children interact with their caretakers; child and caretaker act upon and react to each other. This reciprocity involves an exchange of signals each to the other. The child responds differentially (e.g. with smiles or cries) to different maternal actions, such as different facial expressions (Bruner, 1975). For example, the caretakers endeavour to decode distress signals and cease to search for further solutions when their actions result in signals of satisfaction. It is out of this interchange of communication through body movements, gestures, facial expressions, and vocalizations that verbal communication emerges; it does not arise suddenly with a first 'word'.

Claim 2. Initial functions of language are social interactional

If we distinguish broadly between language uses which attempt to comment upon the nature of things, for instance making statements which are either true or false, and those which appear to be attempts to regulate the states or behaviour of self and others or to define role relationships (see Robinson, 1978), then in Halliday's child, Nigel, the former only began to appear over nine months after the first socially relevant language units had emerged. Halliday found that instrumental (getting things for self), regulatory (making others do things), interactional (encounter-regulation), and personal (reactions to events or states) units were the first to appear. Among these were nã (give me that), bø (give me my bird), ৯ (do that again), do (nice to see you), nŋ (that tastes nice) (see glossary under phonology). This child began to talk, it seems, because verbal interaction with others was pleasurable; it was not because he was hungry or in pain. The design of the baby includes an impetus to interact with people, an impetus to interact with other features of the environment, and an impetus to develop the schemes of interaction. If one wishes to say that the reasons babies begin to talk are biological, then they are socio-biological: joint action with care-takers. That being so, the promotion of co-ordinated joint action may be one form of inducement to develop communicative skills.

As Halliday illustrates, Nigel later expanded his functional range to include the heuristic (finding out) and imaginative (let's pretend) functions, and he increased the number of communicative acts associated with each of these until, by the age of one-and-a-half, he had over 50 in his repertoire. This 50 is a misleading figure because from the outset the child had both general and specific variants of each function, such as nã (give me that - general), and bø (give me my bird - specific). The general form may be an important growth point as well as having general utility, in that it affords the caretaker an opportunity to respond non-verbally with the appropriate action, verbally to label the unspecified object, and to continue the conversation, all at the same time. The opportunity to learn a specific referent for the particular 'that' can be fitted into the sequence of activity, without this constituting a major diversion.

About the time Nigel reached his 50 meanings he also ceased to rely solely upon inventing his own units (mainly un-English in form and actually heavily reliant on tone); two important changes occurred.

First, Nigel interpolated a third level of linguistic structure, the lexico-grammatical, between soundings and meanings. Individual sounds ceased to be expressive of individual meanings. Combinations of sounds were used to form 'words', words and tones were sequenced to create 'meanings'. Thus the tri-stratal essence of language became established. (At some later point in time the child has also to learn to distinguish between the semantic and pragmatic levels; different forms can serve the same general func-tions, the same form can serve different functions, the appropriate choice requiring knowledge of the cultural norms of the society.)

Claim 3. The child makes deliberate efforts to learn language

Second, Nigel's speech began to distinguish between using

language and learning language. He deliberately solicited
from his caretakers 'names' of objects, attributes and
actions and he practised combinations and alterations both
in monologue and dialogue. Whether all children do this we
do not yet know. How do caretakers respond to these enquiries about words (and structures)? On the principles of
any associative theory of learning (see de Cecco, 1968),
supplying the requested items emphatically, clearly and with
some measure of repetition and extension should increase the
chances of individual children learning the language feature
and its use. It should also encourage them in the process of
finding out more. Not supplying the requested information,
or supplying it in a form that the child cannot assimilate
in the short run, forgoes an opportunity for learning about
the specific matter in hand and in the long run should
result in the child ceasing to make enquiries.

Claim 4. Units and structures are accumulated piecemeal but inexorably

An extreme position might argue that units are mastered one
at a time, always being linked to some unit or structure
already in the child's repertoire. They may be learnt and
lost again. The cycle may be repeated until the unit dis-
appears or becomes established. The units which become
finally established and relatively stable will be those in
the speech of the child's circle of interactants, particularly of those with whom the child is most frequently in a
learning and interactive relationship.

By 'unit' is meant any feature of the language at any
level: for example, phonemes (individual sounds), tonic
stresses, pitches, intonation patterns, morphemes, words,
groups, clauses, sentences, utterances, rules of expli-
citness, rules of politeness, rules of differential social
status. (It should be remembered that a unit at one level
can be a structure at another, e.g. a sequence of particular
pitches can form an intonation pattern, but this pattern
serves as a unit if it serves to form an interrogative; a
principle or rule can become a unit when treated as such.)

A new unit will be more likely to enter and remain in
a child's repertoire if that child is intellectually capable
of grasping some aspect of its approximate meaning or significance. Capability is not the only factor; a unit is more
likely to be mastered if its meaning and significance is
relevant to something the child wishes to communicate or
comprehend. Reasons for a unit not entering would be that
the child may already be using his energies and available
capacity to develop other units or structures of verbal or
non-verbal behaviour. The child may also be performing and
living rather than learning; there is more to life than
learning. A unit will only become stabilized in use if it is
encouraged to do so by others (see claim 6).

Claim 5. The new is often first learnt in terms of the old

An ancient Greek paradox points to the impossibility of

change, and this principle is sometimes invoked as a reason why children cannot learn language! If understanding a word must precede the learning of that word, how can it be learnt? If learning must precede understanding how can the child come to understand something that has no meaning? And yet children clearly do learn. One of several lines of escape from the paradox is to argue that the child can express new meanings 'badly' with old, already available units and structures, and that caretakers can reformulate the child's meaning with the new units and structures which the child may then be able to assimilate to the meaning intended. Evidence is consistent with the idea that the child learning to associate the various kinds of negation in English with the appropriate adult lexical and syntactic structures can rely on adults continuing to supply the new forms upon the occasions of the child using those already in its repertoire.

Since syntactic systems such as interrogation and negation are compound and complicated, it may follow that the developing child will only master them piecemeal, generating transitional forms, if claim 4 is valid. The evidence pointing to the many transitional forms of syntactic construction (e.g. Why it is raining?; see Brown, 1973) is probably consistent with the idea that these variants are best left to correct themselves unless particular examples of them appear to have stabilized over many months. If a child cannot learn quickly from a correction there is probably little point, and there may be harm, in pursuing it.

Claim 6. Caretakers control the probability of new features being learned and remaining in the child's repertoire

Montessori is responsible for the last observation made in claim 5 and a second injunction of hers may be used to introduce claim 6. Her 'cycle of three' for teaching was: This is an X - Show me the/an X - What is this? (pointing at X). The first labels the activity, event, object or attribute. The second checks the child's capacity for recognition. The third encourages the production of the label. She adds that a repeated failure to elicit appropriate reactions from the child is best taken as a suggestion for dropping the matter and returning to it later. This model can easily be abused if taken too literally, but it has considerable value if used as a framework to bear in mind when combining instruction with conversation. How is a child to find out the conventional linguistic means of expressing meanings unless from caretakers? Why should caretakers leave children to extract features as best they can from their discourse? Why not structure their learning opportunities as clearly as possible leaving them to accept or reject them? (Many mothers object to viewing themselves or being viewed as teachers. Whether or not they are to be seen as teaching is contingent only upon the definition of 'teach'. If the provision of opportunities for learning is enough to be called 'teaching' then all people interacting with children are teachers. If this provision has to be intended to help learning, then fewer people are teachers of children, but presumably there are some things all mothers intend that their children should learn. Our own view is that mothers should accept that there is much they can teach their children and that they enjoy this role to the benefit of all concerned.)

Two studies can be quoted to illustrate the power of caretakers at the relatively early period of language development when the child's utterances are on average between 1.5 and 3 words (MLU: mean length of utterance; at this stage of development the number of morphemes is closely related to the number of words).

Ellis and Wells (1980) contrasted the maternal inter-action characteristics of slow language developers (12 months to move from MLU 1.5 to MLU 3.5) with those of early fast developers (less than 6 months to make this change and achieved before 21 months old). At the outset mothers of the two groups differed, the former talking generally more during routine household activities, issuing more instructions and commands, being more likely to acknowledge their child's utterance, and more likely to repeat or correct these. By the time the children had reached 3.5 MLU, maternal differences were still present, but they were different in type, the early fast children's mothers using more statements and questions, particularly teaching-type questions, to which the mother already knew the answers. Cross (1978) found in a contrast between faster and slower developers that different maternal speech vari-ables discriminated at different ages. The implications of these two studies are several. Optimal facilitation of development may require the employment of different tactics at different points in development and may also require the application of different principles.

More basic principles are also relevant. Mothers whose speech is more unintelligible in that it is mumbled and incoherent with no clear breaks and stresses at customary points are likely to have children whose speech is developing more slowly.

In a study of the mother-child interaction among six year olds (see Robinson, forthcoming), it was found that children who asked more questions, more complex questions, and revealed more verbally mediated knowledge about an assortment of objects, games, and toys had mothers who were more likely to:

* set any remark in a previously shared context;
* answer any question with a relevant, accurate reply that extended somewhat beyond the question posed;
* confirm children's utterances which were true and well-formed and to point out or correct errors;
* maintain themes over several utterances.

The findings probably need qualification and supplementation. Pointing out and correcting errors is likely to be productive only if children can learn from this and provided they do not become afraid to make mistakes. One feature of maternal behaviour that was unrelated to children's performance was the mother's questioning of the child; it seemed that at least in this context questioning may have been intended to re-focus the interest of children who were already actively attending to something else and were unwilling to be distracted. On the other hand, questioning can be viewed as motivating and others have found it to be positively associated with more advanced performance, but perhaps in their case the questioning was creating and achieving concentration rather than trying to re-direct attention. Questioning which encourages extension of interest may have different consequences from questions which are failed attempts to direct the child. (These two may be distinguishable in terms of quality of voice and intonation.)

If two words were to be used to sum up the contrast they would be 'push' versus 'pull'. Pushing did not work, pulling did: adults could set up the context of situation in which activity took place, but beyond that children decided what they were interested in. Adults can set the scene, offer suggestions, and tempt the child; but children direct the form and content of the scripts. The 'push' is already there; it is a design characteristic of human children. By their reactive behaviour adults can encourage and develop both this intrinsic motivation and the learning which results from its activity. They may also be able to treat it in ways which may slow down, check, deflect, distort, prevent or otherwise impede development.

Providing, tempting and modelling appear to be the main activities caretakers can offer to facilitate language (and general) development. How far the success of these actions depends upon the caretaker's genuine concern with the child and the child's behaviour remains unknown. One would have to say, as an act of faith, that caring in action, realized as an expression of a sincere liking and cheerful interest in what children find important, is certainly desirable, if not necessary. Entering both intellectually and emotionally into the spirit and perspective of the child's orientation to the child's own world must make the processes easier to achieve.

Claim 7. Coming to 'know that' reorganizes the possibilities developing 'know how'

Halliday (1975) noted that at an early age young Nigel discriminated between using the language and learning the language. Some children of four already 'know that' there are rules governing how things are to be said and can say something about their nature. We can also ask how children come to realize that speech can be ambiguous, that a speaker may send messages too vague for correct comprehension and appropriate action. At an early stage children do not realize a message should refer uniquely to its referents if it is to be acted upon appropriately. In a situation where speaker and listener have identical sets of cards, each set depicting stick-men holding flowers differing in size and colour, they will pick up a card in response to 'A man with a flower' without necessarily asking for more information. If their choice turns out to be wrong they will state that the speaker had said enough (told properly) and that it was their fault that the mismatch had occurred (phase 1 below). When older they will be more likely to demand more information by asking questions and if a mismatch does still occur they can blame the inadequacy of the message and the speaker for the failure. They 'know that' messages can be inadequate. They can reflect upon and analyse the efficiency and precision of their own speech and that of others (phase 2 below).

At present we can only speculate about the general significance of this work, but the possible implications are considerable and can be represented roughly in a three-phase model that could apply to any aspects of language development. Let X be a truth, principle or fact about language.

* PHASE 1: children are mainly victims of X. Their capacities for being agents with control over X are limited by their ignorance of the character of X and how it functions in the language in communication. However, they achieve a measure of mastery of X in use (know how) as a result of associative learning both in its classical and instrumental conditioning guises, and they may also learn about X in use through observation. They are additionally an agent and can purposefully use X, relying on corrective feedback from others for the development of context-bound rules of use. These various processes acting separately and in combination may lead to a child using X successfully much of the time. However, limitations of intellectual capacity and an absence of opportunities and/or capacities for reflecting upon the workings of X will be manifested when the child's rules for using X fail. They will not be able to diagnose the reasons for failure and will not be able to formulate a diagnosis and act effectively upon it.

* PHASE 2: either through their own reflective efforts or as a result of a competent other teaching and telling them about the workings of X children will come to realize how (and perhaps why) X works as it does. As a result of reflective analysis in particular new situations or through a consideration of past events, or through imaginative rehearsing of situations involving X, they will consciously develop and organize their knowledge about X. We might expect an associated period of learning practice in which the use of X is tried out with care and awareness. Individual children (or adults) have become reflecting agents in respect of X organizing their 'knowledge that', and perhaps temporarily less efficient in their 'know how'.

*   PHASE 3: the use of X will become reduced to an auto-
    mated skill except for situations where, for various
    reasons, it might be important not to make mistakes with
    X and for situations where trouble in using X occurs. In
    the face of trouble the problem can be raised to a con-
    scious reflective analysis, diagnoses made, and correc-
    tive action taken: other things being equal. The 'know
    how' is greater than at the transition from phase 1 to
    phase 2 and is in a potential dialectic relation to a
    'knowing that' of understanding.

We are thinking in this fashion only about the child's
control of ambiguity in verbal referential communication,
but see a range of possible application to a whole variety
of behaviours within the orbit of language in communication:
learning the meanings of words, rules of spelling in the
written language, rules of pronunciation in the oral, rules
of grammar, rules for varying forcefulness and politeness
of requests, rules of etiquette more generally, rules for
taking the listener into account and rules for telling jokes
well.

Perhaps one important set of reasons why schoolchildren
have difficulty in learning to use language more competently
is that we ourselves cannot formulate the rules for them.
Instead we leave them to continue to operate at a particular
and concrete level, learning many instances rather than
fewer principles and rules. And when we do find out the
rules and principles we do not necessarily set up conditions
of learning and practice that carry the child's competence
through to the phase of out-of-awareness efficient use, with
reflective facilities for analysis when trouble occurs or is
anticipated. It is worth comparing the ease of learning a
game, like chess or tennis, with and without the help of
information about rules. To learn how to play will require
observation, practice, and correction, but knowing the rules
renders these easier. Discovering them for yourself could be
simply a frustrating waste of time and effort.

Erroneous beliefs

The most fundamental, and possibly the most common, false
assumption is that the rate and extent of younger and older
children's learning how to use language is not affected by
the behaviour of their caretakers; that some innate features
of the child's brain or temperament determine what emerges.
(We have avoided mentioning ages of children at points where
readers might have preferred them to be specified. The
arguments in the section on backwardness offer some reasons
why it is misleading and dangerous to hold firm expectations
as to what individual children ought to have achieved at
particular ages. The educational problems with children are
to advance their knowledge, understanding, values and
motivation, not to categorize them.) While systematic
investigations of parents' and teachers' beliefs about
language development have yet to be made, it is quite clear
that within some cultures, some parents believe that the

child will become what it will become regardless of what they do. The empirical evidence is that these beliefs do not correspond to reality: while many facts about relations between caretaker behaviour and language development have yet to be discovered, the positive results already established are too numerous and theoretically plausible to be discounted.

Unfortunately, academic thinking about these matters is still dominated by a simplicity that is naïve. One common assumption in research seems to be that if a certain kind of caretaker behaviour can be shown to be beneficial then it follows that the more of it the better: and that its efficacy will hold true for all children at all phases of language development regardless of the context of operation and the state of relationship between caretaker and child. Neither the basic assumption nor its presumed generality is likely to be true.

For example, it is likely that caretakers can talk too much with children as well as too little. And they can over-teach particular features. Developmental social psychologists have been slow to appreciate that many relations between variables are likely to be curvilinear rather than monotonic. 'The more the better' may have a limit beyond which 'more' may mean worse or nothing and not better.

Just as caretakers may talk too much as well as too little, they can talk 'at' or 'past' children instead of with them. They can initiate and control without responding. Some adults seem anxious to hurry their replies, without having listened first: they act but do not react or interact. One of the first lessons to be learned in dealing with young children is not to impose oneself too quickly upon them, and this applied to continuing as well as initial encounters. While children have to learn how and when to listen, they also need to be listened to. It has been argued that mothers listen attentively to children trying to decipher the meanings of their cries, but one can be sceptical about the continuing and pervading applicability of such parental commitment to all children as they grow older. Brown (1973) showed that 40 per cent of his children's questions were met with replies that were unrelated to the sense of the question; one therefore wonders how many caretakers make serious efforts to listen to children, encourage them to talk about their activities, and maintain interest and cohesion in such conversations. Those caretakers who are concerned to promote development may push too hard or pull too hard. On the evidence to date 'pushing' is not productive, whereas 'pulling' pitched at the right level with not too high or low a frequency is an important facilitator of development. Caretakers can pitch their initiations and reactions to children at too low a level or too high a one. Too low may be generally uncommon, but certainly some mentally retarded children appear to be kept at a lower standard of performance by adults unwilling to extend their conversation with them. But how are caretakers to judge what is too much, too often, or too hard?

Caretakers can solve these problems only in context. A monitoring of the child's actions and reactions in combination with an appraisal of the verbal interaction itself should suffice to indicate whether the child is attentively involved. Adults should be able to appraise whether or not their remarks are understood by the child both from the non-verbal reactions and from the succeeding remarks. Adults should be able to judge whether they themselves are understanding and reacting appropriately to the child's utterances. Does the child have great difficulty constructing replies? Are there many disfluencies and intervening silences? Are themes maintained over a succession of utterances? In short, does the conversation have an orderly structure? Does the talk relate to the contextual features of the situation in which it is occurring? If it does, and if the adult is injecting new information about the world and about language at such a rate that the child can take up and use some of the features being introduced, the worst mistakes are being avoided.

This capacity to adjust speech to a developing child is itself a skill that has to be learned. Child-rearing manuals (Leach, 1978) or pre-school teacher's advice (Tough, 1977) offer much constructive (and some wrong!) advice on such matters. Perhaps both under-estimate the value of two activities: conversation as such and the appropriate injection of small doses of teaching about languages during conversation.

Finally, the conversation has to be anchored to the outside world of actions and events and/or the inner personal worlds of wishes, intentions, feelings and ideas. The talk has to be more than wordings. Experiences have to be arranged and/or exploited. Topics have to be selected. If they are not, individual children are in danger of separating rhetoric from reality (or fantasy). They might come to believe there is a world of wordings and a world of events and things and fail to appreciate that the two should interact with each other.

Why enhance development?

Taken at its most abstract interpretation the question becomes tautological, but given the inaccuracy and inadequacy of the explicit or implicit theories guiding the behaviour of many caretaker educators, we may have to argue for a number of advantages that greater knowledge might bring. Given a goodwill towards children and a correlated desire not to let them suffer unnecessarily, the substitution of knowledge for ignorance affords greater possibilities of reducing difficulties for them.

A child's own ignorance and incompetence ensures a dependence on others; to be dependent renders children open to exploitation and leaves them less able to assume responsibility for control over their actions. Increasing mastery of

language helps to free children from superfluous dependence;
it enables them to gain satisfaction from both self-reliant
and joint activity. They are better placed to communicate
explicitly their wants and wishes. They are better equipped
to perform each of the functions for which language can be
used (see, for example, Robinson, 1978). Language can also
provide a vehicle of representation for learning and for
problem-solving, a tool whose appropriate use can promote
their own development. We have yet to ascertain how language
mastery enters into the human capacity for turning round
upon one's own schemata, for viewing oneself as both object
and subject, for reflecting about oneself as well as others.
It is quite possible that the emergence of the self-concept
and self-esteem and the subsequent growth of both personal
and social identity are intimately bound up with language
development. Certainly it would be both mad and bad to
assume that language development was irrelevant to these
processes.

Advocates of delay might point to the potential dangers
of excessive hurrying, straining children beyond their
capacity and denying them the joys of childhood. While that
can be agreed, delays may also have disadvantages. There is
an impetus to develop in young babies which can be overstretched or understretched; our problem is to create
opportunities for learning which optimize the application of
this intrinsic motivation. If children can enjoy learning,
why deny them opportunities? If children enjoy the exercise
of mastery of skills and understanding, why remove such
sources of satisfaction? Too few people seem to have observed the vigour of the infant's impetus to interact
constructively and adaptively; too many adults think children enjoy only play and treats. Perhaps the sometimes quoted
view has substance; that adults often kill off rather than
encourage motivation to learn.

Caretakers who are not promoting language development
in children are not only doing their children a disservice,
they are probably making child-rearing harder than it need
be. Lovable as a pre-linguistic child may be, parents
generally find crying upsetting and full-scale screaming
harrowing and pitiful. And yet these can frequently be
switched off very rapidly by the provision of 'it'. Is 'it'
food, drink, teddy, the green plastic spoon, daddy sitting
in his proper chair or what? What is the event which will do
the trick? A single unambiguous word from the child could
prevent the incident occurring or defuse it at the outset.
How many such incidents might be avoided by equipping children with the facility to communicate more effectively with
their caretakers? While effectiveness of communication does
not preclude the occurrence of or resolve conflicts, it does
enable frustrations and conflicts to be defined. While there
is as yet no hard evidence that improved communication
between children and parents eases relations between them,
the assumption that it probably does is a wiser bet than the
reverse.

Many of us probably see young babies as dull jelly-like blobs requiring intermittent but frequent attention, whose salvation lies in the instinctual affection of their parents. We are not sufficiently aware of the details of the changes that take place day by day, week by week, and month by month. Does it make a difference to parental satisfaction if they become aware of, attend to, and take an interest in these features? To claim that it did for oneself may certainly be true. To claim that it can for others is a belief which is empirically testable. Such child-watching could degenerate into a detached cognitively-based curiosity, but if the observer is simultaneously a loving participant the activity is transformed into a profound and continuing appreciation of the wonderful complexity of human growth. Too few parents are informed enough to enjoy this experience. Fromm wrote, 'Love is the active concern for the life and growth of that which we love'. To act upon this principle requires knowledge about the growing and how to help it to occur.

Special problems

Backwardness

Before we comment upon backwardness in language development, it is essential that we note a too-often forgotten fact. Backwardness is not an absolute concept but a relative one. Backwardness can exist only where a norm* is defined. For various reasons our society has selected biological age from birth as a reference point. For many aspects of growth and development we have devised ways of measuring characteristics of children that give a spread of scores about an average or norms of some kind for children of a particular age. Then we use our tests to obtain scores for individual children. However, to expect then that each individual child should score close to the average is importantly irrational: such an expectation is logically and empirically inconsistent with the spreading procedures adopted to construct the test.

This is not to say that it is foolish to ask why a child or group of children is below (or above) average. Answers to such questions may enable us to take constructive action to facilitate the development of particular children who are unnecessarily and undesirably backward in certain respects.

Many people in our society may also adopt a moral position that special efforts should be made to promote more rapid development in some sub-sample of the population defined as 'backward': say the lowest 10 per cent. That is defensible. However, it is not logically or empirically possible to eliminate a bottom 10 per cent. We can take action to raise the absolute performance or characteristics of children. What we cannot do is use norm-referenced tests and eliminate the variation about the norm.

We must also accept the fact that at any moment in any society there are limits both to what can be done and what the members of society think it is important to do. There

are biological, sociological-historical and economic limits
to what can be done. There are moral limits as to what we
might consider it proper or fair to do.

We can also observe that there are wrong ways of con-
ceptualizing these problems. Over the last 20 years, and
before, questions have been asked about why children fail at
school. Some have blamed the biology and psychology of
failing children. Others have blamed bad homes. Bad teaching
and bad schools have been cited, as have curricula. The
governments and the social structure of the society have
been blamed. In reality the sole reason why n per cent of
children fail CSE, O level or A level is that the examiners
have agreed a fail rate of n per cent. We can sensibly ask
why children from certain identifiable groupings are particularly at risk for failure. We can also note that explanations for such failure have generally been 'deficiency
models' of some kind, deficiency in language being a frequently cited factor. Oddly, we have only resorted to this
kind of explanation within age groups, particularly for
social categories such as social class, rurality and cultural minorities, and psychological categories such as the
mentally retarded or the maladjusted. We do not see infant
schoolchildren as language-deficient adults who need to
be brought up to a state of adult competence forthwith.
Education is normally seen as promoting and facilitating
development, not in terms of removing deficiencies. And yet
within a particular age cohort we tend to use the deficiency
model, even for 'normal' children. Whether a glass of water
is seen as half full or half empty is a fact about the
observer, not the water. The fate of the water may not be
affected by that perception. However, when children are seen
as more empty (or filled with the wrong stuff) than they
ought to be, there are likely to be consequences for themselves, their families, their teachers and ultimately the
society of which they are to become citizens.

Another possible error in conceptualization is to think
of children's personality being made up of stable traits and
dispositions that will remain invariant with respect to
their age peers. A complex variety of assumptions is
involved in such a belief and no simple variant of it
corresponds that closely to reality, at least so far as
educational decisions about normal individual children are
concerned.

But need we even consider a developing child norma-
tively; and, if so, against which norms? If we are to make
special educational or other provision for those in particular need then testing individuals against norms of intellectual achievement or social behaviour is essential as a
diagnostic means of some objectivity. Test scores help to
define the characteristics of a child. Age-based norms
constitute the single most efficient screening frame of
reference for operation. Once the presenting characteristics
are defined by reference to test scores the hard work of
explanation and decision-making starts. Are the scores

deviant enough from what might be expected from this individual to warrant further enquiry? If either is true, are the scores themselves what are important, or are they symptoms of something else? Pronouncing /r/ as /w/ may be the only oddity: an omission in education perhaps remedied speedily. If the scores are judged to be indicators of problems rather than the problems in themselves, are these best treated by being left to remedy themselves with subsequent monitoring? There are certain to be ebbings and flowings in normative positioning, and it would seem to be important not to treat backwardness or oddity that will be changed by individual children themselves as something requiring intervention. On the other hand, where intervention is judged as desirable, the use of norm-referenced tests is likely to have played a crucial role in detection and perhaps diagnosis; they do not in themselves provide either an explanation or a rationale for the adoption of particular educational activity in respect of the children tested.

Educational programmes for language development
The mid-1960s witnessed the construction and implementation of a large number of educational programmes, particularly in the USA, which were intended to raise special groups of children to a state from which they could enter the infant school curriculum on terms of equality (of opportunity) with the average of the population. The programmes were to help children whose families were economically, ethnically, or otherwise socially disadvantaged.

Rumour has distorted, simplified and caricatured the reality of the outcomes of these endeavours in a summary judgement of total failure. This rumour is not accompanied by explanations for the supposed failures and, sadly, equality of opportunity in education has itself faded as an issue of public concern. Certainly some programmes failed. This was to be expected when too little of the wrong thing was done in the wrong way. Buying a new car for the sheriff was unlikely to boost IQ scores in the local kindergarten. Neither was a 20-minute session of drilling for 30 days, especially over the longer term. In fact, programmes that were 'sensible' were very successful (see Stallings, 1975).

We have long known that the life chances of the disadvantaged can be dramatically altered by changing environmental conditions and, more generally, it is extraordinarily arrogant to assume that our upbringing and education of children has reached perfection in 1981. Successful ventures mounted programmes consistent with the claims made in this chapter. Unsuccessful ones failed in one or more of the following respects.

* The contents and/or materials of the curriculum were not matched closely enough to the contemporary knowledge, understanding, values or motivation of the children. Materials, for example, were sometimes unfamiliar or too advanced or too elementary.

* The implementation of the curriculum failed to use instructional techniques appropriate to the nature of the problems to be solved or the psychology of the children learning. For example, the formation of concepts or principles requires that the child actively construct hypotheses; understanding requires more than rote learning. Brophy and Evertson (1975) have shown that the kinds of teacher-child interaction most promotive of learning in the low socio-economic status (SES) groups in their study were different from those benefitting high SES children. Crudely, the former benefitted from greater structuring of the learning by the teacher.

* Insufficient attention was paid to the social influence of peers and parents. Children learn better when they are with other children who are also disposed to learn. The relevance of active parental support and interest has long been established as a significant facilitator of educational achievement and the effects of integration of parents into programmes are highlighted in several successful American programmes.

* The social significance of any difference between the language or dialect of the school and those of the home were not appreciated. In the section on dialects we mention but not develop the idea that the dialect or language of the school can be one that is hated by children and parents; it can be seen as a vehicle of oppression and as the language of the oppressors. To speak the language as it is taught could be to deny one's social identity.

* As the switch in title of programmes from 'Head Start' to 'Follow Through' implies, it was realized that a brief boost to achievement may represent an inadequate conceptualization of education. Programmes that were seen as priming capacity for a take-off typically revealed subsequent regression, which is what one would generally expect. Those who maintained their endeavour maintained the gains.

* Too much return was expected from too little investment. Programmes have expected changes in general intelligence from 10 hours of instruction! Training experiments have sometimes lasted only half an hour.

Successful programmes made fewer of these mistakes. There is no doubt that very large changes could still be induced in the educability of young children and in their competence with language, but such changes would require appropriate and persisting changes in the character of child-parent interaction, as well as in the schools.

It would be improper not to refer to the other main educationally disadvantaged group: the mentally retarded. Contributions to the literature on these children (e.g. Schiefelbusch and Lloyd, 1974) show how their language development can be facilitated. A common reaction to the general quality of the instructional techniques typically used is to assert that they are too minutely structured, concentrate too heavily on learning bits and pieces of language at the expense of language in use in communication, and rely too heavily on incentives which are not customary constituents of parent-child conversation. If these strictures are valid, however, they point to ways of developing the approach rather than reasons for abandoning it. As with the other special educational programmes, those for the mentally retarded work when they are sensible and sustained, and both serve to highlight the content and process of language learning in settings other than the home.

Dialects and accents

'Standard English' (SE) can be usefully thought of as that dialect of British English whose rules of prosody, grammar, lexis, semantics and pragmatics have become institutionalized as the variety of English towards whose mastery the educational endeavour aspires. 'Received Pronunciation' (RP) refers to the accent that defines the corresponding phonology. The components of SE stressed most frequently are its grammar and lexis; it is usually in respect of those characteristics that SE is contrasted with other regional and social dialects. When a variety is accorded the status of a dialect is not closely defined. Dialectologists have mapped out the distribution of regional dialects in Britain, particularly rural ones. Socially stratified dialects have not been well investigated. And for both we have yet to learn what their similarities and differences are. Are dialects more alike than they are different in each of their components? The number of differences in grammatical rules is probably few in relation to the total in the language.

Those responsible for educating children need to distinguish between features in their speech which indicate ignorance of language and its workings, and those which mark social identity through the dialect of the child's home. If teachers denigrate the local dialect while teaching SE they are potentially denigrating the people who speak that dialect and may eventually force children to choose between SE and the local dialect. Are they to equip themselves for upward social mobility at the cost of social separation from their families and local community? But why create conditions where a choice has to be made?

One false belief is that people can master only one dialect. Where the need for mastery of two different languages exists, children learn two, often without the benefit of schools to teach them. The factors that operate to prevent children mastering several dialects are mainly socio-cultural and not biological-cognitive.

If education is to open up opportunities rather than to close them down, that system has to facilitate the development of control of the dialects and languages of greatest potential significance to individual children, of which the two most important are their local social/regional dialects or language and SE, so that they may be able to use each as and when appropriate.

Similarly, arguments can be advanced for the educational support of more than one accent. It is now well documented that people do not always utter the same sound in the same way; it is a matter of proportion. And the proportions vary: this has been shown most frequently through manipulations of the formality-casualness of the situation.

Moreover, we also converge towards and diverge away from the speech of our fellow conversationalists (Giles and Powesland, 1975, chapter 9), such movements being interpreted as indicative of goodwill and separateness respectively. Giles and Powesland (1975, chapter 3) review studies which show how accents are evaluated in Britain. Evaluation can be along more than one dimension, and in this case two emerge that may be most simply summarized as expertness and trustworthiness. Unfortunately, these are not independent, RP speakers being seen as untrustworthy experts and broadly-accented countryfolk as trustworthy but ignorant. But children as well as adults are judged by their accents, and it must be incumbent upon the expert caretakers to increase their knowledge and understanding about these matters.

In sum, we need to extend and disseminate our knowledge about the ways language functions in our community. We need to develop and act upon policies that enable children to master in sufficient measure those varieties of language that will both promote their learning and enable them to retain or gain access to membership of those social groups in and through which their identity is realized.

Conclusions

One common complaint made by members of the public, their elected representatives, and their paid servants is that academics address problems rather than solve them; they spend too much time posing questions and too little answering them. At least in language development we have now moved to a position where the types of question being asked begin to embrace a comprehensive functional-structural framework. We have begun to ask how children learn units and structures to communicate meanings which have significance for action. We are confronting language in use as a four-component system (language in its pragmatic, semantic, lexico-grammatical and phonological aspects) just as the developing children themselves confront, cope with and learn to use all four interdependently. We have appreciated that although function may be a primary focus, we have also to note that a child who can distinguish between 'knowing how to' and 'knowing that' is in a strong position to hold and develop both structures and functions in a dynamic inter-active relation to each other, and that this capacity in fact predates the conscious onset of the discrimination. The questions being posed are now more likely to lead to progress than some of those narrower and stranger questions of 20 years ago.

Furthermore, we have begun to answer quite a number of questions. The claims made here are a distillation focussing on processes and mechanisms of development rather than content. What is now known about the content and sequence of language development is considerable, especially in young children. The claims made are couched in a form at as low a level of abstraction as appears to be compatible with the evidence. To be more specific would require the prior specification of more details of the particular children, caretakers, context of situation, and learning problems under consideration; the claims are principles that may guide practice but cannot prescribe its concrete characteristics. They also mark a departure from what might be called the 'one-answer-only' mentality. Psychologists have tried to look for 'the' process that converts all substances to gold, or in this case all pre-linguistic babies to verbally competent toddlers. We have seen the invalid logic that takes the form of arguing that because process X may not be invariably necessary for mastering Y, it has no relevance. It is likely that all learning processes are relevant or can be made relevant to some aspects of language development in some children. Once we ask whether, when and how a process can be used to facilitate development, our answers may become more positive and useful.

But are the claims made here any improvement on common sense? They are, in two ways. Unfortunately, a particular form of sense is not common to all people, as can be speedily demonstrated by revealing the extent of individual subcultural and cultural differences as to what it is sensible to believe. At present we know next to nothing about parents' (or even teachers') beliefs about language development, but we do know they differ. Some are wrong. This is not to insult them. We are all wrong in some of our beliefs, and none of us is omniscient. Common sense will not yield the truth. At present too the experts continue to disagree among themselves as to ways and means likely to facilitate language development. If we mean by 'common sense' the accumulated wisdom of experienced caretakers, then experts would surely be well-advised to solicit their opinions; if they have learned through observing the consequences of their teaching methods then they are the prime populations for ideas. But the convictions that have derived from their private experience have then to be checked in the publicly demonstrable contexts of systematic investigation. While the evidence obtained through scientific procedures is prone to errors of various kinds, investigators are trained to try to avoid these. Hence the evidence and the interpretations they offer should be less prone to error, especially when empirical studies conducted in a variety of settings yield results which can be shown to be consistent. The claims put forward have been subject to systematic scrutinizing activity, and that is why they rather than others are presented.

Glossary

Accommodation
A Piagetian term referring to the development of new schemes arising out of the failure of current schemes to regulate action. Hence sensori-motor schemes for sucking will not enable an infant to drink from a cup: new schemes have to be constructed.

Adaptation
In Piagetian development adaptation is the combination of the processes of assimilation and accommodation.

Assimilation
The application of currently available schemes to inter-action with the environment. If a baby has a sucking scheme used for breast feeding, it may readily assimilate the sucking of a bottle teat to this scheme. The sucking scheme will also be applied to fingers and toys but this transfer will not, in the long run, be adaptive. New schemes will be required to accommodate to the use of toys.

Intonation
Patterns of variation in pitch and stress that distinguish (i) between what is believed to be accepted already by conversation partners and what is new, and (ii) the character of utterance as questions, statements, commands, etc.

Lexico-grammar
The rules governing what is generally acceptable within a morphology and syntax. Rules in morphology define changes to words themselves as their functions in sentences change; for example, 'he' is subject, 'him' is the form for object. Syntax defines the possible sequences, substitutions and co-occurrences of words, phrases and clauses permitted in the construction of sentences.

About 150 special words in English (conjunctions, prepositions, pronouns, etc.) are sometimes seen as having predominantly grammatical/semantic significance. The remaining 500,000 or so are lexical items. Both are listed in dictionaries.

Morpheme
The smallest unit of meaning in a language.

Norm
In its descriptive sense norm refers to the typical or most common behaviour of members of a group. It is also used evaluatively to assert what is to be expected of such members. The failure to separate the two can lead to the idea that everyone has to be average, which is self-contradictory.

Phoneme
The individual sounds of a language that make a difference to meaning.

Phonology

The study of sound systems of languages. Within a language, which sounds make a significant difference to meaning? What are the rules which define which combinations of sounds can occur? To aid these descriptions linguists have devised an International Phonetic Alphabet that attempts to write down sounds so that their pronunciation is defined. This does not yet include conventions that represent stress or pitch.

Pragmatics (see semantics)

Pragmatics is concerned with the significance for action of utterances. To use language effectively people have to be able to interpret the speech of others and to know how their own utterances are likely to be interpreted. This requires a knowledge of rules of the culture and not just the semantics.

Psycholinguistics

The study of the psychological processes that underlie speech performance. The main focus in child development has been upon the encoding and decoding of syntax, but a comprehensive study would include comparable analyses of sounds and written symbols and meanings. Some people would also include pragmatics.

Scheme

The procedures that regulate an action or set of actions. Hence, if an infant has a sucking scheme, his brain must contain a set of instructions for action that result in a co-ordinated sequence of movements that relate his body, mouth and hands to nipples. Not all schemes relate to sensori-motor skills; they can also relate to intellectual products.

Semantics

Units at and above the level of morpheme have meanings. A cat is not a dog; 'on' does not mean the same as 'in'. It is through their combinations, in accordance with lexico-grammatical rules, that sequences of sounds come to have meaning. Some people have difficulty in grasping the distinction between semantics and pragmatics; pragmatics is concerned with action. 'The door is open', uttered by a teacher in a classroom, means what it says. The semantics declares a state of affairs to be true. The pragmatic significance could be 'The last child to have come in should get up and shut the door'. Unfortunately, we can use the question 'What did he mean?' to refer to both the semantics and the pragmatics. 'Meaning' is ambiguous.

Sociolinguistics

Traditionally the study of language variation in relation to variations in the nature of the setting, participants, ends, aesthetics, key, modality, norms, and genre, with a speech community. The focus is upon pragmatics and how functions relate to the forms used. Sociolinguistics and psycholinguistics overlap.

Syntax
The rules for combining words into phrases, clauses and sentences.

References

Brown, R. (1973)
A First Language: The early stages. London: Allen & Unwin.

Brophy, J.E. and Evertson, C.M. (1975)
Learning from Teaching. New York: Allyn & Bacon.

Bruner, J.S. (1975)
The ontogenesis of speech acts. Journal of Child Language, 2, 1-19.

Cross, T.G. (1978)
Mother's speech and its association with role of linguistic development in the young child. In N. Waterson and C. Snow (eds), The Development of Communication. Chichester: Wiley.

De Cecco, J.P. (1968)
The Psychology of Learning and Instruction. Englewood Cliffs, NJ: Prentice-Hall.

De Villiers, P.A. and De Villiers, J. (1979)
Early Language. Glasgow: Fontana/Open Books.

Ellis, R. and Wells, C.G. (1980)
Enabling factors in adult-child discourse. First Language, 1, 46-62.

Giles, H. and Powesland, P.F. (1975)
Speech style and social evaluation. London: Academic Press.

Halliday, M.A.K. (1975)
Learning How to Mean. London: Arnold.

Leach, P. (1978)
Baby and Child. London: Michael Joseph.

Robinson, W.P. (1978)
Language Management in Education. Sydney: Allen & Unwin.

Robinson, W.P. (ed.) (forthcoming)
Communication in Child Development. London: Academic Press.

Schiefelbusch, R.F. and Lloyd, L.L. (1974)
Language Perspective: Acquisition, retardation and intervention. Baltimore: University Park Press.

Stallings, J. (1975)
Implementation and child effects of teaching practices in follow-through classrooms. Monographs of the Society for Research in Child Development, 40, No. 163.

Tough, J. (1977)
Talking and Learning. London: Ward Lock.

Turner, J. (1975)
Cognitive Development. London: Methuen.

Questions

1. What can adults do to facilitate language development in young children?

2. In what ways can adults make language learning by children more difficult than is necessary?
3. Write a government leaflet giving advice to young mothers about language development in their children.
4. If mothers wish to facilitate language development in their children, which is it more important for them to know: details about the nature of language, or rules of interaction?
5. Can children be 'linguistically deprived'?
6. Is it the ignorance of parents and teachers rather than the incapacity of children that delays their development?
7. Under what conditions will practice not make perfect? Discuss in relation to language development.
8. Describe and comment upon the child's development of syntax.
9. How can young children control their own language development?
10. How can we distinguish between speech errors that mark development and those which indicate failures to learn?
11. What learning processes underlie which aspects of language development?
12. What roles can imitation play in language development?
13. Why do children stretch familiar units to cope with new meanings?
14. Does ability to play with aspects of language indicate or facilitate mastery?
15. What do experiments with retarded children reveal about natural language development?
16. Why encourage language development in children?
17. What could be the advantages and disadvantages of systematic teaching of language to pre-school children?
18. Ought we to concern ourselves with 'backwardness' in language development?
19. What should be done in infant schools about the dialects of children?

Annotated reading

Ausubel, D.P. (1978) Theory and Problems of Child Development (2nd edn). New York: Grune & Stratton.
    A general textbook about child development from an educational perspective.

Coulthard, C.M. (1977) An Introduction to Discourse Analysis. London: Longmans.
    What are the relations between linguistic form and the discourse functions of speech? Coulthard offers some suggestions.

De Stefano, J.S. (ed.) (1973) Language, Society and Education. Worthington, Ohio: Charles Jones.
    A collection that brings life to varieties of American English and discusses learning simply and clearly. No comparable book on British English, alas.

De Stefano, J.S. (1978) Language, the Learner and the School. New York: Wiley.
>Introductory books about language are still liable to concentrate upon syntax and ignore language in use. This is a welcome exception. Examples of language varieties are mainly American.

De Villiers, J.G. and de Villiers, P.A. (1978) Language Acquisition. Cambridge, Mass.: Harvard University Press.
>The most balanced, comprehensive clear, introduction to language acquisition. Cognitive rather than social emphasis.

De Villiers, J.G. and de Villiers, P.A. (1979) Early Language. London: Fontana/Open Books.
>A simplified and highly readable version of the authors' more substantial text. Compulsory reading.

Moerk, E.L. (1977) Pragmatic and Semantic Aspects of Early Language Development. Baltimore: University Park Press.
>The emphasis on pragmatics is compatible with contemporary concerns.

Waterson, N. and Snow, C. (eds) (1978) The Development of Communication. Chichester: Wiley.
>A collection of papers illustrating the kinds of questions being posed and answers being offered in respect of the communicative development in young children.

Part three
Individual Psychology

Psychometrics

The success of any scientific venture lies in its ability to offer accurate and reliable measurements of the phenomena under study. Psychology has a long psychomentric tradition: that is, a tradition of endeavouring to describe mental functioning through the use of objective, reliable tests. Advances in mathematics have led to increasingly sophisticated analyses of test scores, the intention being that such analyses should lead to complex discriminations between different patient groups and between different types of personality organization and hence allow access to the individual mind. Mental testing has evoked considerable controversy since its inception at the turn of the century. Nowhere is this debate more heated than in the field of human intelligence. Many workers argue that intelligence tests adopt a rather arbitrary (and often socially and culturally biassed) definition of 'intelligence'. Important decisions about individuals are then made on the basis of test evidence. Others object to the more general statements made about different populations of individuals on the basis of their test score patterns. It is often argued that reducing an individual to a cluster of test scores fails to capture the essential nature of being human; in the midst of statistical correlations the individuality of a person is lost.

In a great number of cases the critics of psychometrics do not acknowledge the major purposes of mental testing. Psychometric devices include indices of mental abilities (intelligence tests), personality inventories which investigate social and emotional functioning, attitude scales describing the values of different individuals, and behavioural observation scales for helping to state objectively what an individual actually does in particular situations. The techniques used include the use of personal interviews, self-report questionnaires, paper and pencil reasoning tasks, and observer rating scales. The purposes of these different types of measurement vary widely. It may be that a particular theoretical model predicts that individuals who experience high levels of anxiety in social situations can best be helped by a particular form of therapy. At the same time, in order to demonstrate the validity of this prediction, we must gain evidence about changes in the individual's anxiety during the course of therapy. Hence clinicians need valid and reliable indices of social anxiety so that a decision can be made about the most appropriate forms of therapy. It will also help clinicians to demonstrate the effectiveness of their intervention. In other cases it may be necessary to establish whether particular individuals have any specific learning difficulties at school, or whether their disruptive behaviour is mainly due to emotional factors. Here we would need a reliable measure of general school attainment together with specific measures of various learning skills. Young children who are referred to speech therapists for language or speech difficulties also require a broad range of assessments to determine whether their difficulties are general or specific. In short, the limitations of psychometric assessment are obvious; and to claim that the personalities and abilities of individuals can be fully described by a relatively simple measuring instrument is nonsense. What psychometric devices do offer is valuable information for making decisions about the extent of handicap, for assisting in the selection of appropriate treatment methods, and for collecting evidence about the value of treatments.

The success of clinical psychometric assessment depends on the validity and reliability of the devices employed. Many instruments require strict administration and rigorous scoring to satisfy the need for reliability. The ability to administer tests is a clinical skill in itself. But it is no substitute for the intelligent interpretation of what the test scores mean in practical and individual terms. Psychometric assessment of the individual case requires an understanding of the limitations of mental testing, as well as an understanding of the clinical significance of test scores.

The self

Many psychometric devices provide an opportunity to compare one individual with others along some dimension. But each individual possesses a unique view of the world which cannot lend itself easily to comparison with others. This unique aspect can be termed the 'self': that part of us which escapes ability tests or personality inventories. When we interview stutterers we may obtain an objective measurement of the severity of their dysfluency, or their anxiety levels in different situations and their personal histories; but how can we gain an objective measurement of how individuals feel, what they think about, and how they see the future? Many models of psychopathology stress the importance of gaining access to the self and assisting individuals gain insight into their own unique personalities. For many years this level of intervention was considered 'unscientific' as it required an interpretation of what particular individual experience in their personal but private consciousness. The pioneering work of George Kelly on personal construct theory offered a new view of the self, and a new means of gaining access to the self, which does not violate the principles of scientific enquiry. The use of repertory grids has now become widespread in clinical practice and particularly in the treatment of stuttering. Often this type of investigation can take place without any real appreciation of how it feels to be on the receiving end of the enquiry. Freud was amongst the first to acknowledge the possibility that a clinician's own views and biasses often colour judgements about patients, and he advocated a personal analysis for all psychoanalysts in order that these biasses would be faced and acknowledged. Whilst the influence of psychoanalysis may have waned, the fact remains that clinical workers need to examine their own prejudices and their own motivation in choosing to work with other people. Only then can patients receive a high standard of care. Self-exploration is not just for those who have problems in living, but for everyone interested in self-development and personal growth.

In chapter 6 Paul Kline discusses the issues involved in psychometric assessment and the range of assessment procedures commonly used in clinical practice. In chapter 7 Don Bannister offers some suggestions for those interested in exploring the self both as a professional clinician and as an ordinary person.

6

Personality and Individual Assessment
P. Kline

In this chapter we examine individual differences among human beings, how such differences are measured, and the psychological implications of such differences for understanding personality and behaviour. First of all we discuss psychological tests and testing techniques, for it is by the application of these measures that individual differences have been discovered.

The characteristics of good psychological tests and how these may be achieved

Efficient testing devices must be (i) reliable, (ii) valid and (iii) discriminating.

Reliability
Reliability has two meanings: first, self-consistency. Tests must be self-consistent; each item should measure the same variable. An instrument, for example, which measured in part pressure as well as temperature would not give a reliable measurement of either of these. The second meaning is consistency over time: that is, test-retest reliability. If a test is administered a second time to a person then, unless a real change has taken place, the score on the two occasions should be the same. Reliability is measured by the correlation coefficient, an index of agreement running from +1 (perfect agreement) to -1 (perfect disagreement). A correlation of 0 shows random agreement. Good tests should have a reliability coefficient of at least 0.7 which represents 49 per cent agreement (square the coefficient).

1. FACTORS INFLUENCING RELIABILITY

* Test length: it can be shown that reliability increases with the length of a test. The typical university essay exam has only four items (four essays) and is thus not highly reliable. To increase reliability, most psychological tests have a large number of items. Twenty items are about the minimum necessary for reliability.
* Objective scoring: scores should be objective: that is, there should be no personal judgement required of the scorer. Where judgement is required, as in essays, differences arise, often large, between different markers and with the same markers if they rescore the

test. A good test has items that are objectively scored.

If a test is reliable then it can be valid. Notice the 'can'. It is possible to devise a highly reliable test that measures virtually nothing. A test for measuring the length of people's noses would be easy to devise and would be highly reliable, but it is unlikely to be a valid test of intelligence or personality. On the other hand, an unreliable, inconsistent test which gives different scores on different occasions cannot possibly be valid.

Validity

A test is said to be valid if it measures what it claims to measure. This may sound obvious but many tests are quite invalid. For example, essay-type tests of scientific subjects are highly unlikely to be valid since essay writing demands verbal ability, and ability in physics is somewhat different from this. The term validity is used in psychological testing (psychometrics) in several ways.

1. FACE VALIDITY: this refers to the appearance of a test which is said to be face valid if it looks as if it measures what it claims to measure. This is important in testing adults who may balk at doing tests which look absurd. They may simply refuse to co-operate or even treat the test as a bit of a joke. Children, however, are used to overlooking such niceties. Face validity is not usually related to true validity.

2. CONCURRENT VALIDITY: this refers to studies of the validity of a test made on one occasion. For example, the concurrent validity of a new test of intelligence would be assessed by its correlation with well-established intelligence tests; does the new test give a similar score to the score on an existing test? Concurrent validity studies are beset by problems of criteria: what tests or other measurement should be used in establishing the concurrent validity of a test? If other similar tests are used, and the correlation is very high, the question arises as to what value the new test has since it is measuring the same variable as the old.

3. PREDICTIVE VALIDITY: this refers to the capacity of a test to correlate with some future criterion measure. This can be the most powerful evidence for the validity of a test. Some examples will clarify this point. A good test of anxiety should be able to predict future attendance at the psychiatric clinic, and a good test of intelligence given at 11 years of age should correlate with future academic performance in GCE examinations and subsequently. Thus the test predicts events external to itself.

4. CONSTRUCT VALIDITY: the construct validity of a test

is defined by taking a large set of results obtained with the test and seeing how well they fit in with our notion of the psychological nature of the variable which the test claims to measure. Thus it embraces concurrent and predictive validity. In effect, we set up a series of hypotheses concerning the test results and put these to the test. For example, if our test was a valid measure of intelligence we might expect:

* high-level professional groups would score more highly than lower-level professionals;
* children rated highly intelligent by teachers would score more highly than others;
* scores would correlate positively with level of education;
* scores would correlate highly with scores in public examinations;
* scores would correlate highly with scores on other intelligence tests;
* scores would not correlate with scores on tests not claiming to measure intelligence.

If all these hypotheses were supported then the construct validity of our test would be demonstrated. It is deserving of note that it is always useful to show (as in the final point above) what tests do not measure, a technique used by Socrates in his examination of the meaning of words.

Unlike reliability, for which there can be clear unequivocal evidence, the validity of a test is to some extent subjective. Nevertheless, most well-known tests, especially of ability, have now accumulated so much evidence relating to validity that there is no dispute about them. It is more difficult to demonstrate the validity of personality tests but, as we see later, it can be done. Many psychological tests have little support for their validity and a large number are clearly invalid.

Discriminatory power

Good psychological tests should be discriminating: that is, they should produce a wide distribution of scores. For example, if we test 10 children and all score 15 we have made no discriminations at all. If four score 13, three score 12 and three score 14 then we have made only three discriminations. If, on the other hand, each child scores a different score, then the distribution of scores is wide. The scatter of scores in a distribution is known as the variance and the standard deviation is the usual measurement. A good test has a large standard deviation.

With reliable, valid and discriminating tests it is possible to investigate the nature of individual differences in human beings. In fact, this has been going on since the turn of the century when Binet began the assessment of the educability of Parisian children.

Types of tests and categories of individual differences

Individual differences among human beings fall into relatively independent categories for which different types of tests have been developed.

Intelligence and ability tests

The most important ability as studied by psychometrists is general intelligence, the ability to educe correlates; a general reasoning ability which underlies much problem-solving ability. Modern studies of this general reasoning factor (e.g. Cattell, 1971) tend to reveal two aspects: (i) fluid ability which is close to inherited reasoning ability; and (ii) crystallized ability, which is fluid ability as it is evinced in a culture. The old-fashioned 11+ intelligence tests were largely concerned with crystallized ability. More will be said later about intelligence.

Other typical abilities are: verbal ability, V; numerical ability, N; and spatial ability, K. Performance on various tasks will depend upon our status on these variables. For example, a writer and an engineer may both score much the same on general intelligence, but on verbal ability the writer should be higher, whereas on numerical and spatial ability the engineer should be superior. Intelligence can be thought of as a general factor, while verbal and numerical ability are group factors. Intelligence plays its part in almost all skills, while verbal ability is involved only in certain groups. Some factors are more narrow than this; auditory pitch discrimination would be an example.

Aptitude tests

Aptitude tests comprise a group of tests related to tests of ability. Aptitude tests tend to be of two different kinds. One type may be identical with the group tests discussed above. Thus it would be difficult to distinguish between verbal ability and verbal aptitude. However, computer aptitude tests are clearly different; they should test the collection of traits (perhaps more than just abilities) necessary for this particular job. In some instances, such as clerical aptitude, the necessary skills are quite disparate and unrelated to each other. Generally, aptitude tests measure the separate abilities demonstrated to be important for a particular job or class of jobs.

Personality tests

Personality tests can be divided into tests of temperament, mood and dynamics. Temperament tests measure how we do what we do. Temperamental traits, such as dominance or anxiety, are usually thought of as enduring and stable. Dynamic traits are concerned with motives; why we do what we do. These attempt to measure drives such as sexuality or pugnacity. Moods refer to those fluctuating states that we all experience in our lives: anger, fatigue or fear.

Temperament tests

The most used type of temperament test is the personality

questionnaire. These consist of lists of items concerned with the subject's behaviour. Typical items are: do you enjoy watching boxing? Do you hesitate before spending a large sum of money? Items come in various formats. Those above would usually require subjects to respond 'Yes' or 'No'; or 'Yes', 'Uncertain' or 'No'. Sometimes items are of the forced choice variety; for example, 'Do you prefer: (i) watching boxing; (ii) going to a musical; or (iii) sitting quietly at home reading?'

The disadvantages of questionnaires are considerable, yet in spite of them many valid and highly useful personality questionnaires have been constructed. These disadvantages are outlined below.

*   They are easy to fake: that is, subjects may not tell the truth for one reason or another. This makes them difficult to use in selection, although for vocational guidance or psychiatric help, where subjects have no reason to fake, this is not too serious.
*   They require a degree of self-knowledge and some subjects, while attempting to be honest, may respond quite unrealistically.
*   They are subject to response sets. An important set is social desirability, the tendency to endorse the socially desirable response. People like to present themselves in the best possible light. For example, to the item 'Do you have a good sense of humour?', the response 'Yes' would be given by about 95 per cent of subjects. The other serious response set is that of acquiescence; the tendency to put 'Yes' or 'Agree' to an answer, regardless of content. Balanced scales, with some responses keyed 'No', obviate this to some extent.

OBJECTIVE TESTS: these, defined by Cattell (cf. Cattell and Kline, 1977) as tests of which the purpose is hidden from the subject and which can be objectively scored (see the section on reliability), have been developed to overcome the disadvantages of questionnaires. Ironically, because their purpose is hidden from subjects, considerable research is necessary to establish their validity and as yet most are still in an experimental form. These tests will probably take over from questionnaires when the necessary research has been done. The following examples indicate their nature.

*   Balloon blowing: subjects are required to inflate a balloon as much as they can. Measures taken are the size of the balloon, time taken in blowing it up, whether they burst it, and delay in beginning the task. This test may be related to timidity and inhibition.
*   The slow-line drawing test: subjects are required to draw a line as slowly as possible. The measure is the length of line over a fixed time.

In fact more than 800 such tests have been listed and more can easily be developed, depending upon the ingenuity of the researcher. The technique is to administer a large battery of such tests and to determine experimentally by so-called validity studies what each of them measures.

PROJECTIVE TESTS: these essentially consist of ambiguous stimuli to which the subjects have to respond. These are some of the oldest personality tests and one, the Rorschach test (the inkblot test), has achieved a fame beyond psychology. The rationale of projective tests is intuitively brilliant: if a stimulus is so vague that it warrants no particular description, then any description of it must depend on what is projected on to it by the subject. Projective testers believe that projective tests measure the inner needs and fantasies of their subjects.

A serious problem with projective tests lies in their unreliability. Responses have to be interpreted by scorers and often considerable training, experience and expertise is necessary. Inter-marker reliability is low. Generally, too, it is difficult to demonstrate test validity. However, the present writer has experimented with entirely objective forms of scoring these tests and some evidence has now accrued that this is a useful procedure.

PROJECTIVE TEST STIMULI: although any ambiguous stimulus could be used as a test, the choice of stimulus is generally determined by the particular theory of personality which the test constructor follows. For example, a psychoanalytically-orientated psychologist would select stimuli relevant to that theory, such as vague figures who could be mother and son (the Oedipus complex) or figures with knives or scissors (the castration complex). The TAT (Thematic Apperception Test) developed by Murray uses pictures which, it is hoped, tap the inner needs held by Murray to be paramount in human behaviour.

Mood and motivation tests
Mood and motivation tests are essentially similar to temperament tests, but relatively little work has been done with these and their validity is not so widely attested as that of temperament tests.

Mood tests generally use items that concentrate, as might be expected, on present feelings rather than on usual ones. With these, high test-retest reliability is not to be expected. However, fluctuations in scores should not be random but should be related to external conditions. Thus experiments can be conducted in which the tests, if they are valid, can be retaken. If the experimental manipulations are good and the tests valid, the relevant scores should change in response to these changes in mood.

The results of motivation tests should be similarly fluctuating, according to whether drives are satisfied or frustrated. In one study the scores of a single subject over a 28-day period were related to a diary recording all that happened to her and everything she felt or thought (Kline and Grindley, 1974). In fact, the relation of scores to diary events was close. For example, the fear drive rose each weekend when the subject went touring in a dangerous car. The career drive was flat except on the day when the subject was interviewed for a course in teacher-training, and so on.

Motivation tests can be of the questionnaire variety, although objective and projective tests are more frequently used. For moods, questionnaire tests are more usually employed though they suffer, of course, from the same response sets as bedevil questionnaire measures of temperamental traits.

Interest tests

The tests of motivation described above are very general: that is, they measure variables thought to account for a wide variety of human behaviour. Vocational and industrial psychologists, however, have long felt the need for more specific measures of motivation, assessing the variables which seemed of immediate relevance to them: for instance, interests. We all know of motoring enthusiasts who seem to have an all-embracing interest in cars, which seems to account for much of their behaviour and conversation.

A number of interest tests have been developed which attempt to assess the major interests such as outdoor, mechanical, or interest in people. In some tests, the scoring of items is in terms of occupational groups. The performance of particular occupational groups on the tests is known and if, for example, foresters score high on a particular item then this item contributes to the 'interest in forestry' score. In other tests, the scoring involves little more than subjects having to rank jobs. In other words, interest tests of this type are like formalized interviews.

Generally, the correlations of interest test scores with success in a job relevant to those interests are modest and little better than the correlation obtained between job success and the subject's response to the question of whether the job would be enjoyable or not.

Attitude tests

Social psychologists have attempted to measure attitudes for many years now. Usually, the attitudes tested apply to important aspects of an idnividual's life: for example, attitudes to war, or to coloured people (in white populations) or to religion. Obviously, if efficient measures of such attitudes are possible then progress can be made in understanding how such attitudes arise or are maintained; important knowledge, it is thought, in a complex multi-racial society. There are three kinds of attitude test, differing in their mode of construction.

1. THE THURSTONE SCALES: in these tests items are given to the judges to rank 1-11 (favourable-unfavourable) in respect of an attitude. Items on which there is good agreement among the judges are then retained. The subject then taking the test is given the highest judged rank score of the items with which he agrees. The reason for this is clear if we consider a few examples. (1) 'War is totally evil' would probably be ranked high as unfavourable to war. (2) 'Wars sometimes have to be fought if there is no alternative': this is clearly against war, but not strongly. (3) 'Wars are not always wrong': this is yet further down the scale, while the item (4) 'Wars are good: they select the finest nations' is favourable. Thus a subject who agreed with (1) would not agree with (2), (3) or (4). Similarly, a subject agreeing with (3) would not agree with (4). These tests are difficult to construct because much depends on obtaining a good cross-section of judges. A more simple alternative is the Likert scale.

2. LIKERT SCALES: in the Likert scales statements relevant to the attitude being measured are presented to the subject who has to state on a five-point scale the extent of his agreement. Thus a 'Hitler' would score 100 on a 20-item attitude to war scale. A 'Ghandi' would score zero, one presumes. To make the scale less obvious, items are so written that to agree with items represents both poles of the attitude.

3. THE GUTTMAN SCALE: this is a scale constructed so that if the items are ranked for positive attitude, then any subject who endorses item 10 will also endorse items 1-9 below it. While this tends to happen by nature of its construction with the Thurstone scale, such perfect ordering of items can usually only be achieved by leaving huge gaps between the items (in terms of attitude) which means few items and rather coarse measurement.

Such, then are the main types of psychological tests with which individual differences are measured in psychology. Needless to say, these are not the only kinds of test. In the remainder of this chapter we briefly describe some intelligence tests, discuss some of the substantive findings that have emerged from these tests and examine their application in practical psychology.

Intelligence tests

Intelligence has been most widely studied of all test variables and, since it is a topic of considerable importance in applied psychology and education, let us examine in detail some intelligence tests to help us to understand the nature of intelligence as conceptualized by psychologists.

Individual intelligence tests

Some intelligence tests are given to subjects individually. This enables the tester to measure not only the intelligence of the subject but also to see whether a child panics at difficulties or goes on and on obsessionally even when it is obvious that no solution will result. Similarly, it can be seen whether an individual is easily distracted, and all this is valuable in attempting to understand any educational difficulties which may arise.

The WISC

The Wechsler Intelligence Scale, WISC (Wechsler, 1938), consists of the following sub-tests which fall into two groups: verbal tests and non-verbal tests. A total IQ score is obtainable, as are a verbal IQ and a performance IQ. Large differences between these two sub-scores are of some psychological interest and call for further study. Some of our examples are taken from Kline (1976).

1. THE VERBAL TESTS

* Vocabulary: a straightforward vocabulary test. Vocabulary is highly related to intelligence although social class differences in reading habits do, obviously, affect this particular sub-test. Nevertheless, if forced to make a selection of intelligent children or adults as quickly as possible, the vocabulary sub-test would be about the best measure obtainable.
* Information: a test of general knowledge.
* Arithmetic: an ordinary arithmetic test.

These three tests are heavily affected by school learning and social class. They therefore reflect what Cattell called crystallized intelligence, or the result of cultural influences upon innate ability.

* Comprehension: this is an interesting test because it presents problems which are dependent upon how much the child is capable of making sensible decisions on its own initiative. One example (which is not in the test) might be a question like 'What would you do if you saw a burglar in the house next door?' Two points would be scored by a response such as 'Phone the police - dial 999'; one point by the response 'Run and tell Mummy', and no points by 'Shoot him with my bow and arrow' or 'Push his car over'. At the higher level this sub-test requires abstract analytical reasoning on such questions as 'Why is there a Hippocratic oath?'
* Similarities: a common form of intelligence test item, simple to write and easy to vary the level of difficulty. For example, 'What is similar about peaches and prunes?' The correct response requires that the essential similarity (fruit) is recognized.
* Digit span (forward and reverse): digits are read out and the subjects repeat them immediately. Seven or eight digits is the usual span for bright adults.

In the majority of cases most psychologists give five of the six tests, the last two of which in part measure fluid ability.

2. THE NON-VERBAL TESTS: these are generally quite novel to most subjects, so they are more a measure of fluid (inherited) ability than are the verbal tests. Large disparities between the verbal and performance score are often found in middle-class children whose upbringing is highly verbal. The performance sub-tests are as follows.

* Block design: patterns are presented to the child in a booklet and he must then make them up by arranging building blocks such that their top surfaces represent the pattern. This test can be made of varying difficulty. It is also one which indicates well how a child tackles a strange problem.
* Picture arrangement: here series of strip cartoons tell stories. Each series is presented in jumbled order and the child must put them in their correct sequence: a neat way of testing a child's ability to work out the relationships involved.
* Object assembly: this is a timed jigsaw-like task of arranging broken patterns.
* Mazes: the child is required to trace the way through pencil and paper mazes.
* Coding: here the key to a simple cipher system is given. The child then completes as many examples as possible (presented in random order) in a fixed time.
* Picture completion: pictures with a missing element, often only a small detail, are shown to the subject who is required to spot this.

This, then, is the Wechsler Intelligence Scale, one of the standard individual intelligence tests. The verbal and performance IQ scores are highly reliable, as is the total score: all around 0.9 or beyond.

The WISC is an individual test. It is obviously not suitable for group administration. Let us now look at some item types used in group intelligence tests (rather than examine any one test in detail) since these are widely used in applied psychology.

Group intelligence tests

Items can be verbal or non-verbal, testing largely fluid or crystallized ability.

1. ANALOGIES

Easy: a is to c as g is to ...
              sparrow is to bird as mouse is to ...

Difficult: Samson Agonistes is to Comus as the Bacchae are to ...

With analogy items all kinds of relationships may be tested, as in the examples where we find sequence, classification, double classification (by author and type of play, for example), and opposites. Analogy is thus a useful form for encapsulating a wide variety of relationships. We can use shapes for this type of item, as distinct from verbal forms.

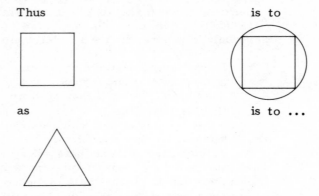

Thus ... is to ...

as ... is to ...

Here we would supply possible answers in multiple choice form, for example:

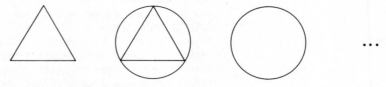

...

2. ODD-MEN-OUT

Odd-men-out items also allow us to test wide varieties of relationships in many materials. Some examples are given below.

* carrot, turnip, swede, beetroot, cabbage
* valley, coomb, hillock, gorge, chasm
* early, greasy, messy, swiftly, furry

For these three examples some knowledge is required of vegetables, geography and grammar, but this alone is not enough.

3. SIMILARITIES

These are essentially the same item form (where the common relationship must be worked out), but are more difficult to write for a group test, because the multiple choice answer will give the game away.

Non-verbal odd-men-out items are simple to produce; see the following examples.

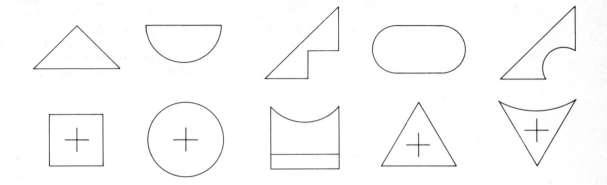

4. SEQUENCES AND MATRICES

Numbers, of course, offer easy ways of creating complex relationships without needing any special knowledge of mathematics and hence sequences are a useful item form. For example, 20, 40, 60, 80 ... is entirely unequivocal. Sequences allow also for the development of highly complex or multiple relationships.

A matrix involving several sequences might be of the following form:

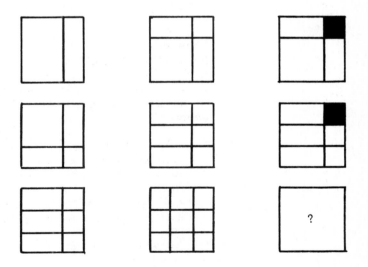

followed by a multiple choice

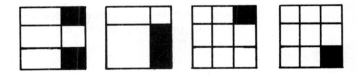

Raven's Matrices is an example of a test composed entirely of such sets of non-verbal items. Many forms have been produced and it is capable of extending the intelligence of subjects from about five years upwards to the limits. It is one of the best single measures of fluid ability. Despite its non-verbal appearance, however, it is related to some extent to verbal ability, presumably because verbalization improves performance.

These, then are typical items in tests of intelligence. From our description of these and of the WISC scale, it should be possible to get an insight into what it is that intelligence tests measure.

We have concentrated on intelligence tests in our more detailed study of tests because they have been at the centre of so much controversy, both in respect of their use as selection devices for secondary school education and more recently in respect of the heritability of success in these tests. It is to this latter topic, which is of great social importance and intellectual interest, that we now turn, a further reason for ensuring that the nature of such tests is fully appreciated.

The heritability of intelligence test scores

This is so large and complex a subject that inevitably our summary must be somewhat assertive and dogmatic. To make it even more difficult, well-known writers reviewing the same evidence come to opposite conclusions. For example, Cattell (1971) and Eysenck (1971) conclude that about 80 per cent of the variance in intelligence test scores is heritable, at least in the west. Kamin (1974), reviewing the same evidence, comes to the conclusion that there are no sound data to reject the hypothesis that differences in test scores are determined by different life experiences.

To make our discussion of this matter comprehensible rather than comprehensive let us first establish a number of important points.

* All results of heritability studies refer only to the population from which the sample was drawn. Thus results in Great Britain are not applicable in other cultures. If culture has any effect, then in a country with a diverse cultural background (such as India) the heritability index would be smaller than in a more homogeneous culture.
* All workers in the field argue that there is an interaction between genetic and environmental determinants of intelligence test scores. Where there is disagreement is in the matter of how large is the influence of each factor.
* In principle, an ideal method of studying the topic is to investigate the differences in intelligence test scores of monozygotic twins (i.e. twins with the same genetic endowment) reared apart. All differences in test scores within such pairs must be environmentally

determined (ignoring differential effects of placental deprivations, etc., in such pairs which would exaggerate any differences).

Critics of this approach argue that it is vitiated by the fact that twins are, by definition, a different population from singleton children. Furthermore, there is a tendency for identical twins to be placed in foster homes similar to each other, thus making their scores similar.

* Burt carried out the most extensive twin studies. His data, however, must be ignored. It appears, alas, that he doctored the figures.
* However, other twin studies show the same results, namely that in America and Great Britain there is a substantial hereditary component in the determination of test scores, the critical finding being that identical twins reared apart show less differences in intelligence test scores than do non-identical twins reared together.
* Kamin's (1974) arguments attempting to refute these results are statistically weak, as has been fully exposed by Fulker (1975).
* More sophisticated methods of statistical analyses known as biometric genetic methods, which have been demonstrated as powerful in animal work, have been employed in the study of human intelligence test scores. These can assess the kind of gene action and the mating system in the population by analysing within and between family differences and their interactions. The results of these methods are difficult to impugn and it appears from such studies that: (i) around 70 per cent of the variance in IQ score is heritable in Great Britain and the USA; (ii) there is a polygenic dominance for IQ and that assortative mating is an important influence.
* Such biometric methods can be applied to any variable to reveal its heritability. The major personality variables such as extraversion, neuroticism and psychoticism, are also similarly highly genetically determined.

The factorial description of personality

Factor analysis is a statistical technique for simplifying correlations: this is extremely useful in the study of personality by questionnaires, of which there are very large numbers. Factor analysis reveals dimensions which can mathematically account for the observed correlations. For example, almost all tests of ability are highly correlated together. Factor analysis reveals that this is largely due to the operation of two related factors: fluid and crystallized ability.

Personality questionnaires have been subjected, over the years, to factor analyses in the hope of discovering what are the basic temperamental dimensions. The main researchers in this area have been Cattell (working in Illinois), Eysenck (in London), both students of Burt, and Guilford (in

California). Although superficially each has produced what looks like a separate set of factors, recent research in this field has enabled some sort of consensus to be arrived at (see Cattell and Kline, 1977, and Kline, 1979, for a full discussion of this work). In effect, the study of individual differences has led to the establishment of the main dimensions of personality. These dimensions are therefore those that demand study. They are outlined below.

Extraversion

The high-scoring extravert is sociable, cheerful, talkative and does not like to be alone. He enjoys excitement, takes risks and is generally impulsive: an outgoing optimist, active and lively. The introvert is the opposite of this: cold, retiring and aloof. This dimension has been related by Eysenck to the arousability of the central nervous system. Scores on tests of this factor have a large genetic component.

Neuroticism (or anxiety)

The highly anxious subject is one who worries a lot, is moody and often depressed. He is highly emotional and takes a long time to calm down. He tends to sleep poorly and to suffer from psychosomatic disorders. This variable is claimed to be related to the lability of the autonomic nervous system. These variables are both measured by the Cattell 16PF test and Eysenck's EPQ. If we know an individual's status on these two factors, then already we know a good deal about his temperament.

Psychoticism

This variable has not been as extensively studied as extraversion and anxiety and only recently (1975) has it appeared in a published questionnaire: the EPQ. Nevertheless, the nature of psychoticism is clear. The high scorer on this dimension is solitary, uncaring of people, troublesome, lacking in human feeling and empathy, thick skinned and insensitive. He is cruel, inhumane, hostile and aggressive, reckless to danger, and aggressive even to his own family. Naturally enough, most normals score low on P but many criminals score high. This factor has been related by Eysenck to masculinity, and to be related to levels of male sex hormones.

It is to be noted that these three factors have not only been clearly identified from the factor analysis of questionnaires: there is also a considerable mass of experimental data supporting their identification and nature.

These are the three second-order factors claimed by Eysenck to be the most important in accounting for temperamental differences. (Second-order factors are factors arising from the correlations among first-order factors; i.e. the factors accounting for the original correlations.) The first-order or primary factors are more problematic than the second-orders but, as the work of Cattell has shown, can be of considerable power in applied psychometrics.

In brief, the factorial analysis of personality has revealed three basic dimensions, each tied to the basic physiology of Man and hence largely heritable.

The application of findings in applied psychology

The study of individual differences, described in this chapter, has implicit within it a model of Man which might be called the psychometric model. Explanation of this model, which is remarkably simple, will make the application of results obvious.

The implicit psychometric model

This model states that any given piece of behaviour is related to that individual's status on the main factors in the sphere of ability, temperament, motivation and mood. This model does not ignore past experience because this itself affects status on these variables. The psychometric model is therefore a variant of a trait model of behaviour. Thus, for example, performance on GCE examinations depends upon intelligence, verbal and numerical ability, extraversion, anxiety, psychoticism, mood at the time of taking the exam and the various motivation variables discussed above (to take the main variables). Obviously, for different behaviours (e.g. exam passing and serving well behind a bar) different weights for each of the factors is required.

How important each factor is - that is, what its weight is - has to be determined empirically. In fact, the statistical technique of multiple correlation or regression does this precisely. Thus, the argument runs, we put all the test variables into a multiple correlation with the criterion and these are then weighted to achieve the highest possible correlation. These weights (beta weights) indicate the relative importance of the variable for the behaviour in question. Cattell and Butcher (1968) have done exactly this with academic success both in America and Great Britain and found multiple correlations around 0.7.

Thus in educational guidance and selection we find the beta weights of the variables and select and guide children accordingly. If X, Y and Z have the highest weights for academic success, then we select and encourage children high on these variables. In industrial psychology, we can choose and guide people to various jobs according to their scores on the highest weighted variables. In clinical psychology, too, we can find the tests most related to psychiatric breakdown or diagnose into clinical groups. Then we know who in the population is at risk and can avoid putting them into stressful conditions.

References

Cattell, R.B. (1971)
Abilities: Their structure, growth and action. New York: Houghton-Mifflin.
Cattell, R.B. and Butcher, H.J. (1968)
The Prediction of Achievement and Creativity. New York: Bobbs Merrill.

Cattell, R.B. and Kline, P. (1977)
   The Scientific Analysis of Personality and Motivation.
   London: Academic Press.
Eysenck, H.J. (1971)
   Race, Intelligence and Education. London: Temple-
   Smith.
Fulker, D. (1975)
   The science and politics of IQ. American Journal of
   Psychology, 88, 505-537.
Kamin, L.J. (1974)
   The science and politics of IQ. Harmondsworth: Penguin.
Kline, P. (1976)
   Psychological Testing. London: Malaby Press.
Kline, P. (1979)
   Psychometrics and Psychology. London: Academic Press.
Kline, P. and Grindley, J. (1974)
   A 28-day case study with the MAT. Journal of
   Multivariate Clinical Experimental Psychology, 1, 13-32.
Wechsler, D. (1938)
   The Wechsler Intelligence Scale for Children. New York:
   Psychological Corporation.

Questions

1. What is meant by test reliability, and why should psychological tests be reliable?
2. What is the meaning of test validity?
3. What factors contribute to the efficiency of psychological tests?
4. What are the main types of psychological test? Give a brief description of them.
5. Compare projective and questionnaire personality tests.
6. Discuss the main types of attitude tests.
7. Outline the main arguments concerning the heritability of intelligence.
8. Discuss the concept of intelligence as factorially defined.
9. What are the main factors of personality?
10. Compare the work of Eysenck and Cattell on the factor analysis of personality.
11. Give a simple description of factor analysis.
12. If individuals are unique, how can they be measured by tests of universal dimensions?
13. If individuals are unique, how can there be a science of personality?

Annotated reading

Cattell, R.B. and Kline, P. (1977) The Scientific Analysis of Personality and Motivation. London: Academic Press.
   A full account of the factor analysis of personality where the results are related to clinical theories.

Cronbach, L. (1976) Essentials of Psychological Testing. Chicago: Harper & Row.
   A clear comprehensive discussion of psychological testing and tests.

Freud, S. (1978) New Introductory Lectures. Harmondsworth: Penguin.

A brilliantly told account of Freudian theory by the Master himself.

Hall, G.S. and Lindzey, G. (1973) Theories of Personality. New York: Wiley.

A good summary of a variety of personality theories.

Vernon, P.E. (1979) Intelligence, Heredity and Environment. San Francisco: Freeman.

Vernon is well-known for his balanced account of issues relating to intelligence, its measurement, and social significance. This is one of the most recent reviews of topics in the field and is written in a lucid style.

7

Knowledge of Self
D. Bannister

Definition is a social undertaking. As a community we
negotiate the meaning of words. This makes 'self' a
peculiarly difficult term to define, since much of the
meaning we attach to it derives from essentially private
experiences of a kind which are difficult to communicate
about and agree upon. Nevertheless, we can try to abstract
from our private experience of self qualities which can
constitute a working definition. Such an attempt was made
by Bannister and Fransella (1980) in the following terms.

**Each of us entertains a notion of our own separateness from
others and relies on the essential privacy of our own
consciousness**
Consider differences between the way in which you communicate with yourself and the way in which you communicate with
others. To communicate with others involves externalizing
(and thereby blurring) your experience into forms of speech,
arm waving, gift giving, sulking, writing and so on. Yet
communicating with yourself is so easy that it seems not to
merit the word communication: it is more like instant recognition. Additionally, communicating with specific others
involves the risk of being overheard, spied upon or having
your messages intercepted and this contrasts with our
internal communications which are secret and safeguarded.
Most importantly, we experience our internal communications
as the origin and starting point of things. We believe that
it is out of them that we construct communications with
others. We know this when we tell a lie because we are aware
of the difference between our experienced internal communication and the special distortions given it before transmission.

**We entertain a notion of the integrity and completeness of
our own experience in that we believe all parts of it to be
relatable because we are, in some vital sense, the
experience itself**
We extend the notion of me into the notion of my world. We
think of events as more or less relevant to us. We distinguish between what concerns and what does not concern us.
In this way we can use the phrase 'my situation' to indicate
the boundaries of our important experience and the ways in

which the various parts of it relate to make up a personal world.

We entertain the notion of our own continuity over time; we possess our biography and we live in relation to it

We live along a time line. We believe that we are essentially the 'same' person now that we were five minutes ago or five years ago. We accept that our circumstances may have changed in this or that respect, but we have a feeling of continuity, we possess a 'life'. We extend this to imagine a continuing future life. We can see our history in a variety of ways, but how we see it, the way in which we interpret it, is a central part of our character.

We entertain a notion of ourselves as causes; we have purposes, we intend, we accept a partial responsibility for the consequences of our actions

Just as we believe that we possess our life, so we think of ourselves as making 'choices' and as being identified by our choices. Even those psychologists who (in their professional writing) describe humankind as wholly determined, and persons as entirely the products of their environments, talk personally in terms of their own intentions and purposive acts and are prepared to accept responsibility, when challenged, for the choices they have made.

We work towards a notion of other persons by analogy with ourselves; we assume a comparability of subjective experience

If we accept for the moment the personal construct theory argument (Kelly, 1955, 1969) and think not simply of 'self' but of the bipolar construct of self versus others, then this draws our attention to the way in which we can only define self by distinguishing it from and comparing it to others. Yet this distinction between self and others also implies that others can be seen in the same terms, as 'persons' or as 'selves'. Our working assumption is that the rest of humankind have experiences which are somehow comparable with, although not the same as, our own and thereby we reasonably assume that they experience themselves as 'selves'.

We reflect, we are conscious, we are aware of self

Everything that has been said so far is by way of reflecting, standing back and viewing self. We both experience and reflect upon our experience, summarize it, comment on it and analyse it. This capacity to reflect is both the source of our commentary on self and a central part of the experience of being a 'self'. Psychologists sometimes, rather quaintly, talk of 'consciousness' as a problem. They see consciousness as a mystery which might best be dealt with by ignoring it and regarding people as mechanisms without awareness. This seems curious when we reflect that, were it not for this problematical consciousness, there would be no psychology to have problems to argue about. Psychology itself is a direct expression of consciousness. Mead (1925) elaborated this point in terms of the difference between 'I' and 'me', referring to the 'I' who acts and the 'me' who reflects upon the action and can go on to reflect upon the 'me' reflecting on the action.

Do we or do we not know ourselves?

The question 'do you know yourself?' seems to call forth a categorical 'yes' by way of answer. We know, in complete and sometimes painful detail, what has happened to us, what we have to contend with and what our thoughts and feelings are. We can reasonably claim to sit inside ourselves and know what is going on.

Yet we all have kinds of experience which cast doubt on the idea that we completely know ourselves. A basic test (in science and personal life) of whether you understand someone is your ability to predict accurately what they will do in a given situation. Yet most of us come across situations where we fail to predict our own behaviour; we find ourselves surprised by it and see ourselves behaving in a way we would not have expected to behave if we were the sort of person we thought we were.

We also sense that not all aspects of ourselves are equally accessible to us. There is nothing very mysterious in the notion of a hidden storehouse. We can confirm it very simply by reference to what we can readily draw from it. If I ask you to think about what kind of clothes you wore when you were around 14 years old you can probably bring some kind of image to mind. That raises the obvious question: where was that knowledge of yourself a minute ago, before I asked you the question? We are accustomed to having a vast knowledge of ourselves which is not consciously in front of us all the time. It is stored. It is not a great step to add to that picture the possibility that some parts of the 'store' of your past may not be so easily brought to the surface. We can then go one stage further and argue that although parts of your past are not easily brought to the surface they may nevertheless influence the present ways in which you feel and behave.

The best known picture of this kind of process is the Freudian portrait of the unconscious. Freud portrayed the self as divided. He saw it as made up of an id, the source of our primitive sexual and aggressive drives; a super-ego, our learned morality, our inhibitions; and an ego, our conscious self, struggling to maintain some kind of balance between the driving force of the id and the controlling force of the super-ego. Freud argued that the id is entirely unconscious and a great deal of the super-ego is also unconscious, and that only very special strategies such as those used in psychoanalytic therapy can give access to the contents of these unconscious areas of self. We do not have to accept Freud's particular thesis in order to accept the idea of different levels of awareness, but it may well be that the enormous popularity of Freudian theory is due to the fact that it depicts what most of us feel is a 'probable' state of affairs; namely, that we have much more going on in us than we can readily be aware of or name.

Indeed, if we examine our everyday experience then we may well conclude that we are continually becoming aware of aspects of ourselves previously hidden from us.

A great deal of psychotherapy, education and personal and interpersonal soul-searching is dedicated to bringing to the surface hitherto unrecognized consistencies in our lives.

How do we know ourselves?

There is evidence that getting to know ourselves is a developmental process: it is something we learn in the same way that we learn to walk, talk and relate to others. In one study (Bannister and Agnew, 1977), groups of children were tape-recorded answering a variety of questions about their school, home, favourite games and so forth. These tape-recordings were transcribed and re-recorded in different voices so as to exclude circumstantial clues (names, occupations of parents and so forth) as to the identity of the children. Four months after the original recording the same children were asked to identify their own statements, to point out which statements were definitely not theirs and to give reasons for their choice. The children's ability to recognize their own statements increased steadily with age, and the strategies they used to pick out their own answers changed and became more complex. Thus, at the age of five, children relied heavily on their (often inaccurate) memory or used simple clues such as whether they themselves undertook the kinds of activity mentioned in the statement; 'That boy says he plays football and I play football so I must have said that'. By the age of nine, they were using more psychologically complex methods to identify which statements they had made and which statements they had not made. For example, one boy picked out the statement 'I want to be a soldier when I grow up' as definitely not his because 'I don't think I could ever kill a human being so I wouldn't say I wanted to be a soldier'. This is clearly a psychological inference of a fairly elaborate kind.

Underlying our notions about ourselves and other people are personal psychological theories which roughly parallel those put forward in formal psychology. A common kind of theory is what would be called in formal psychology a 'trait theory'. Trait theories hinge on the argument that there are, in each of us, enduring characteristics which differentiate us from others, who have more or less of these characteristics. The notion that we or someone else is 'bad-tempered' is closely akin to the notion in formal psychology that some people are constitutionally 'introverted' or 'authoritarian' and so forth. The problem with trait descriptions is that they are not explanatory. They are a kind of tautology which says that a person behaves in a bad-tempered way because he is a bad-tempered kind of person.

Such approaches tend to distract our attention from what is going on between us and other people by firmly lodging 'causes' in either us or the other person. If I say that I am angry with you because I am 'a bad-tempered person' that relieves me of the need to understand what is going on specifically between you and me that is making me angry.

Environmental and learning theories in psychology have their equivalents in our everyday arguments about our own nature. The fundamental assertion of stimulus-response psychology, that a person can be seen as reacting to his environment in terms of previously learnt patterns of response, is mirrored in our own talk when we offer as grounds for our actions that it is all 'due to the way I was brought up' or 'there was nothing else I could do in the circumstances'. Those theories and approaches in formal psychology which treat the person as a mechanism echo the kinds of explanation which we offer for our own behaviour when we are most eager to excuse it, to deny our responsibility for it and to argue that we cannot be expected to change.

Any theory or attempt to explain how we come to be what we are and how we change involves us in the question of what kind of evidence we use. Kelly (1955) argued that we derive our picture of ourselves through the picture which we have of other people's picture of us. He was arguing here that the central evidence we use in understanding ourselves is other people's reactions to us, both what they say of us and the implications of their behaviour towards us. He was not saying that we simply take other people's views of us as gospel. Obviously this would be impossible because people have very varying and often very disparate reactions to us. He argued that we filter others' views of us through our view of them. If someone you consider excessively rash and impulsive says that you are a conventional mouse, you might be inclined to dismiss their estimate on the grounds that they see everyone who is not perpetually swinging from the chandelier as being a conventional mouse. However, if someone you consider very docile and timid says that you are a conventional mouse, then this has quite different implications. You do not come to understand yourself simply by contemplating your own navel or even by analysing your own history. You build up a continuous and changing picture of yourself out of your interaction with other people.

Do we change ourselves?

That we change in small ways seems obvious enough. Looking at ourselves or others we readily notice changes in preferred style of dress, taste in films or food, changes in interests and hobbies, the gaining of new skills and the rusting of old and so forth.

Whether we change in large ways as well as small involves us in the question of how we define 'large' and 'small' change. Kelly (1955) hypothesized that each of us has a 'theory' about ourselves, about other people, and about the nature of the world, a theory which he referred to as our personal construct system. Constructs are our ways of discriminating our world. For many of them we have overt labels such as nice-nasty, ugly-beautiful, cheap-expensive, north-south, trustworthy-untrustworthy and so forth. He also distinguished between superordinate and subordinate constructs. Superordinate constructs are those which govern large areas of our life and which refer to matters of central concern to us, while subordinate constructs govern the minor detail of our lives.

If we take constructs about 'change in dress' at a subordinate level then we refer simply to our tendency to switch from sober to bright colours, from wide lapels to narrow lapels and so forth. If we look at such changes superordinately then we can make more far-reaching distinctions. For example, we might see ourselves as having made many subordinate changes in dress while not changing superordinately because we have always 'followed fashion'. Thus at this level of abstraction there is no change because the multitude of our minor changes are always governed and controlled by our refusal to make a major change, that is, to dress independently of fashion.

Psychologists differ greatly in their view of how much change takes place in people and how it takes place. Trait psychologists tend to set up the notion of fixed personality characteristics which remain with people all their lives, which are measurable and which will predict their behaviour to a fair degree in any given situation. The evidence for this view has been much attacked (e.g. Mischel, 1968). Direct examination of personal experience suggests that Kelly (1955) may have been right in referring to 'man as a form of motion and not a static object that is occasionally kicked into movement'.

Psychological measurement, to date, suggests that people change their character, if only slowly, and have complex natures so that behaviour is not easily predictable from one situation to another. Psychologists have also tended to argue that where change takes place it is often unconscious and unchosen by the person. The issue of whether we choose change or whether change is something that happens to us is clearly complex. One way of viewing it might be to argue that we can and do choose to change ourselves, but that often we are less aware of the direction which chosen change may eventually take.

A person in a semi-skilled job may decide to go to night-school classes or undertake other forms of training in order to qualify themselves for what they regard as more challenging kinds of work. They might be successful in gaining qualifications and entering a new field. Up to this point they can reasonably claim to have chosen their direction of personal change and to have carried through that change in terms of their original proposal. However, the long-term effect may be that they acquire new kinds of responsibility, contacts with different kinds of people, new values and a life style which, in total, will involve personal changes not clearly envisaged at the time they went to their first evening class.

On the issue of how we go about changing ourselves, Radley (1974) speculated that change, particularly self-chosen change, may have three stages to it. Initially, if we are going to change, we must be able to envisage some goal; we must have a kind of picture of what we will be like when we have changed. He argued that if we have only a vague picture or no picture at all then we cannot change; we need to be able to 'see' the changed us in the distance. He went on to argue that when we have the picture then we can enact the role of a person like that. That is to say, we do not at heart believe that we are such a person but we can behave as if we were such a person, rather like an actor playing a role on stage or someone trying out a new style. (This may relate to the old adage that adolescence is the time when we 'try out' personalities to see which is a good fit.) He argued that if we enact in a committed and vigorous way for long enough then, at some mysterious point, we become what we are enacting and it is much more true to say that we are that person than that we are our former selves. This is very much a psychological explanation, in that it is about what is psychologically true, rather than what is formally and officially true. Thus the student who qualifies and becomes a teacher may officially, in terms of pay packet and title, be 'a teacher'. Yet, in Radley's terms, the person may still psychologically be 'a student' who is enacting the role of teacher, who is putting on a teaching style and carrying out the duties of a teacher but who still, in his heart of hearts, sees himself as a student. Later, there may come a point at which he becomes, in the psychological sense, a teacher.

However, we are also aware that there is much that is problematic and threatening about change. The set expectations of others about us may have an imprisoning effect and restrict our capacity to change. People have a picture of us and may attempt to enforce that picture. They may resist change in us because it seems to them unnatural, and it would make us less predictable. Phrases such as 'you are acting out of character', or 'that is not the true you', or 'those are not really your ideas' all reflect the difficulty people find and the resistance they manifest to change in us. Often the pressure of others' expectations is so great that we can only achieve change by keeping it secret until the change has gone so far that we can confront the dismay of others.

This is not to argue that we are simply moulded and brainwashed by our society and our family so that we are merely puppets dancing to tunes played by others. We are clearly influenced by others and everything, the language we speak, the clothes we wear, our values, ideas and feelings, is derived from and elaborated in terms of our relationships with other people and our society. But the more conscious we become of how this happens, the more likely we are to become critical of and the less likely automatically to accept what we are taught (formally and informally), and the more we may independently explore what we wish to make of ourselves as persons.

Equally, when we attempt to change we may find the process personally threatening. We may lose sight of the fact that change is inevitably a form of evolution: that is to say, we change from something to something and thereby there is continuity as well as change. If we lose faith in our own continuity we may be overwhelmed by a fear of some kind of catastrophic break, a fear of becoming something unpredictable to ourselves, of falling into chaos. Whether or not we are entirely happy with ourselves, at least we are something we are familiar with, and quite often we stay as we are because we would sooner suffer the devil we know than the unknown devil of a changed us. Fransella (1972) explored the way in which stutterers who seem to be on the verge of being cured of their stutter often suddenly relapse. She argued that stutterers know full well how to live as 'stutterers'; they understand how people react and relate to them as 'stutterers'. Nearing cure they are overwhelmed with the fear of the unknown, the strangeness of being 'a fluent speaker'.

Monitoring of self

One of the marked features of our culture is that it does not demand (or even suggest) that we formally monitor our lives or that we record our personal history in the way in which a society records its history. True, a few keep diaries, and practices such as re-reading old letters from other people give us glimpses into our past attitudes and feelings. For the most part, our understanding of our past is based on our often erratic memory of it. Moreover, our memory is likely to be erratic, not just because we forget past incidents and ideas but because we may actively 're-write' our history so as to emphasize our consistency and make our past compatible with our present.

Psychologists have tended to ignore the importance of personal history. The vast majority of psychological tests designed to assess the person cut in at a given point in time; they are essentially cross-sectional and pay little heed to the evolution of the person. It would be a very unusual psychology course that used biography or autobiography as material for its students to ponder. There are exceptions to this here-and-now preoccupation. In child psychology great emphasis is laid on the notion of 'development' and a great deal of the research and argument in child psychology is about how children acquire skills over a period, how they are gradually influenced by social customs and how life within the family, over a period of years, affects a child's self-value. Additionally, clinical psychologists involved in psychotherapy and counselling very often find themselves engaged in a joint search with their clients through the immediate and distant past in order to understand present problems and concerns. This does not necessarily argue that a person is simply the end product of their past. We need to understand and acknowledge our past, not in order to repeat it but in order either to use it or to be free of it. As Kelly (1969) put it, 'you are not the victim of your autobiography but you may become the victim of the way you interpret your autobiography'.

Obstacles to self-knowledge and self-change

To try and understand oneself is not simply an interesting pastime, it is a necessity of life. In order to plan our future and to make choices we have to be able to antici-pate our behaviour in future situations. This makes self-knowledge a practical guide, not a self-indulgence. Some-times the situations with which we are confronted are of a defined and clear kind so that we can anticipate and predict our behaviour with reasonable certainty. If someone asks you if you can undertake task X (keep a set of accounts, drive a car, translate a letter from German and so forth) then it is not difficult to assess your skills and experience and work out whether you can undertake the task or not. Often the choice or the undertaking is of a more complex and less defined nature. Can you stand up in conflict with a powerful authority figure? Can you make a success of your marriage to this or that person? Can you live by yourself when you have been used to living with a family? The stranger the country we are entering the more threatening the prospect becomes; the more we realize that some degree of self-change may be involved, the more we must rely upon our under-standing of our own character and potential.

In such circumstances we are acutely aware of the dangers of change and may take refuge in a rigid and inflexible notion of what we are. Kelly (1955, 1969) re-ferred to this tendency as 'hostility'. He defined hos-tility as 'the continued effort to extort validational evidence in favor of a type of social prediction which has already been recognized as a failure'. We cannot lightly ab'andon our theory of what we are, since the abandonment of such a theory may plunge us into chaos. Thus we see someone destroy a close relationship in order to 'prove' that they are independent or we see teachers 'proving' that their pupils are stupid in order to verify that they them-selves are clever.

Closely connected to this definition of hostility is Kelly's definition of guilt as 'the awareness of dis-lodgement of self from one's core role structure'. Core constructs are those which govern a person's maintenance processes; they are those constructs in terms of which identity is established and the self is pictured and under-stood. Your core role structure is what you understand yourself to be.

It is in a situation in which you fail to anticipate your own behaviour that you experience guilt. Defined in this way guilt comes not from a violation of some social code but from a violation of your own personal picture of what you are.

There are traditional ways of exploring the issue of 'what am I like?' We can meditate upon ourselves, ask others how they see us, or review our history. Psychologists have devised numerous tests for assessing 'personality', though in so far as these are of any use they seem to be designed to give the psychologist ideas about the other person rather than to give the people ideas about themselves. Two relatively recent attempts to provide people with ways of exploring their own 'personality' are offered by McFall (in Bannister and Fransella, 1980) and Mair (1970).

McFall offers a simple elaboration on the idea of talking to oneself. His work indicated that if people associate freely into a tape-recorder and listen to their own free flow then, given that they erase it afterwards so that there is no possible audience other than themselves at that time, they may learn something of the themes, conflicts and issues that concern them; themes that are 'edited out' of most conversation and which are only fleetingly glimpsed in our thinking. Mair experimented with formalized, written conversation. Chosen partners wrote psychological descriptions of each other (and predictions of the other's description) and then compared and discussed the meaning and the evidence underlying their written impressions.

Although we have formal ways of exploring how we see and how we are seen by others (the encounter group), and informal ways (the party), it can be argued that there is something of a taboo in our society on direct expression of our views of each other. It may be that we fear to criticize lest we be criticized, or it may be that we are embarrassed by the whole idea of the kind of confrontation involved in telling each other about impressions which are being created. Certainly if you contemplate how much you know about the way you are seen by others, you may be struck by the limitations of your knowledge, even on quite simple issues. How clear are you as to how your voice tone is experienced by other people? How often do you try and convey to someone your feelings and thoughts about them in such an oblique and roundabout way that there is a fair chance that they will not grasp the import of what you are saying?

Psychologists are only very slowly seeing it as any part of their task to offer ways to people in which they may explore themselves and explore the effect they have on others.

Role and person

Social psychologists have made much use of the concept of 'role'. Just as an actor plays a particular role in a drama it can be argued that each of us has a number of roles in our family, in work groups, in our society. We have consistent ways of speaking, dressing and behaving which reflect our response to the expectations of the group around us. Thus within a family or small social group we may have inherited and developed the role of 'clown' or 'hardheaded practical person' or 'sympathizer'. Jobs often carry implicit role specifications with them so that we perceive different psychological requirements in the role of teacher from the role of student or the role of manager from the role of worker. We are surprised by the randy parson, the sensitive soldier, the shy showbusiness person. Society also prescribes very broad and pervasive roles for us as men or women, young or old, working-class or middle-class and so forth. It is not that every word of our scripts is pre-written for us, but the broad boundaries and characteristics of behaviour appropriate to each role are fairly well understood. These social roles can and do conflict with personal inclinations and one way of defining maturity would be to look on it as the process whereby we give increasing expression to what we personally are, even where this conflicts with standard social expectations.

Kelly chose to define role in a more strictly personal sense in his sociality corollary which reads: 'to the extent that one person construes the construction processes of another he may play a role in a social process involving the other person'. He is here emphasizing the degree to which, when we relate to another person, we relate in terms of our picture of the other person's picture of us. Role then becomes not a life style worked out by our culture and waiting for us to step into, but the on-going process whereby we try to imagine and understand how other people see the world and continuously to relate our own conception to theirs.

The paradox of self-knowing

We reasonably assume that our knowledge of something does not alter the 'thing' itself. If I come to know that Guatemala produces zinc or that the angle of incidence of a light ray equals its angle of reflection, then this new knowledge of mine does not, of itself, affect Guatemala or light. However, it alters me in that I have become 'knowing' and not 'ignorant' of these things. More pointedly, if I come to know something of myself then I am changed, to a greater or lesser degree, by that knowledge. Any realization by a person of the motives and attitudes underlying their behaviour has the potential to alter that behaviour.

Put another way, a person is the sum of their understanding of their world and themselves. Changes in what we know of ourselves and the way in which we come to know it are changes in the kind of person we are.

This paradox of self-knowledge presents a perpetual problem to psychologists. An experimental psychologist may condition a person to blink their eye when a buzzer is pressed, simply by pairing the buzzer sound with a puff of air to the person's eyelid until the blink becomes a response to the sound of the buzzer on its own. But if the person becomes aware of the nature of the conditioning process and resents being its 'victim' then conditioning may cease, or at least take much longer. Knowledge of what is going on within that person and between the person and the psychologist has altered the person and invalidated the psychologist's predictions. Experimental psychologists seek to evade the consequences of this state of affairs by striving to keep the subject in ignorance of the nature of the experimental process or by using what they assume to be naturally ignorant subjects: for example, rats. But relying on a precariously maintained ignorance in the experimental subject creates only a mythical certainty in science. Psychotherapists, on the other hand, generally work on the basis that the more the person (subject, patient, client) comes to know of themselves, the nearer they will come to solving, at least in part, their personal problems.

This self-changing property of self-knowledge may be a pitfall for a simple-minded science of psychology. It may also be the very basis of living, for us as persons.

References

Bannister, D. and Agnew, J. (1977)
The Child's Construing of Self. In A.W. Landfield (ed.), Nebraska Symposium on Motivation 1976. Nebraska: University of Nebraska Press.

Bannister, D. and Fransella, F. (1980)
Inquiring Man (2nd edn). Harmondsworth: Penguin.

Fransella, F. (1972)
Personal Change and Reconstruction. London: Academic Press.

Kelly, G.A. (1955)
The Psychology of Personal Constructs, Volumes I and II. New York: Norton.

Kelly, G.A. (1969)
Clinical Psychology and Personality: The selected papers of George Kelly (ed. B.A. Maher). New York: Wiley.

Mair, J.M.M. (1970)
Experimenting with individuals. British Journal of Medical Psychology, 43, 245-256.

Mead, G.H. (1925)
The genesis of the self and social control. International Journal of Ethics, 35, 251-273.

Mischel, W. (1968)
Personality and Assessment. New York: Wiley.

Radley, A.R. (1974)
The effect of role enactment on construct alternatives. British Journal of Medical Psychology, 47, 313-320.

Questions

1. Discuss the problem of defining 'self'.
2. Examine the way in which a person's idea of 'self' is affected by the nature of their work.
3. Discuss the nature of sex differences in ideas about 'self'.
4. How can we 'keep track' of ourselves?

5. What does Kelly mean by 'hostility'? Give examples.
6. Outline one theory of 'self' you have read about.
7. Describe some way in which you have increased your knowledge of yourself.
8. Comment on Radley's idea of change through role enactment.
9. Outline Freud's picture of self as made up of id, ego and super-ego.
10. How would you go about teaching a course in 'self-knowledge'?
11. How do parents influence their children's ideas about 'self'?
12. To what extent is our picture of our self influenced by our physical state and appearance?
13. Some institutions require their staff to meet regularly and formally to discuss how their personal differences affect their work. Is this a good idea?
14. We come to understand ourselves through our relationship with others. Discuss.
15. Examine the way in which social customs inhibit our revealing of 'self'.
16. Self is just a product of our environment. Discuss.
17. People are born with a fixed character which they cannot alter. Discuss.
18. Adolescence is the time when we experiment with self. Discuss.
19. Write an essay on 'roles'.
20. Can psychologists measure personality?
21. What, in your view, are the main hindrances of self-knowledge?
22. Write an essay on 'guilt'.
23. 'He is not himself today.' What triggers off this kind of comment, and does it say more about the speaker than the person of whom it is said?
24. How can we go about changing ourselves?
25. What idea about 'self', proposed by anyone (psycho-logist, poet, friend or whatever) has impressed you most? Why?
26. Your family teaches you what to think of yourself. Discuss.
27. Your job enables you to express yourself. Your job prevents you being yourself. Discuss.

Annotated reading

Axline, V.M. (1971) Dibs: In search of self. Harmondsworth: Penguin.
    A finely written description of a withdrawn and disturbed child who in the process of psychotherapy comes vividly to life. It casts light on our early struggles to achieve the idea of being a 'self'.

Bannister, D. and Fransella, F. (1980) Inquiring Man: The psychology of personal constructs. Harmondsworth: Penguin.
    The second edition of a book which sets out the way

George Kelly sees each of us as developing a complex personal view of our world. The book describes two decades of psychological research based on the theory and relates it to problems such as psychological breakdown, prejudice, child development and personal relationships.

Bott, M. and Bowskill, D. (1980) The Do-It-Yourself Mind Book. London: Wildwood House.
A lightly written but shrewd book on the ways in which we can tackle serious personal and emotional problems without recourse to formal psychiatry.

Fransella, F. (1975) Need to Change? London: Methuen.
A brief description of the formal and informal ways in which 'self' is explored and change attempted.

Rogers, C.R. (1961) On Becoming a Person. Boston: Houghton-Mifflin.
Sets out the idea of 'self-actualization' and describes the ways in which we might avoid either limiting ourselves or being socially limited, and come to be what Rogers calls a fully functioning person.

Part four

Social Psychology

Introduction

Social influence

In recent years the link between particular social influences and basic aspects of health has been demonstrated. The passive disease model, once widely accepted in medicine, has been seriously undermined. According to the model the body becomes invaded by some alien organism which attacks tissue; this results in the appearance of consistent, overt symptoms. Several groups of workers have shown how depression in middle-aged women is linked to their immediate social circumstances. Of even more dramatic impact are studies which link resistance to particular kinds of illness with psychological state. Here it is argued that the body's immune system, which protects it from attack by foreign organisms, is seriously impaired when mental state is disturbed. Such studies imply that the response to infection is a much more active process than the established model had predicted. So, by examining the social influences which lead to changes in self-concept and mood, we can prevent or alleviate various types of illness.

This line of reasoning is still in the very early stages of development, and does not imply that all forms of illness are linked to poor psychological adjustment. However, there is sufficient evidence to suggest that in investigating possible sources of individual variation in health we must be alert to the role played by social factors. We would readily accept that first and foremost Man is a social animal. From an evolutionary point of view we see co-operation, and the development of language, as evidence of this fact. Further evidence of the powerful influence social pressures can exert on individuals comes from experimental studies in social psychology during the 1950s and 1960s. Here group pressures led to conformity and obedience to authority, in spite of the individual's better judgement. These studies contributed to the practice of group therapy with individuals who held maladaptive or irrational ideas. Social influence was harnessed and put to therapeutic use.

However, social influence is a double-edged sword and it became clear that not all social groups achieve positive effects. Studies of large organizations and institutions revealed that in some circumstances social influence could lead to the adoption of a maladaptive role, the 'institutionalization syndrome'. Here individuals assume a passive,

211

apathetic role because they cannot influence the system. Also certain modes of behaviour are selectively reinforced by those in authority. Chronic, long-stay psychiatric patients are those most prone to institutionalization, and it was amongst these populations that the first programmes of 'community therapy' were initiated. The social skills training (SST) movement is a modern development for those who have lost the capacity to relate effectively to others, either through extended periods of mental disturbance and hospitalization, or through avoiding social situations because of excessive anxiety. Michael Argyle and others have designed training programmes which have now been applied to a number of patient groups and are aimed at maximizing these interactional abilities. SST has had a profound influence on the treatment of adolescent and adult communication disorders where a significant social dimension is involved.

Family processes
In the past decade the family unit has received new attention from therapists. Changing attitudes to health have resulted in a movement away from a focus on the individual patient separated from his immediate social environment. This trend is particularly apparent in the treatment of handicapped children. Where social and emotional difficulties exist it is paramount to determine the extent to which changes in the patterns of family care could result in immediate improvement. Where specific cognitive deficits exist there is a need to engage family members in the intervention process through carrying out the necessary therapy on an intensive basis. The training of parents as principal therapists is not just a means of maximizing scarce resources, but a recognition of the need for intensive treatment, carried out in the natural environment for 24 hours a day, seven days a week.

Family systems differ radically, and so a starting point may be the systematic analysis of the family in question to establish the lines of power and communication that exist. This information allows therapists to decide how best to design an intensive intervention strategy and minimize any negative influences that may exist in the system. Professional therapists can then assume a supervisory role for the family. This shift in emphasis can be seen in recent publications on the treatment of childhood language disorders but is, as yet, in early stages of development. The difficulties encountered in developing home-based treatment programmes are considerable, and require a first-hand systematic analysis of the particular family involved. New skills need to be acquired by professional therapists if these new methods of treatment are to succeed.

In chapter 8 Michael Argyle offers a detailed introduction to the nature of social skills training and illustrates how training schemes are set up for individuals experiencing social difficulties. In chapter 9 Neil Frude discusses recent research on family processes and the types of problem which can arise in the family system.

8

Social Behaviour
Michael Argyle

Introduction: social behaviour as a skill

We start by presenting the social skill model of social behaviour, and an account of sequences of social interaction. This model is relevant to our later discussion of social skills and how these can be trained. The chapter then goes on to discuss the elements of social behaviour, both verbal and non-verbal, and emphasize the importance and different functions of non-verbal signals. The receivers of these signals have to decode them, and do so in terms of emotions and impressions of personality; we discuss some of the processes and some of the main errors of person perception. Senders can manipulate the impressions they create by means of 'self-presentation'. The processes of social behaviour, and the skills involved, are quite different in different social situations, and we discuss recent attempts to analyse these situations in terms of their main features, such as rules and goals.

We move on to a number of specific social skills. Research on the processes leading to friendship and love makes it possible to train and advise people who have difficulty with these relationships. Research on persuasion shows how people can be trained to be more assertive. And research on small social groups and leadership of these groups makes it possible to give an account of the most successful skills for handling social groups.

Social competence is defined in terms of the successful attainment of goals, and it can be assessed by a variety of techniques such as self-rating and observation of role-played performance. The most successful method of improving social skills is role-playing, combined with modelling, coaching, videotape-recorder (VTR) playback, and 'homework'. Results of follow-up studies with a variety of populations show that this form of social skills training (SST) is very successful.

Harré and Secord (1972) have argued persuasively that much human social behaviour is the result of conscious planning, often in words, with full regard for the complex meanings of behaviour and the rules of the situations. This is an important correction to earlier social psychological views, which often failed to recognize the complexity of individual planning and the different meanings which may be given to stimuli, for example in laboratory experiments.

However, it must be recognized that much social behaviour is not planned in this way: the smaller elements of behaviour and longer automatic sequences are outside conscious awareness, though it is possible to attend, for example, to patterns of gaze, shifts of orientation, or the latent meanings of utterances. The social skills model, in emphasizing the hierarchical structure of social performance, can incorporate both kinds of behaviour.

The social skills model also emphasizes feedback processes. A person driving a car sees at once when it is going in the wrong direction, and takes corrective action with the steering wheel. Social interactors do likewise; if another person is talking too much they interrupt, ask closed questions or no questions, and look less interested in what is being said. Feedback requires perception, looking at and listening to the other person. Skilled performance requires the ability to take the appropriate corrective action referred to as 'translation' in the model: not everyone knows that open-ended questions make people talk more and closed questions make them talk less. And it depends on a number of two-step sequences of social behaviour whereby certain social acts have reliable effects on another. Let us look at social behaviour as a skilled performance similar to motor skills like driving a car (see figure 1).

Figure 1

The motor skill model (from Argyle, 1969)

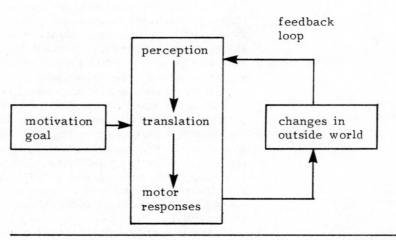

In each case the performer is pursuing certain goals, makes continuous response to feedback, and emits hierarchically-organized motor responses. This model has been heuristically very useful in drawing attention to the importance of feedback, and hence to gaze; it also suggests a number of different ways in which social performances can fail, and suggests the training procedures that may be effective, through analogy with motor skills training (Argyle and Kendon, 1967; Argyle, 1969).

The model emphasizes the motivation, goals and plans of interactors. It is postulated that every interactor is trying to achieve some goal, whether or not there is awareness of that. These goals may be, for example, to be liked by another person, to obtain or convey information, to modify the other's emotional state, and so on. Such goals may be linked to more basic motivational systems. Goals have sub-goals; for example, doctors must diagnose patients before they can be treated. Patterns of response are directed towards goals and sub-goals, and have a hierarchical structure: large units of behaviour are composed of smaller ones, and at the lowest levels these are habitual and automatic.

The role of reinforcement

This is one of the key processes in social skills sequences. When interactor A does what B wants done, B is pleased and sends immediate and spontaneous reinforcements: smile, gaze, approving noises, etc., and modifies A's behaviour, probably by operant conditioning; for example, modifying the content of subsequent utterances. At the same time A is modifying B's behaviour in exactly the same way. These effects appear to be mainly outside the focus of conscious attention, and take place very rapidly. It follows that anyone who gives strong rewards and punishments in the course of interaction will be able to modify the behaviour of others in the desired direction. In addition, the stronger the rewards that A issues, the more strongly other people will be attracted to A.

The role of gaze in social skills

The social skills model suggests that the monitoring of another's reactions is an essential part of social performance. The other's verbal signals are mainly heard, but non-verbal signals are mainly seen; the exceptions being the non-verbal aspects of speech and touch. It was this implication of the social skills model which directed us towards the study of gaze in social interaction. In dyadic interaction each person looks about 50 per cent of the time, mutual gaze occupies 25 per cent of the time, looking while listening is about twice the level of looking while talking, glances are about three seconds, and mutual glances about one second, with wide variations due to distance, sex combination, and personality (Argyle and Cook, 1976). However, there are several important differences between social behaviour and motor skills.

* Rules: the moves which interactors may make are governed by rules; they must respond properly to what has gone before. Similarly, rules govern the other's responses and can be used to influence behaviour; for example, questions lead to answers.
* Taking the role of the other: it is important to perceive accurately the reactions of others. It is also

necessary to perceive the perceptions of others; that is, to take account of their points of view. This appears to be a cognitive ability which develops with age (Flavell, 1968), but which may fail to develop properly. Those who are able to do this have been found to be more effective at a number of social tasks, and more altruistic. Meldman (1967) found that psychiatric patients are more egocentric (that is, talked about themselves more than controls), and it has been our experience that socially unskilled patients have great difficulty in taking the role of the other.

* The independent initiative of the other sequences of interaction: social situations inevitably contain at least one other person, who will be pursuing personal goals and using social skills. How can we analyse the resulting sequences of behaviour? For a sequence to constitute an acceptable piece of social behaviour, the moves must fit together in order. Social psychologists have by no means discovered all the principles or 'grammar' underlying these sequences, but some of the principles are known, and can explain common forms of interaction failure.

Verbal and non-verbal communication

Verbal communication

There are several different kinds of verbal utterance.

* Egocentric speech: this is directed to the self, is found in infants and has the effect of directing behaviour.
* Orders, instructions: these are used to influence the behaviour of others; they can be gently persuasive or authoritarian.
* Questions: these are intended to elicit verbal information; they can be open-ended or closed, personal or impersonal.
* Information: may be given in response to a question, or as part of a lecture or during problem-solving discussion.

(The last three points are the basic classes of utterance.)

* Informal speech: consists of casual chat, jokes, gossip, and contains little information, but helps to establish and sustain social relationships.
* Expression of emotions and interpersonal attitudes: this is a special kind of information; however, this information is usually conveyed, and is conveyed more effectively, non-verbally.
* Performative utterances: these include 'illocutions' where saying the utterance performs something (voting, judging, naming, etc.), and 'perlocutions', where a goal is intended but may not be achieved (persuading, intimidating, etc.).

* Social routines: these include standard sequences like thanking, apologizing, greeting, etc.
* Latent messages: in these, the more important meaning is made subordinate ('As I was saying to the Prime Minister ...').

There are many category schemes for reducing utterances to a limited number of classes of social acts. One of the best known is that of Bales (1950), who introduced the 12 classes shown in figure 2.

Non-verbal signals accompanying speech

Non-verbal signals play an important part in speech and conversation. They have three main roles:

* completing and elaborating on verbal utterances: utterances are accompanied by vocal emphasis, gestures and facial expressions, which add to the meaning and indicate whether it is a question, intended to be serious or funny, and so on;
* managing synchronizing: this is achieved by head-nods, gaze-shifts, and other signals. For example, to keep the floor a speaker does not look up at the end of an utterance, keeps a hand in mid-gesture, and increases the volume of his speech if the other interrupts;
* sending feedback signals: listeners keep up a continuous, and mainly unwitting, commentary on the speaker's utterances, showing by mouth and eyebrow positions whether they agree, understand, are surprised, and so on (Argyle, 1975).

Other functions of non-verbal communication (NVC)

NVC consists of facial expression, tone of voice, gaze, gestures, postures, physical proximity and appearance. We have already described how NVC is linked with speech; it also functions in several other ways, especially in the communication of emotions and attitudes to other people.

A sender is in a certain state, or possesses some information; this is encoded into a message which is then decoded by a receiver.

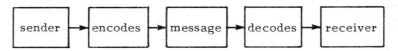

Encoding research is done by putting subjects into some state and studying the non-verbal messages which are emitted. For example Mehrabian (1972), in a role-playing experiment, asked subjects to address a hat-stand, imagining it to be a person. Men who liked the hat-stand looked at it more, did not have hands on hips and stood closer.

Non-verbal signals are often 'unconscious': that is, they are outside the focus of attention. A few signals are unconsciously sent and received, like dilated pupils,

Figure 2

The Bales categories (from Bales, 1950)

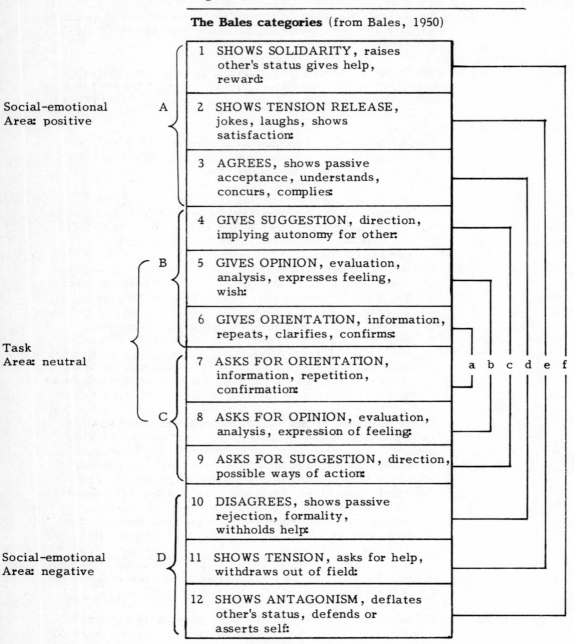

KEY

a problems of communication   A positive reactions
b problems of evaluation   B attempted answers
c problems of control   C questions
d problems of decision   D negative reactions
e problems of tension reduction
f problems of reintegration

signifying sexual attraction, but there are a number of other possibilities as shown in table 1.

Table 1

Awareness of non-verbal signals

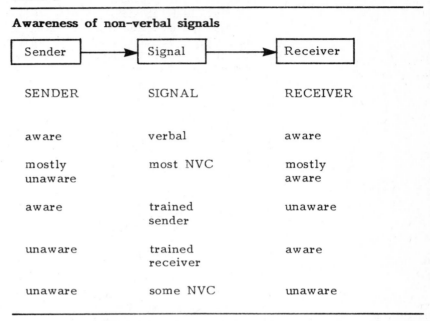

SENDER	SIGNAL	RECEIVER
aware	verbal	aware
mostly unaware	most NVC	mostly aware
aware	trained sender	unaware
unaware	trained receiver	aware
unaware	some NVC	unaware

Strictly speaking pupil dilation is not communication at all, but only a physiological response. 'Communication' is usually taken to imply some intention to affect another; one criterion of successful communication is that it makes a difference whether the other person is present and in a position to receive the signal; another is that the signal is repeated, varied or amplified if it has no immediate effect. These criteria are independent of conscious intention to communicate, which is often absent.

* Interpersonal attitudes: interactors indicate how much they like or dislike one another, and whether they think they are more or less important, mainly non-verbally. We have compared verbal and non-verbal signals and found that non-verbal cues like facial expression and tone of voice have far more impact than verbal ones (Argyle, Salter, Nicholson, Williams and Burgess, 1970).
* Emotional states: anger, depression, anxiety, joy, surprise, fear and disgust/contempt, are also communicated more clearly by non-verbal signals, such as facial expression, tone of voice, posture, gestures and gaze. Interactors may try to conceal their true emotions, but these are often revealed by 'leakage' via cues which are difficult to control.

Person perception   In order to respond effectively to the behaviour of others

it is necessary to perceive them correctly. The social
skills model emphasizes the importance of perception and
feedback; to drive a car one must watch the traffic outside
and the instruments inside. Such perception involves selecting certain cues, and being able to interpret them correctly. There is evidence of poor person perception in
mental patients and other socially unskilled individuals,
while professional social skills performers need to be
sensitive to special aspects of other people and their
behaviour. For selection interviewers and clinical psychologists the appraisal of others is a central part of the
job.

We form impressions of other people all the time, mainly
in order to predict their future behaviour, and so that we
can deal with them effectively. We categorize others in
terms of our favourite cognitive constructs, of which the
most widely used are:

* extraversion, sociability;
* agreeableness, likeability;
* emotional stability;
* intelligence;
* assertiveness.

There are, however, wide individual differences in the constructs used, and 'complex' people use a larger number of
such dimensions. We have found that the constructs used vary
greatly with the situation: for example, work-related constructs are not used in purely social situations. We also
found that the constructs used vary with the target group,
such as children versus psychologists (Argyle, Furnham and
Graham, 1981).

A number of widespread errors are made in forming
impressions of others which should be particularly avoided
by those whose job it is to assess people:

* assuming that a person's behaviour is mainly a product
  of personality, whereas it may be more a function of
  situation: at a noisy party, in church, etc.;
* assuming that behaviour is due to the person rather than
  the person's role; for example, as a hospital nurse, as
  a patient or as a visitor;
* attaching too much importance to physical cues, like
  beards, clothes, and physical attractiveness;
* being affected by stereotypes about the characteristics
  of members of certain races, social classes, etc.

During social interaction it is also necessary to perceive
the emotional states of others: for example, to tell if
they are depressed or angry. There are wide individual
differences in the ability to judge emotions correctly
(Davitz, 1964). As we have seen, emotions are mainly
conveyed by non-verbal signals, especially by facial expression and tone of voice. The interpretation of emotions is

also based on perception of the situation the other person is in. Lalljee at Oxford found that smiles are not necessarily decoded as happy, whereas unhappy faces are usually regarded as authentic.

Similar considerations apply to the perception of interpersonal attitudes, for instance who likes whom, which is also mainly based on non-verbal signals, such as proximity, gaze and facial expression. Again use is made of context to decode these signals: a glance at a stranger may be interpreted as a threat, an appeal for help or a friendly invitation. There are some interesting errors due to pressures towards cognitive consistency: if A likes B, then A thinks that B likes A more than B on average actually does: if A likes both B and C, A assumes that they both like each other more than, on average, they do.

It is necessary to perceive the on-going flow of interaction in order to know what is happening and to participate in it effectively. People seem to agree on the main episodes and sub-episodes of an encounter, but they may produce rather different accounts of why those present behaved as they did. One source of variation, and indeed error, is that people attribute the causes of others' behaviour to their personality ('He fell over because he is clumsy'), but their own behaviour to the situation ('I fell over because it was slippery'), whereas both factors operate in each case (Jones and Nisbett, 1972). Interpretations also depend on the ideas and knowledge an individual possesses: just as an expert on cars could understand better why a car was behaving in a peculiar way, so also can an expert on social behaviour understand why patterns of social behaviour occur.

Situations, their rules and other features

We know that people behave very differently in different situations; in order to predict behaviour, or to advise people on social skills in specific situations, it is necessary to analyse the situations in question. This can be done in terms of a number of fundamental features.

Goals
In all situations there are certain goals which are commonly obtainable. It is often fairly obvious what these are, but socially inadequate people may simply not know what parties are for, for example, or may think that the purpose of a selection interview is vocational guidance.

We have studied the main goals in a number of common situations, by asking samples of people to rate the importance of various goals, and then carrying out factor analysis. The main goals are usually:

* social acceptance, etc.;
* food, drink and other bodily needs;
* task goals specific to the situation.

We have also studied the relations between goals, within and between persons, in terms of conflict and instrumentality.

This makes it possible to study the 'goal structure' of situations.

Rules

All situations have rules about what may or may not be done in them. Socially inexperienced people are often ignorant or mistaken about the rules. It would obviously be impossible to play a game without knowing the rules and the same applies to social situations.

We have studied the rules of a number of everyday situations. There appear to be several universal rules; to be polite, friendly, and not embarrass people. There are also rules which are specific to situations, or groups of situations, and these can be interpreted as functional, since they enable situational goals to be met. For example, when seeing the doctor one should be clean and tell the truth; when going to a party one should dress smartly and keep to cheerful topics of conversation.

Special skills

Many social situations require special social skills, as in the case of various kinds of public speaking and interviewing, but also such everyday situations as dates and parties. A person with little experience of a particular situation may find that he lacks the special skills needed for it (cf. Argyle et al, 1981).

Repertoire of elements

Every situation defines certain moves as relevant. For example, at a seminar it is relevant to show slides, make long speeches, draw on the blackboard, etc. If moves appropriate to a cricket match or a Scottish ball were made, they would be ignored or regarded as totally bizarre. We have found 65-90 main elements used in several situations, like going to the doctor. We have also found that the semiotic structure varies between situations: we found that questions about work and about private life were sharply contrasted in an office situation, but not on a date.

Roles

Every situation has a limited number of roles: for example, a classroom has the roles of teacher, pupil, janitor, and school inspector. These roles carry different degrees of power, and the occupant has goals peculiar to that role.

Cognitive structure

We found that the members of a research group classified each other in terms of the concepts extraverted and enjoyable companion for social occasions, but in terms of dominant, creative and supportive for seminars. There are also concepts related to the task, such as 'amendment', 'straw vote' and 'nem con', for committee meetings.

Environmental setting and pieces

Most situations involve special environmental settings and

props. Cricket needs bat, ball, stumps, and so on; a seminar requires a blackboard, slide projector and lecture notes.

How do persons fit into situations, conceived in this way? To begin with, there are certain pervasive aspects of persons, corresponding to the 20 per cent or so of person variance found in P x S (personality and situation) studies. This consists of scores on general dimensions like intelligence, extraversion, neuroticism and so on. In addition, persons have dispositions to behave in certain ways in classes of situations; this corresponds to the 50 per cent or so of the P x S variance in relation to dimensions of situations like formal-informal, and friendly-hostile. Third, there are more specific reactions to particular situations; for example, behaviour in social psychology seminars depends partly on knowledge of social psychology, and attitudes to different schools of thought in it. Taken together these three factors may predict performance in, and also avoidance of, certain situations - because of lack of skill, anxiety, etc. - and this will be the main expectation in such cases.

Friendship

This is one of the most important social relationships: failure in it is a source of great distress, and so it is one of the main areas of social skills training. The conditions under which people come to like one another have been the object of extensive research, and are now well understood.

There are several stages of friendship: (i) coming into contact with the other, through proximity at work or elsewhere; (ii) increasing attachment as a result of reinforcement and discovery of similarity; (iii) increasing self-disclosure and commitment; and, sometimes, (iv) dissolution of the relationship. Friendship is the dominant relationship for adolescents and the unmarried; friends engage in characteristic activities, such as talking, eating, drinking, joint leisure, but not, usually, working.

Frequency of interaction
The more two people meet, the more polarized their attitudes to one another become, but usually they like one another more. Frequent interaction can come about from living in adjacent rooms or houses, working in the same office, belonging to the same club, and so on. So interaction leads to liking, and liking leads to more interaction. Only certain kinds of interaction lead to liking. In particular, people should be of similar status. Belonging to a co-operative group, especially under crisis conditions, is particularly effective, as Sherif's robbers' cave experiment (Sherif, Harvey, White, Hood and Sherif, 1961) and research on inter-racial attitudes have shown.

Reinforcement
The next general principle governing liking is the extent to which one person satisfies the needs of another. This was

shown in a study by Jennings of 400 girls in a reformatory (1950). She found that the popular girls helped and protected others, encouraged, cheered them up, made them feel accepted and wanted, controlled their own moods so as not to inflict anxiety or depression on others, were able to establish rapport quickly, won the confidence of a wide variety of other personalities, and were concerned with the feelings and needs of others. The unpopular girls on the other hand were dominating, aggressive, boastful, demanded attention, and tried to get others to do things for them. This pattern has been generally interpreted in terms of the popular girls providing rewards and minimizing costs, while the unpopular girls tried to get rewards for themselves, and incurred costs for others. It is not necessary for the other person to be the actual source of rewards: Lott and Lott (1960) found that children who were given model cars by the experimenter liked the other children in the experiment more, and several studies have shown that people are liked more in a pleasant environmental setting.

Being liked is a powerful reward, so if A likes B, B will usually like A. This is particularly important for those who have a great need to be liked, such as individuals with low self-esteem. It is signalled, as discussed above, primarily by non-verbal signals.

Similarity
People like others who are similar to themselves, in certain respects. They like those with similar attitudes, beliefs and values, who have a similar regional and social class background, who have similar jobs or leisure interests, but they need not have similar personalities. Again there is a cyclical process, since similarity leads to liking and liking leads to similarity, but effects of similarity on liking have been shown experimentally.

Physical attractiveness
Physical attractiveness (p.a.) is an important source of both same-sex and opposite sex liking, especially in the early stages. Walster, Aronson, Abrahams and Rottmann (1966) arranged a 'computer dance' at which couples were paired at random: the best prediction of how much each person liked their partner was the latter's p.a. as rated by the experimenter. Part of the explanation lies in the 'p.a. stereotype'. Dion, Berscheid and Walster (1972) found that attractive people were believed to have desirable characteristics of many other kinds. However, people do not seek out the most attractive friends and mates, but compromise by seeking those similar to themselves in attractiveness.

Self-disclosure
This is a signal for intimacy, like bodily contact, because it indicates trust in the other. Self-disclosure can be measured on a scale (1-5) with items like:

What are your favourite forms of erotic play and sexual lovemaking? (scale value 2.56)

What are the circumstances under which you become depressed and when your feelings are hurt? (3.51)

What are your hobbies, how do you best like to spend your spare time? (4.98) (Jourard, 1971).

As people get to know each other better, self-disclosure slowly increases, and is reciprocated, up to a limit.

Commitment

This is a state of mind, an intention to stay in a relationship, and abandon others. This involves a degree of dependence on the other person and trusting them not to leave the relationship. The least committed has the more power.

Social skills training

The most common complaint of those who seek social skills training is difficulty in making friends. Some of them say they have never had a friend in their lives. What advice can we offer, on the basis of research on friendship?

* As we showed earlier, social relations are negotiated mainly by non-verbal signals. Clients for social skills training who cannot make friends are usually found to be very inexpressive, in face and voice.
* Rewardingness is most important. The same clients usually appear to be very unrewarding, and are not really interested in other people.
* Frequent interaction with those of similar interests and attitudes can be found in clubs for professional or leisure activities, in political and religious groups, and so on.
* Physical attractiveness is easier to change than is social behaviour.
* Certain social skills may need to be acquired, such as inviting others to suitable social events, and engaging in self-disclosure at the right speed.

The meaning and assessment of social competence

By social competence we mean the ability, the possession of the necessary skills, to produce the desired effects on other people in social situations. These desired effects may be to persuade the others to buy, to learn, to recover from neurosis, to like or admire the actor, and so on. These results are not necessarily in the public interest: skills may be used for social or antisocial purposes. And there is no evidence that social competence is a general factor: a person may be better at one task than another, for example, parties or committees. SST for students and other more or less normal populations has been directed to the skills of dating, making friends and being assertive. SST for mental patients has been aimed at correcting failures of social competence, and also at relieving subjective distress, such as social anxiety.

To find out who needs training, and in what areas, a detailed descriptive assessment is needed. We want to know, for example, which situations individual trainees find difficult (formal situations, conflicts, meeting strangers, etc.), and which situations they are inadequate in, even though they do not report them as difficult. And we want to find out what individuals are doing wrong: failure to produce the right non-verbal signals, low rewardingness, lack of certain social skills, etc.

Social competence is easier to define and agree upon in the case of professional social skills: an effective therapist cures more patients, an effective teacher teaches better, an effective salesperson sells more. When we look more closely, it is not quite so simple: examination marks may be one index of a teacher's effectiveness, but usually more is meant than just this. Salespersons should not simply sell a lot of goods, they should make the customers feel they would like to go to that shop again. So a combination of different skills is required and an overall assessment of effectiveness may involve the combination of a number of different measures or ratings. The range of competence is quite large: the best salesmen and saleswomen regularly sell four times as much as some others behind the same counter; some supervisors of working groups produce twice as much output as others, or have 20-25 per cent of the labour turnover and absenteeism rates (Argyle, 1972).

For everyday social skills it is more difficult to give the criteria of success; lack of competence is easier to spot: failure to make friends, or opposite sex friends, quarrelling and failing to sustain co-operative relationships, finding a number of situations difficult or a source of anxiety, and so on.

Methods of social skills training

Role-playing with coaching

This is now the most widely-used method of SST. There are four stages:

* instruction;
* role-playing with other trainees or other role partners for 5-8 minutes;
* feedback and coaching, in the form of oral comments from the trainer;
* repeated role-playing.

A typical laboratory set-up is shown in figure 3. This also shows the use of an ear-microphone for instruction while role-playing is taking place. In the case of patients, mere practice does no good: there must be coaching as well.

For an individual or group of patients or other trainees
a series of topics, skills or situations is chosen, and introduced by means of short scenarios. Role partners who can
be briefed to present carefully graded degrees of difficulty
are used.

It is usual for trainers to be generally encouraging,
and also rewarding for specific aspects of behaviour, though
there is little experimental evidence for the value of such
reinforcement. It is common to combine role-playing with
modelling and video-playback, both of which are discussed
below. Follow-up studies have found that role-playing
combined with coaching is successful with many kinds of
mental patients, and that it is one of the most successful
forms of SST for these groups.

Role-playing usually starts with 'modelling', in which a
film is shown or a demonstration given of how to perform the
skill being taught. The feedback session usually includes
videotape-playback and most studies have found that this is
advantageous (Bailey and Sowder, 1970). While it often makes
trainees self-conscious at first, this wears off after the
second session. Skills acquired in the laboratory or class
must be transferred to the outside world. This is usually
achieved by 'homework': trainees are encouraged to try out
the new skills several times before the next session. Most

Figure 3

A social skills training laboratory

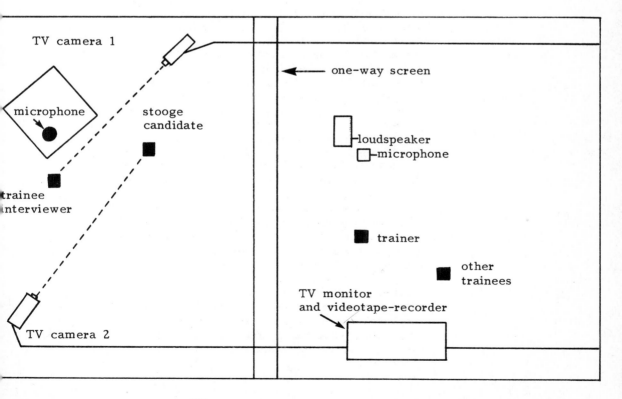

trainers take people in groups which provides a source of role partners, but patients may need individual sessions as well for individual problems.

Other methods of training

TRAINING ON THE JOB: this is a widely used traditional method. Some people improve through experience but others do not, and some learn the wrong things. The situation can be improved if there is a trainer who regularly sees the trainee in action, and is able to hold feedback sessions at which errors are pointed out and better skills suggested. In practice this method does not appear to work very well, for example with trainee teachers (see Argyle, 1969).

GROUP METHODS: these, especially T-groups (T standing for training), are intended to enhance sensitivity and social skills. Follow-up studies have consistently found that 30-40 per cent of trainees are improved by group methods, but up to 10 per cent are worse, sometimes needing psychological assistance (e.g. Lieberman, Yalom and Miles, 1973). It has been argued that group methods are useful for those who are resistant to being trained.

EDUCATIONAL METHODS: these, such as lectures and films, can increase knowledge, but to master social skills it is necessary to try them out, as is the case with motor skills. Educational methods can be a useful supplement to role-playing methods.

Areas of application of SST

NEUROTIC PATIENTS: role-playing and the more specialized methods described above have been found to be slightly more effective than psychotherapy, desensitization, or other alternative treatments, but not much (Trower, Bryant and Argyle, 1978). Only one study so far has found really substantial differences: Maxwell (1976), in a study of adults reporting social difficulties and seeking treatment for them, in New Zealand, insisted on homework between training sessions. However, SST does produce more improvement in social skills and reduction of social anxiety. A few patients can be cured by SST alone, but most have other problems as well, and may require other forms of treatment in addition.

PSYCHOTIC PATIENTS: these have been treated in the USA by assertiveness training and other forms of role-playing. Follow-up studies have shown greater improvement in social behaviour than from alternative treatments. The most striking results have been obtained with intensive clinical studies of one to four patients, using a 'multiple baseline' design: one symptom is worked on at a time over a total of 20-30 sessions. It is not clear from these follow-up studies to what extent the general condition of patients has been improved, or how well they have been able to function outside the hospital (Hersen and Bellack, 1976). It has been argued by one practitioner that SST is more suitable than psychotherapy for working-class patients in view of their poor verbal skills (Goldstein, 1973).

Other therapeutic uses of SST

ALCOHOLICS have been given SST to improve their assertiveness, for example in refusing drinks, and to enable them to deal better with situations which they find stressful and make them drink. Similar treatment has been given to drug addicts. In both cases treatment has been fairly successful, though the effects have not always been long-lasting; SST is often included in more comprehensive packages.

DELINQUENTS AND PRISONERS have often been given SST with some success, especially in the case of aggressive and sex offenders. SST can also increase their degree of internal control.

TEACHERS, MANAGERS, DOCTORS, etc.: SST is increasingly being included in the training of those whose work involves dealing with people. The most extensive application so far has been in the training of teachers by 'micro-teaching'. They are instructed in one of the component skills of teaching, such as the use of different kinds of question, explanation or the use of examples; they then teach 5-6 children for 10-15 minutes, followed by a feedback session and 're-teaching'. Follow-up studies show that this is far more effective than a similar amount of teaching practice, and it is much more effective in eradicating bad habits (Brown, 1975). In addition to role-playing, more elaborate forms of simulation are used, for example to train people for administrative positions. Training on the job is a valuable addition or alternative, provided that trainers really do their job.

NORMAL ADULTS: students have received a certain amount of SST, especially in North American universities, and follow-up studies have shown that they can be successfully trained in assertiveness (Rich and Schroeder, 1976), dating behaviour (Curran, 1977), and to reduce anxiety at performing in public (Paul, 1966). Although many normal adults apart from students have social behaviour difficulties, very little training is available unless they seek psychiatric help. It would be very desirable for SST to be more widely available, for example in community centres.

SCHOOLCHILDREN: a number of attempts have been made to introduce SST into schools, though there are no follow-up studies on its effectiveness. However, there have been a number of successful follow-up studies of training schemes for children who are withdrawn and unpopular or aggressive, using the usual role-playing methods (Rinn and Markle, 1979).

Conclusion

In this chapter we have given an account of those aspects of social psychology which are most relevant to the work of teachers, social workers and others, both in understanding the behaviour of their clients and also in helping them with their own performance. We have used various models of social behaviour, such as the social skills model and the model of social behaviour as a game. Some of the phenomena described cannot be fully accounted for in terms of these models: for example, the design of sequences of interaction. A number of practical implications have been described; in particular, discussion of the skills which have been demonstrated to be the most effective in a number of situations, and the methods of social skills training which have been found to have most impact. It should be emphasized that much of this research is quite new and it is expected that a great deal more will be found out on these topics in the years to come.

References

Argyle, M. (1969)
Social Interaction. London: Methuen.
Argyle, M. (1972)
The Social Psychology of Work. London: Allen Lane and Penguin Books.
Argyle, M. (1975)
Bodily Communication. London: Methuen.
Argyle, M. and Cook, M. (1976)
Gaze and Mutual Gaze. London: Cambridge University Press.
Argyle, M., Furnham, A. and Graham, J.A. (1981)
Social situations. London: Cambridge University Press.
Argyle, M. and Kendon, A. (1967)
The experimental analysis of social performance. In L. Berkowitz (ed.), Advances in Experimental Social Psychology, Volume 3. London: Academic Press.
Argyle, M., Salter V., Nicholson, H., Williams, M. and Burgess, P. (1970)
The communication of inferior and superior attitudes by verbal and non-verbal signals. British Journal of Social and Clinical Psychology, 9, 221-231.
Bailey, K.G. and Sowder, W.T. (1970)
Audiotape and videotape self-confrontation in psychotherapy. Psychological Bulletin, 74, 127-137.
Bales, R.F. (1950)
Interaction Process Analysis. Cambridge, Mass.: Addison-Wesley.
Brown, G.A. (1975)
Microteaching. London: Methuen.
Curran, J.P. (1977)
Skills training as an approach to the treatment of heterosexual-social anxiety. Psychological Bulletin, 84, 140-157.
Davitz, J.R. (1964)
The Communication of Emotional Meaning. New York: McGraw-Hill.
Dion, K., Berscheid, E. and Walster, E. (1972)
What is beautiful is good. Journal of Personality and Social Psychology, 24, 285-290.
Flavell, J.H. (1968)
The Development of Role-taking and Communication Skills in Children. New York: Wiley.

Goldstein, A.J. (1973)
Structured Learning Therapy: Toward a psychotherapy for the poor. New York: Academic Press.

Harré, R. and Secord, P. (1972)
The Explanation of Social Behaviour. Oxford: Blackwell.

Hersen, M. and Bellack, A.S. (1976)
Social skills training for chronic psychiatric patients: rationale, research findings, and future directions. Comprehensive Psychiatry, 17, 559-580.

Jennings, H.H. (1950)
Leadership and Isolation. New York: Longmans Green.

Jones, E.E. and Nisbett, R.E. (1972)
The actor and the observer: divergent perceptions of the causes of behavior. In E.E. Jones, D. Kanouse, H. Kelley, R.E. Nisbett, S. Valins and B. Weiner (eds), Attribution: Perceiving the causes of behavior. Morristown, NJ: General Learning Press.

Jourard, S.M. (1971)
Self Disclosure. New York: Wiley Interscience.

Lieberman, M.A., Yalom, I.D. and Miles, M.R. (1973)
Encounter Groups: First facts. New York: Basic Books.

Lott, A.J. and Lott, B.E. (1960)
The formation of positive attitudes towards group members. Journal of Abnormal and Social Psychology, 61, 297-300.

Maxwell, G.M. (1976)
An evolution of social skills training. (Unpublished, University of Otago, Dunedin, New Zealand.)

Mehrabian, A. (1972)
Nonverbal Communication. New York: Aldine-Atherton.

Meldman, M.J. (1967)
Verbal behaviour analysis of self-hyperattentionism. Diseases of the Nervous System, 28, 469-473.

Paul, G.L. (1966)
Insight v. Desensitization in Psychotherapy. Stanford, Ca: Stanford University Press.

Rich, A.R. and Schroeder, H.E. (1976)
Research issues in assertiveness training. Psychological Bulletin, 83, 1081-1096.

Rinn, R.C. and Markle, A. (1979)
Modification of social skill deficits in children. In A.S. Bellack and M. Hersen (eds), Research and Practice in Social Skills Training. New York: Plenum.

Sherif, M., Harvey, O.J., White, B.J., Hood, W.R. and Sherif, C. (1961)
Intergroup Conflict and Cooperation: The Robbers' Cave experiment. Norman, Oklahoma: The University of Oklahoma Book Exchange.

Trower, P., Bryant, B. and Argyle, M. (1978)
Social Skills and Mental Health. London: Methuen.

Walster, E., Aronson, E., Abrahams, D. and Rottmann, L. (1966)
Importance of physical attractiveness in dating

behavior. Journal of Personality and Social Psychology, 5, 508–516.

Questions

1. Is it useful to look at social behaviour as a kind of skill?
2. What do bad conversationalists do wrong?
3. What information is conveyed by non-verbal communication?
4. In what ways do non-verbal signals supplement verbal ones?
5. How is the perception of other people different from the perception of other physical objects?
6. What information about a social situation would a newcomer to it need to know?
7. Do we like other people primarily because they are rewarding?
8. Why do some people have difficulty in making friends?
9. Can social competence be measured?
10. How can the effectiveness of social skills training be assessed?
11. Is social skills training successful with mental patients?
12. If someone has inadequate social behaviour, what else may be required in addition to SST?
13. What criticisms have been made of experiments in social psychology? What other methods are available?
14. Does social behaviour take the same form in other cultures?
15. Are there fundamental differences between social behaviour in families, work-groups and groups of friends?

Annotated reading

Argyle, M. (1978) The Psychology of Interpersonal Behaviour (3rd edn). Harmondsworth: Penguin.
Covers the field of the chapter, and related topics at Penguin level.

Argyle, M. and Trower, P. (1979). Person to Person. London: Harper & Row.
A more popular account of the area covered by the chapter, with numerous coloured illustrations.

Argyle, M. (1975). Bodily Communication. London: Methuen.
Covers the field of non-verbal communication in more detail, with some illustrations.

Berscheid, E. and Walster, E.H. (1978). Interpersonal Attraction (2nd edn). Reading, Mass.: Addison-Wesley.
A very readable account of research in this area.

Bower, S.A. and Bower, G.H. (1976). Asserting Yourself. Reading, Mass.: Addison-Wesley.

An interesting and practical book about assertiveness, with examples and exercises.

Cook, M. (1979). Perceiving Others. London: Methuen.
A clear account of basic processes in person perception.

Goffman, E. (1956). The Presentation of Self in Everyday Life. Edinburgh: Edinburgh University Press.
A famous and highly entertaining account of self-presentation.

Trower, P., Bryant, B. and Argyle, M. (1978). Social Skills and Mental Health. London: Methuen.
An account of social skills training with neurotics, with full details of procedures.

9

The Family
Neil Frude

Psychology and the family

The psychologist may regard the family as a background against which to view the individual, asking perhaps how the parents influence the development of a child or how families of alcoholics may help the individual to overcome his or her difficulties, or alternatively the family itself may be the unit of study. The family is a small group and we can observe the patterns of communication within it, the process of mutual decision making, and so forth. It is a system, with individuals as sub-units or elements within. Typically, psychologists have focussed their interests on the biological and social nature of the individual, but they are now becoming increasingly concerned not only with individuals or even 'individuals in relationships' but with the relationships themselves.

Clinical and educational psychologists, for example, are increasingly working within the family context and some problems which were initially identified as 'belonging' to the individual adult or child are now seen, more appropriately, as problems of the 'family system'. Also, psychologists working, for example, with handicapped children have come to recognize that the powerful influence and involvement of the parents means that they can be harnessed as highly potent sources of training, and such clinicians are increasingly using these strategies to establish a far more effective educational programme than they themselves could possibly provide. But the needs of parents, and the stresses which such a high level of involvement may place upon them, are also recognized and so the psychologists may well regard themselves as involved with the problems of the family as a whole.

So there are vital problems in the area and there are some impressive results. Let us look at some of these, choosing some of those areas which relate to major social problems and some innovations which suggest methods for their alleviation.

Family planning

Current surveys of the plans of young married couples for families have shown a high level of conscious control and active planning, a reflection of the wide availability of highly effective contraceptive techniques. The number and spacing of children are controlled with varying degrees of skill and success. The number of couples who opt for voluntary childlessness seems to be increasing. In about half of such cases the couple have planned from the start not to have children, while the other half postpone pregnancy and eventually decide to remain childless.

Contraceptive use varies greatly. Despite the numerous methods available, none is perfect, for various reasons. Some men find that the sheath reduces pleasurable sensation, the pill may have side effects on health or mood, and a number of women find methods such as the cap bothersome and distasteful. The coil may involve a painful initial fitting and an extensive gynaecological involvement which some find embarrassing and disturbing. Sterilization or vasectomy may be advisable for the older and highly stable couple, but a number of people who have undergone such surgery later change their partners. They may then request reversal surgery and in many cases successful reversal will not be possible. The solution to the contraception problem is thus by no means always simple and family planning counselling, and the tailoring of recommendations to the particular needs and life stage of the couple, is a task requiring considerable skill and insight as well as knowledge of the technical features of the particular methods.

Different couples have different 'ideal family structures', often specifying not only the number of children but also their spacing and sex. There is still some preference, overall, for boys and current research makes it likely that in the near future couples will be able, with some accuracy, to determine the sex of their baby. Many will prefer to 'leave it to nature' but others will choose one option or the other. This is likely to result in a relative excess of boys, with longer-term social results which can only be guessed.

Reactions to pregnancy range from unqualified delight to profound despair. The option of abortion is now increasingly available. Reactions to this also vary from relief to regret and while, overall, the evidence is that there are rarely long-term negative consequences for the women, several studies have suggested the need for pre- and for post-termination counselling. A number of women miscarry, some repeatedly, and again this can be a very stressful experience requiring skilled intervention.

Birth and early interaction

The process of birth is biological, but the importance of social variables is also apparent. The pregnant woman may anticipate the sex and looks of her baby, but initial acceptance is by no means inevitable. Premature babies, for example, may look very unlike the baby-food advertisements which may have conditioned the mothers' expectations.

Fathers are now often present at the delivery and there is evidence that this helps the woman in the birth process itself and also helps the couple to feel that the baby is

part of both of them. The demands which the baby makes may
not have been fully anticipated and the initial period with
the infant may call for a difficult process of adaptation
and adjustment, just as the first period of the couple
living together calls for give and take and the setting-up
of new norms of interaction.

Not all babies are the same: they differ in their activity level, their crying and their patterns of sleep and
wakefulness. Some are not easy to care for, and may be
unresponsive and difficult to soothe. Baby-care makes great
demands and the mother may be totally unprepared for the
energy and level of skill required. Surveys show that many
of them find the period of early childhood highly stressful.
They may be tired and feel inadequate and, at times, very
angry. If mothers fail to understand and control their
babies, their treatment of them may be poor and sometimes
harsh.

The level of medical care in pregnancy and around the
time of the birth may be high, but many mothers then feel
isolated with the baby, unsure about such matters as
feeding, toileting and weaning.

In assuming that a 'mother's instinct' will aid her in
these tasks we may have seriously under-estimated the extent
to which, in earlier times, the informal training opportunities offered to the young girl by larger family units
and the close neighbourhood community helped her in her own
parenting.

The developing child

In the early years interactions with parents form the major
social background for the child. There is a good deal of
informal teaching and the child learns by example. Guidance
and discipline help the infant to establish a set of internal rules and encouragement and praise help to develop
skills and intellectual abilities. Overhearing conversations
between adults enables the child to learn about the structure of language and conversation and the rules of social
interaction. Watching the parents' interactions and reactions enables children to develop their own emotional
repertoire and social skills, and they will experiment and
consciously imitate the behaviour of their parents. The
child may identify strongly with a particular parent. Games
of pretence enable youngsters to practise complex tasks and
build a repertoire of interactive styles, and in collabor-
ation with other young children they may rehearse a number
of roles. In both competitive and co-operative play social
interaction patterns are devised and perfected, children
learn about rule-following and discover their strengths and
weaknesses relative to their peers.

Different parents treat their children differently, and
there are many styles of parenting. Some parents are warm
and affectionate, others are more distant, and some are
openly hostile. Some give the child a lot of freedom and
exercise little control while others are very restrictive.

Not surprisingly, the children reared in such atmospheres
develop somewhat differently. The children of highly
restrictive parents tend to be well-mannered but lack
independence, the children of warm parents come to have a
confident high regard for themselves, and the children of
hostile parents tend to be aggressive. There are various
ways in which such findings can be explained. Do the aggressive children of hostile parents, for example, behave in
that way because they are reacting against the pressures
which their parents put on them, are they simply imitating
the behaviour of the adults around them and picking up their
interactive styles, or is there perhaps some hereditary
biological component which makes both parents and children
hostile?

Probably, as in so many cases of such overall correlations, there is a combination of such factors. It is also
possible, of course, that hostility originating in the
children themselves causes a parental reaction. We must be
wary of the conclusion that children simply respond to the
atmosphere of their home. They also help to create that
atmosphere and the relationship between parents' behaviour
and the child's behaviour is a fully interactive one.
Children are not shapeless psychological forms capable of
being moulded totally in response to their social environment, but have dispositions and levels of potential of their
own which they bring into the family.

Children have certain psychological needs which the
family should be able to provide. They need a certain
stability, they need guidance and a set of rules to follow
and the feeling needs to be conveyed to them that they are
'prized' by their parents. In the traditional system with
two parents there may be a certain safeguard for the constant provision of these needs by one or other of the
parents, and for the prevention of total lack of interest or
of rejection. But if the natural family with two parents is
ideal in many ways as an arrangement in which to provide for
the child's development, this is not to say that the child's
best interests cannot also be met in alternative contexts.
Most children in single-parent households fare well and
develop happily. For the child living apart from the natural
parents adoption seems a better option than does fostering
(though long-term fostering seems to share many of the
positive features of adoption) and fostering seems to be
better for the child than a continued stay in an institution. Even this context, however, can provide reasonably
well for the child's needs if there is stability, a high
level of staffing, high intimacy between staff and children
and the provision of high levels of verbal and other types
of stimulation.

The family and stress

Just as the family is a principal source of a person's
happiness and well-being, it can also be the most powerful
source of stress. Research has now been done to try to

establish inventories of the life stresses which people experience and in even a cursory glance through such a list it is difficult not to be struck by the extent to which the relationships within the family are bound up with personal change. Some of these events, like the birth of a handicapped child or the death of a child, happen to only a few people, but others, such as the older child leaving home, marital conflict, sexual problems, and the death of a parent happen to many or most. Stress precipitated by such life events has been shown to have a marked effect on both physical and mental health, and if illness is the result then this in turn will provide added hardship.

It is not only particular events which cause stress. The constant presence of ill-health, handicap or marital conflict can similarly take its toll over the years. On the other hand, the stability and comfort of the family setting and the constant presence of others seems to provide much that is beneficial. Marriage reduces the risk of alcoholism, suicide and many forms of psychological ill-health, and interviews with separated and widowed people reveal the elements which they feel they are now missing in their lives, and which in turn may help to explain why living in relative isolation tends to be associated with a greater risk of experiencing psychological problems. As well as providing the opportunity to discuss problems and providing stability, the presence of a spouse reduces loneliness. It also facilitates discussion of a variety of issues and so enables the partners to forge a consensus view of the world: it provides extra interest and social contact, the opportunity to give love and express concern, and provides constant feedback to the individuals about themselves, their value and their role. Practical tasks may be shared and the person may be aware of being prized by the other. This then fosters the sense of self-worth which has been found to be very important for overall well-being.

Of course, not all marital relationships are good and some may lead to far greater problems than those of living in isolation. Certainly recent family changes and conflict seem, in many cases, to be a trigger factor leading to subsequent admission to a psychiatric hospital. Overall, however, it seems that the emotional impact of an intimate relationship, in adult life as in childhood, is likely to involve many more gains for the individual than losses, that people value the protection which such relationships provide and that they often suffer when such support ends.

Schizophrenia, depression and the family

There is a popular notion that schizophrenic illness originates in family relationships, and that certain forms of family communication, in particular, may cause an adolescent or young adult to become schizophrenic. A considerable number of studies have now been carried out to establish whether or not there is a firm evidential basis for such an assumption and, at this point, it looks as if the decided lack of positive evidence should lead us to abandon the hypothesis that such relationship problems constitute the major cause of the illness. While no strong data have been forthcoming to support the family interaction claim, a great deal of evidence implicating the role of genetics in schizophrenia has been found and it now looks as if a predominantly biological explanation may eventually be given. But while there is no good evidence that family relationships are formative in schizophrenia, there is strong support for the notion that family interaction markedly influences the course of a schizophrenic illness and the pattern of relapses and remission from symptoms over the years. It seems that the emotional climate in the home and particular family crisis events often trigger renewed episodes of schizophrenic breakdown.

On the other hand, it seems that depression often has its origin in severe life events and difficulties and that the family context provides many of these. In a recent study conducted in London, Brown and Harris (1978) found that depression was more common in those women in the community who had recently experienced a severe event or difficulty. Many of the events involved loss. Women with several young children were more vulnerable than others, as were the widowed, divorced and separated. Social contact seemed to provide a protective function against the effects of severe life events and the rate of depression was lower in those women who had a close intimate relationship with their husbands. Women without employment outside the home were found to be more vulnerable and the loss of a mother in childhood also seemed to have a similar effect. Brown and Harris suggest that such early loss through the death of a parent may change the way in which the person comes to view the world and attempts to cope with the problems that arise. The study provides clear evidence that family relationship factors may make a person more or less susceptible to clinical depression, and again illustrates how the contribution of family life to personal problems is two-sided. The family may be the source of much stress, but a close supportive marital relationship will enable the individual to cope with many problems without succumbing to the threat of clinical depression.

Sexual behaviour and sexual problems

Married couples vary greatly in the frequency of their sexual contact and in the style and variety of their sexual interaction. The rate of intercourse does not seem to be related to overall satisfaction with the marriage, except that where a marriage is failing for other reasons sexual contact may be low or absent. If there is a marked discrepancy, however, between the expectations or needs of the partners then this may lead to conflict and dissatisfaction. Sex is also one of the factors which can cause problems in the early stages of adjustment to marriage.

Although several medical men and women wrote 'marriage manuals' during the nineteenth century and in the early part of this century, our knowledge of human sexuality was very

limited before the studies of people such as Kinsey and
Masters and Johnson. Using interviews, and later observational and physiological techniques, researchers have now
provided us with extensive information about sexual practices. Masters and Johnson (1966, 1970), in particular, have
supplied a thorough and detailed account of human sexual
behaviour, and they have also provided insights into such
questions as sexuality in the older person and sexual
behaviour during pregnancy.

It has become clear that problems of sexual dysfunction
affect a great many people at some stage in their marriage.
Masters and Johnson have produced a range of therapies which
has been shown to be highly effective, and many of these
have now been adopted by other psychologists, psychiatrists
and marriage counsellors. The couple, rather than the
individual man or woman, is considered to be the most
appropriate treatment unit, and discussion and detailed
advice are followed up with 'homework assignments' which
the partners carry out in the home. Anxiety about sexual
performance can have a serious effect on behaviour and a
vicious circle can easily form, for example, between anxiety
and failure to achieve erection. Awareness of the female
orgasm has increased considerably in recent years and it
appears that the pattern of problems for which advice is
sought has changed. Whereas the majority of sexual problems
encountered by counsellors some decades ago involved a
mismatch of sexual appetites, with the woman complaining
about her husband's excessive demands, a dominant problem
now seems to be that of the woman's dissatisfaction with her
husband's ability to bring her to orgasm.

Opinions differ about how much the 'couple unit' is
always the appropriate focus for treatment and how far
deep-seated relationship difficulties, rather than specific
sexual skills and attitudes, underlie the problems presented. It does appear that in about half of the cases seen
there are other serious marital difficulties in addition to
the sexual dysfunction being treated by sex therapy which is
aimed at improving other aspects of the relationship.

Family conflict and violence

There is open conflict at times in most families. Sometimes
the focus of disagreements is easily apparent; it may
centre, for example, on matters concerning money, sex or
the handling of children; but at other times the row seems
to reflect underlying resentments and difficulties in the
relationship. Studies have been made of how arguments start,
how they escalate and how they are resolved, and some
research in this area has been successful in identifying
patterns of conflict which seem to predict later marital
breakdown. It appears that there are right ways and wrong
ways to fight with other family members. In some marriages
there may be constant conflict which, however, is successfully worked through and which does not endanger the basic
relationship.

Inter-generational conflict is also common. In the early years the parents have the power and may use discipline to settle matters of disagreement. Again, the way in which this is done is important and it seems that parents should not use their power in such a way that the child feels rejected. Children should be made to feel that their behaviour, rather than their whole personality, is the target of the parents' disapproval. In the adolescent years, the child's struggle for power and independence is often the focus of conflict. Adolescence is frequently a period of stress and young people may have doubts about their status and future. It is also a time when peer-influence may conflict with that of the parents.

Marital conflict sometimes leads to physical assault and a number of wives have to receive medical attention for injuries inflicted by their husbands. Many such wives choose to return to the home after such an incident although some seek the haven of a women's refuge. Even where there is repeated violence, the wife often feels that her husband is not likely to treat her badly in the future; she may feel that drinking or stress triggered the assault, and such wives often report that the man is generally caring and responsible and that his violent outbursts are out of character. Jealousy and sexual failure or refusal are also associated with attacks on the wife, though it is also true that for some couples physical assault or restraint represents a modal response in conflict situations, and that in some marriages (and indeed in some sub-cultures) there are few inhibitions against the couple hitting one another.

Violence against children also occurs with alarming frequency in families, and it is estimated that about two children die each week in England and Wales as a result of injuries inflicted by their parents. The children involved are often very young, and it does not take much physical strength to seriously injure a small child or baby. Only a small proportion of the parents involved in these attacks have a known psychiatric history and, contrary to one popular image, they often provide well for the general needs of their children. Sadistic premeditated cases do occur but they are relatively rare. Generally the attack occurs when a child is crying or screaming or has committed some 'crime' in the eyes of the parent. The mother or father involved is often under considerable stress, and there are frequently severe marital difficulties. The parents involved are often young and may have little idea of how to cope with the crying child, and there is evidence that many abused children are themselves difficult to handle. They may be disturbed, over-active or unresponsive although, of course, many such problems may themselves be the result of longer-term difficulties in the family.

Family therapy

There has recently been a considerable growth of interest in 'family therapy'. This is practised in a variety of ways and

with a number of alternative theoretical underpinnings but
it claims, in all its forms, that when there is a psychological disturbance it is useful to work with the 'family
system' rather than with the individual identified client.
The view is often expressed that the symptom should properly
be seen as an attribute not of the individual but of the
family as a whole. By focussing on the structure of the
group, on the emotional climate and on the pattern of
relationships and communication, an attempt is made to bring
about a fundamental change which will result in a well-
functioning family and an alteration in the circumstances
which have maintained the symptom.

Thus a child who is truanting from school may be
presented as the only problem by a family who, in fact, have
a number of difficulties. By focussing on or scapegoating
the child in this way, the family system may preserve itself
from serious conflict between other members or between the
family group and another part of the wider social system.
The child's problem with school is therefore in some way
'useful' to the family and any direct attempt to deal with
the truanting may be directed at reducing the underlying
conflict or at changing a disordered style of communication
which has led to the family 'needing' the child's symptom.

In the therapeutic sessions family members are seen
together. The focus is largely on the group processes
operating and involves the observations of such interactional elements as coalitions, stratagems and avoidances.
As these are further analysed, they may be revealed to the
family or they may be simply 'corrected' by the direct
authoritative action of the therapist. The periods intervening between treatment sessions are seen as being of
primary importance for the family, who may then revert to
original dysfunctional patterns or may continue in the
direction of therapeutic change.

The role of the therapist is varied. Some therapists
regard themselves primarily as analysts and concentrate on
making the family aware of its interactional style, whereas
some regard themselves as mediators or referees or may take
sides with one or more family members to provide a necessary
balance of power. If two or more therapists work as a team
then they may present their own relationship as a model of
open communication and in this way try, for example, to
illustrate the constructive potential of conflict.

The professional background of family therapists is
highly varied and their original training may be in psychology, social work or psychiatry. The theoretical concepts
used similarly cover a wide range including psychoanalysis,
communications theory and behavioural analysis. Concepts
have also been borrowed freely from general systems theory,
which is predominantly a mathematical theory with applications in cybernetics and biology. In behavioural family
therapy the focus is on the manipulation of the family
consequences of individual behaviour and the attempt is made
to analyse and modify social reinforcement patterns and
observational learning.

Because family therapy involves a varied and often subtle set of procedures, it is very difficult to carry out satisfactory studies to measure its effectiveness. Many of the variables said to be involved are rather intangible and the processes underlying changes in social systems are highly complex. Preliminary evidence suggests that it is often useful but this can also be said of many other forms of therapy, and the 'cost-effectiveness' considerations which play a part in treatment choice sometimes make it difficult to support a strong case for the use of family therapy. Many critics would return a general verdict of 'not proven', but the level of interest by professionals is undoubtedly high and growing. One special difficulty has been the failure of those working in this area to provide an adequate means of identifying the cases which may be most appropriately treated in this way. Any attempt to treat all conditions with a uniform approach is unlikely to return a high overall rate of effectiveness. With a more limited set of identified problems this mode of treatment may in future prove to be the optimal means of effective intervention for a range of cases. At present, family therapy reflects just one aspect of the increasing awareness of the importance of understanding the social context when dealing with a presented psychological symptom.

The effects of marital breakdown

Divorce statistics represent a very conservative estimate of marital failure and a still more conservative estimate of marital unhappiness and disharmony, but the rates are high and increasing. There are various estimates of the likely divorce rate of currently made marriages but one in four is a frequently encountered figure. There are certain known predictors of marital breakdown. It is more frequent, for example, when the couple married at an early age, when they have few friends, when they have had relatively little education and when their life style is unconventional. The marital success or failure of their own parents also bears a direct statistical relationship to the couple's chances of breakdown.

Psychological studies have shown that certain measures of personality and social style are also predictors of failure. If the wife rates her husband as being emotionally immature, if the husband's self-image is lacking in coherence and stability, or if either of the partners is emotionally unstable then marital breakdown is more likely than if the reverse holds. Good communication, a high level of emotional support and the constructive handling of conflict situations are, not surprisingly, features of relationships which are associated with high levels of marital happiness and low rates of breakdown. In many of these studies it is, of course, difficult to disentangle cause and effect.

The process of adjustment to a marriage may be a long and difficult one, and some marriages never successfully 'take'. The highest rates of breakdown therefore occur in the first years, but many relationships are stable and

satisfactory for a while and are then beset with difficulties at a later stage. Divorce is usually preceded by
months or years of intense conflict and may eventually come
as a relief, but the evidence suggests that generally the
whole process is a very painful one for many members of the
family involved, both adults and children.

Research with divorcees has revealed a high degree of
stress and unhappiness which may last for a very long time.
On the whole, it appears that the experiences of women in
this situation result in rather more disturbance than those
of men, but for both sexes the status of divorce is associated with higher risk of clinical depression, alcoholism
and attempted suicide. The psychological effects of a
marriage breakdown may stem largely from lack of social
support, the absence of an intimate relationship and a loss
of self-esteem, but there are often additional pressures
relating to the loss of contact with the children or of
having to bring them up alone. There is a high rate of
remarriage among the divorced; and divorce itself, for
all the apparent risks which it brings, is still often
preferable to continuing in a marriage which has failed.

The 'broken home' is associated with increased aggressiveness and delinquency in children, but there seems to be
only a weak association with neurotic and other psychiatric
problems of childhood. While the rate of conduct problems in
the children of divorce is considerably higher than that for
children of stable marriages, there is apparently little
increase in such antisocial behaviour for children whose
homes have been broken by the death of a parent. This
suggests that it is the discord in the home which produces
the effect rather than the mere absence of one parent. This
is supported by the finding that conduct problems also occur
with increased frequency in homes with continual discord,
even when there is no separation or divorce.

Single-parent families

Children are raised in single-parent families when the
mother has not married, when there has been a divorce or
separation, or when one parent has died. 'Illegitimacy' is a
somewhat outmoded term and an increasing number of single
women now feel that they want to rear their child on
their own. Social attitudes against illegitimacy and
single parenthood have softened over the years and this has
encouraged more mothers to keep the baby rather than have it
adopted.

Single parenthood appears to be more stressful for the
remaining parent than sharing the responsibilities with a
partner. Lack of emotional support and of adult company are
some of the reasons for this but there are also likely to be
increased financial hardships, and the homes of single
parents have been shown to be overcrowded and often lack
both luxuries and basic amenities. During times of parental
illness there may be few additional social resources to call
upon, and the single parent is less likely to be able to

organize a social life for herself (about 90 per cent of single parents are women). A number of self-help organizations have now been formed to fulfil some of the special needs of the single parent.

One-parent families are viable alternatives to the more traditional nuclear families, and most of the children raised in such circumstances do not appear to show any signs of disturbance or impaired development. There have been suggestions that the boy without a father might tend to be more effeminate but it has been found that most boys brought up by their mothers are as masculine as the rest. If anything, they tend to make fewer sex-identity based assumptions about tasks and roles. We could say that they seem to be less 'sexist' than other boys. Similarly, the girl brought up with the father alone does not seem to lack feminine identity. These findings reflect a more general conclusion that children seem to base their own stereotypes on the wider world around them rather than on the conditions prevailing in their own immediate family.

The family life of old people

Old age is marked by declining health and mobility and by a process of disengagement from several life enterprises, notably employment. There may be low income and financial difficulties, contemporaries are likely to die, and the old person may find it difficult to replace such contacts with the result that they live in a shrinking social world. The high emphasis which some old people place on privacy may reduce the uptake of potential neighbourhood and community resources.

The major exception made to such concern with privacy is with the immediate family. Typically, contacts with children and grandchildren are highly prized and may be a major focus of interest in their lives. While there is likely to be an increase in dependency, however, this is often recognized by the old and they often respect the independence of the younger family and feel a crushing sense of obligation if they are forced through circumstance to accept aid from them. In some families there is an informal 'exchange of services' between generations with the older person, for example, looking after the grandchildren while parents are working or having a short holiday.

Recent social change has resulted in fewer three-generation households, but with increasing age and decreasing health, and perhaps the death of one of the parents, the younger couple may want to offer the surviving partner a place in their home. There may be doubts about how well this will work out and conflict may be initiated between the marital partners over how far feelings of duty should lead to changes which might disrupt the family. As the children become older the pressure on space may build up, and with increasing health difficulties the burden of the older person may become too great. Deafness may become an irritation, there may be restricted mobility and the elderly parent may become incontinent.

The increased strain on the family may lead to harsh feelings or even violence towards the old person as well as to a detrimental effect on the health of other members of the family. Eventually the pressure may become unmanageable and the old person may be forced to enter an institution. For many elderly people, living with a child is a halfway stage between having a home of their own and living in an old people's home. Both moves may involve their giving up possessions and pets. The quality of institutions varies greatly, but a frequent reaction is one of withdrawal, depression and depersonalization. Despite having many people around the old person may suffer from a deep sense of loneliness and isolation.

While it seems inevitable that old age will always bring unhappiness to some people, for many it is a time of contentment and fulfilment and in a number of cases the positive aspects centre on activities and memories of relationships within the family. Older women, for example, may play a major role in organizing family get-togethers and may act as a social secretary for members of the extended family, and grandmothers and grandfathers may gain great satisfaction from their relationships with their grandchildren. Many of the recent social changes in housing organization and mobility, it is true, militate against a high level of interaction between the generations, and there seems as yet little awareness by policy-makers of the social costs which such changes entail.

The future of intimate life styles

Contact with intimates in the family group seems to provide the individual, overall, with considerable benefits. Significant relationships are highly potent and there may be dangers, but generally the benefits far outweigh the costs. A variety of psychological needs are very well fulfilled in the traditional family setting. The child growing in the caring and stable family setting can generally develop skills and abilities and achieve a potential for happiness better than in any other setting, and the adult can fulfil with the marital partner the needs of emotional support, freedom from loneliness, sex, stability, and the building of a mutually comfortable 'social reality'. When the basic family pattern is disturbed there can be grave consequences for each of the people involved.

There is no uniform change in western society to a single alternative life style arrangement but there is rather an increasing diversity. There are now fewer children in families, more single-parent families, more divorces and separations, and there is a high incidence of transitory relationships and less contact between generations. Several lines of evidence suggest that children are valued less than in the recent past; that women, in particular, are looking more outside the family for their role-orientation and their life satisfactions; that there is now less 'family feeling'; and that family duties and responsibilities impinge upon individual decision making less than was the case some decades ago.

We may expect this variety to increase further as ideas regarding the roles of men and women evolve, as changes in biological and 'hard' technology take place and as patterns of employment and leisure alter. It would be premature to forecast, at this stage, what effects such changes will bring to interpersonal relationships and personal life styles. What does seem certain, however, is that there will be important effects. To some extent these can be affected by direct social intervention and some undesirable effects may be prevented.

Family life, then, is a key variable in society and adverse changes may inflict an enormous social bill. For this reason the effects on individuals must be carefully monitored. Psychologists are just one of the groups which will be involved in this vitally important enterprise.

References

Brown, G.W. and Harris, T. (1978)
Social Origins of Depression. London: Tavistock Publications.
Masters, W. and Johnson, V. (1966)
Human Sexual Response. Boston: Little, Brown.
Masters, W. and Johnson, V. (1970)
Human Sexual Inadequacy. London: Churchill.

Questions

1. Write an essay on 'The family and psychology'.
2. Assess the importance of personal relationships in the lives of individuals, referring to psychological and other studies to support the analysis you present.
3. Consider some of the factors which might lead a couple to decide to remain childless.
4. Now that there are a number of highly effective contraceptive methods why do so many unwanted pregnancies occur, and how might this be changed?
5. How is a relationship between the mother and her baby likely to differ from that between the father and his baby? Why is this so?
6. Many mothers find looking after a young baby a difficult and stressful experience. Why is this?
7. Hospital births may be medically the safest, but are there likely to be psychological dangers in treating birth more as a biological than as a social and family process?
8. What are 'the needs of children' and how may they be met?
9. Critically assess the evidence relating to the effects of a mother's work outside the home on the children.
10. Write an essay on 'The family as a source of stress'.
11. Some people have maintained that schizophrenia arises as a result of problems within the family. Critically assess the evidence relating to this issue.

12. Describe current approaches to the treatment of sexual dysfunction.
13. The family seems to be the context for a good deal of violence, particularly towards children and wives. Why should this be so?
14. Write an essay on 'The after-effects of divorce'.
15. Consider the special problems of the single-parent family.
16. 'The natural social setting for old people is with their younger family.' How true is this statement? Consider the problems which may arise in a three-generation household.
17. Is the family an institution worth preserving?
18. Are there 'experts' in child-rearing? Is this process too important to be left to parents?
19. Some authors have claimed that the family is oppressive and that people should be liberated from the limits that it places on them. How far do you share this view? Give reasons.

Annotated reading

Belliveau, F. and Richter, L. (1971) Understanding Human Sexual Inadequacy. London: Hodder & Stoughton.
> Non-technical report of the work of Masters and Johnson on sexual behaviour and sexual problems, including details of treatment methods.

Herbert, M. (1975) Problems of Childhood. London: Pan.
> A comprehensive account of the problems of the early years, their treatment and prevention.

Kellmer Pringle, M. (1980) The Needs of Children (2nd edn). London: Hutchinson.
> Important review of children's needs and how they may be met both inside and outside the family. Readable and authoritative book with important implications for social policy.

Kempe, R. and Kempe, E. (1978) Child Abuse. London: Fontana/Open Books.
> The nature of treatment of violence and sexual assault on children in the family, with an account of methods of treatment and prevention.

Rutter, M. (1976) Helping Troubled Children. Harmondsworth: Penguin.
> Leading British child psychiatrist examines the nature of the more severe problems of childhood. Provides good coverage of the importance of family factors and related methods of treatment.

Part five

Abnormal Psychology

Mental health

The concept of 'mental illness' remains enigmatic even after more than a century of vigorous research effort. The idea that mental disturbance can be compared to bodily disease sprang from instances where known disease processes occurred in the CNS and resulted in profound changes in consciousness. These organic syndromes with their accompanying mental disturbances had suggested that all forms of mental disturbance had some physical aetiology in the CNS. Contemporary psychiatry no longer holds this simple view. The influence of social and emotional development, as well as potential physical factors, are now recognized as highly significant in mental disturbance. The notion of 'mental illness' is therefore something of an anachronism. Healthy psychological functioning not only depends on stable neural metabolism but also on effective interchange between individuals and their environments. The nature of these interchanges has been studied from a variety of theoretical perspectives, each differing in the assumptions they make about the nature of Man and the nature of mental processes. It is these theoretical models which generate the range of psychological therapies available to clinicians.

One of the most distinctive features of mental disturbance is the gradual breakdown in communicative abilities which effectively distinguishes the healthy individual from those in need of help. Many types of communication disorder have, in the absence of physical pathology, been seen as symptoms of psychological disturbance. Given the lack of evidence that chemotherapy is of value in the treatment of such communication disorders there is indeed no alternative to seeking a psychological explanation for the problem. Once a tentative explanation has been reached there will be an opportunity to test this explanatory hypothesis through the application of derived therapeutic techniques. In the case of the aphonic, with no overt physiological damage, it may be advisable to seek evidence of psychological disturbance by switching the focus of enquiry from specific voice difficulties to an assessment of personality, emotional state and current social functioning.

Psychological treatment

Psychological therapies have been derived from the different schools of psychology presented earlier in the book. Although the various treatment approaches highlight the diversity available in psychology there is a growing trend towards integration of previously disparate techniques. In the past there was a very distinct division between behavioural therapy on the one hand and 'insight' therapy on the other. In the former approach emphasis is placed on modifying overt behavioural patterns such as temper tantrums in children or obsessive-compulsive rituals in adults. In insight therapy the focus is on the thoughts and feelings held by individuals about themselves and others in their social world. As will become apparent, there are serious criticisms of both these models of therapy. However, a new movement is emerging. It attempts to combine behavioural and cognitive approaches, resulting in the modification of actual behaviour as well as thoughts and feelings. The new cognitive-behaviour therapies present a challenge both to clinicians and theoreticians. Clinicians have yet to demonstrate the superiority of these treatments over the well-established forms of psychological therapy; the theoreticians must try to explain any differential outcomes seen in clinical practice.

In many ways psychological methods of treatment are 'coming of age'; seldom has the literature of psychotherapy been more alive with healthy debate which recognizes the validity of different theoretical positions. Previously there was a tendency for dogma to supplant informed argument but the modern trend moves away from entrenched positions towards a more open study of different treatment tehniques. As the quality of therapy evaluation increases there will be opportunities to pioneer new treatments for different patient groups. Clinical workers must try to master a variety of treatment techniques, and make decisions about the most appropriate approach for a given patient's difficulties. Clinical reality contains not only different conditions but also unique individuals, presenting specific difficulties. Rather than treating a case of X, we actually find ourselves treating person X suffering from a unique problem, or set of problems. At this fine level of clinical practice broad treatment techniques may have to be supplemented by specific forms of intervention, tailored to the personality and interests of the individual patient.

In chapter 10 David Shapiro reviews the major models of psychopathology which try to account for the varieties of difficulties experienced by people suffering from psychological distress. In chapter 11 we outline several forms of psychological treatment which have found application both in abnormal psychology and speech therapy.

10

Psychopathology
D. A. Shapiro

'Psychopathology', literally defined, is the study of disease of the mind. Our society entrusts most of the care of individuals whose behaviour and experience are problematic or distressing to medical specialists (psychiatrists). Being medically trained, psychiatrists see their work as requiring diagnosis and treatment of 'patients'. Psychologists, on the other hand, have sought alternative means of understanding abnormal behaviour, and the aim of this chapter is to outline the progress that has been made in this direction.

The varieties of psychopathology

A good way to appreciate the great variety of problems we are concerned with is to examine the system of classification used by psychiatrists, summarized in table 1. Readers requiring more detailed descriptions of these should consult a psychiatric textbook. In the NEUROSES, the personality and perception of reality are fundamentally intact, although emotional disturbances of one kind or another, usually involving anxiety or its presumed effects, can make life very difficult for the individual. The PSYCHOSES, on the other hand, are characterized by gross impairments in perception, memory, thinking and language functions, and the individual is fundamentally disorganized, rather than merely emotionally disturbed. However, there is no clear-cut brain disease, and so the disorder cannot be explained in purely biomedical terms. The layman's conception of 'madness' is based on the symptoms of schizophrenia, including delusions (unshakeable, false beliefs), hallucinations (such as hearing 'voices') and thought disorder (manifested in 'garbled' speech). The third category of table 1, personality disorders, comprises deeply ingrained, motivational and social maladjustments. Table 1 also includes organic syndromes, which are behaviour disorders associated with identified brain disease. Not included in the table are the important group of psychosomatic illnesses. These are characterized by physical symptoms whose origins are in part psychological (emotional). They include asthma, high blood pressure, gastric and duodenal ulcers. More generally, psychological stress is increasingly implicated in many physical illnesses.

Table 1

Major category	Neuroses (milder disturbances)				
Illustrative syndromes	Anxiety state	Obsessive-compulsive disorders	Phobias	Conversion reactions	Neurotic depression
Characteristic symptoms	Palpitation, tires easily, breathlessness, nervousness anxiety	Intrusive thoughts, urges to acts or rituals	Irrational fears of specific objects or situations	Physical symptoms, lacking organic cause	Hopelessness dejection

Major category	Psychoses (severe Non-organic disturbances		Personality disorders (antisocial disturbances)	Organic syndromes		
Illustrative syndromes	Affective disorders	Schizophrenia	Psychopathic personality	Alcoholism and drug dependence	Epilepsy	Severe mental handicap
Characteristic symptoms	Disturbances of mood, energy and activity patterns	Reality distortion, social withdrawal, disorganization of thought, perception and emotion	Lack of conscience	Physical or psychological dependence	Increased susceptibility to convulsions	Extremely low intelligence, social impairments

The medical model of psychopathology

Before describing psychological approaches to behaviour disorder, it is necessary to examine critically the predominant medical approach. This makes three major assumptions, which are considered in turn.

The diagnostic system

The first assumption of the medical model is that the various kinds of abnormal behaviour can be classified, by diagnosis, into syndromes, or constellations of symptoms regularly occurring together. This diagnostic system has already been summarized in table 1. It has a number of disadvantages. First, some disorders appear to cut across the boundaries of the system. Thus an individual whose severe anxiety is associated with fears of delusional intensity may defy classification as 'neurotic' or 'psychotic'. Second, scientific studies of the ability of psychiatrists to agree on the diagnosis of individuals have suggested that the process is rather unreliable, with agreement ranging from about 50 per cent to 80 per cent depending upon the circumstances (Beck, Ward, Mendelson, Mock and Erlbaugh, 1962). Third, research also suggests that the diagnosis given to an individual may bear little relationship to the symptoms the individual has (Zigler and Philips, 1961). Fourth, the diagnosis of psychiatric disorder is much more subjective and reflective of cultural attitudes than is the diagnosis of physical illness; one culture's schizophrenic might be another's shaman; similar acts of violence might be deemed heroic in battle but psychopathic in peacetime. Careful comparisons of American and British psychiatrists have shown that the two groups use different diagnostic criteria and hence classify patients differently.

Despite these limitations, the psychiatric classification persists. This is largely because no better descriptive system has been developed, whilst improvements have been obtained in the usefulness of the system by refining it in the light of earlier criticisms. For example, agreement between psychiatrists has been improved by standardization of the questions asked in diagnostic interviews and the use of standard decision-rules for assigning diagnoses to constellations of symptoms. But it is still necessary to bear in mind that the diagnostic system is not infallible and the 'labels' it gives individuals should not be uncritically accepted.

Physiological basis of psychopathology

The second assumption of the medical model is that the symptoms reflect an underlying disease process, physiological in nature like those involved in all illnesses, causing the symptoms. Three kinds of evidence are offered in support of this. First, the influence of hereditary factors has been assessed by examining the rates of disorder among the relatives of sufferers. To the extent that a disorder is heritable, its origins are considered biological in nature. For example, comparison between the dizygotic (non-identical) and monozygotic (identical) twins of sufferers suggests that there is some hereditary involvement in schizophrenia, anxiety-related disorders, depression and antisocial disorders, with the evidence strongest in the case of schizophrenia (Gottesman and Shields, 1973). Studies of children adopted at birth also suggest that the offspring of schizophrenic parents are more liable to suffer from schizophrenia than other adopted children, despite having no contact with the biological parent. On the other hand, the evidence also shows that hereditary factors alone cannot fully account for schizophrenia or any other psychological

disorder. Even amongst the identical twins of schizophrenics, many do not develop the disorder. Both hereditary
and environmental influences are important.

The second line of evidence for a 'disease' basis of
psychopathology concerns the biochemistry of the brain. This
is a vastly complex subject, and one whose present methods
of investigation are almost certainly too crude to give
other than an approximate picture of what is going on. Over
the years, a succession of biochemical factors have been
suggested as causes for different forms of psychopathology.
Unfortunately, the evidence is not conclusive, as biochemical factors found in sufferers may be consequences
rather than causes. Hospital diets, activity patterns or
characteristic emotional responses may influence the brain
biochemistry of disordered individuals.

Despite these problems, there are some promising lines
of biochemical research. For example, it has been suggested
that schizophrenia may be caused by excess activity of dopamine, one of the neurotransmitters (substances with which
neurons stimulate one another: see Snyder, Banerjee, Yamamura and Greenberg, 1974). This suggestion is supported by
the similarity in molecular structure between dopamine and
the phenothiazine drugs which are used to alleviate schizophrenia, suggesting that these drugs block the reception of
dopamine by taking its place at receptors which normally
receive it. These drugs also cause side effects resembling
the symptoms of Parkinson's disease, which is associated
with dopamine deficiency. Although this and other evidence
support the dopamine theory of schizophrenia, some research
has failed to support it, and so the theory has yet to be
universally accepted. In sum, biochemical evidence is suggestive, and consistent with presumed physiological origins
of psychopathology, but it is not conclusive, nor can such
evidence make a psychological explanation redundant. It is
best seen as an important part of our understanding of
psychopathology, whose causal significance varies from one
disorder to another.

The third line of evidence for the physiological basis
of psychopathology concerns disorders with clear organic
causes. Disease or damage to the brain can result in severe
disturbance of behaviour. A classic example of this is
'general paresis of the insane', whose widespread physical
and mental impairments were discovered in the last century
to be due to the syphilis spirochete. This discovery encouraged medical scientists to seek clear-cut organic causes
for other psychological abnormalities. A large number of
organic brain syndromes have been established, in which
widespread cognitive and emotional deficits are associated
with damage to the brain by disease, infection, or injury.
Epilepsy, in which the individual is unusually susceptible
to seizures or convulsions, is associated with abnormal
patterns of brain activity measured by the electro-
encephalogram (EEG) even between seizures. Many individuals
with severe mental handicap (cf. Clarke and Clarke, 1974),

who attain very low scores on tests of general intelligence and show minimal adaptation to social requirements and expectations, suffer from clear-cut organic pathology, often accompanied by severe physical abnormalities.

On the other hand, all of these disorders are affected by the person's individuality, experience and environment. For example, similar brain injuries result in very different symptoms in different individuals. Those suffering from epileptic seizures can make use of their past experience to avoid circumstances (including diet and environmental stimuli) which tend to trigger their convulsions. Most mentally handicapped people do not have clearly identifiable organic illnesses. Even amongst those who do, the environment can make a big difference to the person's ability to learn the skills of everyday living. Psychologists have found that special training can help mentally handicapped people who might otherwise appear incapable of learning.

Medical treatment of psychopathology

The third assumption of the medical model concerns how psychopathology should be managed. Physical treatments are offered in hospitals and clinics to persons designated 'patients'. It is beyond our present scope to describe the extensive evidence supporting the effectiveness of drugs and electro-convulsive therapy (ECT), the major physical treatments currently employed. However, there are several reasons why psychologists are often inclined to question the support this evidence gives to the medical model. First, individuals differ in their responsiveness to physical treatments, and nobody really understands why some individuals are not helped. Second, the fact that abnormal behaviour can be controlled by physical means does not prove that its origins are physical. Third, the physical treatments often lack a convincing scientific rationale to explain their effects.

The medical model: conclusions

In sum, the medical model gains some support from the evidence, but is sufficiently defective and incomplete to warrant the development of alternative and complementary approaches. Although the diagnostic system is of some value, it must be used with caution. Although hereditary influences, biochemical abnormalities and organic pathology have a part to play in our understanding of psychopathology, they cannot explain its origins without reference to environmental and psychological factors. The apparent efficacy of physical treatment does not establish the physical origins of what they treat. The remainder of this chapter is concerned with five alternative approaches developed by psychologists and social scientists, and assesses their contribution with respect to some of the most important kinds of psychopathology. The evidence presented is, of necessity, very selective, and a full appreciation of these approaches can only follow more extensive study. It should also be borne in mind that the present emphasis on origins of disorder entails a relative neglect of research on treatment.

The statistical model

The statistical model identifies individuals whose behaviour or reported experience is sufficiently unusual to warrant attention on that basis alone. Abnormal individuals are those who greatly differ from the average with respect to some attribute (such as intelligence or amount of subjective anxiety experienced). For example, according to Eysenck (1970), people who score highly on dimensions known as 'neuroticism' (very readily roused to emotion) and 'introversion' (quick in learning conditioned responses and associations) are likely to show what the psychiatrist calls 'anxiety neurosis'. Although this approach is commendably objective, it is not very helpful alone. Not all unusual behaviour is regarded as pathological. Exceptionally gifted people are an obvious case in point. Some statistically abnormal behaviours are obviously more relevant to psychopathology than are others, and we need more than a statistical theory to tell us which to consider, and why. But the model is of value for its suggestion that 'normal' and 'abnormal' behaviour may differ only in degree, in contrast to the medical model's implication of a sharp division between them.

The psychodynamic model

The psychodynamic model is very difficult to summarize, based as it is on theories developed early in the century by Freud, and revised and elaborated by him and subsequent workers within a broad tradition (Ellenberger, 1970). Like the medical model, it seeks an underlying cause for psychopathology, but this is a psychological cause, namely, unconscious conflicts arising from childhood experiences. Freudians have developed a general theory of personality from their study of psychopathology. Freud viewed the personality as comprising the conscious ego, the unconscious id (source of primitive impulses) and partly conscious, partly unconscious super-ego (conscience). The ego is held to protect itself from threat by several defence mechanisms. These are a commonplace feature of everyone's adjustment, but are used in an exaggerated or excessively rigid manner by neurotic individuals, and are overstretched to the point of collapse in the case of psychotic individuals.

For example, neurotic anxiety is learnt by a child punished for being impulsive, whereupon the conflict between wanting something and fearing the consequences of that desire is driven from consciousness (this is an example of the defence mechanism known as repression). According to this theory, pervasive anxiety is due to fear of the person's ever-present id impulses, and phobic objects, such as insects or animals, are seen as symbolic representations of objects of the repressed id impulses. Dynamic theory views depression as a reaction to loss in individuals who

are excessively dependent upon other people for the maintenance of self-esteem. The loss may be actual (as in
bereavement) or symbolic (as in the misinterpretation of a
rejection as a total loss of love). The depressed person
expresses a child-like need for approval and affection to
restore self-esteem. In psychotic disorders such as schizophrenia, the collapse of the defence mechanisms leads to the
predominance of primitive 'primary process' thinking.

Despite its considerable impact upon the ways in which
we understand human motivation and psychopathology, psychodynamic theory has remained controversial. Most of the
evidence in its favour comes from clinical case material, as
recounted by practising psychoanalysts, whose work is based
on the belief that unconscious conflicts must be brought to
the surface for the patient to recover from the symptoms
they have engendered. Whilst this method often yields com-
pelling material which is difficult to explain in other
terms (Malan, 1979), it is open to criticism as insuf-
ficiently objective to yield scientific evidence. It is all
too easy for the psychoanalyst unwittingly to influence
material produced by the patient, and the essential distinction between observations and the investigator's interpretations of them is difficult to sustain in the psychoanalytic
consulting-room. The abstract and complex formulations of
psychodynamic theory are difficult to prove or disprove by
the clear-cut scientific methods favoured by psychologists,
and the patients studied, whether in Freud's Vienna or
present-day London or New York, are somewhat
unrepresentative.

There is some scientific evidence which is broadly
consistent with psychodynamic theory; for example, the
defects in thinking found in schizophrenia are compatible
with the dynamic concept of ego impairment, and loss events
of the kind implicated by dynamic theory are associated with
the onset of depression. Although psychologists hostile to
dynamic theory can explain these findings in other terms,
there is little doubt that the theory has been fruitful,
contributing to psychology such essential concepts as
unconscious conflict and defence mechanism.

The learning model

The learning model views psychopathology as arising from
faulty learning in early life, and conceptualizes this
process in terms of principles of learning drawn from
laboratory studies of animals and humans. The most basic
principles are those of Pavlovian or 'classical' conditioning (in which two stimuli are presented together until
the response to one stimulus is also evoked by the other),
and 'operant' conditioning (whereby behaviour with favourable consequences becomes more frequent). According to
proponents of the learning model, the symptoms of psychopathology are nothing more than faulty habits acquired
through these two types of learning. The 'underlying pathology' posited by the medical and psychodynamic models is
dismissed as unfounded myth.

For example, it is suggested that phobias are acquired by a two-stage learning process; first, fear is aroused in response to a previously neutral stimulus when this stimulus occurs in conjunction with an unpleasant stimulus; then the person learns to avoid the situation evoking the fear, because behaviour taking the person away from the situation is rewarded by a reduction in fear. Another learning theory is that schizophrenic patients receive more attention and other rewards from other people, such as hospital staff, when they behave in 'crazy' ways, thereby increasing the frequency of this behaviour. Again, depressed people are seen as failing to exercise sufficient skill and effort to 'earn' rewards from situations and from other people; a vicious circle develops and activity reduces still further in the absence of such rewards.

In general, the learning model provides a powerful set of principles governing the acquisition of problem behaviour. But it has severe limitations. For example, the fact that fears and phobias can be established by processes of conditioning in the laboratory does not prove that this is how they come about naturally. The theory cannot readily explain how people acquire behaviours which lead to such distress (it is hardly 'rewarding' to suffer the agonies of depression or anxiety, and learning theorists acknowledge their difficulty over this fact by referring to it as the 'neurotic paradox'). Recently, learning theorists have examined the important process of imitative learning or modelling, whereby the behaviour of observers is influenced by another's actions and their consequences. Fear and aggression can be aroused in this way, with obvious implications for the transmission of psychopathology from one person (such as a parent) to another. But human thinking is considered by many psychologists too complex to be understood in terms of these relatively simple learning theories. Hence the development of the cognitive approach, to which we now turn.

The cognitive model

The cognitive model focusses upon thinking processes and their possible dysfunctions. 'Neurotic' problems are seen as due to relatively minor errors in reasoning processes, whilst 'psychotic' disorders are held to reflect profound disturbances in cognitive function and organization.

For example, it is well known that depressed people hold negative attitudes towards themselves, their experiences and their future. According to cognitive theory, these attitudes give rise to the feelings of depression (Beck, 1967). Although an episode of depression may be triggered by external events, it is the person's perception of the event which makes it set off depressed feelings. Experiments in which negative beliefs about the self are induced in non-depressed subjects have shown that a depressed mood does indeed follow. But whether similar processes account for the more severe and lasting depressive feelings of clinical patients is another matter, although the promising results of 'cognitive therapy', in which the attitudes of depressed patients are modified directly, may be taken as indirect evidence for the theory.

Cognitive theory also embraces people's beliefs about the causation of events (known as attributions). For example, it has been suggested that the attributions one makes concerning unpleasant experiences will determine the impact of those experiences upon one's subsequent beliefs about oneself; thus, if a woman is rejected by a man, this is much more damaging to her self-esteem if she believes that the main cause of the event is her own inadequacy, than if she attributes the event to the man's own passing mood. An attributional approach suggests that failure experiences are most damaging if individuals attribute them to wide-ranging and enduring factors within themselves. Consistent with this, depressed people have been found to attribute bad outcomes to wide-ranging and enduring factors within themselves, whilst they attribute good outcomes to changeable factors outside their control.

Psychologists have devoted considerable efforts to precise descriptions of the cognitive deficits of schizophrenic patients through controlled laboratory experiments. For example, schizophrenics have difficulty performing tasks requiring selective attention to relevant information and the exclusion from attention of irrelevant information. Schizophrenics are highly distractable. This may help to explain how irrelevant features of a situation acquire disproportionate importance and become interpreted as part of their delusional systems of false beliefs, or how speech is disorganized by the shifting of attention to irrelevant thoughts and mental images which other people manage to ignore.

The cognitive approach is of great interest because it combines the systematic and objective methods of experimental psychology with a thoroughgoing interest in an important aspect of human mentality. It is a very active 'growth area' of current research, and shows considerable promise. It is perhaps too soon to evaluate many of its specific theories, however, and it does carry the risk of neglecting other aspects of human behaviour.

The socio-cultural model

The final model to be considered attributes psychopathology to social and cultural factors. It focusses upon malfunctioning of the social or cultural group rather than of an individual within that group.

In terms of the socio-cultural model schizophrenia, for example, has been considered both in relation to the quality of family life and to larger socio-economic forces. Within the family, behaviour labelled schizophrenic is seen as a response to self-contradictory emotional demands ('double binds') from other family members, notably parents, to which no sane response is possible. Although graphic accounts have been offered of such patterns in the family life of schizo-phrenic patients, there is no evidence that these are peculiar to such families. If anything, the research evidence suggests that abnormalities of communication within the families of schizophrenics arise in response to the behaviour of the patient, rather than causing the disorder. Looking beyond the family, the higher incidence of schizophrenia amongst the lowest socio-economic class, especially in inner city areas, is attributed to the multiple deprivations suffered by this group. Episodes of schizophrenia are triggered by stressful life events, some of which are more common, or less offset by social and material supports, amongst lower-class people. On the other hand, cause and effect could be the other way round, with persons developing schizophrenia 'drifting' into poverty-ridden areas of the city. Indeed, schizophrenic patients tend to achieve a lower socio-economic status than did their parents.

The socio-cultural approach is of undoubted value as a critical challenge to orthodox views, and has generated useful research into social and cultural factors in psychopathology. Its proponents have also made valuable contributions by bringing a greater humanistic respect for the personal predicament of troubled individuals, and to the development of 'therapeutic communities' and family therapy as alternatives to individually-centred treatments. However, many of its propositions concerning cause-effect relationships have not stood the test of empirical research.

The psychology of illness

It is well known that certain physical illnesses are related to psychological factors. These 'psychosomatic disorders' include ulcerative colitis, bronchial asthma and hypertension. It is not so widely appreciated, however, that psychological factors may be involved in any physical illness. This is because the physiological changes associated with stress (for instance, the release of the 'stress hormones' such as adrenalin) can suppress immune responses and so increase the individual's susceptibility to many diseases, ranging from the common cold to cancer (Rogers, Dubey and Reich, 1979). Many aspects of a person's life have been implicated in ill-health, presumably because of their effects on such physiological mechanisms. These include physical stresses such as noise, highly demanding and/or repetitive jobs (whether physical or mental), catastrophic life events (such as accidents, illness or bereavement) and major emotional difficulties (such as marital discord).

However, for physical illness as for psychopathology, the cause-effect relationship is not simple. Some individuals are more constitutionally stress-prone than others, it appears. Some people live in congenial and supportive surroundings, enabling them to withstand pressures which might otherwise lead to illness. Most of the events implicated in psychological distress and ill-health are in part the results of the individual's own state and behaviour. For example, marital conflict may reflect prior strains felt by the individuals involved. Furthermore, the impact of a stressful event or circumstance depends on the individual's appraisal of it. For example, noise is less distressing if we know we can silence it should it become unbearable. Thus consideration of psychological factors in ill-health demonstrates clearly the interaction between features of individuals and of their surroundings. For physical illness as for psychopathology, we must realize that there are many interacting causes rather than imagine that any one factor is alone responsible for the problem at issue.

Conclusions

Each of the approaches surveyed has contributed to our understanding of psychopathology. The evidence presented for each can only illustrate the massive amounts of research which have been carried out. Nonetheless, several clear themes emerge which have profound implications for our present and future knowledge of psychopathology.

First, the system of classification is inadequate, and research shows that different people within the same broad diagnostic group (such as schizophrenia) behave very differently; it therefore follows that different causes may be found for the difficulties experienced by these sub-groups of people.

Second, the different approaches could profitably be integrated rather more than they have been in the past. For example, elements of the medical, statistical, socio-cultural and cognitive approaches have been combined in recent work on schizophrenia, in which the vulnerability of an individual to the disorder is seen as reflecting both heredity and environment; this vulnerability determines whether or not a person experiences schizophrenia when faced with stresses which are too much to cope with (Zubin and Spring, 1977). The fact that psychopathology generally has multiple causes lends particular urgency to the need to construct broad theories incorporating the facts which were hitherto regarded as supporting one or another of the competing approaches.

Third, the different approaches have more in common than is often acknowledged. In relation to schizophrenia, for example, the breakdown of ego functioning described by psychodynamic theory resembles the inability to process information identified by cognitive theory.

Fourth, the limitations of existing models have encouraged the growth of alternative approaches. For example, the 'transactional' approach emphasizes the importance of the individual's active part in bringing about apparently external stressful events and pressures (Cox, 1978). This approach views the individual as neither a passive victim of circumstances, nor as irrevocably programmed from birth to respond in a particular way. Person and environment are seen as in continuous interaction, so that one-way cause-effect analysis is inappropriate. For example, harassed executives and mothers of small children bring some of the stress they suffer upon themselves as they respond sharply to colleagues or children and thus contribute to a climate of irritation or conflict. Research using this approach has only recently begun, but it holds considerable hope for the future.

Finally, what can this psychological study of psychopathology offer the professional? There are as yet no certain answers to such simple questions as 'What causes schizophrenia?' or 'Why does Mrs Jones stay indoors all the time?' If and when such answers become available, they will not be simple. They will involve many interacting factors. Meanwhile, the psychological approach teaches us a healthy respect for the complexity of the human predicament, and is a valuable corrective to any tendency to offer simplistic or unsympathetic explanations of human distress. Furthermore, professionals will often find it illuminating to apply some of the approaches outlined here to help understand distressed individuals they encounter in their daily work.

References

Beck, A.T. (1967)
Depression: Clinical, experimental and theoretical aspects. New York: Harper & Row.

Beck, A.T., Ward, C.H., Mendleson, M., Mock, J.E. and Erlbaugh, J. (1962)
Reliability of psychiatric diagnosis II: a study of consistency of clinical judgments and ratings. American Journal of Psychiatry, 119, 351-357.

Clarke, A.M. and Clarke, A.D.B. (1974)
Mental Deficiency: The changing outlook (3rd edn). London: Methuen.

Cox, T. (1978)
Stress. London: Macmillan.

Ellenberger, H.F. (1970)
The Discovery of the Unconscious. London: Allen Lane/ Penguin.

Eysenck, H.J. (1970)
The Structure of Human Personality. London: Methuen.

Gottesman, I.I. and Shields, J. (1973)
Genetic theorising and schizophrenia. British Journal of Psychiatry, 122, 15-30.

Malan, D.H. (1979)
Individual Psychotherapy and the Science of Psychodynamics. London: Tavistock.

Rogers, M.P., Dubey, D. and Reich, P. (1979)
The influence of the psyche and the brain on immunity and disease susceptibility: a critical review. Psychosomatic Medicine, 41, 147-164.

Snyder, S.H., Banerjee, S.P., Yamamura, H.I. and Greenberg, D. (1974)
Drugs, neurotransmitters and schizophrenia. Science, 184, 1243-1253.

Zigler, E. and Philips, L. (1961)
Psychiatric diagnosis and symptomalogy. Journal of Abnormal and Social Psychology, 63, 69-75.

Zubin, J. and Spring, B. (1977)
Vulnerability – a new view of schizophrenia. Journal of Abnormal Psychology, 86, 103–126.

Questions

1. Outline the psychiatric system of classification.
2. What problems are raised by the diagnostic system used by psychiatrists? Can it be improved?
3. What can the study of twins tell us about psychopathology?
4. Outline the evidence for a biochemical basis for schizophrenia.
5. Give an example of psychopathology with a known organic cause, and explain what this cause is. Do environmental factors play any part in the disorder you have described?
6. How useful is the medical model of psychopathology? Does it have any disadvantages?
7. Outline the statistical approach to psychopathology, indicating its value and limitations.
8. What are defence mechanisms, and how are they involved in psychopathology?
9. Compare and contrast the explanations of phobias offered by psychodynamic and learning theories.
10. What is wrong with psychoanalysis as a scientific method of investigating psychopathology?
11. Outline some differences between neurotic and psychotic disorders.
12. How might you recognize depression in a client or pupil you encountered in the course of your professional work?
13. Is psychopathology simply behaviour which has been learnt because it produces rewards?
14. What is the importance of self-esteem in psychopathology?
15. How can family life affect well-being and psychopathology?
16. Which of the models of psychopathology do you prefer? Give your reasons.
17. How can psychological factors affect susceptibility to physical illness?
18. 'The child is father to the man.' Does this statement gain support from psychological research into psychopathology?
19. Sometimes people confuse 'mental illness' and 'mental handicap'. How would you explain the difference to a colleague or student?
20. Which forms of psychopathology would be particularly disabling to a person employed in your profession, and why?

Annotated reading

Bannister, D. and Fransella, F. (1980) Inquiring Man (2nd edn). Harmondsworth: Penguin.
A persuasive account of George Kelly's personal

construct approach to psychology and psychopathology, written by two of its leading exponents.

Davison, G.C. and Neale, J.M. (1977) Abnormal Psychology: An experimental clinical approach (2nd edn). New York: Wiley.
> The chapter can provide no more than an introduction to psychopathology. This is the best of the textbooks available: it is readable, comprehensive and, in general, accurate. It is useful in teaching, and has been drawn upon extensively for drafting the chapter. If you want to follow up any aspect of the chapter in more detail, look up the topic in the Index of this book.

Hilgard, E.R., Atkinson, R.L. and Atkinson, R.C. (1979) Introduction to Psychology (7th edn). New York: Harcourt Brace Jovanovich (chapters 14, 15 and 16).
> Intermediate in length between the present chapter and the Davison and Neale book, this group of chapters gives a good general account. Chapter 14 reviews conflict and stress in terms of both experimental and psychoanalytic work; chapter 15 gives a good outline of much of the ground covered in this chapter; and chapter 16 discusses methods of treatment.

Inechen, B. (1979) Mental Illness. London: Longman.
> This reviews the field from a sociological viewpoint, and covers a good deal of research on social factors in psychopathology.

Seligman, M.E.P. (1975) Helplessness: On depression, development and death. New York: Freeman.
> Seligman presents his theory of learned helplessness in a very stimulating and engaging book. Although the theory was based on laboratory studies with animals, Seligman has injected a great deal of 'human interest' into this account. Students who are especially interested in the theory of depression should note, however, that Seligman's ideas have moved on since the book was written to incorporate attributional concepts.

Spielberger, C. (1979) Understanding Stress and Anxiety. New York: Harper & Row.
> A very readable and well-illustrated introduction to experimental and clinical work on stress and anxiety, recommended for the student wishing to look further into these aspects.

Stafford-Clark, D. and Smith, A.C. (1979) Psychiatry for Students (5th edn). London: Allen & Unwin.
> The present chapter does not attempt to do full justice to psychiatry. This is the most readable of the general textbooks on psychiatry, written for students rather than practitioners. It is a good source for more details of psychiatric symptoms, disorders and treatments.

11

Psychotherapy
Harry Purser

What is psychotherapy?

In the preceding chapter David Shapiro outlined the major approaches found in the field of psychopathology. These range from the traditional medical 'disease' model, which generates organic forms of intervention, to the social models which emphasize the importance of interpersonal processes in the aetiology and treatment of psychopathology. The evidence for a purely physiological account of psychological distress remains suggestive rather than conclusive; some forms of psychopathology do seem to have a strong genetic bias, but the isolation of a specific physiological deficit in such conditions has yet to be achieved. Modern psychopathology favours an interactive model of psychological distress by postulating that certain individuals ('vulnerable' individuals), may be genetically predisposed to psychological dysfunction, but it takes further environmental and social stresses to precipitate a breakdown. This interactive model has been termed the 'diathesis-stress' paradigm (Davison and Neale, 1978), where it is suggested that different forms of psychopathology may have a different diathesis-stress balance. Some conditions may have a strong genetic component which is triggered by minimal environmental stress; others may have a weak and general genetic vulnerability which only leads to dysfunction in more extreme environmental circumstances.

Two distinct forms of treatment have emerged in psychopathology. Somatic treatment for the supposed physiological dysfunction underlying psychopathology has consisted of drugs, ECT (electro-convulsive therapy) and neurosurgery. The second treatment approach consists of viewing psychological dysfunction from a completely different perspective: as the result of unconscious mental conflict, exemplified by the theorizing of Freud. Psychoanalysis was the first systematic treatment of psychological dysfunction from a purely psychological analysis. Freud recognized that the id, ego and super-ego were brain processes and that physiological dysfunction could disrupt the tripartite energy balance, but he argued that, in general, psychopathology was the result of particular interactions between a developing biological system - the id, ego and super-ego - and the external social environment. Repression of id impulses led to anxiety and neurotic disorders; treatment was aimed at releasing these repressed ideas by giving the individual 'insight' into the

nature of their repressed impulses. Freud pointed the way
to a psychological, rather than physiological, account of
psychopathology which implied that therapy should be conducted at the psychological level rather than manipulating
the underlying somatic processes.

A 'psychotherapy', in the broadest sense, is any form of
intervention which aims to change the psychological functioning of an individual by purely psychological means. In
this broad sense everyone is a 'psychotherapist' because we
try, through communication, to influence each other without
resorting to physiological stimulation. Teachers can be
regarded as 'psychotherapists' because they attempt to
structure psychological input to achieve some change in
psychological processing. Even the simple act of giving
advice may constitute 'psychotherapy' by this broad definition. More specifically, a number of psychological sciences
have given rise to a range of psychological treatment techniques which have been applied and evaluated in clinical
practice. Over the years continuing theoretical developments
have led to a diversity of treatment approaches and this has
caused some confusion in defining 'psychotherapy'.

This confusion led London (1964) to classify psychological therapies along two dimensions: insight therapies
and action therapies. Insight therapies focus on the internal cognitive and emotional processes of the individual
with the aim of understanding these processes and diagnosing
pathology in their functioning. The therapy aim is to give
the individual 'insight' into these pathological processes
in order to improve psychological functioning. Action therapies are characterized by focussing on the individual's disordered behaviour which is then directly modified using
experimental techniques. The first approach is typical of
psychoanalysis and the second of behaviour therapy and behaviour modification. This distinction retains the generic
term 'psychotherapy' for all forms of non-somatic treatment
but distinguishes the 'talking' therapies from the 'behavioural' therapies. Contemporary psychotherapy has evolved
since London first put forward this distinction. A clear
trend can be seen in recent publications that clinical
science has moved to a more integrated view of psychological
treatment, retaining the rigour of behaviouristic analysis
with more cognitive investigations of the individual patient. This move towards more integrated treatment methods
is largely the result of dissatisfaction amongst practitioners with any single approach to psychological treatment.
Evaluative studies which have compared the efficacy of
different kinds of psychological therapies have concluded
that there is little to choose between different treatments.
Some forms of therapy achieve better results with certain
types of problem, but in general the same end result can be
reached from a range of views. (See Sloane, Staples,
Cristol, Yorkston and Whipple, 1975, for a full discussion
of the effects of different psychotherapies.)

Psychotherapy and human communication

There is a generally accepted definition of psychotherapy which states: psychotherapy is an interpersonal process designed to bring about modifications of feelings, cognitions, attitudes and behaviour which have proven troublesome to the person seeking help from a trained professional.

This definition emphasizes that psychotherapy consists of a special kind of transaction that takes place between a therapist and a patient. The exact nature of that transaction will vary from one therapy to another, but the communication process between therapist and patient is clearly a very significant part of psychotherapy. For the speech therapist, who must effectively communicate with the communication-handicapped, this is a doubly challenging task. Approaches must be found which offer guidance on how to maximize this communication exchange if any form of therapy is to be successful.

A general feature of psychopathology is the extent to which it disrupts interpersonal communication. Acute forms of psychotic illness can present a totally mute state, whereas in manic conditions there may be 'press of speech' where words and ideas gush forth in an almost uncontrollable fashion. Certain specific forms of communication disorders such as stuttering, voice disorders and language disorders have, in the absence of any physiological damage, been seen as primary instances of psychopathology. This has led to the exclusive use of psychotherapeutic treatment for these conditions. Speech therapists, in addition to being 'psychotherapists' in the broad sense, are also psychotherapists in the narrower sense when treating communication disorders of a psychological nature.

Insight therapies

Four forms of insight therapy are outlined: psychoanalysis, client-centred therapy, PCT and group therapies. The common feature of these therapies is the emphasis they place on gaining insight into an individual's cognitive, emotional and social life in order to detect dysfunction and encourage change.

Psychoanalysis

Freudian 'depth' psychology has been largely responsible for the growth and acceptance of psychological treatments during this century. Freud's general theory of human development stressed the importance of early life events for later psychological adjustment in adulthood. Although Freud believed his theory had been derived through scientific enquiry, his reliance on case history evidence (and introspection about his own childhood) has been seriously criticized by philosophers of science (Cioffi, 1970). But if Freud's ideas cause controversy amongst modern scientists it is slight in comparison to the hostility he experienced from the medical establishment of the time. His theory of infantile sexuality was furiously condemned as an outrage. Yet psychoanalysis survived these attacks and flourished as an 'alternative medicine' throughout this hostile period. The original ideas of Freud have been subject to revision by his pupils and further elaboration by his successors and there are now several 'schools' of psychoanalysis with differing views of the psychopathological process. Freud's basic theory highlights the main thread of psychoanalysis.

Causes of psychopathology
In Freudian psychology the causes of psychological stress can be found in an imbalance in the energies of the mind. The reasons for these imbalances must be investigated and treatment aims to restore the normal equilibrium. Briefly, classical psychoanalysis is based on Freud's second theory of anxiety which states that neurotic anxiety is the reaction of the ego when a previously punished and repressed id impulse strives for expression in adulthood. These repressed impulses are usually sexual in nature and can lie dormant for many years under constant repression. But if some current environmental situation is sufficiently similar (either physically or symbolically) to the original situation which resulted in repression, then these childhood impulses are reactivated and strive for expression with renewed zeal.

In order to cope with this new surge of expression, and the resultant ego anxiety that is evoked, a number of defence mechanisms come into play which control the impulse but result in a behavioural or psychological dysfunction. The defence mechanism of conversion is responsible for the condition of hysteria where sensory losses are the result of converting emotional energy into a physical symptom. The task of the therapist is to discover the exact nature of the id impulse which has led to the need for an ego defence mechanism. In order to achieve this insight, the therapist must gain access to the patient's unconscious mind where the id impulse resides. A number of techniques were developed to allow access to the unconscious.

* FREE ASSOCIATION: this consists of asking the patient to give free reign to his thoughts and to verbalize those thoughts. It was assumed that under these conditions unconscious processes might influence verbal output. By making the individual feel safe and secure during this exercise, it was reasoned that defence mechanisms would be lowered and clues about the nature of the unconscious conflict would emerge.
* STUDY OF DREAMS: Freud supposed that during sleep the ego defence mechanisms would be at their lowest ebb. It was reasoned that repressed material from the unconscious would therefore be represented in dream content. Such material would, however, be highly distorted through symbolism.

* PROJECTIVE TECHNIQUES: a later development in probing the unconscious was the use of highly unstructured or ambiguous stimuli to elicit an interpretation from the patient. This interpretation might reveal insight into the person's unconscious processes if the defence mechanism of projection was being employed. Projection is where we externalize worries on to objects and people in the environment. Two of the best-known projective techniques are the Rorschach Ink Blot technique and the Thematic Apperception Test (TAT).
* HYPNOSIS: a further means of access to the unconscious mind was through the use of hypnosis. Hypnosis is assumed to place the individual in a 'twilight zone' of consciousness, where the conscious and unconscious meet. Analysts could 'regress' their patients to recall childhood incidents which could be of clinical significance.

The process of psychoanalysis

The initial stages of analysis involve probing the unconscious mind for some clue as to the causes of repression. In order to attain this goal the analyst adopts a 'blank screen' approach to the patient. The patient projects his worries and insecurities on to the analyst because of this non-directive, non-interactive presentation. Once the analyst believes he has sufficient evidence of the likely conflict the treatment moves to an interpretive stage. The analyst is now more active in exploring the emotional significance of early remembered life experiences and current symptoms. The patient's reactions during this phase are carefully noted since it is believed the threat of uncovering repressed impulses brings new defence mechanisms into play: for example, denial and hostility. Only when the ego is beginning to accept the validity of the analyst's interpretation does the specific phase of transference neurosis emerge. This term describes a point in treatment where the patient reacts to the analyst as if he were some emotionally significant figure from the patient's past (mother, father, etc.). By acting childishly towards the analyst the patient is marking the final phase of therapy where repressed material is coming into consciouness and allowing resolution in the light of adult reality. When resolution of these conflicts has been achieved by the patient the need for ego defence mechanisms is removed and the restoration of mental equilibrium attained.

Critique of psychoanalysis

Objections to the scientific credibility of Freudian psychology have already been outlined by Paul Kline in chapter 6 and by David Shapiro in chapter 10, as well as others elsewhere (Wolpe and Rachman, 1960; Eysenck, 1966; Cioffi, 1970; Fisher and Greenberg, 1977). It is argued, however, that the fact that this approach to psychopathology has curative effects is sufficient evidence of the validity of the theory. If analysis can help people with 'problems in living' then surely we should not reject it because it fails to live up to our usual standards of scientific rigour. But the efficacy of psychoanalysis has been questioned and Rachman and Wilson (1980), in a review of the published effects of psychoanalysis, concluded that it was difficult to muster clear evidence of its curative powers. Even if evidence did suggest a particular therapy has beneficial effects this evidence might not be sufficient to validate the particular theory on which the therapy was based. It may be that therapies 'work' for totally different reasons than the underlying theory suggests. Much will depend on how we define 'beneficial' (i.e. what constitutes 'improvement') and how accurately the therapy has been derived from the theory.

One further point to consider is the 'range of convenience' of a particular therapy. The 'success' of analysis is usually cited for cases classified as 'neurotic disorders'. Outside this group of relatively mild conditions there has been little attempt to apply psychoanalysis (although the theory does address the aetiology of the more severe disorders, such as schizophrenia and manic depression). The account of depression given by Freud is rather curious in its reasoning. Having postulated that depression results from the loss through bereavement of a loved one, Freud introduced the notion of 'symbolic loss' to account for cases where depression was seen in the absence of recent, close bereavement. Such inventions are commonplace in Freud's theorizing whenever it seemed that the theory could not fully account for a particular phenomenon. This tendency to pure speculation and the lack of clear evidence for the efficacy of the therapy has resulted in a growing dissatisfaction with psychoanalysis amongst scientific clinicians. When claims are made of the beneficial effects of the treatment we are left uncertain as to whether the theory is valid or if these effects are simply produced by a very intimate form of relationship between patient and therapist.

Psychoanalysis and human communication
Psychoanalysis as an approach to psychopathology can afford to ignore the actual symptoms of dysfunction (the loss of hearing or sensations of anxiety) and concentrate on the more fundamental, underlying dysfunction which has caused these overt symptoms. A number of instances of human communication disorder have been seen as the resultant symptoms of an anxiety neurosis and thus treated by the methods of psychoanalysis. The most celebrated example is the condition of conversion hysteria.

In aphonia, hearing loss and dyspraxia (where no organic reasons have been discovered), psychoanalysis has offered an explanation in terms of the ego defence mechanism of conversion. Treatment is then aimed at resolving the repressed and converted impulses which have resulted in the functional communication disorder. Stuttering has also been scrutinized by depth psychology and several causal mechanisms have been postulated from oral fixation to projected aggression. But psychoanalysis has also had more general implications for the treatment of human communication disorders. The nature of the patient-therapist relationship in speech therapy has been of particular concern. Psychoanalysis warns of the danger of patient and therapist projecting their anxieties on to each other, resulting in distorted views of the relationship. The advice has been 'not to get involved' with the patient; by maintaining a relatively 'blank screen' approach the difficulties of mutual projection can be avoided. The possibility of a 'transference neurosis' occurring during therapy has also been highlighted and therapists were warned to be alert to this possibility.

Classical psychoanalysis and its modern equivalent of ego analysis have enjoyed a prestigious place in modern psychotherapy despite a relatively narrow range of convenience. The time scale of analysis can be as long as five or ten years, and thus it is an extremely expensive form of therapy in terms of resource input. Recently, a few short-term variants of analysis have emerged which show some promise and may offer a more realistic alternative to several years of expensive treatment.

Depth psychology has introduced the notion of the 'unconscious mind' and ego defence mechanisms which have had a major impact on the development of theory in psychopathology. Some have argued that both concepts are 'unscientific' because they are, by definition, unobservable entities. Others have accepted the idea of non-conscious forces influencing behaviour and the existence of methods of 'defence' against environmental reality.

Rogers' client-centred therapy
After Freud it is perhaps Carl Rogers who is most identified with the 'insight' approach to psychotherapy. Rogers was also amongst the first clinicians who tried to de-mystify the nature of the patient-therapist interaction by conducting research into the dynamics of the relationship. This work has been extended by Rogers (1951) and his co-workers to form the basis of training programmes designed to maximize positive therapeutic qualities in psychotherapists. Rogers developed his 'self theory' after the Second World War and offered a much simpler account of psychological distress than was available from psychoanalysis. This account gave rise to the 'counselling movement' both in the USA and in Britain. Rogers' theory stressed the social and emotional nature of the therapeutic interaction rather than reliance on any specific professional techniques and so a number of lay individuals could be quickly trained as effective counsellors. The term 'patient' was replaced by the term 'client' which, with its legal overtones defined the new therapy role as an objective counsellor rather than as an omnipotent psychical healer.

Causes of psychopathology

Rogers arrived at his self theory through considerable clinical experience with a student advisory service at the University of Chicago. He was struck by the fact that when his 'clients' arrived for help they would often make observations like: 'I feel I'm not being my real self', 'I wonder who I am, really', 'I wouldn't want anyone to know the "real" me'. These observations led Rogers to conclude that it was necessary to explore the subjective awareness of individuals - to find out what they are thinking and feeling at that time - without recourse to any defined norms or values, and without resorting to postulating unconscious processes. By studying how individuals perceive themselves (and their problems), the therapist can help them to talk through their worries and reach realistic conclusions about themselves and their lives.

'Healthy' people, who do not suffer from anxieties and insecurities, are aware of themselves. This self-knowledge allows them to understand their motivation in behaving as they do. People who suffer psychological distress do not have a coherent view of themselves and thus are not aware of their own motivation. According to Rogers each of us has an innate tendency to 'actualize'. Actualization refers to a process of striving towards realizing our full potential as human beings. We seek out new intellectual, social and emotional challenges which further develop our personal self-concept and lead to greater self-knowledge. Rogers described this process as 'personal growth' which culminates in a well-adjusted, confident personality with a cheerful outlook on life. Deviations from this ideal state occur when self-actualization ceases due to a faulty self-concept or unrealistic view of the world. For example, in the course of everyday existence we are constantly evaluating our performance in situations in order to build up an accurate self-concept of ourselves. Problems arise when we begin to accept the evaluations of others as more valid than our own perception. If the evaluations of others disagree with our own intuitive evaluation we begin to develop a distorted self-concept which will prevent further self-actualization.

Such acceptance leads to a state of incongruence between our own perceptions and those of others. This incongruence will be experienced as anxiety and we will end up not really knowing who we are or where we are going. We may also be unaware that we are so dependent on the evaluations of others; the therapy goal is to facilitate the gaining of insight by the individual into his 'real' self. This positive and optimistic theory of psychological functioning stresses the need to be personally responsible for our lives and to seek active solutions in situations of incongruence. The approach also focusses on the present, rather than delving into the past, as the main source of insight into personal problems.

Treatment

This self-actualizing view of Man suggests that social and

environmental factors are responsible for psychological dysfunction. The aim of treatment is to create a 'mini environment' within the therapy session where suitable conditions for honest self-evaluation and self-actualization are provided. To be consistent with the emphasis on self-responsibility and self-determination the therapist adopts a non-judgemental, non-directive approach to treatment. The client raises the subject matter of the session whilst the therapist concentrates on creating a suitable social and emotional climate for the client to resolve his problems. This 'safe' environment allows the client to explore his self-image and acknowledge the discrepancy between his current view of self and his ideal self; the self he is capable of becoming through further self-actualization.

Rogers has defined a number of characteristics typical of client-centred therapy. The therapist must display an accepting, non-judgemental attitude towards the client which recognizes the value of the individual, acknowledges his 'innate goodness' and offers 'unconditional positive regard' towards the individual. This implies total acceptance of the client and his present difficulties through accurate empathy with his feelings and emotions. Within this secure, trusting and warm therapeutic relationship the client can experiment with his ideas of self without the fear of censure that might occur in real life. The therapist further tries to clarify the individual's thoughts and feelings, both about himself and others, to facilitate self-knowledge. By avoiding interpretations the therapist encourages the client to talk in an honest and realistic way about his current insecurities. This focus on the subjective experience of the client in a non-directive fashion is the hallmark of client-centred therapy (CCT). The client is the agent of personal change and re-evaluation; the therapist is the provider of a safe and empathic relationship rather than the master of specific therapeutic techniques.

Client-centred therapy, whilst de-emphasizing specific therapeutic techniques, places a heavy emotional burden on the therapist. The need for accurate empathy with the client and 'unconditional positive regard' means the therapist has to become 'more involved' with the individual client than was previously acknowledged. In order to train therapists to cope with this burden and become effective clinicians, Rogers studied the personal characteristics of effective therapists in order to maximize these capacities in trainees. Truax and Mitchell (1971) identified three main characteristics of the effective therapist:

* being genuine and non-defensive in therapeutic transactions;
* providing a non-threatening, safe, trusting or secure atmosphere for the client by his own acceptance, positive regard, love, valuing or non-possessive warmth for the client;
* having a high degree of accurate empathic understanding of the client on a moment to moment basis.

These three personal qualities of genuineness, accurate empathy and non-possessive warmth have been seen as the essential attributes of all professional therapists who attempt, on an individual or group basis, to change psychological functioning. Training programmes have been designed which are claimed to increase an individual's awareness of these qualities through the use of group methods. Such training schemes have found application both in health care and in industry and commerce. The use of role-play and group encounters are the main methods of increasing these essential characteristics.

Critique of client-centred therapy (CCT)

A major criticism of Rogers' CCT lies in the fact that in keeping with its phenomenological viewpoint it uses the client's self-report of improvement as the basic measurement of efficacy. No attempt is made to see if the client really does show an improvement in his everyday functioning. If an individual claims he is anxious, particularly in social situations, we have no proof that therapy has actually improved his ability to manage social encounters. It may be that therapy creates a highly artificial environment within which the client feels 'improved', but that such an environment is seldom encountered outside therapy and thus real difficulties may actually persist, but the client is less worried about them. A further source of uncertainty is the notion of an 'innate actualizing tendency'. Rogers sees evidence for this notion in the fact that people often go out of their way to take on daunting and arduous tasks but, having said that, Rogers uses the notion of a 'self-actualizing' tendency to explain the actual behaviour. This form of circular reasoning is not convincing. Rogers also has difficulty in explaining why only some people accept the evaluations of others. A fuller account of how such individual differences in functioning come about would be necessary for a full understanding of psychological distress. It will be difficult to empathize if we have no developmental account of individual differences. The range of convenience of Rogerian theory is also rather narrow. Much of the research has been carried out on marginal personality problems and mild neurotic conditions. The extent to which this approach can assist in the more severe disorders is open to question.

Rogerian therapy and human communication

The Rogerian counselling movement has influenced a range of helping professions from social work to psychiatry. The very generality of the approach (rather than any specific explanations of psychological distress which arise) has ensured a broad following. This account of therapeutic relationships is a valuable pointer towards effective therapy and effective therapists. It emphasizes the emotional style of the therapist as a major influence on the establishment of rapport. The genuineness, positive regard and empathy of the therapist will influence the trust and honesty with which the patient will approach therapy. These principles will apply to all phases of a particular therapy, from initial assessment through treatment and reassessment phases.

Therapists must also communicate with relatives and friends of patients who may have no psychological dysfunction but who may still be in very anxious states. During these encounters the principles of CCT may allow the therapist to communicate with sensitivity and accuracy. Recent findings in the study of doctor(GP)-patient communications suggests that patients only retain a tiny fraction of the information they receive. In part this poor retention may be due to the fact that the information is too technical and the individual is often anxious when such information is being given. A client-centred approach to clinical communication suggests a very careful analysis of the recipient of such information.

Personal construct theory

George Kelly's PCT shares the phenomenological approach of CCT, but goes much further in exploring individual differences between self-concepts. The idea of 'man the scientist', actively construing future events on the basis of current construct systems, captured the imagination of many clinicians and also offered the means to explore an individual's phenomenological world using objective methods: the repertory grid technique. Grids representing construct systems could be analysed in several ways to generate a sequence of therapeutic transactions. Simple grids showed up inconsistency and loose construing; here the therapist may focus on several specific constructs which require modification. This in turn may lead to the eliciting of a further construct system which can be analysed in the same way. Implication grids (Hinkle, 1965) allow single pictures to be built up of how individuals currently see themselves (core role constructs or self-concept) and how they would ideally like to be. It is these grids which have led to therapy advocating 'personal change' as a way of coping with psychological distress.

Treatment in personal construct theory

Clinicians approaching therapy from the PCT viewpoint are aware of the reflexive nature of the theory; it applies as much to the therapist as to the patient, so therapists must find their own 'personal' approach to helping others. The therapist will be actively building up a construct system about the patient whilst the patient builds a system around the therapist. In addition to investigating the construct system which brought the patient along in the first place, emphasis is placed on reaching some degree of mutual construction between therapist and patient. Once this stage has been reached, the therapist assumes the role of 'research supervisor' who monitors the progress of his

'student' as he experiments within the therapeutic situation
with alternative constructions of his experience and behaviour. As in Rogerian therapy, the clinician does not
begin with any assumptions about what is 'normal' in any
objective sense; he will simply start from the point that
the person's current state of personal experience is giving
rise to psychological distress. The therapist encourages
the individual to construe things differently in order to
achieve a happier state of affairs. If one alternative fails
to work, other alternatives can be considered.

One means of achieving such change is through the use
of 'fixed role therapy'. Here the person adopts a completely
new set of constructs about himself and behaves in a way
that would be predicted by such constructs. The individual
may adopt this new role for a finite period of time (perhaps
a day, week or month) as part of an 'experiment in living'.
Within this new self-identity the individual can experience
things he would not have tried before. Such a diversion from
the usual self allows the patient a new view of life and a
new perspective on himself. The therapist himself may adopt
different roles from one session to another in order to
assist the patient evaluate his assumptions (constructs).
The focus of PCT, then, is to give individuals insight into
their current construct system and encourage the adoption of
a modified construct system which allows personal prediction
to become more accurate and reduce incongruence between core
role constructs and actual behaviour. In this sense there
is little real difference between the aims of Rogerian and
Kellian therapy. The difference lies in the role of the
therapists. From the non-directive approach of Rogers we
move to the more directive methods of construct theorists
who actively structure and encourage personal change. Grid
techniques provide both a means of access to the phenomenal
experience of the individual and a means of recording
personal change in an individual.

Critique of personal construct theory

Does construct theory place too much emphasis on the subjective experience of the patient and not enough on the more
practical aspects of living, such as becoming a skilled social communicator? No matter what the state of an individual's construct system there are still social tasks to be
performed, such as co-operation at work. Does construct
theory pay too little attention to these behavioural skills?
Fixed role therapy may indeed include a number of behavioural tasks which the individual can explore, practise
and become more proficient at, but it is also possible that
the search for self-knowledge could become an intellectual
pursuit alone. All of us experience a variety of 'one off'
situations where our construct systems are only capable of
very general predictions, and as a consequence we must rely
on our more automatic social skills to get us through
difficult patches.

Critics also seem dubious of the rather arbitrary nature of construct elicitation where a number of techniques (triad, laddering, etc.) are used to elicit construct topography. How do we know that the most significant constructs will emerge? If the Freudian notion of the 'unconscious' has any real basis, then to rely on consciously-generated constructs may well miss much of significance. Construct theorists dismiss such misgivings by claiming that the notion of an 'unconscious mind' is an unnecessary postulate. We can, by definition, only be aware of what is conscious and so we can only change through conscious processes.

Personal construct theory and human communication

Construct theory throws out a challenge to all professional therapists to explore their own construct systems before attempting to gain access to the systems of others. In this sense construct theory is consistent with psychoanalysis, which insisted all analysts should have undergone analysis themselves to prevent their own 'neuroses' becoming intermeshed with those of the patient. Construct theory suggests that there is a more practical reason for undertaking this self-exploration. In therapy the clinician must attempt to construe the patient and help the patient construe the therapeutic relationship. This means that not only do therapists have to get to know their patients, they must also try to make themselves known to their patients. Don Bannister in chapter 7 outlined how self-knowledge may be pursued whether or not one conducts therapy from the PCT approach. Construct theory is not simply a way of viewing psychopathology; it is a continuous process of self-evaluation for all individuals.

Construct theory has gained rapid acceptance in the treatment of communication disorders. The work of Fransella (1970, 1972) and Brumfitt and Clarke (1982) illustrates two applications in the areas of stuttering therapy and aphasia rehabilitation. Beech and Fransella (1968), in an extensive review of theoretical accounts of stuttering, concluded that little hard evidence could be amassed for any of the traditional positions. The view that dysfluent speech represents a temporary dysfunction which, through the application of specific training methods, can restore dormant fluency, is rejected by Fransella. She has argued that stutterers have had little real experience of fluency during their lives and so the sudden termination of stuttering and the establishment of fluency could place individuals in alien territory. In order to make this transition from dysfluency to fluency a whole new way of life must be established. Fransella sees stuttering as a psychological process and not simply a behavioural symptom of some underlying physiological dysfunction. Stutterers have therefore chosen to stutter as a way of predicting both themselves and their social worlds. By stuttering they can make accurate predictions of how people will react to them and how they will react to others.

Although this approach to construing the world may be eccentric, it may also eliminate any discrepancy between self and actual behaviour or self and other people. But the world of fluency is a new territory where previous predictions (as a stutterer) are no longer valid.

Fransella (1970) reports a study of 20 stutterers who were given the opportunity to construe themselves as nonstutterers on an implication grid. This invitation to build up a construct system of fluency rather than dysfluency was seen as a preparatory stage to becoming a permanently fluent speaker. Patients were asked to think of a recent situation in which they had been fluent and to recall everything that had happened in that situation. They reconstructed the situation, their feelings, and so on, to gain some appreciation of what it would feel like to be a completely fluent speaker. The implication grid provided a description of the constructs used by the stutterers to construe themselves both as stutterers and as fluent speakers.

What I have called the 'stutterer grid' is made up of constructs elicited in the following way. The patient is shown photographs of two men along with a card on which is written 'the sort of person people see me as being when I am stutterering'. He is told to try and think of himself in these terms along with the two other men and to decide in what important ways two of them might be seen as being alike and thereby different from the third. He might say that two are shy and the other self-confident. That is a construct. The same procedure is repeated with six different pairings of photographs, but always with the third person being himself as others see him when he is stuttering. Having elicited these constructs he is asked to consider each in turn and to decide which pole he would like to be seen as - for instance, 'shy' or 'self-confident' - and which pole he thinks best describes him as he is now. When he has done this he is asked why he prefers to be described by the pole of his choice rather than by the other. The answer he gives is another construct.

A second grid is developed in just the same way but with one essential difference. The card with which the photographs are paired has written on it 'the sort of person people see me as when I am NOT stuttering' (Fransella, 1970).

Fransella found that without any specific work on the actual symptom of stuttering the number of 'non-stutterer' implications increased and the number of 'stutterer' implications decreased with a corresponding decrease in actual dysfluent speech. This kind of evidence suggests that a personal construct approach to stuttering can control dysfluency as effectively as mechanical training techniques. Thus personal change in self-concept (core role constructs) can lead to the reduction of dysfunctional behaviour.

Brumfitt and Clarke (1982) have explored the use of PCT in the rehabilitation of adult brain-damaged patients. In aphasia, for example, individuals experience dramatic changes in their core role constructs by virtue of their sudden handicap. At one moment a man may consider himself a dynamic, confident sales director of a large firm; at the next a helpless, speechless individual, confused and frightened by what has happened. Adjustment to this handicap must be made without the usual social support of the family since communication has been lost. Accounts from individuals who have recovered from aphasic disorders present a harrowing picture of this process of adjustment. Emotional confusion, depression, frustration and a variety of other negative emotions can be experienced, some of which may be caused by the actual lesion; others are a direct consequence of being 'lost for words'. The minimal communicative effort involved in grid development allows discrepancies and implications to emerge from the phenomenological experience of brain damage which enables therapists to assist in the process of self-reconstruction. Only when some reasonable level of coherence is re-established in the construct system can more specific forms of communicative therapy be attempted.

Construct theory has both general and specific implications for the clinician involved in human communication disorders. Perhaps the most provocative aspect of personal construct theory concerns the therapist's exploration and reconstruction of himself and the discovery of the constructs used by patients to view the therapeutic interaction. Construct theory suggests that more accurate clinical communication could result if a detailed analysis of these areas was undertaken by clinical scientists in their construction of their role.

Group therapies

The three preceding forms of therapy, despite their social implications, are primarily individual forms of treatment. The therapeutic relationship becomes a social vehicle for personal change. Group therapies stemmed from the early research in social psychology which demonstrated the power of group processes to effect change in individual participants. Several theoretical positions have developed which offer a description of how change in groups occurs, the kinds of psychological problems amenable to group treatment and the role of the therapist in such groups. The pioneering work of Rogers (1970) and Truax and Carkhuff (1967) established group methods of therapist training and 'personal growth' through the rise of encounter groups. Group therapies are seldom simply economical ways of treating large numbers of patients, although some evidence suggests that many forms of individual therapy can be carried out as effectively in group settings.

The use of groups in psychiatric settings has revolutionized concepts of rehabilitation and shifted the emphasis on residential care for the psychologically distressed.

Maxwell Jones (1953) introduced the idea of 'therapeutic communities' where residential patients become actively involved in the decision taking and organization of their residential environment. Non-residential applications of group methods range from the creation of self-help groups for specific problems such as alcoholism, depression, brain damage and kidney disease to groups designed to foster self-awareness in normal individuals. Four types of group therapy are briefly outlined.

Psychodrama

Moreno and Kipper (1968) are credited with being the pioneers of group treatment for psychiatric disturbance. Their approach was to ask individuals to 'act out' their feelings and anxieties about themselves and other people in their lives as if they were actors in a play. Other patients play the parts of significant characters - mother, father, boss, wife, husband, son, daughter, etc. - and so a personal 'play' is enacted as a way of getting individuals to give a more concrete account of their problems. Thus the treatment group becomes a company of actors (often using a real stage to heighten the drama) who portray the difficulties of an individual's life. Group members who are not involved in this production form an 'audience' who offer feedback on specific aspects of the play. At various points in psycho-drama, group members play each other in order to give feedback about the way they are seen by the group. This 'mir-roring' technique allows an individual to see himself as others do. The therapist becomes a 'director' in these productions, actively setting up new 'scenes' and encouraging the expression of feelings. Further description of the theory and therapy of psychodrama can be found in Greenberg (1974).

Gestalt therapy

The creation of Gestalt therapy is usually attributed to Perls (1969) who advocates the need for continuous 'personal growth' throughout the life span both for individuals suffering psychological distress and for 'normal' people as well. This extension of therapy to the non-psychiatrically disturbed is referred to as the humanistic movement in psychology. Humanistic psychology acknowledges that it is not only the psychiatrically disturbed who experience self-doubt, guilt and other negative emotions in their lives; everyone is prone to these states, but can be helped to come to terms with them through appropriate training. It is assumed that by exchanging experiences, expectations, feelings and attitudes with others, in a secure emotional and social climate, a great deal of these negative sensations can be eliminated.

To achieve this personal growth a number of 'ground rules' are laid down in Gestalt therapy by which individual participants must agree to abide.

* Emphasis is placed on becoming aware of the present experience of the individual as a whole. The focus is therefore on current feelings and thoughts on a moment to moment basis including awareness of how the body is being used to convey these feelings and ideas.
* Emphasis is placed on self-responsibility and self-determination. Individuals are encouraged to work towards self-acceptance; allowing themselves to become the people they really are and thus removing the need for a social 'front'.
* Emphasis is placed on the creative and expressive aspects of the individual rather than the negative frustrations and emotions that interfere with personal growth.

Gestalt therapy is, of course, an extension of Gestalt psychology which concentrated on the perception of 'wholes' rather than constituent 'parts'. Gestalt therapy is concerned with making the person 'whole' by putting him in contact with the range of intrapsychic and bodily processes which make up individual totality rather than focussing on one specific emotional or intellectual difficulty.

A variety of techniques are employed in Gestalt therapy to attain this goal of self-integration. One involves asking group members to talk always in the present tense to emphasize the current state of the person. Personal responsibility is stressed by the use of personification: rather than say 'my hands are shaking' the member is asked to accept responsibility for his hands by saying 'I am shaking'. Another technique consists of asking people to externalize their feelings and then speak to them as if they were objects in the environment. This procedure is said to assist in 'getting in touch' with one's feelings. Group members often pair up and play 'games' designed to foster personal responsibility and achieve more accurate empathy with other people. (See Shepherd and Fagan, 1970, for further discussion of Gestalt therapy.)

Training groups (T-Groups)

Training groups resulted from the efforts of social psychologists in the 1940s to improve interpersonal communication in business; 'group talk' methods were used to increase an individual's self-awareness of the impact his style of communication was having on other group members. Training groups were later developed as educational experiences for individuals in the counselling and psychotherapy fields. Aronson (1972) states the following aims for T-Groups:

* to develop a willingness to examine one's own behaviour and to experiment with new ways of behaving;
* to learn more about people in general;
* to become more authentic and honest in interpersonal relationships;

*   to work co-operatively with people rather than assuming an authoritarian or submissive manner;
*   to develop the ability to resolve conflicts through logical and rational thinking rather than through coercion and manipulation of others.

The T-Group leader tries to encourage individuals to be less guarded in their self-presentation and to highlight shared emotions and attitudes which develop in the group. Group tasks are set which require co-operation, leadership and support amongst participants. More recently these groups have been developed along more radical lines. More emphasis has been placed on the use of the 'body techniques' such as massage and yoga as an additional pathway to self-integration and sensitivity. A variety of non-verbal methods of communication such as miming, sculpting and eye contact, together with group 'games' have been introduced to 'break the ice' in new groups and promote trust and acceptance between participants.

Family therapy

Family therapy explores a very special set of individual relationships which can become disturbed and result in specific instances of psychological distress. Therapy attempts to re-organize and give insight into the effects of such intra-family dynamics and thus remove the presumed causative factors of the 'identified patient's' problem. Family therapists come from a number of different theoretical backgrounds, from psychoanalytic to behaviouristic therapy. However, despite these differences, there is general agreement on the value of the family approach. Psychological distress does not just occur spontaneously in a given individual; the 'identified patient' in the family system may only represent the tip of the iceberg. Clinical practitioners do not regard the patient as 'ill' but rather the scapegoat in a family with ineffective internal communication and anxiety-provoking relationships. Therefore the patient is a public representation of the underlying turmoil in family processes. Neil Frude gives a more detailed account of family systems in chapter 9, and Walrond-Skinner (1976) provides an excellent introduction to family therapy. A comprehensive review of the efficacy of family therapy has been undertaken by Gurman and Kniskern (1981).

Insight groups and human communication

Speech therapists regularly employ group methods of treatment both for specific communication problems and as an adjunct to individual therapy where distinct social and emotional problems exist. The aims of such treatments therefore range in specificity from general supportive functions (stroke clubs, parents' groups) to the more specific acquisition of new skills (social skills groups, assertion training groups). These group treatments have grown in popularity as therapists have acknowledged the need to treat 'the whole patient'. Communication breakdown seldom occurs in isolation from other aspects of individual functioning. Very significant social and emotional disturbances invariably accompany such a handicap either as potential causative factors or as the product of the inability to communicate.

Group treatment techniques have been developed for children and adolescents, mature adult patients and geriatric patients both as weekly and intensive forms of treatment. Further reading in the area of group therapies can be found in Harris (1977), Walton (1971), and Andolfi (1979).

Action therapies

Behaviourism

Behaviouristic psychology has generated a formidable array of treatment methods during the past three decades. Two main streams of action therapies can be distinguished. The radical behaviourism of Skinner has been systematically translated into clinical action under the title of 'behaviour modification'. The neo-behaviouristic approach of Clark Hull has been developed by Wolpe and Eysenck into an explanatory system of the human neuroses and a variety of techniques to eliminate these conditions, usually termed the behaviour therapies. Both approaches stress the need for rigorous scientific analysis of problems to identify likely causative factors which can then become amenable to treatment. Action therapies derive their name from the emphasis on a direct attack on problem behaviours rather than discussion of the significance of symptoms and reliance on the patient's account of improvement.

Radical behaviouristic therapy: behaviour modification

Skinner's analysis of human learning virtually prickled with therapeutic implications. It encompassed the acquisition of motor skills as well as higher mental functions, (such as language acquisition) and psychiatric disturbance. The simplicity of Skinner's emphasis on modifying actual overt behaviour through manipulation of environmental reinforcement contingencies offered an extremely practical method of tackling human problems. For radical behaviourists psychopathology consists of a cluster of 'faulty behaviours' which can be objectively described and treated using systematic reinforcement. Therapists must analyse where the likely sources of social and emotional reinforcement lie in the individual's environment which are assumed to be maintaining the actual behavioural symptoms. When these sources have been identified, therapy concentrates on weakening the associations between behaviour and reinforcement to decrease the problem behaviour and then build up new, adaptive operant responses by the further application of reinforcement.

Assessment in radical behaviour modification is a process (rather than any specific psychometric device) known as 'functional analysis'. Cullen et al (1977) have outlined the main features of functional analysis as follows:

* an identification and description of the behavioural
  episode and its part in the individual's total behaviour
  organization. This is essentially an exercise in data
  collection which may involve a number of methods including direct observation, interview, and standardized
  formal psychological testing.
* an interpretation of the data in terms of a conceptual
  framework derived explicitly from an experimental analysis of behaviour (Skinner, 1953, 1972). This involves
  the specification of functional relationships between
  the behaviour stream and the environment. It may include
  a retrospective (developmental) analysis of causes and a
  projected analysis of a behavioural solution (targets).
* an intervention based on the interpretative stage involves the manipulation of the functional relationships
  to predicted ends, and thus is a process which is
  experimental in nature.
* an assessment of the effects of intervention.

This kind of analysis provides a framework for clinical
action in distinct stages which may interact at certain
points in treatment. Thus if the results of the fourth stage
are not what was predicted on the basis of the third stage,
then the therapist must return to the first two stages in an
attempt to reformulate the problem.

Causes of psychopathology

Psychopathology is seen as a set of maladapative learned
responses which are maintained by environmental reinforcement. Phobic conditions are learned responses which receive
environmental reinforcement. Phobic behaviour consists of a
number of avoidance responses which receive direct environmental reinforcement; thus a child may make excuses why he
should not attend school (colds, pains, etc.) and if these
excuses are accepted by parents the child is directly reinforced for his avoidance behaviour. In the same way obsessive compulsive disorders and hysteria have been seen by
Ullmann and Krasner (1969) as learned behaviours reinforced
by reduced demands and increased attention from others.
Depression has also been viewed from this perspective by
Eastman (1976) and Ullmann and Krasner (1975). The central
feature of depression is seen as a sudden reduction in
available environmental reinforcement. This could follow
bereavement, marital discord or work problems. The reduction
in environmental reinforcement leads to a reduction in operant behaviour, but as a consequence of this lowered activity
level the individual may receive new kinds of reinforcement
in the form of increased social and professional concern.
This new source of reinforcement might serve to maintain the
depressive behaviour unless specific action is taken to get
the patient to establish new social and individual contacts
which will result in replacement reinforcement.

Behavioural disorders can result from faulty learning
under contingent environmental reinforcement. Language can

be viewed as 'verbal behaviour', anxiety as 'fear behaviour' and stuttering as 'speech behaviour'. Behaviour modification using full functional analysis can be programmed for many types of disordered behaviour and a range of modification principles have been derived from Skinnerian theory which emphasize the experimental nature of intervention.

Treatment: behaviour modification

Functional analysis yields a set of hypotheses (predictions) about the possible sources of reinforcement which may be maintaining current behaviour and thus suggests 'experiments' which will either confirm or disconfirm the predictions. It is these empirical studies which constitute behaviour modification treatments, or contingency management as it is sometimes called. Functional analysis provides a detailed account of the actual problem behaviours, their rate of occurrence under different reinforcement conditions and specifies target behaviours which intervention will attempt to establish. Each modification programme is therefore unique to each individual patient. Accounts of the process of functional analysis can be found in Haynes (1978) and Kazdin (1978). The application of operant conditioning principles to problem behaviours can take several forms.

Individual conditioning paradigms

The most common application of behaviour modification is to the individual case manifesting distinct episodes of maladaptive behaviour. Children may have self-injurious tendencies, aggressive episodes towards peers and adults or some specific developmental problem which is open to functional analysis. Treatment consists of identifying the sources of maintaining reinforcement and removing this source of reinforcement through physical means or through replacing it with aversive reinforcement. New adaptive behaviours can be built up in the place of these maladaptive ones through the systematic application of new reinforcement contingencies. This training may occur in the psychological laboratory or in the 'real life' environment of the child. Functional analysis is usually conducted in the 'real life' situation, but the initial stages of treatment may need the control of the laboratory for the fading of problem behaviour. Treatment is a continuous process which is established in the eventual target environment.

Group conditioning paradigm: token economy

Although operant procedures for the individual case are the most common form of behaviour modification, the use of group procedures with specific populations has grown in popularity over the past decade. Ayllon and Azrin (1965, 1968) demonstrated how the principles of behaviour modification could be applied to residential environments for chronic psychiatric patients. Staats and Staats (1963) pioneered the use of group principles in their work with mentally retarded and behaviourally disordered children. Ayllon and Azrin designed a programme for an entire ward of chronic, long-stay psychiatric patients. By using plastic tokens which could be 'cashed in' for more tangible rewards such as extra television time, food, drink and other privileges, a practical method of delivering individual reinforcement was achieved. The aim then was to manipulate available reinforcement using the tokens to reduce undesirable behaviour and promote self-help and social behaviour. The outcome of this study was remarkably successful; patients who had previously remained in bed, failed to attend to personal hygiene and seldom interacted in a social fashion were seen to engage in more adaptive behaviour after a few weeks of the token programme.

Following this early work a number of token economies have been set up for a range of problems. The need for an institutional setting for such programmes is obvious if complete control over reinforcement contingencies is to be attained. In recent years there has been some pointed criticism of the token economy on the basis that it confuses management with rehabilitation (Cullen et al, 1977). The use of tokens as a handy means of controlling reinforcement contingencies is still a central feature of many behaviour modification programmes which aim to change specific symptoms (Liberman and Teigen, 1979).

Neo-behaviouristic therapy: behaviour therapy
Neo-behaviourism represents a clear break with the breadth explanations of learning put forward by radical behaviourists. Neo-behaviouristic theory seeks the causes of behaviour both in the external environment and in the internal functioning of the individual. The most significant aspect of this neo-behaviourism has been the reinterpretation of 'reinforcement' to refer to any event which results in the reduction of internal drive states. This development attempts to explain why some individuals are prone to faulty learning in an environment whilst others are not. The individual who presents some behavioural disorder may have learnt a maladaptive response because he was in a state of high emotional activity, which was alleviated by engaging in a particular behavioural activity. Specific behavioural activity is 'learned' because it is associated with drive reduction. It is assumed that there are biological differences in the level of internal physiological activity, which interact with the external environment to result in a series of 'adaptive' responses, yet these may be socially maladaptive. Behaviour therapy attempts to dissolve these defensive associations between internal states (such as anxiety) and overt behavioural activity (such as avoidance responses).

Causes of psychopathology
Anxiety is the central concept in behavioural therapy and is seen as an energizer of new behaviour. The anxiety drive mediates between environmental input and behavioural output to achieve internal equilibrium. New behaviours are learnt

and employed in everyday living because they have drive reduction properties. This analysis of psychopathology suggests that behavioural symptoms arise because they have drive reduction properties. A new focus for treatment is suggested which assumes symptoms can be reduced by directly tackling the underlying drive state (usually anxiety). Neobehaviourism does not differ from radical behaviourism in the rigour with which it pursues the scientific explanation and treatment of behavioural problems.

Assessment shifts from a purely environmental description to measurement of the underlying psychological state of anxiety. Three kinds of measurement are employed to quantify anxiety.

* Direct observation of the individual can reveal a great deal of information about his psychological state. Sweating, breathing, yawning, sighing, agitation and other nervous habits can be quantified in a time sample as a measurement of drive state.

* Self-report questionnaires have been developed and standardized on clinical and normal samples to provide objective indices of anxiety. One such instrument is the IPAT Anxiety Scale (Krug, Scheier and Cattell, 1976) which has been derived from Cattell's work on the factorial description of personality. This instrument offers a rapid, objective way of eliciting clinical information in patients from the age of 14 upwards. It consists of two scales containing 20 items which measure (i) unrealized, covert anxiety and (ii) an overt, symptomatic conscious anxiety. Each question has three possible answers to choose between, which yield a total score plus an overt-covert discrepancy which can be analysed for abnormality.

* Physiological measurement of anxiety and related states has greatly increased in popularity in recent years. A number of psychophysiological indices can be utilized to build up a direct, objective profile of the individual's drive state; (i) heart rate: increases and decreases in heart rate can be used to estimate the emotional significance of various situations; (ii) skin conductance: as anxiety and arousal increase sweating occurs which results in changes in the electrical conductivity of the skin and by taking continuous measurements of these conduction changes in areas of horny skin (fingers, palm of hand) a picture can be gained of arousal states; (iii) muscle tension: the electromyograph can record tiny changes in muscle tension by picking up the electrical currents associated with muscle movement. These measures are particularly useful when patients report a specific muscular focus of tension, such as a headache.

Anxiety measurement can assist in exploring the individual's drive activation in general as well as his response to specific kinds of environmental input. A further advantage of such measures lies in their ability to detect change as a consequence of intervention.

Conditions such as phobias and obsessive-compulsive neuroses are instances of learnt behaviour because the actual behaviour has drive reduction properties. A compulsive hand washer who is plagued by obsessive ideas of contamination by germs has adopted the ritual because it leads to anxiety reduction (lowers anxiety about contamination). The association between anxiety and contamination can be further weakened by the application of specific behavioural therapy. Hysteria is seen as a learnt way of coping with internal anxiety. The actual symptoms, such as deafness, hoarseness, paralysis, etc., are maintained because of their drive reduction properties. Seligman (1974) has offered an account of depression which suggests that anxiety is the usual initial response to any stressful situation. If no effective behavioural means are available to cope with such stressful situations a resultant state of 'learned helplessness' occurs which is characterized by lethargy, blunting of affect and anhedonia (inability to experience pleasure). This account of depression has emerged from experimental work with dogs, although a number of theoretical predictions have since been confirmed in Man.

Treatment: behaviour therapies

Four kinds of behaviour therapies are outlined which have been derived from neo-behaviouristic learning theory. These treatments have wide applications in the field of health care where anxiety management is required.

Systematic desensitization

Systematic desensitization has its roots in the early conditioning work of Watson and Rayner (1920). The 'counter conditioning' technique used by these workers to alleviate the phobic reaction of 'Little Albert' was refined by Wolpe (1958) as a general method of reducing learnt anxiety and was called 'reciprocal inhibition'. The basic aim of this therapy is to induce a response in the individual patient which is incompatible with anxiety and then expose the patient to a hierarchically graded sequence of anxiety provoking situations. As long as the competing response outweighs the anxiety response, the association between environmental stimuli and the anxiety response will be weakened. Wolpe settled on muscular relaxation as the ideal competing response to anxiety and adopted the methods of Jacobsen (1927) to induce a state of deep muscle relaxation in his anxiety patients. Someone with a phobia about heights would be interviewed to find out in what situations this fear was experienced. The individual volunteers around a dozen or so examples and then is asked to rate each on a 'fear thermometer', an arbitrary scale from 1 to 100, which indicates the relative fear in each. This information allows the therapist to construct a hierarchy of situations from least to most fearful which can be used in treatment. The patient is then taught deep muscle relaxation and asked to imagine (in his mind's eye) the least anxiety-provoking situation on the hierarchy. Once any anxiety is experienced the patient is asked to stop imagining the scene and go through the relaxation sequence once more. As each scene is imagined without anxiety progress is made up the hierarchy until the most threatening situation can be envisaged without discomfort. At this stage it is assumed the patient has extinguished his fear of heights.

Systematic desensitization is the modern term for this technique although a major difference is the use of 'in vivo' (as opposed to imaginal) treatment. A patient with a fear of heights would go through the usual procedure, but rather than imagine items in his fear hierarchy he would be accompanied by a therapist to a real-life situation which corresponds with his hierarchy items. Imaginal desensitization is still the only practical treatment for more diffuse fears, or rare fears, where in vivo treatment is impossible. Modern desensitization has also developed modified forms of relaxation training which avoid the lengthy procedures of Jacobsen, such as Wolpe and Lazarus (1966) and Bernstein and Borkovec (1973). For a broad review of behaviour therapy in clinical practice, see Wolpe (1969).

Flooding

During the 1960s encouraging reports of an inverse procedure of desensitization was given by Stampfl and Lewis (1967) where anxiety patients were asked to experience very intense anxiety-provoking situations without a gradual build up. Individuals treated in this way seemed to display a much faster recovery from their fears than was achieved with systematic desensitization. Rachman (1969) offered an explanation of this finding in terms of an inbuilt self-limiting mechanism which comes into operation when intolerable levels of anxiety are experienced. From very high levels of anxiety the individual paradoxically enters a state of low anxiety where the anxiety response simply habituates.

In flooding, the patient is confronted with a high anxiety-provoking situation derived from his presenting complaint. He is asked to endure these situations (perhaps with the help of some coping technique such as rapid relaxation) until the anxiety response subsides. Although a highly traumatic technique, clinical evidence does suggest it provides a rapid method of controlling disabling anxiety.

Modelling

Bandura (1969), in his investigations of imitation learning, came across the phenomenon of modelling which resulted in the development of the clinical technique of anxiety control. He described the effects as 'vicarious conditioning' which occur when phobic individuals are simply allowed to observe another person (model) engaging in the activity that is feared. The original studies employed snake phobic patients who were shown both filmed and 'live' sequences of other people handling snakes with no sign of fear. Self-report and physiological measures of anxiety in these patients showed a reduction in anxiety levels as a direct consequence of watching others in fear-arousing situations. Rachman and colleagues (Rachman, Hodgson and Marzillier, 1970; Rachman, Hodgson and Marks, 1971; Rachman, Marks and Hodgson, 1973) have extensively investigated the use of modelling techniques for a variety of anxiety conditions and conclude that this simple procedure does indeed have lasting effects on anxiety levels. Therapists act as a model by engaging in the feared activities of the patient who at first simply watches and is gradually asked to participate in the activity. This may extend over several treatment sessions until the patient reports he no longer experiences anxiety when fully participating in the previously feared activity.

Aversion therapy
Aversion therapy is based on the classical conditioning paradigm where an innate reflex response of pleasure has been associated with some form of environmental stimulus. When this association is considered maladaptive the pleasurable response is replaced by an aversive response through further conditioning. Subsequent presentations of the original pleasure-evoking stimulus results in an aversive internal response. Early work in aversion therapy used electric shock as the aversive stimulus which was paired with the presentation of the pleasure evoking stimulus. Chemical aversive agents such as disulfiram (Antabuse) have been employed in cases of alcoholism where ingestion of the drug results in nausea and vomiting (innate reflex responses) when alcohol (CS) is consumed. Thus the previous CR of pleasure is replaced by a UCR of nausea and vomiting to the CS of alcohol. Similar experiments have been shown to have the same effect for smoking and a number of preparations are currently available to inhibit and extinguish 'smoking behaviour'.

One further area where aversion therapy has been extensively employed is the treatment of sexual offenders. Aversive olfactory stimulation is used to extinguish pleasurable responses to the sight of some sexual object. In a typical conditioning set-up the patient is shown slides of scenes which are pleasurable followed by aversive stimulation. After a number of trials this paradigm can be supplemented by providing a button which, if pushed within a few seconds, changes the pleasurable (now aversive) scene to a more adaptive scene (normal heterosexual stimuli) and also avoids the presentation of the aversive stimulation. In this way pleasurable responses to the 'wrong' stimuli are extinguished, and, because of the anxiety-reducing effect of viewing the 'right' stimuli, increased attractiveness results.

Aversion therapy has generated some controversy since its introduction, both on theoretical and ethical grounds. Critics argue that the classical conditioning paradigm is

severely stretched in this form of therapy and the unpleasant nature of the treatment may not be justified by the ends
it achieves. There is no doubt, however, of the power of
conditioning under these circumstances and, although humane
levels of aversion stimulation are employed, this power
could well be increased by raising the level of aversive
stimulation. It is perhaps this latter hypothesis that
causes most discomfort to the critics of aversion therapy.
Further detailed discussion of this technique can be found
in Rachman and Teasdale (1969).

Critique of behaviouristic therapies

Behaviour therapies, both radical and neo-behaviouristic,
have found application in mental health, education, special
education and a variety of other spheres for the past 30
years. A vast literature on techniques and their effectiveness with a wide range of populations has grown. Behavioural
techniques provide a practical and effective means of modifying overt and intrinsic responses to environmental stimuli
with commendable scientific control and rigour. Despite this
impressive series of applications there has been serious
doubt expressed about the use of these techniques which fall
into three main categories:

* the adequacy of the theoretical basis of the behavioural
  techniques;
* the extent to which these treatments have lasting
  effects;
* the impersonal nature of the treatment.

Theoretical adequacy

1. RADICAL BEHAVIOURISM: Skinner's rather simple paradigm
made a number of assumptions which were necessary for objective, scientific enquiry. He began with the assumption
that all behaviour is 'learned'; each species is born, in
Locke's terms, a tabula rasa: a blank slate on which experience (learning) writes. This assumption was made because
the notion of 'innate behaviour' was an unscientific concept. He went on to take a fairly arbitrary species (the
laboratory rat, chosen for its ease of storage) and placed
it in a very arbitrary 'learning environment' (the Skinner
Box, designed for the maximization of experimental control).
It was further assumed that what would emerge from this
paradigm would be general laws governing the acquisition of
new responses. As Seligman (1970) pointed out, an arbitrary
species in an arbitrary environment may give rise to specific laws which only apply to arbitrary situations. After
all, Skinner's view of the 'general laws of learning' does
not make a great deal of sense from an evolutionary
viewpoint.

His theory suggests that species must learn survival
skills through the application of environmental reinforcement, but in many situations this is simply not feasible.

Imagine a mouse out foraging at night and a hungry owl perched in a nearby tree. Are we to assume our mouse learns to associate the sound of the owl's wings with being eaten? In these circumstances only a tiny proportion of mice could escape such trauma and 'learn' this association. Closer attention to how mice survive in natural habitats reveals that they typically 'freeze' on the spot when any novel stimulus is presented. This innate 'freezing' reaction is highly adaptive. When the mouse 'freezes' in grass the owl has a very difficult task to locate him. When the mouse is moving it provides a clearly visible track through the grass which can be easily followed from the air. We assume mice who have tried running away from strange sounds or movements have been caught by predators and have not survived to reproduce.

This simple point illustrates Seligman's notion of biological 'preparedness' for learning. He contends that animals are equipped with a range of species-specific behaviour which is genetically programmed for essential survival skills such as courtship and reproduction, food getting and escape from predators. These innate behaviours are examples of 'prepared' learning; the CNS and hormonal systems of the species are designed to recognize certain stimuli and behave in a highly stereotyped way. A number of examples of this kind of behaviour were noted by Breland and Breland (1966) in a series of conditioning experiments to train animals for use in television commercials. These workers found that certain behaviours which they attempted to shape would degenerate into unmodifiable sequences which were actually species-specific behaviours. In one example they cite how a racoon was being trained to pick up coins and deposit them in a nearby toy 'bank'. This is a rather simple matter of shaping responses through food rewards until a more complex sequence is built up. The racoon was trained to pick the coins up but could not be persuaded to put them down again despite the application of reinforcement. Instead it would rub the coins together in a miserly fashion between its front paws. Breland and Breland found this rubbing activity in wild racoons when they hunt crayfish. The fish is rubbed between the front paws to remove the horny shell. Their racoon seemed to be displaying the innate sequence as a result of receiving a food reward and therefore Breland and Breland termed this phenomenon 'instinctual drift'. So species are biologically 'prepared' to make certain associations which lead to the performance of innate, species-specific forms of behaviour.

Seligman describes 'unprepared' behaviour as the kind of learning which requires a number of trials to establish an association between a specific input and a particular behavioural output. All operant conditioning studies therefore involve 'unprepared' learning. Finally, Seligman proposes a third type of 'preparedness': 'contra prepared' learning. Here the animal either never learns a particular association or only learns it after a very great number of trials. He cites cases from the literature, particularly Thorndike's early work, when it was found certain responses could not be established in an animal no matter how much reinforcement is applied. For example, it is relatively easy to train a pigeon to peck at a coloured disc to obtain food reward (unprepared learning) because the association between pecking and food getting is 'prepared'. A coloured disc is not an actual food source, but it leads to food reward and is therefore learnt after a few trials. But if we try to train a bird to fly away from some stimulus in order to gain food reward this is contra prepared because the bird cannot make such an association.

Seligman's analysis has posed difficult problems for 'general process' learning theory. The assumption that any species can learn to make an association between any stimulus and any response has been shown to be quite wrong. All species bring along to an experiment a set of highly specialized sensory and motor capacities and a highly specialized associative apparatus. To predict accurately how that animal will learn we must recognize not only its sensory and motor capabilities, but also its innate species-specific behaviour, which will reflect a specialized set of associative capacities.

In a more practical example we can consider Skinner's analysis of 'verbal behaviour'. For Skinner the acquisition of language is no different from the acquisition of any other new response. Verbal behaviours are shaped by environmental reinforcement into recognizable phonological output associated with particular environmental objects. Chomsky (1959), as noted earlier, highlighted the difficulty this account experienced given that child language displays features like creativity: new words and word forms (e.g. 'cutted' as a past tense of 'to cut') which the child may never have heard before. Skinner's account implies that children can only learn what they have heard previously and so any novel output is very difficult to explain. Chomsky argues that the only way to explain such examples of creativity in child language is by postulating that rather than learning specific responses the child applies certain 'rules' to the generation of language. A rule may be learnt in one situation and generalized to different situations: thus 'ed' added to the end of a word may be a rule for the formation of past tenses. Such a rule will then be generally applied. Chomsky further argued that these 'rules' were the product of an innate capacity (Language Acquisition Device or LAD) for the analysis of speech and language, which was genetically programmed to process input in a highly structured fashion and generated 'rules' of language which guided actual output. A similar view is reached by biological theorists of communication. The study of animal communication suggests a significant genetic component, and it is proposed by Lenneberg (1967) that human language is a species-specific capacity which is dependent on the state of maturation of the CNS. Only when the CNS has reached a particular stage of maturation (e.g. myelinization of the nerve axons) does language acquisition take place. He too argues for an innate CNS programming which processes input in a highly specific way to generate language output.

These views are in agreement with Seligman's notion of 'prepared learning'; language is a species-specific phenomenon genetically programmed to result in a specific form of CNS processing. One prediction this view makes is that this capacity will not be found in any other species and it will not be amenable to training schemes derived from 'unprepared' learning experiments.

2. NEO-BEHAVIOURISM: early accounts of the acquisition of phobias by Watson and Rayner (1920) were problematic because conditioning theory predicts that in the absence of further UCS pairings (loud noise) the CR (of fear) should extinguish. The fact of phobias is that they do not extinguish; if anything they 'get worse' as time passes. In order to account for this, Mowrer (1939) proposed what has become known as 'two-factor' learning theory of neuroses. Mowrer postulated that anxiety responses are initially learnt in classical conditioning situations. A person who has a nasty experience in a lift will experience those same nasty feelings in future when lifts are encountered. This conditioned fear (anxiety) response becomes a Hullian drive which can energize behaviour, leading to drive reduction. Thus the person with a lift phobia may 'learn' to avoid lifts in future, and as a consequence may not have an opportunity to experience non-reinforced 'lift trials'. This new instrumental response of avoidance prevents the individual from receiving further modification of the fear response leading to extinction, and so the anxiety does not dissipate. This view can account for how some phobias are acquired and even for the failure of the anxiety to dissipate, but it cannot explain why only some individuals react in this way whereas others do not; nor why anxiety seems to increase rather than decrease with the passage of time. Two further lines of theoretical reasoning have been put forward by Eysenck (1967, 1976) to explain these findings. Eysenck points to individual differences in conditionability (extraversion-introversion) and in emotional reactivity (neuroticism-stability) as a source of variation in the acquisition of anxiety conditions. Highly reactive and conditionable individuals are more likely to acquire fear responses to previously neutral stimuli. Eysenck also puts forward the notion that anxiety increases over time because of an 'incubation' process. Anxiety and fear responses grow in strength each time an unreinforced presentation of the original CS is encountered. Seligman (1970) has proposed that phobias represent special cases of 'prepared' learning where traditional general process theories break down. He points to the fact that the vast majority of phobias can be seen as biological in nature: fear of loss of support, heights, spiders, cats, mice, snakes, enclosed spaces, etc.

He notes that instances of 'lamb phobias' are extremely rare, presumably because we are not 'prepared' to fear such harmless creatures, whereas the 'prepared' phobic objects have dangerous implications.

In short a number of problems exist with the neo-behaviouristic account of the development of neuroses. This has led to a new era of theory which focusses on the cognitive and emotional processes of the individual in response to fear-arousing situations.

Further criticism has been directed at the theoretical adequacy of the derived techniques in behaviour therapy. Breger and McGaugh (1965) argue that there is only a very loose association between academic theories of learning and the actual form of behaviour therapy. They point out that in systematic desensitization the 'stimulus' is an imagined scene from a hierarchy: an unobservable, unquantifiable entity. The desired 'response' is relaxation; and this again is not an easy thing to observe or measure. Given these unquantifiable elements can it really be claimed that systematic desensitization is truly an application of scientific theory? This point has been taken by many clinical workers who accept that behavioural techniques work, but have doubts about the interpretation of how such treatments actually work. London (1972) highlights this gulf between theory and therapy and proposes that new explanations be sought for the effectiveness of behavioural treatments.

Both radical and neo-behaviouristic therapies have demonstrated their efficacy in alleviating psychological distress, but have yet to produce coherent theoretical arguments for such efficacy. Modern developments in therapy are now moving away from theoretical dogma and concentrating on a scientific investigation in order to develop more comprehensive treatments with an acceptable underlying theoretical framework.

Generalization of treatment effects

Although the effectiveness of behaviouristic treatments has been established in controlled environments, there is a paucity of longitudinal evidence on their continuing effectiveness. For radical behaviourists the problem of maintaining treatment gains after therapy has been tackled by the use of intermittent reinforcement schedules. When establishing some new response through behaviour modification, continuous and then fixed interval reinforcement schedules are used. In order to make this reinforcement more similar to the real world, an intermittent schedule is eventually used which will approximate more closely the real-life situation. People do not usually reinforce every single instance of 'social behaviour'; rather they occasionally say 'thank you' or offer some other form of positive reinforcement. But the problem of generalization is more complex than this; not only is the frequency of reinforcement different between laboratory and real world, but the nature of available reinforcement may also be quite different.

The 'token economy' is perhaps the best example of this distinction. This application of radical behaviourism has proved extremely effective in influencing the social and individual behaviour of children and adults in institutional environments. In most cases only very basic self-help and co-operative skills are trained through this approach. Kazdin and Bootzin (1972) demonstrated how such behaviour is very much tied to the availability of token reinforcement. When tokens are withdrawn behaviour returns to pre-token levels. Cullen et al (1977) point out that these applications have confused simple management techniques with a genuinely rehabilitative aim. Token economies introduced to chronic long-stay institutional environments have shown quite dramatic gains in management of these patients. If a genuinely rehabilitative aim is contemplated, in the sense of preparing people to leave institutional life and return to the community, then token systems have proved spectacularly unsuccessful.

For Cullen et al (1977) this problem of generalization of learning from one environment to another hinges on the nature of the reinforcement used during the training scheme. A careful functional analysis of the target environment is required to identify the natural sources of reinforcement to which the individual will eventually be exposed. By then working back to the current institutional environment, a series of graded reinforcers can be planned which begin with the basic token system and then move to more natural forms of reinforcement at each stage in the programme. By the end of the scheme the individual may have progressed from ward to community house to hostel and will be sensitive to the natural reinforcement in each environment.

This argument also applies to any other form of operant programme where tangible reinforcement is used to establish specific adaptive behaviours. From work on language learning to control of temper tantrums, the aim would be to examine the natural reinforcement available in the natural environment and design a graded programme which varies the actual nature of the reinforcement in planned stages. This point is illustrated by Ferster (1974):

Teaching a child how to dress himself by synthesizing the performances by successive approximations - a procedure frequently carried out with food or token reinforcement - is a convenient context in which to illustrate natural reinforcement. If we begin with a child who is inclined to go outside and play on a cold day, we have two natural events - the outside play activity, and the temperature - as the reinforcers to sustain the performances. To start with, reinforcement occurs when the child is intercepted at a time when he is inclined to go outside to play. His arm is put into the sleeve of the coat and his other arm put halfway in the other sleeve while he is kept loosely and good naturedly in the vicinity of the therapist by the crook of the arm and the position of the body. Under most conditions the child will push his hand the remaining distance, perhaps 3 inches, into the coat sleeve. As the coat goes on, the therapist says 'Fine, Timmy, let's go outside' and he is out in a flash. The reinforcer is immediate, natural and effective. On the next occasion for going outside, the child's hand is only started into the sleeve so that this time he has to extend it farther in order to get the coat on. Step by step, less of the activity is supplied by the therapist and more is controlled by its contribution to getting the coat on, until the child eventually takes full responsibility for dressing reinforced by getting the coat on, which in turn is reinforcing because it is an occasion when he can go to the playground dressed warmly. The procedure emphasises reinforcers derived from the child's own natural inclinations.

Realizing the need to use natural reinforcers has encouraged therapists to train parents rather than children. Much more emphasis is now placed on training children in their natural environments rather than in institutional or in-patient environments. By training parents in the use of behaviour modification techniques and by ensuring the eventual use of natural reinforcement rather than token or other artificial reward systems, the learning of 'token responses' can be avoided and behavioural gains maintained in the target environment.

Generalization of treatment effects in neo-behaviouristic therapy has also been investigated. In systematic desensitization we may ask whether by imagining feared situations and mastering anxiety in these situations we can expect this mastery to generalize to real-life situations and to related anxiety-provoking stimuli. It may be that anxiety reduction is tied to the safe, secure therapeutic environment. Much may depend on the capacity of the patient to generate vivid internal imagery. This problem has been tackled by, as far as possible, using 'in vivo' desensitization procedures where real-life fears are confronted in the course of therapy. Further, a wide range of anxiety-provoking situations are tackled to ensure a broad range of anxiety reduction.

These efforts to tackle the problem of treatment generalization fail to convince those insight theorists who argue that behaviouristic treatments only treat the behavioural symptoms of psychological distress rather than remove the underlying causes of such distress. For radical behaviourists the 'problem behaviours' are maintained by environmental reinforcement and there is therefore no need to probe for intrapsychic causes: the behaviour is the problem. Neo-behaviourists take the view that overt behavioural problems are a consequence of an underlying cause: anxiety. By directing behavioural therapy at this anxiety the overt behavioural symptoms are removed. Insight theorists maintain that in addition there must be some further psychological reason for this anxiety which results in behavioural problems. By tackling the specific behaviour, the actual cause of the anxiety may remain and result in further behavioural problems: the so-called 'symptom substitution' phenomenon.

Conclusion

Bannister (1966) has likened the behaviouristic 'model of man' to 'a ping-pong ball with a memory'. Many clinicians have felt uncomfortable with the mechanistic view of Man that behaviourism suggests; people are the victims of environmental stimuli and reinforcement, resulting in behavioural disorders which require further S-R manipulation for restoration to normality. This approach, it is said, ignores the personal experience of the individual and focusses instead on behavioural symptoms. It denies the need for any particular patient-therapist relationship; the findings of Rogers would be an irrelevance in behaviour therapy. These criticisms were levelled by theorists and clinicians who saw behaviour therapy as a denial of the unique make-up of the individual patient. Behaviour therapists replied that their methods were as effective, if not more, in treating psychological distress, were not surrounded with any mystique requiring extensive training, and could be carried out on a much shorter time scale than the more traditional insight therapies.

In recent years this kind of criticism has waned as a new eclecticism has spread through clinical practitioners. It is now obvious that there is more similarity between therapies than their theoretical positions would imply. For example, the 'fixed role therapy' in PCT looks very like behaviour therapy. By behaving differently as well as construing differently, the PCT patient may be acquiring new behavioural skills as well as new social and emotional viewpoints. In the same way we may wonder what really goes through a patient's mind in systematic desensitization. Could it be that during desensitization he is giving new thought to his irrational fears resulting in some kind of cognitive restructuring?

One further point concerns the patient-therapist relationship in psychological treatment. Whereas psychoanalytic theorists make much of 'transference' and other patient-therapist exchanges, and PCT stresses the 'supervisory' nature of personal construct therapy, behaviour therapists have emphasized the objectivity of their approach to the patient as conforming to scientific standards. But close examination of behaviour therapies gives ground for supposing that this objectivity may apply to measurement and technique application, but that therapists still form warm relationships with their patients. After all, systematic desensitization is a rather intimate form of therapy; patients discuss their intimate fears, are taught relaxation skills and place themselves in the hands of their therapist with confidence and trust. As a consequence of this kind of reasoning, and the awareness that each theoretical/clinical approach has its own range of convenience, a new group of therapies has emerged in recent years which attempts to synthesize theory into more realistic and practical treatments: the cognitive-behaviour therapies.

Cognitive-behaviour therapies

This modern synthesis of cognitive and behavioural therapies began in the 1960s with the clinical ideas of Albert Ellis (1962), Aaron Beck (1964) and later Bandura (1969). Ellis and Beck emphasized the importance of phenomenological investigation of the individual case: how the patient processes information in his belief system. Bandura, whilst recognizing the value of behavioural procedures in psychological therapy, argued that the basic processes of behavioural change involve cognitive and symbolic mechanisms. This shift in emphasis from overt behavioural responses to internal cognitive states recognizes the importance of beliefs and attitudes in generating emotional and behavioural responses to environmental events. The cognitive-behavioural movement was welcomed by insight therapists who had always maintained the importance of subjective experience in understanding psychological distress; but this new position implied that neither talk alone (insight therapy) nor behavioural action alone (behaviour therapy) could adequately tackle psychological dysfunction. A combination of these approaches was needed for a truly comprehensive psychological intervention.

The notion of self-control is pervasive in cognitive-behaviour therapies; in traditional insight therapies it was enough to create self-awareness and in behaviour therapies it was the therapist who wielded control through the manipulation of environmental contingencies. Self-control is very much emphasized by Seligman (1974) in his theory of depression as 'learned helplessness'. In depression it is proposed that the individual cannot perceive any way of gaining control over environmental events. In bereavement there is no course of action open to the individual to undo what has occurred. In these cases the individual falls into 'helplessness'. In less obvious cases, some event - for example, redundancy - may initially generate anxiety because the event is outside the individual's control. As time progresses and no future possibilities seem to exist, the person may come to believe that he has no control over the situation and this may result in a state of 'learned helplessness' or depression. Hiroto and Seligman (1975) have tested this hypothesis on students by subjecting them to a variety of insoluble problems. On later testing, when soluble problems were presented, it was found that these subjects made little attempt to reach solutions and they rated themselves as depressed on the Beck Depression Inventory (Beck, 1967). Seligman has recently extended his theory of 'learned helplessness' to explain differences in the course of terminal illness, school achievement and susceptibility to psychosomatic diseases.

The central theme of Seligman's theory is the extent to which people believe they have control over the events surrounding them. This phenomenological position suggests that even if some degree of objective control exists in a particular situation, it will be no comfort to the individual who really cannot accept that a solution (in the form of control) is available. This position has been reached by other cognitive-behaviour theorists such as Beck, who has also extensively investigated depression. Beck (1970) has conducted a systematic analysis of the belief system of depressed individuals and has noted the existence of irrational thoughts in his patient groups. He sees several types of cognitive patterns distinguishing different patient groups. Depressive patients tend to distort their personal experience in the direction of selfblame and view negative events as catastrophic. Several characteristic logical errors are found in their cognitive processing.

* ARBITRARY INFERENCE: this refers to the tendency to draw illogical conclusions from events. The individual may feel it is because he is such a worthless individual that it rains while he is washing his car!
* SELECTIVE ABSTRACTION: conclusions are drawn based on one out of many elements in a situation. He may conclude that if a cat is killed by a car whilst he is walking towards it, it is his fault.
* OVERGENERALIZATION: here a very general conclusion is reached on the basis of a single, perhaps trivial, event. Thus if the person breaks a cup he feels overcome with feelings of uselessness and worthlessness.
* MAGNIFICATION AND MINIMIZATION: magnification occurs when an individual exaggerates a particular event out of all proportion. A scratch on the car will be seen as the car being 'totally wrecked'. Minimization occurs when, despite massive objective evidence of competence and worth, the individual is plagued by self-doubt and insecurity.

Beck sees the depressive as someone who commits logical errors in processing information in the direction of negative self ideas. The form of therapy Beck has developed involves obvious cognitive components by getting the individual to analyse these negative thoughts and ideas about himself and compare them with objective reality. By identifying examples of negative cognitions, the patient is encouraged to replace these with more positive ideas. An essential component of this therapy is the setting of behavioural 'homework' which requires the patient to gather 'evidence' of his negative and positive thinking and compare it with his actual behavioural performance. If depression has led to social isolation and inactivity then therapist and patient will set behavioural activities to be achieved each day in order to break the cycle of isolation. The patient will be asked to note the difficulties associated

with each task and this account will form the basis of
further discussion. This goal setting and feedback allows
the individual to become aware of his own self-control.

One further celebrated example of cognitive-behaviour
therapy is Albert Ellis' Rational Emotive Therapy (RET).
Ellis (1962) begins with the assumption that unpleasant
feelings are caused by maladaptive thoughts. He also lists
a number of maladaptive thoughts which lead to emotional
disturbance:

*   it is a dire necessity for any adult to be loved by
    everyone for everything he or she does;
*   certain acts are awful or wicked and people who perform
    such acts should be severely punished;
*   it is horrible when things are not exactly the way one
    would like them to be;
*   it is easier to avoid than to face life difficulties;
*   because something once affected one's life in the past
    it should continue to affect one's life indefinitely;
*   one has virtually no control over one's emotions and one
    cannot help feeling certain things.

Ellis proposes that it is thoughts such as these which are
responsible for feelings of anxiety, guilt and hopelessness.
The aim of the RET therapist is to assist the individual
to become aware of these beliefs and to alter such maladaptive cognitions. Mahoney and Arnkoff (1978) list five therapeutic activities practised by RET therapists to achieve
this aim.

*   Direct instruction and persuasion toward the basic RET
    premise (i.e. that irrational thoughts play an important
    role in subjective distress).
*   Recommendations to monitor one's thought patterns.
*   Modelling of a rationalistic evaluation and modification
    of personal thought patterns.
*   Candid feedback (positive and negative) on reported
    changes in thinking patterns and self-evaluation.
*   Performance assignments and rehearsal tasks to improve
    discrimination and evaluation of performance-relevant
    cognitions.

The work of Seligman, Beck and Ellis supports the analysis
of Rogers and Kelly in emphasizing the need for a phenomenological analysis of the individual case, but employing
actual behavioural performances as a valuable way of modifying internal cognitions and beliefs about oneself and
one's environment. Two further areas of contemporary
research are also relevant to this new paradigm.

Social skills training (SST)
The growth of the social skills movement in the last five
years owes much to the pioneering work of Argyle (e.g.
Trower, Bryant and Argyle, 1978). SST starts from the

premise that social interaction takes place along a continuum of competence. In part an individual's position on this continuum will be the result of his early social experience and development. A great deal of our social presentation is the result of modelling: imitating the behaviour, mannerisms and characteristics of people we admire. Our actual social performance, however, may be affected by a variety of excitatory and inhibitory factors; we may adopt a specific role depending on whom we are talking to and the situation in which we find ourselves. Certainly our social capacities will vary according to our own self-perception. If we see ourselves as worthless and uninteresting our self-presentation will reflect this belief. If we are then 'social failures', this feedback will tend to further reinforce our beliefs about self.

SST assumes that a number of individual 'skills', such as eye-contact, smiling, questioning, etc., can be taught like any other behavioural response through systematic reinforcement and direct feedback of performance using videotape. Some individuals may simply have reached the stage where they have such a poor self-image that they can no longer attain a reasonable social performance. They may be so self-concerned that their social awareness has been gradually eroded, resulting in further negative feedback about themselves. Others may never have had much social fluency. Skills training can be seen as a way of modifying internal cognitive functioning through eliminating negative self-perception in social situations. By teaching an individual the various skills which lubricate social interaction and increase interpersonal attraction, he receives positive feedback which alters his internal self-conception. This notion of perceived self-efficacy is the central theme of Bandura's new theory of modelling. In practice, skills training is often used by clinicians in a joint approach to an individual's problems. Psychotherapy may be utilized to alter beliefs and attitudes, whilst skills training helps reinforce this change and also provides a more effective means of social interaction. This two-pronged attack on psychological distress not only addresses cognitive and emotional change, but also enhances the individual's capacity to form satisfying interpersonal relationships.

Biofeedback training

One further level of therapeutic integration has been achieved by introducing direct feedback of internal physiological states whilst undergoing cognitive and behavioural therapy. Biofeedback became a popular therapeutic technique for anxiety management and a variety of other somatic complaints during the 1960s. This development owed much to the theoretical work of Miller (1969), who apparently demonstrated that, contrary to current belief, voluntary control was not restricted to skeletal muscle activity but also occurs in autonomic nervous system activity. A distinction had grown up between the involuntary classical conditioning of the autonomic nervous system (ANS) and the voluntary operant conditioning of skeletal responses. This led to the view that conscious, voluntary control of the ANS was impossible. In a series of ingenious experiments, Di Cara and Miller (1968) and Miller (1969) seemed to disprove this distinction through demonstrating that heart rate, blood pressure and even renal blood flow could all be controlled through instrumental conditioning. This work stimulated a great deal of further research on autonomic control, but Miller's later inability to replicate these results cast doubt on the earlier work (Miller and Dworkin, 1974).

Since then a great deal of psychophysiological research (see Porges and Coles, 1976, for a useful review) has led to the clinical application of both CNS and ANS measures such as the EEG (electro-encephalogram: measures surface cortical activity), the EMG (electromyogram: measures muscular activity), the ECG (electrocardiogram: measures heart-rate), and the GSR (galvanic skin response: measures the electrical conductance of the skin which varies during different states of arousal). These devices allow direct feedback of bodily activity which can be used to train individuals to bring these processes under conscious control. Psychophysiological measures have been employed successfully in the treatment of tension and migraine headaches, gastro-intestinal disorders and even in the control of epilepsy (see Yates, 1980, for a review of techniques and applications in clinical psychophysiology). Meyer and Reich (1978) have described how physiological, cognitive and behavioural variables can be integrated in the treatment of anxiety to produce a high degree of self-control in phobic conditions. This use of multi-model therapy techniques is a continuing trend in clinical practice and a further spur to theoretical integration.

Behaviour therapy and human communication
Modern clinical practice in both insight and behavioural therapy demonstrates an acceleration of the process of integration. Recent contributions by Meichenbaum (1979), Mahoney and Arnkoff (1978), Stern (1978) and Wilson (1978) attest to the growth of the cognitive behaviour therapy movement. Garfield and Bergin (1978), in their recent review of the state of psychological therapy, see this trend as a positive development after many years of entrenched theoretical and clinical dogma. They see the outcome of this movement being a more efficient and effective delivery of psychological therapy to distressed individuals.

There is little doubt that a great deal of therapeutic procedures in speech therapy owe much to the radical and neo-behavourist models of learning. Behaviour modification principles have been extensively applied to speech, language and social/emotional disorders in children. A similar enthusiam can be seen in the treatment of adult acquired disorders from dysfluency to dysphasia. The attractiveness of these behaviourist models is understandable since they generate clear implications for clinical practice, even if the theoretical account they propose of the aetiology of communication disorders is sometimes lacking. A brief outline of the major paradigms is now given with particular emphasis on future directions which the advent of cognitive behavioural therapies has opened up.

Radical behaviourism

Stuttering

A number of accounts have been given of the detailed application of operant techniques to the problem of stuttering: Damsté, Zwaan and Shoenaker (1968), Gray and England (1969), Sloane and MacAuly (1968) and Van Riper (1963). The premise for this intervention is that stuttering is a 'learned habit', initially established and currently maintained by environmental reinforcement in the same way that Ullmann and Krasner (1975) view obsessive compulsive disorders. Indeed, stuttering is seen by some as essentially an obsessive-compulsive condition. Operant procedures are employed to sever the reinforcement-response bond and shape new, more adaptive responses in place of the stutter. A number of case studies of this approach can be found in the literature: Beattie (1973), Goldiamond (1965), Martin (1968), Curlee and Perkins (1969) and Seigal (1970). These techniques utilize negative reinforcement to decrease the rate of dysfluency and systematic positive reinforcement to maintain fluency. Using 'time out' from speech, the stutterer, upon producing a dysfluency, must stop speaking and wait for a defined period of time before continuing. Reports have also been made of the use of token economies with adult stutterers in intensive treatment programmes.

The literature implies these techniques are very effective in the treatment of stuttering, but closer examination of sample size, improvement measures and lack of adequate control groups casts some doubt on the generality of these findings. The outstanding omission with much of this work is the singular failure to employ adequate follow-up procedures to ascertain the extent of generalization and the duration of treatment effects.

Voice disorders

Greene (1972) suggests a number of 'teaching methods' for dysphonias and articulation disorders which look very much like operant procedures. Graded goals are set for therapy, repetition of specific responses is stressed and the need for encouragement is given particular emphasis. A purely behaviourist approach to dysphonia in the absence of organic damage would be to regard this behaviour as caused and maintained by environmental reinforcement. Functional analysis might reveal the sources of such reinforcement which could then be subject to the usual extinction and shaping procedures. In cases where organic damage has occurred, therapists are still faced with the need to find a psychological level of intervention. In the absence of obvious psychiatric disturbance two approaches are available:

behaviour modification techniques and a cognitive information processing model. The latter would concentrate on supplying feedback information to the patient against which an 'ideal' model could be compared. By specifying graded performance goals and utilizing modern technology such as the laryngograph, electromyograph and sound spectrogram (and displaying these patterns visually on a television screen through computer enhancement), a much more detailed set of therapeutic objectives could be specified.

Aphasia

Ince (1973, 1976) and Goodkin (1969) have both reported small-scale studies on the use of operant procedures to re-establish word and sentence production in aphasic adults. Although a purely behaviouristic rationale for such an approach remains uncertain (clearly the individual's lack of communication is not being maintained by environmental reinforcement), it could well be that the systematic design of these programmes contributes greatly to their apparent success. Operant programmes attempt to shape behavioural responses in gradual steps by presenting a reduced input and output demand to the individual under reinforcement conditions. Gradually this input and output demand is built up and elaborated under more refined reinforcement conditions. This simplification of input-output structure, together with reinforcement (which may act as feedback information), may be responsible for the progress patients make in this paradigm. Recently Powell (1981) has proposed that the experimental investigation of individual brain damage provides more specific opportunities for therapeutic intervention than a general 'blanket treatment' approach.

Neo-behaviourist approaches

The relationship between communication disorders and anxiety has a long history in clinical practice. Freud's theoretical system made much of this by proposing that neurotic anxiety was the root cause of many communication dysfunctions. This relationship has not always been viewed as causal, since clinicians are aware of the anxiety-provoking nature of handicap. Two lines of therapeutic application have emerged where anxiety is either a major causal factor in communication breakdown or a product of breakdown. In both positions the need for anxiety management techniques has led to the use of neo-behaviouristic treatment techniques.

Stuttering

An extensive literature on the application of anxiety reduction techniques in stuttering has grown up, represented by Burgraff (1974), Gray and England (1972), Lanyon (1969), Watts (1973) and Wolpe (1969). Wolpe states the position as: 'neurotic anxiety is a determinant of most stuttering'. Other authors have been more cautious in identifying anxiety as a cause of stuttering and consequently classifying stuttering as a neurotic disorder. In a careful review of the relationship between stuttering and neurosis, Beech and

Fransella (1968) conclude that the evidence of a clear relationship is equivocal and difficult to evaluate due to the inadequacy of many research designs. According to Burgraff (1974), Gray (1968), Lazarus (1964), Lanyon (1969) and Webster (1970), however, the application of systematic desensitization has proved a rather effective form of treatment for stuttering (see Ingham and Andrews, 1973, for an extensive review).

Voice disorders

Since many dysphonias have no clear organic base it has been suggested that a psychogenic aetiology is inescapable, and in particular it has been concluded that conversion hysteria is a possible diagnosis. Greene (1972) has advocated the use of relaxation training and supportive counselling whilst psychiatric referral is pursued. The use of systematic desensitization in these cases may be considered if the circumstances surrounding the voice loss indicate obvious precipitating factors. For example, a patient who has suddenly experienced a sudden onset of dysphonia with no organic signs of damage could be further investigated through the use of anxiety and personality measures to establish whether emotional reactivity is a feature of the patient's personality. A careful investigation of the events leading up to voice loss from interviews with the patient and other informants may yield some clue to the precipitating factors. If apprehension about some future communicative act is detected, then systematic desensitization may well assist in dissipating the associated anxiety.

Aphasia

Too often therapists concentrate on re-establishing communicative capacity in brain-damaged patients without acknowledging the social and emotional consequences of this handicap. Ince (1968) and Damon, Lesser and Woods (1979) report the use of systematic desensitization as a means of alleviating emotional disturbance following brain damage. In such cases genuine health fears develop about future cerebrovascular accidents (CVAs) as well as immediate social anxiety due to the communication handicap. In a broad rehabilitative programme this dimension of patient care must be acknowledged, and appropriate therapeutic techniques employed to combat what may be very significant factors in recovery.

Cognitive behaviour therapies

Modern studies of intervention with the communication-handicapped employ more therapy models than was the case ten years ago. This 'broad spectrum' approach has been advocated by Watts (1973) and exemplified by Azrin and Nunn (1974) in their 'habit reversal' procedure for stutterers. This form of therapy consists of several sub-components of which only a few are truly behavioural in form. A lengthy period of 'awareness training' is employed initially which consists of eliciting a phenomenological account of the experience of the individual stutterer. After a further period of relaxation training, the stutterer is instructed in a breathing technique designed to be incompatible with stuttering. A repertoire of further competing activities is built up which allows the person to switch to these activities when stuttering occurs. Role rehearsal procedures and actual behavioural activities are drawn up for the individual to practise, and additional support is sought from friends and relatives to assist in carrying this programme out. It is claimed that this treatment package rapidly brings dysfluency under control and these effects have been maintained up to eight months after treatment. Scrutiny of this approach reveals behavioural techniques, insight techniques, SST, social support and the provision of 'cognitive control' opportunities.

This package approach to stuttering is currently employed in many intensive treatments of one to two weeks' duration. In these cases a further treatment variable is introduced - group dynamics - which may also have a beneficial effect on outcome. Stuttering could be amenable to the 'learned helplessness' analysis of Seligman, where the belief that stuttering is outside personal control results in initial anxiety and later feelings of helplessness. This paradigm would predict that some means of changing this belief is necessary for a lasting solution to the problem. Often stutterers seek help intermittently over a number of years and respond well to any novel form of treatment. It may well be that these initial positive advances owe much to the hope that a reliable method of self-control has been found. If treatment fails to acknowledge the need to carry out simultaneous therapy on the belief system of the individual, then the effects of such treatments may be shortlived once discharge from therapy occurs. Fransella (1970) argues that this 'need to change' from perceiving oneself as a stutterer to a non-stutterer is the crucial therapy task. Certainly a wide range of treatment methods have been shown to have initial positive gains in stutterers, but a theoretical rationale for such improvement has often eluded description.

Beech and Fransella (1968) review a number of treatment methods which they term 'rhythm methods' for stuttering. These range from electronic metronomes, syllable timed speech, slowed speech, smooth speech, DAF (Delayed Auditory Feedback) and, more recently, auditory masking devices. The common feature with these methods is that they emphasize rhythm, stress and rate of speech either through imposing a particular rate or by masking natural feedback which could disrupt these features. A possible explanation for these effects could be that they make conversation a much more predictable affair. The value of prediction is stressed by PCT and may lead to the perception of control in interpersonal communication. Stutterers may lack the ability to predict their performance in conversation and thus do not perceive themselves as being 'in control'. The Azrin and Nunn approach bristles with self-control implications, not only in actual behavioural performance, but also in phenomenological perception and social support.

New directions

Communication disorders, whether of organic or psychological aetiology, are treated at the psychological level by therapists. Clinicians structure input to the patient in a variety of ways, measure output on a number of dimensions and generate theoretical models of the nature of the problem and to guide future intervention. These clinical activities conform to the standards of scientific objectivity, but also constitute a very special form of social and emotional interaction between two people. Until recently psychological therapy has either been shrouded in mystique or has adopted the use of behavioural technology to change specific aspects of functioning. Both these extremes have failed to provide a 'whole person' approach, which acknowledges that handicap is a personal and social phenomenon in addition to having a certain set of overt symptoms. The recent trend towards therapy integration and theoretical reconciliation has provided a clinical climate where experimentation and evaluation have replaced theoretical dogma. (See Martin and Haroldson, 1979, for a review of treatment approaches in stuttering; and Moleski and Tesi, 1976, for comparative outcome research between rational-emotive therapy and systematic desensitization.)

This opportunity to explore the wider aspects of handicap has as many drawbacks as it has advantages. The thoughtless creation of 'therapeutic cocktails' is a major block to progress in this new direction. Theory is the only scientific basis for intervention because it generates predictions which are put to empirical test by accurate translation into clinical action. The outcome of this action can be quantified and described in a variety of ways and marshalled as evidence for the efficacy of the therapy, and as a test of theory. Whereas it has often been debated whether therapy is an 'art' or a 'science', it should be clear that a scientific approach to treatment is the only responsible course open to clinicians. But a scientific approach certainly does not mean that we can ignore the cognitive and emotional experience of our patients and their social situation. Nor should it be assumed that therapy consists of techniques alone; some therapists have been found to achieve better results than others even though they use exactly the same methods. This fact does not imply that therapy is an 'art', but that a more detailed scientific investigation is needed of the variables which make one therapist more effective than another.

Modern psychological therapy seems to be moving towards a more integrated view of psychological distress than has previously been the case. In particular the work of Beck, Ellis, Seligman, Kelly, Bandura and Meichenbaum has opened up exciting new directions for professional therapists. In speech therapy a number of potential applications are suggested. Stuttering therapy may well take on a more cognitive emphasis, with detailed personality and social analyses being conducted alongside phenomenological investigations of the individual patient. Therapy may be geared to several levels of handicap, such as specific cognitive reconstruction along the lines of Ellis and Beck, the setting of behavioural activities which will provide positive and predictable feedback of self-efficacy emphasized by Bandura and thus lead to increased perception of self-control identified by Seligman. Further evidence of self-efficacy may result from social skills programming which may make social predictions more accurate and further increase the notion of self-control. Within the therapy relationship, the interpersonal factors stressed by Rogers and Kelly may play a large part in establishing credibility for the therapist and expectancy for change in the patient.

A similar analysis could be applicable to dysphonic conditions where behavioural, cognitive and interpersonal therapy aims are pursued simultaneously. The use of physiological feedback may make a major contribution to the perception of self-efficacy in achieving control over a previously uncontrollable condition. Even in the treatment of dysarthria and dyspraxia, therapists may have to tackle a deteriorating self-concept in the patient who may feel he is seen as of low intelligence and that others shun him socially. Such conditions may have a dramatic impact on marital relationships with the possibility of depression after a period of time. In brain damage it may not be sufficient to work on communicative performance alone. Patients who suffer such sudden and dramatic handicap have a considerable amount of social and emotional restructuring to achieve if full attention is to be devoted to recovery. The work of Brumfitt and Clarke (1982) highlights both the need and the feasibility of such an approach.

Although these new directions open up new treatment possibilities it is the responsibility of the clinician to demonstrate that new forms of treatment really do represent significant advances over traditional methods. This need for adequate evaluation of therapy brings the clinical scientist up against some of the most difficult problems of professional practice.

The evaluation of therapeutic outcomes

The state of research into therapy outcome has been lamentable until fairly recently. An excess of therapeutic dogma has resulted in a narrow range of outcome measures: behaviourists have examined actual improvements in behavioural performance; insight therapists have taken the word of their clients that they 'feel better'. These limited outcome measures, together with poor experimental design, have resulted in a massive literature that always seems to be in favour of the author's theoretical stance and against

competing approaches. The recent loosening of clinical and
theoretical constraints is leading to improved clinical
science where previously ignored dimensions of change are
now included in the research design. Five basic stages
in therapy evaluation can be distinguished which require
close attention if a valid scientific experiment is to be
achieved. Therapy is an experiment whether it is applied
to a group of individuals or to a single case. Scientific
rigour can be achieved in such experiments only when all
relevant variables have been identified and controlled, and
valid, reliable measurements have been taken both before and
after therapy.

Experimental design and choice of sample

Therapy evaluation can be conducted on a group basis or on
the individual case. In the latter single case study it is
not permissible to generalize findings to other individuals
since the outcome may be specific to the particular individual concerned. Single case studies are usually undertaken
in order to monitor the effects of individual treatment, to
illustrate different forms of treatment or to demonstrate
specific aetiological factors (see Yule and Hemsley, 1977,
for a discussion of single case studies). Where we wish to
ascertain the efficacy of a particular form of therapy in
general we must use a group design where a number of individuals receive the treatment in question and the overall
outcome of this group is analysed. In order to ensure the
external validity of such an experiment our choice of sample
is crucial. When we evaluate a treatment for a specific sub-
population (e.g. adolescent stutterers) we must draw as near
as possible a representative sample of this population.

For adolescent stutters we may have to ensure a balanced
representation of ages from, say 13-18 years, a cross-
section of severity of stutter from mild to severe and
represent such obvious individual differences as sex ratio
in accordance with available epidemiological information.
Having assembled a representative sample of our target population we must consider the kind of statistical analysis
we propose to use, as this may be influenced by the sample
size. In practice we try to assemble as large a sample as
our resources permit. In order to demonstrate the internal
validity of the research it is usual practice to arrange for
a further control group of subjects who do not receive the
experimental treatment, but who are subject to the same research process as the experimental group in order to decide
if non-specific factors (such as increased attention and
passage of time) can account for part of the eventual outcome. In recent years the use of control groups has been
subject to criticism. Subjects in these groups have usually
been set rather irrelevant, non-therapeutic tasks which
often led to the subjects in such control groups actually
deteriorating during the research!

To take a specific example: we might decide to investigate whether relaxation alone has a beneficial effect on

anxiety in dental patients. We could assemble a large sample
of individuals representative of the population of people
who are afraid of the dentist and allocate them at random to
two groups: a relaxation group and a control group. Random
allocation of a sample into two treatment conditions is the
usual method of avoiding experimenter bias. The relaxation
group would have two one-hour sessions per day of relaxation
training for, say, three weeks and the control group might
be asked to do crossword puzzles or simply sit quietly for
the same time. At the end of the experiment we could compare the two groups along some predetermined dimensions of
anxiety to see if the relaxation group is any different from
the control group. Even if the two groups were perfectly
matched along some common dimension before the experiment, could we conclude that differences after the experiment between the two groups were only due to the two kinds
of treatment? On the face of it, yes, but if we imagine the
experience of the two groups we might be more cautious. The
relaxation group and the control group would have been told
the purpose of the experiment and will thus be primed to
expect some change. The relaxation group may well report
themselves as less anxious because they believe the training
has worked. The control group, on the other hand, may see
doing crosswords or just sitting quietly as having no obvious therapeutic advantage and thus they will not have the
same credibility in the treatment or the same expectancy for
change that was generated in the relaxation group. The role
such cognitive factors as expectancy and credibility play in
determining an individual's response to treatment clearly
implies that we cannot directly compare the two groups.

One way of getting around this problem when using control groups is to use deception by designing a credible
'treatment' which is, on all theoretical grounds, thera-
peutically inert. By telling control group members that this
'therapy' will have beneficial effects we could ensure positive credibility and expectancy in both groups. However, if
this kind of design is used we must demonstrate empirically
that expectancy and credibility is comparable in the treatment and 'pseudotherapy' groups. But the very act of trying
to measure how much credibility and expectancy for change is
generated by different treatments will inevitably affect
that credibility.

In many designs the problem of control groups has been
circumvented by the comparison of two or more treatment
approaches. Two groups, matched on all potentially relevant
variables such as age, sex, IQ, personality, etc., are
subjected to different treatment approaches to estimate
which of the two is more effective. Problems again arise
with the relative credibility of the two treatments and in
the deployment of therapists. Individual therapists may have
differential success rates with patients and thus such a
variable would need to be controlled by having a single
group of therapists carry out both forms of treatment. All
therapists would have to be aware of the need to implement

both forms of treatment with equal enthusiasm. If one
therapist has faith in one form of treatment and not in
another this may influence his actual performance in the two
conditions. This experimenter effect can be overcome by
having all therapists go through a uniform training course
on both forms of therapy to attempt to standardize the
therapeutic approach.

Assuming that a design has been arrived at, that matched
representative samples are available and that experimenter
effects have been reduced to a minimum through common
training, we move to the second area of concern.

Measurement of the problem

The specific problem we are interested in may range from an
overt response to a frame of mind. In modern research such
a problem may have several dimensions. A stutter may be
measured in terms of its frequency and duration, its char-
racteristic block pattern and its occurrence under different
conditions. It may vary depending on the social context
(alone, speaking aloud, speaking to a friend, speaking to a
stranger, speaking to a group of individuals, reading aloud,
etc.). Measurements may be taken in a variety of conditions,
but always bearing in mind that naturalistic situations are
needed if valid predictions are to be made about real-life
performance. A number of other measurements may be suggested
by the theoretical stance of the therapist. If anxiety is
seen as a causal or contributory factor then measurements of
this variable will be needed. These measurements could range
from observational description of anxious behaviour on a
check-list, the administration of standardized self-report
questionnaires, a structured personal interview where the
patient rates his anxiety on some phenomenological scale, or
the use of physiological measures of autonomic activity in a
variety of speaking situations. If social factors are believed to play a part in the problem then assessments of
social functioning and social attitudes will be undertaken,
perhaps using video techniques to avoid artificial contamination of social functioning and allow an objective analysis
of social competence to be conducted by a panel of raters.
Attitudes to social functioning may be gathered by self-
report or structured interview technique using repertory
grids.

These measurements are crucial if the detection of
therapeutic change is to be made. Specific problem measurements are repeated after therapy for evidence of the effectiveness of intervention and thus form an operational
definition of 'improvement'. Narrow definitions of improvement result when only a few measurements are taken before
and after therapy. This type of definition may fail to
detect valuable changes which, although not central to the
actual symptom, may provide information on how the individual has responded to treatment. If we define 'improvement'
as simply 'decrease in number of dysfluencies when talking
to another person' we may be disappointed when no real

decrease is observed after treatment. It might be the case that the patient feels less anxious about the stammer, can cope better with talking in groups and feels more confident when meeting people for the first time, but these dimensions of change are not tapped by a narrow definition.

In collecting problem measurements it is good scientific practice to use independent assessors who are not taking part in the actual therapy in case two possible sources of bias are introduced. One type of bias can occur in pre-treatment assessment where the actual therapists carry out the testing; the therapist's expectations of how a given individual will respond to therapy may be influenced. Therapists constantly make predictions (prognoses) of individual responses to treatment and this is a clear source of experimental bias. A second possibility exists when carrying out post-treatment assessment. If the therapist conducts this assessment he may be influenced in scoring a patient's performance by how he thinks the patient has done in therapy. If he feels Mr Jones has made good progress but has made an uncharacteristic mess of his post-treatment assessment, there is temptation to score his performance more leniently. This kind of well-intentioned bias cannot further scientific enquiry. By using independent assessors not participating in the therapy, much more valid and reliable conclusions can be drawn from a study.

Description of the therapeutic procedures
Science advances through careful experimentation and the accumulation of experimental evidence. This means that other workers will, from time to time, try to replicate an experimental study to test the generality of its conclusion. Clinical scientists need to supply detailed information of their experimental investigations if other workers are to design accurate replications. This information must be given both for the therapists and the experimental sample. The step-by-step process of the actual therapeutic techniques needs to be stated clearly and without omitting any potentially significant information. Even factors like the physical accommodation in which the study was conducted could be described, as there may be differences in credibility generated in patients by the prestigiousness of their surroundings and the status of their therapists. The simple act of sending patients an appointment letter may generate expectancies for subsequent therapy. Basic information on the duration of therapy is essential if valid future replications are to be designed.

Outcome measurement
Upon completion of the therapy, re-assessment of the patients is carried out using the pre-therapy measurements. Again, very strict control must be exercised if the results are to be kept free of potential bias and contamination from new variables. One needs to be aware that someone who was a 'stranger' for a stutterer at the initial assessment may

be seen as a familiar person at terminal assessment. Where independent assessors are used it is a good idea to keep a note of who carried out initial assessments on each patient in order that different assessors can carry out the outcome assessments. This avoids the possibility of contamination through familiarity. Some initial measures may have low test-retest reliability because they involve a practice effect. This possibility must be borne in mind when selecting initial assessments and, wherever possible, parallel forms of a psychometric instrument used at re-assessment. One further consideration is the design of future follow-up assessments. Most clinical studies of therapy effectiveness pay lip service to the need for continuing follow-up assessment. It is not enough to demonstrate immediate post-treatment gains for a particular therapy; often quite bizarre forms of 'treatment' can produce such immediate gains. A follow-up assessment at one month, three months, nine months and one year is a realistic structure for most therapies. These measurements allow a graph to be plotted of the increase or decrease in improvement over time for both individuals and the treatment group. This evidence is essential if clinicians wish to claim their treatments have lasting effects rather than short-lived remissions.

Outcome analysis

Assuming a wide spectrum of improvement measures have been taken in both treatment and naturalistic settings, it is a relatively simple matter to subject these data to statistical analysis which will reveal which group of patients made the most progress and which aspects of 'improvement' showed the most dramatic change. Areas where little progress was made may have further implications for future therapy design. One further level of analysis can be conducted where the initial patient variables (age, sex, IQ, personality measures) can be compared with eventual outcome. This analysis may reveal that certain characteristics are associated with a specific response to therapy. Such an analysis may reveal that the more intelligent, more extraverted and less anxious patients did not fare as well in the treatment as the less intelligent, more introverted and anxious patients. This information may have very valuable theoretical implications as well as offering some criteria for future patient selection for that specific form of therapy. Too often this kind of information has either not been obtained or not been analysed in outcome studies. This omission is regrettable given the important implications it could have for both theory and practice. Clinical scientists are increasingly turning to this individual level of analysis rather than simply comparing massed and averaged group data against chance probabilities. At present a major area of ignorance in stuttering theory is the extent to which stutterers form a homogeneous or heterogeneous group. Only an analysis of individual differences can provide an answer to this question.

Therapy and 'therapy'

Recently a number of studies have been conducted which have tried to determine the contribution of non-specific factors to therapeutic outcome. Briefly, these factors refer to all aspects of the therapy which are not unique features of that particular therapy approach. For example, all forms of psychological treatment have a basic social unit of therapist and patient. Before any specific therapy is carried out, several interpersonal factors may be at work which could have profound influences on the eventual treatment outcome. The status (student versus consultant) of the therapist and the emotional style of self-presentation (formal versus informal) could combine with the specific personality (introvert versus extravert) and other unique features of the therapist to evoke a particular attitude to treatment in the patient. In the same way features of the patient will evoke a variety of reactions in the therapist that may also lead to particular expectations of the treatment process.

The physical surroundings in which therapy is carried out could have an influence on outcome independent of the specific therapy being used. To be summoned to a large and modern teaching hospital for treatment may be a far cry from attending the local NHS clinic. As researchers become aware of the influence of these non-specific factors in therapy evaluation, steps can be taken to control them, usually by designing a 'placebo-control' procedure. Past practice has utilized the control group as a means of equating passage of time with therapy outcome. Psychological problems can show 'spontaneous remission' - recovery without treatment - and so it has been necessary to employ no-treatment control groups in order to detect the rate of spontaneous recovery and compare this measure with the treatment measurements. The major drawback to this procedure has already been mentioned. Patients in these groups seldom have the same opportunity to experience all the non-specific factors occurring in the treatment group having therapy.

In order to address this problem, researchers have tried to design placebo 'treatments' which generate the same non-specific factors as the therapy on test. In this way a more reliable conclusion can be reached about the relative merits of different forms of treatment. Shapiro (1978) discusses the use of placebo procedures in psychotherapy and a review by Kazdin and Wilcoxon (1976) warrants particular attention.

Conclusions

The traditional lines of demarcation between different models of psychological therapy have recently begun to buckle under two influences. Our concept of what constitutes scientific investigation has undergone extensive revision in recent years. In part this has been due to new technological advances in psychometrics and insistence from the philosophers of science that psychology, sooner or later, must address itself directly to the problem of phenomenological experience. A further pressure has come from clinical scientists who have felt that many single theoretical paradigms fail to achieve a sufficiently wide range of convenience to offer a comprehensive approach to psychological distress. The result of these dual influences has been a move towards integrated clinical methods with a parallel integration of theoretical models. This development is viewed with caution by some therapists as it could lead to a therapeutic cacophony where 'treatment cocktails' are poured for individual problems with a resulting atrophy of scientific advance. Clinical scientists must assume responsibility for evaluating these new approaches in order to generate new ideas about the aetiology of psychological distress and demonstrate the efficacy of these procedures over a range of problems. By aspiring to new standards of scientific investigation which have not been attained in the past, this trend could lead to major new insights into both normal and abnormal psychology.

References

Andolfi, M. (1979)
Family Therapy: An interactional approach. New York: Plenum.

Aronson, E. (1972)
The Social Animal. San Francisco: Freeman.

Ayllon, T. and Azrin, N.H. (1965)
The measurement and reinforcement of behavior of psychotics. Journal of Experimental Analysis of Behavior, 8, 357-383.

Ayllon, T. and Azrin, N.H. (1968)
The token economy: a motivational system for therapy and rehabilitation. New York: Appleton-Century-Crofts.

Azrin, N.H. and Nunn, R.G. (1974)
A rapid method of eliminating stuttering by a regulated breathing approach. Behaviour Research and Therapy, 12, 279-286.

Bandura, A. (1969)
Principles of Behavior Modification. New York: Holt, Rinehart & Winston.

Bannister, D. (1966)
A New Theory of Personality. In B.M. Foss, New Horizons in Psychology 1. Harmondsworth: Pelican.

Beattie, M. (1973)
A behaviour therapy programme for stuttering. British Journal of Disorders of Communication, 8, 120-130.

Beck, A.T. (1964)
Thinking and depression: 2, theory and therapy. Archives of General Psychiatry, 10, 561-571.

Beck, A.T. (1967)
Depression: Clinical, experimental and theoretical aspects. New York: Harper & Row.

Beck, A.T. (1970)
The core problem in depression: the cognitive triad. In

J. Masserman (ed.), Depression: Theories and therapies. New York: Grune & Stratton.

Beech, H.R. and Fransella, F. (1968)
Research and Experiment in Stuttering. Oxford: Pergamon Press.

Bernstein, D.A. and Borkovec, T.D. (1973)
Progressive Relaxation Training: A manual for the helping professions. Champaign, Ill.: Research Press.

Breger, L. and McGaugh, J. (1965)
Critique and reformulation of 'learning theory' approaches to psychotherapy and neurosis. Psychological Bulletin, 63, 338-358.

Breland, K. and Breland, M. (1966)
Animal Behaviour. New York: Macmillan.

Brumfitt, S. and Clarke, P. (1982)
An application of psychotherapeutic techniques to the management of aphasia. In C. Code and D.J. Müller (eds), Aphasia Therapy. London: Arnold.

Burgraff, R.L. (1974)
The efficacy of systematic desensitisation via imagery as a therapeutic device with stutters. British Journal of Disorders of Communication, 9, 134-139.

Chomsky, N. (1959)
Review of Verbal Behavior by B. F. Skinner. Language, 35, 26-58.

Cioffi, F. (1970)
Freud and the idea of pseudo-science. In R. Borger and F. Cioffi (eds), Explanation in the Behavioural Sciences. Cambridge: Cambridge University Press.

Cullen, C., Hattersley, J. and Tennant, L. (1977)
Behaviour modification - some implications of a radical behaviourist view. Bulletin of the British Psychological Society, 30, 65-69.

Curlee, R.F. and Perkins, W.H. (1969)
Conversational rate-control therapy for stuttering. Journal of Speech and Hearing Disorders, 34, 245-250.

Damon, S.G., Lesser, R. and Woods, R.T. (1979)
Behavioural treatment of social difficulties in an aphasic woman and a dysarthric man. British Journal of Disorders of Communication, 14, 31-38.

Damsté, P.H., Zwaan, E.J. and Schoenaker, T.J. (1968)
Learning principles applied to the stuttering problem. Folia Phoniatrica, 20, 327-341.

Davison, G.C. and Neale, J.M. (1978)
Abnormal Psychology: An experimental clinical approach (2nd edn). New York: Wiley.

Di Cara, L.V. and Miller, N.E. (1968)
Instrumental learning of systolic blood pressure responses by curarised rats: dissociation of cardiac and vascular changes. Psychosomatic Medicine, 30, 489-494.

Eastman, C. (1976)
Behavioural formulations of depression. Psychological Review, 83, 277-291.

Ellis, A. (1962)
Reason and Emotion In Psychotherapy. New York: Lyle
Stuart.

Eysenck, H.J. (1966)
The Effects of Psychotherapy. New York: International
Science Press.

Eysenck, H.J. (1967)
The Biological Basis of Personality. Springfield, Ill.:
Thomas.

Eysenck, H.J. (1976)
The learning theory model of neurosis - a new approach.
Behaviour Research and Therapy, 14, 251-267.

Ferster, C.B. (1974)
The difference between behavioural and conventional
psychology. Journal of Nervous and Mental Disorders,
159, 153-157.

Fisher, S. and Greenberg, R.P. (1977)
The Scientific Credibility of Freud's Theories and
Therapy. Hassocks, Sussex: Harvester Press.

Fransella, F. (1970)
Stuttering: not a symptom but a way of life. British
Journal of Disorders of Communication, 5, 22-29.

Fransella, F. (1972)
Personal Change and Reconstruction: Research on a
treatment of stuttering. London: Academic Press.

Garfield, S.L. and Bergin, A.E. (1978)
Handbook of Psychotherapy and Behavior Change (2nd edn).
New York: Wiley.

Goldiamond, I. (1965)
Stuttering and fluency as manipulable operant response
classes. In L. Krasner and L. Ullman (eds), Research in
Behavior Modification. New York: Holt, Rinehart &
Winston.

Goodkin, R. (1969)
Changes in word production, sentence production and
relevance in an aphasic through verbal conditioning.
Behaviour Research and Therapy, 6, 235-237.

Gray, B.B. (1968)
Some Effects of Anxiety Deconditioning upon Stuttering
Behavior. Monterey, Ca: The Monterey Institute for
Speech and Hearing.

Gray, B.B. and England, G. (1969)
Stuttering and the Conditioning Therapies. Monterey, Ca:
Institute for Speech and Hearing.

Gray, B.B. and England, G. (1972)
Some effects of anxiety deconditioning upon stuttering
frequency. Journal of Speech and Hearing Research, 15,
114-122.

Greenberg, I.A. (ed.) (1974)
Psychodrama - Theory and Therapy. London: Souvenir
Press.

Greene, M. (1972)
The Voice and its Disorders. London: Pitman Medical.

Gurman, A.S. and Kniskern, D.P. (eds) (1981)
Handbook of Family Therapy. New York: Brunner/Mazel.

Harris, G.G. (1977)
The Group Treatment of Human Problems - A social learning approach. New York: Grune & Stratton.

Haynes, S.N. (1978)
Principles of Behavioral Assessment. New York: Gardener Press.

Hinkle, D.N. (1965)
The change of personal constructs from the viewpoint of a theory of implications. Unpublished doctoral dissertation, Ohio State University.

Hiroto, D.S. and Seligman, M.E.P. (1975)
Generality of learned helplessness in man. Journal of Personality and Social Psychology, 31, 311-327.

Ince, L.P. (1968)
Desensitisation with an aphasic patient. Behaviour Research and Therapy, 6, 235-237.

Ince, L.P. (1973)
Behaviour modification with an aphasic man. Rehabilitation Research Practical Reviews, 4, 37-42.

Ince, L.P. (1976)
Behavior Modification in Rehabilitative Medicine. Springfield, Ill.: Thomas.

Ingham, R.J. and Andrews, G. (1973)
Behaviour therapy and stuttering: a review. Journal of Speech and Hearing Disorders, 38, 405-441.

Jacobsen, E. (1927)
Action currents from muscular contractions during conscious processes. Science, 66, 403.

Jones, Maxwell (1953)
The Therapeutic Community. New York: Basic Books.

Kazdin, A.E. (1978)
Methodology of applied behaviour analysis. In A.C. Catania and T.A. Brigham (eds), Handbook of Applied Behaviour Analysis. New York: Irvington.

Kazdin, A.E. and Bootzin, R.R. (1972)
The token economy: an evaluative review. Journal of Applied Behavior Analysis, 5, 342-372.

Kazdin, A.E. and Wilcoxon, L.A. (1976)
Systematic desensitisation and non-specific treatment effects: a methodological evaluation. Psychological Bulletin, 83, 729-758.

Krug, S.E., Scheier, I.V. and Cattell, R.B. (1976)
Handbook for the IPAT Anxiety Scale. Champaign, Ill.: Institute for Personality and Ability Testing.

Lanyon, R.I. (1969)
Behaviour change in stuttering through systematic desensitisation. Journal of Speech and Hearing Disorders, 34, 253-260.

Lazarus, A. (1964)
Objective psychotherapy in the treatment of dysphemia. In H.J. Eysenck (ed.), Experiments in Behaviour Therapy. London: Macmillan.

Lenneberg, E. (1967)
Biological Foundations of Language. New York: Wiley.

Liberman, R.P. and Teigen, J. (1979)
Behavioral group therapy. In P.O. Sjöden, S. Bates and
W. Dockens (eds), Trends in Behavior Therapy. New York:
Academic Press.

London, P. (1964)
The modes and morals of psychotherapy. New York: Holt,
Rinehart & Winston.

London, P. (1972)
The end of ideology in behaviour modification. American
Psychologist, 27, 913-920.

Mahoney, M. and Arnkoff, D. (1978)
Cognitive and self control therapies. In S.L. Garfield
and A.E. Bergin (eds), Handbook of Psychotherapy and
Behavior Change (2nd edn). New York: Wiley.

Martin, R. (1968)
The experimental manipulation of stuttering behaviour.
In H.N. Sloane and B.D. MacAuly (eds), Operant
Procedures in Remedial Speech and Language Training.
New York: Houghton Mifflin.

Martin, R. and Haroldson, S. (1979)
Effects of five experimental treatments on stuttering.
Journal of Speech and Hearing Research, 22, 132-146.

Meyer, V. and Reich, B. (1978)
Anxiety management - the marriage of physiological and
cognitive variables. Behavour Research and Therapy, 16,
177-182.

Meichenbaum, D. (1979)
Cognitive-behavioural modification: future directions.
In P.O. Sjöden, S. Bates, and W. Dockens (eds), Trends
in Behaviour Therapy. New York: Academic Press.

Miller, N.E. (1969)
The learning of visceral and glandular responses.
Science, 163, 434-445.

Miller, N.E. and Dworkin, B. (1974)
Visceral learning: recent difficulties with curarized
rats and significant problems for human research. In
P.A. Obrist et al (eds), Cardiovascular Psychophysiology. Chicago: Aldine.

Moleski, R. and Tesi, D.J. (1976)
Comparative psychotherapy: rational-emotive therapy
versus systematic desensitisation in the treatment of
stuttering. Journal of Consulting and Clinical
Psychology, 44, 309-311.

Moreno, J.L. and Kipper, D.A. (1968)
Group psychodrama and community-centred counselling.
In G.M. Gazda (ed.), Basic Approaches to Group
Psychotherapy and Group Counselling. Springfield, Ill.:
Thomas.

Mowrer, O.H. (1939)
A stimulus-response analysis of anxiety and its role as
a reinforcing agent. Psychological Review, 46, 553-565.

Perls, F. (1969)
Gestalt Therapy Verbatim. Moab, Utah: Real People Press.

Porges, S.W. and Coles, M.G.H. (1976)
Psychophysiology. Stroundsburg, Pa: Dowden, Hutchison & Ross.

Powell, G.E. (1981)
Brain Function Therapy. Farnborough, Hants.: Gower.

Rachman, S. (1969)
Treatment by prolonged exposure to high intensity stimulation. Behaviour Research and Therapy, 14, 349-357.

Rachman, S., Hodgson, R.J. and Marks, I.M. (1971)
Treatment of chronic obsessive-compulsive neurosis. Behaviour Research and Therapy, 9, 237-247.

Rachman, S., Hodgson, R.J. and Marzillier, J. (1970)
Treatment of an obsessive-compulsive disorder by modelling. Behaviour Research and Therapy, 8, 385-392.

Rachman, S., Marks, I.M. and Hodgson, R.J. (1973)
The treatment of obsessive-compulsive neurotics by modelling and flooding in vivo. Journal of Behavioural Therapy and Experimental Psychiatry, 3, 117-123.

Rachman, S. and Teasdale, J. (1969)
Aversion Therapy and the Behaviour Disorders. London: Routledge & Kegan Paul.

Rachman, S. and Wilson, G.T. (1980)
The Effects of Psychological Therapy (2nd edn). Oxford: Pergamon Press.

Rogers, C. (1951)
Client-centered Therapy. Boston: Houghton Mifflin.

Rogers, C.R. (1970)
Carl Rogers on Encounter Groups. New York: Harper & Row.

Seligman, M.E.P. (1970)
On the generality of the laws of learning. Psychological Review, 77, 406-418.

Seligman, M.E.P. (1974)
Depression and learned helplessness. In R.J. Friedman and M.M. Katz (eds), The Psychology of Depression: Contemporary theory and research. Washington, DC: Winston-Wiley.

Shapiro, A.K. (1978)
Placebo effects in medical and psychological therapies. In S. Garfield and A.E. Bergin (eds), Handbook of Psychotherapy and Behavior Change (2nd edn). New York: Wiley.

Shepherd, I. and Fagan, J. (eds) (1970)
Gestalt Therapy Now. Palo Alto, Ca: Science and Behaviour Books Inc.

Seigal, G.M. (1970)
Punishment, stuttering and dysfluency. Journal of Speech and Hearing Research, 13, 4.

Skinner, B.F. (1953)
Science and Human Behavior. New York: Macmillan.

Skinner, B.F. (1972)
Cumulative Record (3rd edn). New York: Appleton-Century-Crofts.

Sloane, H.N. and MacAuly, B.D. (eds) (1968)
Operant Procedures in Remedial Speech and Language
Training. New York: Houghton Mifflin.
**Sloane, R.B., Staples, F.R., Cristol, A.H., Yorkston, N.J.
and Whipple, K.** (1975)
Psychotherapy versus behavior therapy. Cambridge,
Mass.: Harvard University Press.
Staats, A.W. and Staats, C.K. (1963)
Complex Human Behavior. New York: Holt, Rinehart &
Winston.
Stampfl, T.C. and Lewis, D.J. (1967)
Essentials of implosive therapy: a learning therapy
based psychodynamic behaviour therapy. Journal of
Abnormal Behavior, 73, 496-503.
Stern, R. (1978)
Behavioural Techniques - A therapist's manual. London:
Academic Press.
Trower, P.E., Bryant, B.M. and Argyle, M. (1978)
Social Skills and Mental Health. Andover: Methuen.
Truax, C.B. and Carkhuff, R. (1967)
Towards Effective Counselling and Psychotherapy:
Training and practice. Chicago: Aldine.
Truax, C.B. and Mitchell, K.M. (1971)
Research on certain therapist interpersonal skills in
relation to process and outcome. In A.E. Bergin and S.L.
Garfield (eds), Handbook of Psychotherapy and Behavior
Change. New York: Wiley.
Ullmann, L. and Krasner, L. (1975)
A Psychological Approach to Abnormal Behavior (2nd edn).
Englewood Cliffs, NJ: Prentice-Hall.
Van Riper, C. (1963)
Speech Correction. Englewood Cliffs, NJ: Prentice-Hall.
Walrond-Skinner, S. (1976)
Family Therapy: The treatment of natural systems.
London: Routledge & Kegan Paul.
Walton, H. (1971)
Small Group Psychotherapy. Harmondsworth: Penguin.
Watson, J.B. and Rayner, R. (1920)
Conditioned emotional reactions. Journal of Experimental
Psychology, 3, 1-14.
Watts, F. (1973)
Mechanisms of fluency control in stutterers. British
Journal of Disorders of Communication, 8, 131-138.
Webster, L.M. (1970)
A clinical report on the measured effectiveness of
certain desensitisation techniques with stutterers.
Journal of Speech and Hearing Disorders, 35, 369-376.
Wilson, T. (1978)
Cognitive behavior therapy: paradigm shift or passing
phase. In J. Foreyt and D. Rathjen (eds), Cognitive
Behavior Therapy: Research and application. New York:
Plenum.
Wolpe, J. (1958)
Psychotherapy by Reciprocal Inhibition. Stanford, Ca:
Stanford University Press.

Wolpe, J. (1969)
The Practice of Behaviour Therapy. Oxford: Pergamon Press.

Wolpe, J. and Lazarus, A.A. (1966)
Behaviour Therapy Techniques: A guide to the treatment of neuroses. Oxford: Pergamon Press.

Wolpe, J. and Rachman, S. (1960)
Psychoanalytic 'evidence', a critique based on Freud's case of Little Hans. Journal of Nervous and Mental Disease, 131, 135-147.

Yates, A. (1980)
Biofeedback and the Modification of Behavior. New York: Plenum.

Yule, W. and Hemsley, D. (1977)
Single case method in medical psychology. In S. Rachman (ed.), Contributions to Medical Psychology, Volume 1. Oxford: Pergamon Press.

Questions

1. Are all 'insight' therapies based on the same set of assumptions?
2. Describe the various applications of behaviouristic learning theory to clinical problems.
3. Compare and contrast Freudian and behaviouristic explanations of phobias or depression.
4. Outline the main theoretical positions in the new cognitive-behavioural therapies.
5. What is the value of adopting a 'functional analysis' of a given problem?
6. Describe how you would set about using single-case methodology in the treatment of voice disorders.
7. Which factors can influence the process of psychological treatment and what steps can be taken to minimize their effects in group design experiments?
8. What kinds of outcome measure would you consider appropriate in the evaluation of therapy for adult stutterers?
9. Is there a place for the 'talking therapies' in modern speech therapy?
10. Describe how you would set up a support group for the relatives of stroke victims.

Annotated reading

Garfield, S.L. and Bergin, A.E. (1978) Handbook of Psychotherapy and Behavior Change (2nd edn). New York: Wiley.
 The most comprehensive review available of issues and practice in psychological treatment.

Hersen, M. and Barlow, D.H. (1976) Single Case Experimental designs: Strategies for studying behavior change. New York: Pergamon.
 An excellent guide to the practice of single-case methods.

Kazdin, A.E., Bellack, A.S. and Hersen, M. (1980) New Perspectives in Abnormal Psychology. New York: Oxford University Press.
> An up to date review of theory, classification and treatment in contemporary abnormal psychology.

Marks, I. (1981) Care and Cure of Neuroses. New York: Wiley.
> A new psychiatric text which exemplifies behaviouristic intervention over a number of neurotic conditions.

Nay, W.R. (1979) Multimethod Clinical Assessment. New York: Gardener Press.
> This book describes the range of assessment/evaluation strategies available to clinical scientists.

Rachman, S. and Wilson, G.T. (1980) The Effects of Psychological Therapy. Oxford: Pergamon.
> An expert evaluation of psychological treatments covering two decades of research.

Smail, D.J. (1978) Psychotherapy: A personal approach. London: Dent.
> A fascinating account of modern psychotherapy together with discussion of the author's approach to theory and therapy.

Part six

Neuropsychology

Introduction

Body and mind

Neuropsychology stands as a specialist topic at the inter-
face of medicine, psychology, evolutionary biology, linguistics and philosophy. The debate about the relationship
between body and mind is centred on this topic, and it may
seem at first that evidence supports those who argue that
mental processes arise from, and are indistinguishable from,
neurophysiological activity. Any interference in neural
metabolism (for example, through drug administration) or any
disruption of neural tissue can lead to pronounced changes
in consciousness, and it seems that neurophysiological damage is irreversible. But if a simple correspondence exists
between neural and mental functioning, then irreversible
brain injury should lead to permanent deficits in consciousness; but this is not so. At the turn of the century elderly
patients who had suffered sudden and massive cerebral damage
were left with extensive physical and mental deficits which
showed little improvement with time. But later it was observed that younger patients, with less diffuse head injuries, demonstrated considerable recovery of function.

A great deal of anecdotal evidence also suggests that
Man is capable of controlling a great number of bodily functions by simply concentrating on the relevant body system.
The success of biofeedback training attests to this ability
to bring what were thought to be involuntary processes under
voluntary control. However, from the control of heart rate
to the control of neurophysiological processes may seem a
rather large step. Yet just such a step has been proposed by
one of the most eminent neuropsychologists of the twentieth
century. Roger Sperry argues that self-consciousness cannot
be explained from a purely mechanistic standpoint: consciousness can influence physical events in the brain in ways that
we do not yet understand.

With this degree of uncertainty still prevalent in
neuropsychology there is real hope that the effects of brain
damage can be circumvented by appropriate therapeutic techniques. The steady research effort to assist brain-damaged
persons to overcome their handicap, particularly in the
field of aphasia, has gone hand in hand with theoretical
work. Neuropsychologists use information from both normal
and brain-injured populations to construct models of mental

processing. These models range from highly abstract conceptual schemes of memory storage to more tangible theories
of the relationship between specific brain structures and
particular mental abilities. This branch of psychology faces
very considerable practical and philosophical difficulties
yet in recent years, with new advances in modern technology,
a number of these problems have been resolved.

For clinical scientists involved in the care of the
elderly and the brain injured there is an urgent need for
new, therapeutic models of clinical action. In this final
chapter we outline the main features of clinical neuropsychology together with the models of recovery of function
currently available.

12

Clinical neuropsychology
Harry Purser

Human neuropsychology can be defined as the study of neural mechanisms underlying consciousness and behaviour. Neuropsychology attempts to construct models of what Hebb (1949) referred to as the 'conceptual nervous system': the psychological processes taking place in the brain which analyse environmental input and construct behavioural output. Clinical neuropsychology is mainly concerned with studying disturbances in consciousness and behaviour as a result of disease, damage or surgical modification of neural activity. General theories of brain function are put forward from correlating such known damage with the resultant psychological dysfunction.

In formulating models of brain function neuropsychologists have been eclectic in their approach by drawing from research in the physical brain sciences (neuroanatomy, neurophysiology and neurochemistry) as well as the behavioural sciences (behaviouristic and cognitive psychology, psycholinguistics). Evolutionary, developmental and clinical studies have all contributed to the current state of neuropsychology yet, despite 100 years of study, the brain has refused to give away all of its secrets. MacKay (1972) introduces the study of the brain in the following way.

> Of all the natural phenomena to which science can turn its attention none exceeds in its fascination the working of the human brain. Here, in a bare two-handfuls of living tissue, we find an ordered complexity sufficient to embody and preserve the record of a lifetime of the richest human experience. We find a regulator and co-ordinator of hundreds of separate muscle systems of the human body that is capable of all the delicacy and precision shown by the concert pianist and the surgeon. Most mysterious of all, we find in this small sample of the material universe the organ (in some sense) of our own awareness including our awareness of that universe, and so of the brain itself.

The brain

The cerebral hemispheres
The first striking feature of the human brain is the convoluted surface of the two cerebral hemispheres. Beneath

331

these convoluted mantles lie other brain structures which
terminate at the spinal cord (figure 1). When viewed in
cross-section the hemispheres possess an outer layer of
nerve cells known as the cerebral cortex. This crust of
cells is further subdivided into several distinct layers
which have been gradually built up through evolution. The
first rudimentary cortex is seen in reptiles and this has
been elaborated to the level of Man. The convolutions of the
cortex result in a number of distinct ridges (gyri) and fissures (sulci) which form the basis for demarcation between
the four major lobes of the brain: the frontal, parietal,
temporal and occipital areas depicted in figure 1.

Figure 1

**External surface of the left cerebral hemisphere showing
midbrain structures (dotted lines)**

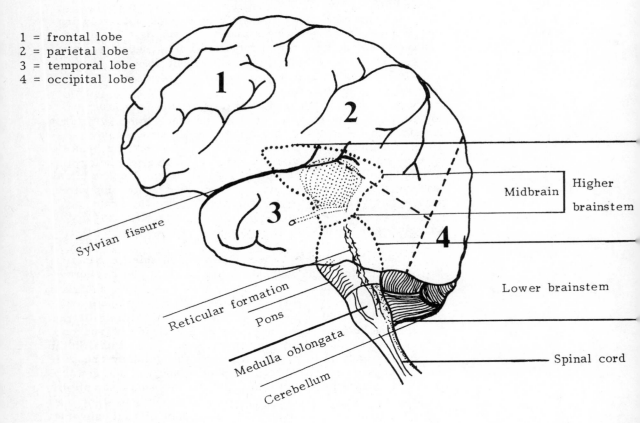

1 = frontal lobe
2 = parietal lobe
3 = temporal lobe
4 = occipital lobe

The two cerebral hemispheres are separated down the midline
by a deep fissure known as the median longitudinal sulcus.
At the base of this fissure lies a thick bundle of myelin-
ated fibres which forms the major interconnecting pathway

between the two hemispheres: the corpus callosum. The cerebral hemispheres therefore make up a dual system, each with four distinct lobes and interconnected to allow transmission of information between the two hemispheres. This structure is the seat of consciousness.

The limbic system

On the inner surface of each hemisphere lies the limbic lobe, a ring of brain structures made up of the septal area, the cingulate gyrus, the hippocampus and the amygdala. These structures interconnect with the hemispheres and with lower, sub-cortical systems. This system has been considered to be involved in both motivational and emotional experience.

The brain stem

The brain stem is the upper extension of the spinal cord and is made up of four distinct structures, as listed below.

* Medulla oblongata: this structure is nearest the spinal cord and is the point at which the cranial nerves enter and leave the brain stem. The medulla is also involved in the maintenance of autonomic activity: mainly breathing and heart action.

* The pons and cerebellum: above the medulla lies the pons which has a central core of cells and fibres with a lattice-like structure known as the reticular formation. This nerve network extends above and below the midbrain and medulla and is involved in the maintenance of arousal in the brain. Behind the pons lies the cerebellum, which closely resembles the convoluted cerebral hemispheres. This structure receives inputs from the hemispheres, the brain stem, the vestibular nuclei (concerned with balance) and the spinal cord. It seems to be concerned with processing feedback information from motor movements and thus guides motor activity.

* The midbrain: above the pons lies the midbrain, a small structure composed of four groups of nuclei known as the colliculi. Two of these nuclei - the superior colliculi - are concerned with the processing of visual input including eye movements, whilst the remaining inferior colliculi process auditory input. These structures form relay stations between the sense organs and the sensory areas in the cerebral cortex.

* The diencephalon: above the midbrain lies the complex structure of the diencephalon. Its main components are the thalamus and the hypothalamus. The thalamus seems to mediate the further projection of sensory information from the colliculi together with relaying motor information to the cerebellum. Fibres are also sent to the association areas of the cortex as well as the various sensory cortices. The hypothalamus consists of several nuclei bilaterally represented on either side of the third ventricle. At the front of the hypothalamus lies the optic chiasma: the junction and cross-over point of

the visual fibres on their way from the retina to the visual cortex. The hypothalamus controls a variety of endocrine functions and integrates information about such functions as water balance, body temperature and autonomic activity. It is further involved in the regulation of metabolism and control of blood pressure. The hypothalamus has also been implicated in the mediation of eating, drinking and sexual behaviour.

The cortical lobes

Over the years clinical observations of brain-damaged individuals have resulted in the mapping of psychological functions on to the four cortical lobes. A drawback to this enterprise is the often inexact information about the extent of the damage that has occurred to a particular structure. One further complication rests in the fact that damage to a specific brain area may disrupt processing at a completely different site. Careful study has, however, resulted in the following picture of cortical functioning.

Frontal lobes

The frontal lobes make up roughly one-third of the mass of the cerebral hemispheres and have been extensively investigated by the Russian neuropsychologist Luria. Both higher cognitive functioning and personality seem to be seriously disrupted when damage occurs. The relationship between frontal damage and changes in personality has been well documented for over 100 years. Moniz in 1935 developed the surgical technique of prefrontal lobotomy, which involves the removal of extensive areas of the frontal lobes, as a means of alleviating chronic states of psychiatric disturbance. After the operation the patient's state of tortured self-concern is removed, but so too is a range of cognitive functioning necessary for planning and problem-solving.

Lesions to the frontal lobes in normal individuals result in very uninhibited behaviour; previously quiet and conscientious individuals may become emotional and irritable and lose their awareness of social convention. Cognitive deficits include the inability to carry out abstract reasoning tasks or plan future strategies, and characteristic perseverance in problem-solving tasks. For example, even simple mental arithmetic may be beyond the scope of the frontal patient since it is an abstract task which requires the development of a computational strategy. Lesions to either the left or right frontal lobe can result in deficits in planning capacities, but specific damage to the left frontal region produces a deficit in the fluent production of linguistic symbols. This impairment of verbal fluency is matched by an impairment of spatial fluency when damage is confined to the right frontal lobe. Verbal fluency can be estimated using simple paper and pencil tests such as writing down in five minutes as many words as possible beginning with a particular letter. As more constraints are placed on what is permissible, so the performance of left frontal cases deteriorates. A similar measure of spatial fluency can be gained by asking patients to draw as many 'doodles' as possible within a given time limit. A feature of the right frontal groups is their tendency to perseverate in their designs. These cognitive deficits may co-exist with profound changes in personality in the direction of euphoria, impulsivity and uninhibited behaviour. In certain patients a general dullness in consciousness can occur, leading to an almost catatonic state.

Temporal lobes

The temporal lobes can be further subdivided into three major areas: the superior, middle and inferior gyri. A very marked asymmetry of function is seen between the two temporal lobes. Lesions to the left temporal lobe result in dysphasia and poor auditory processing. Damage to the right temporal lobe leads to impairments in the perceptual processing of spatial (non-verbal) information. Perhaps the most striking feature of temporal damage is the range of severe memory impairments which result. Verbal and spatial memory can be disturbed by left- or right-sided lesions, but in rare cases of viral encephalitis bilateral damage can take place which leads to the complete destruction of memory.

A great deal has been learned about the functioning of the temporal lobes through surgical procedures aimed at the alleviation of epileptic seizures. Epilepsy can result from unilateral or bilateral damage to the temporal lobes and, in addition to causing seizures, a variety of 'psychic phenomena' are experienced by the patient. Individuals may experience visual and auditory hallucinations and a marked change in consciousness towards a dream state, either before or after a fit. Other disturbances in perception include micropsia, where objects in the environment appear too small, and macropsia, where they appear too large. Even the perception of time can be disrupted. For some individuals temporal lobe seizures are heralded by sudden bouts of apprehension and fear whereas others experience euphoria and deja vu or jamais vu (the 'I've been here before' or 'none of this looks familiar' experience). In the course of investigating surgical procedures for temporal lobe epilepsy Penfield (1958) and Penfield and Roberts (1959) took the opportunity to explore the function of the lobes by applying stimulating electrodes to the surface. This stimulation technique yielded a variety of findings; conscious patients reported very vivid 'memories from the past' when stimulated at certain sites. One patient reported a conversation that had happened a number of years previously although the experience was so vivid it seemed as if it was taking place at that very moment. This recall of past events through stimulation has only been discovered in the temporal lobes, and in particular with stimulation to the superior temporal gyri.

Occipital lobes

Lesions to the occipital lobes invariably result in visual disturbances ranging from complete blindness to very subtle colour vision deficiencies. It was believed that damage to the striate areas of the lobes resulted in 'cortical blindness', but recent animal experimentation suggests that a dual visual system may exist mediated by both cortex and superior colliculus. This secondary visual system allows identification of visual patterns in the absence of the occipital system. In normal functioning these two systems are interdependent such that lesions to one system modify the activity of the other. Even extensive damage to the visual system can leave a great deal of visual functioning intact, although operating in a deficient manner. Different types of lesioning produce a variety of visual agnosias; damage to the posterior cerebral artery can result in extensive disruption of the left occipital region or the fibres of the corpus callosum that connect the two occipital lobes. This type of lesioning leads to a condition called agnosic alexia, or 'pure word blindness', where the individual is unable to read words and sentences or copy printed material.

Penfield and Perot (1963) carried out extensive stimulation work on the occipital lobes and found a majority of cases reported elementary visual hallucinations. These experiences consisted of flashing lights and colours which seemed to be moving across the field of vision. No complex visual experiences were reported (e.g. visualizing some scene from past memory) from occipital stimulation. The temporal lobes remain the only brain site which can generate complex auditory and visual hallucinations.

Parietal lobes

This middle part of the cerebral hemispheres, situated between the other three lobes, displays a variety of functions which are closely related to the functioning of the frontal, temporal and occipital lobes. Consequently a very diffuse range of psychological dysfunction can result from parietal lesioning. One type of disturbance is nearly always indicative of parietal damage: disorders of body image. In these conditions the individual may be unaware of part of his body, or of its position in space. In unilateral neglect the patient fails to use one side of the body when carrying out simple tasks. Although there is no muscular weakness he may use only one hand to put on one shoe. Some patients suffer the experience of perceiving one part of the body as either enlarged or atrophied.

Cerebral dominance

Whilst damage to the motor areas of the cerebral hemispheres results in muscular disruption (hemiplegia) to the side of the body opposite the site of damage, the earliest neuropsychologists noted that disturbances in psychological functioning also seemed related to the site of damage. Following

Broca's (1861) definitive work relating lesions of the left hemisphere to disorders of language it became accepted that the left hemisphere had a dominant role for language over the right hemisphere. This dominance could be seen in having a preferred body side (usually the right) and in the fact that disruption to the hemisphere controlling the preferred side invariably resulted in dysphasia. This loss of communicative ability following brain damage is amongst the most severe clinical conditions that can result from accidental lesioning. Broca's description of this asymmetrical brain functioning began the search to localize different aspects of higher mental processes in the various cortical regions. This notion of a cortical topography related to discrete forms of psychological functioning had been popular in the early nineteenth century when Gall introduced the 'science' of phrenology: 'reading' the bumps on the skull. Broca's observations led to the acceptance that the language hemisphere was dominant over its partner which remained 'dumb' and was seen as a rather passive processor of spatial (non-verbal) information; it passed such information over to the dominant hemisphere for interpretation and action. More recent studies in neuropsychology have now seriously undermined this rather simple picture. Whilst it is still generally true that there is a marked asymmetry of function between the two hemispheres, the role of the 'non-dominant' hemisphere in both language processes and other complex forms of information processing seems more extensive than was previously held.

Broadly, this asymmetry of function can be summarized as follows.

* Left hemisphere lesions produce a range of dysphasic disorders, apraxias, asomatognosias and visual agnosias. Extensive studies of both normal and brain-damaged individuals have established beyond doubt the role of left hemisphere mechanisms in processing verbal material regardless of the particular input modality. It seems then that the left hemisphere contains the neural substrate of all forms of symbolic communication.
* Right hemisphere lesioning results in disorders of spatial orientation like drawing, written language, written calculations and appreciating topographical arrays. Spatial agnosias and body image distortions are also found with right-sided lesioning, together with problems in the perception or recall of non-verbal material or anything having a complex perceptual structure.

Although this functional asymmetry is well established it was only relatively recently that structural asymmetry between the two hemispheres was established. Geschwind and Levitsky (1968) demonstrated that the surface of the planum temporale was significantly greater on the left hemisphere than on the right. A similar asymmetry was observed by Wada, Clarke and Hann (1975) for Broca's motor speech area in the left hemisphere. Electrophysiological studies have also confirmed specialization by each hemisphere in processing different kinds of input. The right temporal region displays greater activity to simple click stimuli than the left; this situation is reversed when meaningful verbal input is made available.

These broad conclusions about hemispheric specialization have been modified in the light of a series of experimental observations made by Sperry in the late 1960s. Sperry (1968) developed the technique of disconnecting the two hemispheres (to relieve intractable epilepsy) by cutting the majority of the corpus callosum fibres. This procedure is extremely effective in preventing convulsions, but also results in the virtual isolation of the two hemispheres. Only sub-cortical pathways remain intact to exchange information between left and right. Neuropsychological studies of such patients have confirmed this functional disconnection, but no significant change occurs in the patient's consciousness. More is said about the split brain procedure later.

The clinical neuropsychologist investigates the relationship between organic damage and resultant psychological functioning in an attempt both to relate specific kinds of functioning to specific brain systems and construct predictive models of the consequences of brain damage. In order to make scientifically valid observations about brain-damaged individuals two problems must be overcome. The first involves accurately discovering the nature and extent of damage that has taken place. Several types of brain damage can occur which result in different patterns of lesioning. In the past the only way to establish the exact extent of brain damage was through post-mortem examination. Recently a number of techniques have been developed which allow the very detailed analysis of neural tissue without resort to surgery. The second problem concerns the design of psychometric assessments of psychological dysfunction. Over the years a number of clinical instruments have been developed which allow the objective description of various patterns of psychological dysfunction. As the picture of cerebral asymmetry of function built up, so these psychological tests were used as a further means of localizing damage in the brain.

Neural lesions

A number of neuropathologies have been identified which each demonstrate a characteristic profile of destruction. Viral infections which selectively attack neural tissues are perhaps the most complex to describe, but three main sources of brain disruption have well-documented effects.

Cerebro-vascular accident (CVA)

CVA refers to some anomaly in the brain's vascular system such as an intracerebral haemorrhage which causes blood to be vented into the surrounding neural tissue (stroke). CVAs are most commonly found in the branches of the middle cerebral artery which results in motor paralysis down the opposite side of the body together with disturbances in higher mental functioning. Ischaemia is a condition where the blood supply to a particular region of the brain is disrupted and so the neural tissue beyond the blockage loses its blood supply and thus dies. This dead tissue is termed a cerebral infarct. The blockages can result from clots (thrombosis) which may be formed in other parts of the body but travel through the system and become lodged in the narrow branches of the cerebral arteries. Arterial disease can also lead to ischaemia through the gradual narrowing of the arterial walls.

Space-occupying lesions

This term is given to any abnormal swellings which occur in neural tissue. Tumours (neoplasms) may begin to grow which are of two types: benign and malignant. Benign tumours are often found growing from the meningeal coverings of the brain (meningiomas); these slow-growing neoplasms can reach a fairly large size before they begin to disrupt physical and psychological functioning. Malignant tumours are more frequently found and these fast-growing neoplasms extensively invade surrounding neural tissue. These malignant growths are further subdivided into primary or secondary neoplasms. The former arise in glial cells or fibres and account for about 40 per cent of adult tumours. Secondary neoplasms arise when a malignancy in another area of the body deposits malignant cells in the brain which leads to a metastic tumour in neural tissue.

Infections of the blood stream or of the cerebro-spinal fluid can result in abscesses which may display signs and symptoms similar to a neoplasm, but can be treated less radically. Collectively the space-occupying lesions result in either local or diffuse damage through pressure, haemorrhaging and ischaemia. Surgical intervention is a necessity in the majority of space-occupying lesions since they often have dramatic effects on physical and mental functioning with a very rapid onset. Often a great deal of surrounding tissue has to be removed to ensure surgical success, and in these cases fairly extensive psychological dysfunction can be seen post-operatively.

Cerebral trauma

Physical blows to the head can cause damage which is very difficult to localize. Penetrating head wounds which lacerate neural tissue may produce a diffuse pattern of destruction, particularly if caused by a high-velocity missile. In a closed head injury the skull is not penetrated although hairline fractures may be seen. Depending on the relative movements of the source and the individual, the brain will be compressed against the inside of the skull resulting in contusion (bruising) of the neural tissue. Sudden loss of consciousness following a blow to the head is due to the shock to the brain stem. Upon recovering consciousness the individual may experience a memory disturbance such as retrograde amnesia (where memory prior to the blow is lost) or anterograde amnesia (post-traumatic memory loss). Following the return of consciousness after cerebral trauma an individual may be disorientated, confused, aphasic, or display heightened sensitivity to sound and light. Where a number of cerebral contusions have occurred over a space of time the 'punch-drunk' syndrome seen in ex-boxers is apparent. The patient may have the greatest difficulties in paying attention and concentrating together with a pronounced dysarthria and labile mood. General intellectual functioning is usually severely impaired.

Physical methods of neural investigation

In order to diagnose the type of brain damage that has occurred to a given individual there is need for methods to investigate the structure and function of the brain 'in vivo'. If surgical intervention is contemplated a very accurate visualization of the internal damage is required. Over the years a number of standard procedures have been developed which allow both the type and the extensiveness of damage to be estimated.

Physical examination

A standard clinical neurological examination concentrates on the patient's sensory channels, reflexes, motor movements and muscle tone. By systematically checking out the end points of the system an estimate can be made of the most likely areas of damage. A neurological examination also involves an estimate of mental status to detect any alterations in consciousness, memory or learning. Such an examination can detect and broadly localize neurological damage but often lacks sufficient specificity for clinical purposes.

Radiological investigation

Arteriography (angiography) consists of introducing a radio-opaque fluid into the blood supply of the brain which is then serially photographed using X-rays. This technique allows the visualization of the circulatory system, which may reveal vascular damage or the presence of a space-occupying lesion when the vessels appear displaced to one side. In a brain scan radio-isotopic compound is injected into the vascular system and travels to the brain. This radioactive material is selectively taken up in sites where tumours, vascular accidents or abscesses are present. Air encephalography is one further technique which allows visualization of the ventricular system. By introducing air into the cerebro-spinal fluid via a syringe the air rises and can be made to fill the ventricular cavities by positioning of the head. X-ray pictures show up this medium allowing visualization of the ventricles which may show displacement or distortion indicative of a nearby space-occupying lesion. Dilation of the ventricular system is consistent with wasting of the surrounding tissue.

CAT scan (computerized axial topography)

Computerized axial topography (EMI Scan) is a recent technological breakthrough which provides computer-enhanced views of the inside of the brain without the need of high levels of radiation. This increase in efficiency of 'reading' radiographic images allows 'slices' of the brain to be represented and built up into a coherent picture. Such an accurate representation of the brain allows detailed examination for pathological deviance.

Electro-encephalogram (EEG)

The EEG records neural activity by means of a series of surface scalp electrodes which are fixed in a standard configuration over both hemispheres. By amplifying the tiny currents at each recording site a visual trace can be produced on a pen recorder. Usually 16 electrodes are attached to the scalp which generates 16 waveforms on the recording equipment. By switching the recording between 'different channels a number of distinct brain areas can be isolated and the waveforms inspected for any abnormality. When a group of nuclei produces abnormal discharges these emerge as 'spike activity' in the EEG, a sudden increase in amplitude in the waveform which occurs periodically. The EEG has been particularly valuable in diagnosing the site of epileptic lesions and in the investigation of sleep and dreaming. During drowsy states the EEG takes on a characteristic slow waveform, indicative of low cortical arousal. When a sleeping individual begins to dream the EEG activity becomes as animated as it would if he were completely conscious. Rapid fast wave activity predominates even though the person is deeply asleep: so-called 'paradoxical sleep'.

Electrical stimulation

The work of Penfield and Roberts (1959) has led to the clinical use of electrical stimulation of neural tissue during the course of surgery to 'map' neuroanatomic functioning. Very fine control can be exercised over this form of direct neural stimulation. The frequency, duration and intensity of the electrical pulses can be varied to give the neurosurgeon wide scope to probe both healthy and damaged tissue.

Neuropsychological investigation

Binet was certainly amongst the first neuropsychologists by introducing the first 'mental test' (Binet and Simon, 1905). The IQ test remains of prime importance to neuropsychological assessment since some reliable index of general mental functioning is necessary in charting recovery after brain damage. Modern IQ tests also yield further implications for more specific assessments of psychological functioning in cases of brain damage.

Wechsler Adult Intelligence Scale (WAIS)

The WAIS (Wechsler, 1955) is perhaps the most common clinical estimate of IQ and provides three measures: a verbal

IQ, a spatial (performance) IQ and a full-scale IQ. These three scores can have implications for further assessment if sufficiently significant differences occur between them.

The majority of cases of brain damage do not have any pre-morbid testing to compare with post-traumatic scores, and so a rather rough clinical judgement must be made about the patient's previous intellectual functioning by considering educational history and employment. Interests, hobbies and reports from friends, relatives and the patient himself allow a picture of pre-morbid adjustment to be built up. If evidence of intellectual impairment is seen together with a history of insidious onset then the initial stages of a dementia might be indicated. If the test is tackled in an unusual way then further clues may be gained about the nature of the patient's impairment.

Large observed differences between the patient's verbal (V) and spatial (S) quotients may be indicative of specific damage to the left (verbal) or right (spatial) hemisphere. A poor performance on V relative to S may simply suggest a poor educational background, but if this possibility is negated by occupational status then damage to the left hemisphere might be concluded. This will in turn suggest further specialized language testing to detect frontal or temporal lesioning. A poor performance on S relative to V may be due to distortions in visual-spatial processing and so would be further investigated using specific frontal and parietal tests.

Tests of cerebral dominance

In cases where surgery may be contemplated, such as relief from temporal lobe epilepsy, it is crucial that the dominant language hemisphere is unequivocally identified. Simple observations of handedness are often not enough. Milner, Branch and Rasmussen (1966) have estimated that in samples of epileptic patients left hemisphere dominance for language is present in 90 per cent of right handers and 70 per cent of left handers. The remaining percentages for both groups are made up by right hemisphere and bilaterally represented language. More accurate methods of establishing language dominance have been derived from experimental psychology: tachistoscopic visual tests and dichotic listening tests.

Tachistoscopic visual field technique
The tachistoscope is an electronic device capable of illuminating a visual stimulus for very brief periods of time. In this technique the visual system is manipulated by means of its anatomical connections. Briefly, one-half of each visual field is routed to each cerebral hemisphere for processing in the occipital lobe. Using the tachistoscope the patient can be asked to focus on a central point on a card with words written to the left and right of this point. When central focussing occurs the information to the right of the point is exclusively delivered to the left hemisphere, and the information on the left is conveyed to the right hemisphere. In everyday life we never encounter a situation

where such a discrete allocation of input occurs. By virtue of head movements, eye scanning and eye tremor, visual information always reaches both hemispheres virtually simultaneously. By locating a central fixation point on a tachistoscopic card and arranging written, verbal stimuli to either side of this point a rapid exposure (under 200 milliseconds) transmits two discrete messages to the left and right hemisphere simultaneously. In this way the differential functioning capacities of the two hemispheres can be compared under different exposure times and using a variety of verbal and non-verbal stimuli. Sperry (1968) and Gazzaniga, Bogen and Sperry (1962) have made extensive use of this technique in investigating split brain patients. Dominance can be allocated to the hemisphere which performs more accurately on visually presented verbal stimuli.

Dichotic listening technique
The dichotic listening test involves the simultaneous presentation of different verbal stimuli to each ear via a stereophonic amplifier. This form of input results in superior recall of the right ear stimuli in right-handed subjects. When competing, non-verbal stimuli (such as tones) are simultaneously presented, a marked left ear superiority results. This can be understood from the special anatomical arrangement of the auditory system. (See Gardener, 1975, p. 272 for discussion of the anatomy of audition.)

This system displays stronger contralateral representation of input than the visual system, and thus Broadbent (1954) demonstrated that when two sets of three digits are presented to each ear simultaneously, a request for recall results in the right ear (for right-handed, left dominant subjects) digits being reported before the left. The dichotic listening test has become one further method of establishing cerebral language respresentation since speech processing capacities can be distinguished from auditory spatial processing.

Special investigation: Wada technique
A further method of establishing the language dominant hemisphere involves delivering a barbiturate fluid, via a catheter, to each cerebral hemisphere in turn. The drug travels in a single carotid artery to a given hemisphere where it produces a unilateral, transitory dysfunction. Such unilateral depression of function results in a pronounced dysphasia when the language dominant hemisphere is treated, whereas language skills remain intact when the non-dominant hemisphere is involved.

Through the use of a variety of object naming, verbal memory and spatial tasks during the unilateral depression, the language dominant hemisphere can be identified. This was the technique used by Milner et al (1966) to arrive at her estimates of dominance in right- and left-handed patients. An updated survey by Milner (1974) further refines these estimates. In a sample of over 200 patients it was found that left hemisphere language was present in 96 per cent of

right handers and in 70 per cent of left handers. In a
further group of patients who sustained brain damage at an
early age it was found that left hemisphere language was
present in 81 per cent of right handers (13 per cent in left
hemisphere, 6 per cent bilateral) and in 30 per cent of left
handers (51 per cent in right hemisphere, 19 per cent bilateral). This discrepancy between early and later brain-
damaged patients may illustrate the brain's capacity for re-
organization following injury. It would seem neural tissue
demonstrates 'plasticity' when damage occurs at an early
age.

Specific psychological tests
Having established language dominance and obtained a general
estimate of the patient's level of intellectual functioning
(which may indicate a left or right hemisphere dysfunction)
a number of more specific psychological tests can be administered to gain more detailed evidence of psychological
dysfunction and attempt to localize the site of damage.
Walsh (1978) lists the major psychological tests commonly
used to identify dysfunction in table 1. In addition to
providing information on the regional significance of different types of dysfunction these assessments provide objective evidence of the nature and extent of psychological
dysfunction in brain-damaged patients. This measurement is
crucial if scientific investigations of brain damage are to
be undertaken.
    Neuropsychological assessment, together with neuro-
logical investigations and case history interviews, result
in a detailed picture of the individual case. The specific
organic pathology (CVA, space-occupying lesion, infarct,
etc.) can be identified and the effects of this damage
objectively reported. Physical, affective and cognitive
dysfunctions can occur which generate hypotheses about the
relationship between damage and psychological functioning
(see Lezak, 1976, for a detailed account of neuropsychological assessment procedures). Although neuropsychology is
based on meticulous assessment of cognitive functioning,
such an account often fails to convey the effects of brain
damage in human terms. Traumatic damage may change a stable
individual into a highly emotional and uninhibited person.
This affective change, together with physical and cognitive
impairment, can seriously strain relationships with friends
and partners. Even where no significant personality changes
occur and when consciousness is intact, the impact of physical and cognitive handicap can be profound; there is a high
incidence of psychiatric disturbance amongst the brain-
damaged population. The extent to which this is a direct
result of damage or the effect of trying to cope with
extensive handicap, is not known. What is known concerns the
relationship between motivation to recover and actual
recovery attained. A number of cases have demonstrated that
where the patient is strongly motivated extensive recovery
of function can take place; where motivation is seriously

Table 1
_____

Neuropsychological assessment techniques
From Walsh (1978). Reproduced by permission.

1. GENERAL EXAMINATION (intelligence, memory, comprehension)
   Wechsler Adult Intelligence Scale (short form; Duke, 1967)
   Wechsler Memory Scale
   Delayed Memory Tasks
   Aphasia Screening test (Russell et al, 1970)
   Token Test (De Renzi and Vignolo, 1962)

2. TEST WHICH MAY PRODUCE INFORMATION WITH REGIONAL SIGNIFICANCE

   (a) Frontal
       * Abstraction, conceptual shift:
         Colour-Form Sorting Test (Goldstein and Scheerer, 1941)
         Milan Sorting Test (De Renzi et al, 1966)
         Halstead Category Test (Halstead, 1947)
         Wisconsin Card Sorting Test (Grant and Berg, 1948)

       * Planning, regulating, checking programmes of action:
         Porteus Maze Test (Porteus, 1965)
         Trail Making Test (Reitan, 1966)
         Complex Figure of Rey (Osterreith, 1944; Rey, 1959)
         Arithmetical problem-solving tests

       * Verbal behaviour and verbal regulation of behaviour (Christensen, 1975):
         Verbal Fluency Test (Benton, 1967)

   (b) Temporal
       * Visual memory tasks:
         Rey Figure (Rey, 1959)
         Benton Visual Retention Test (Benton, 1955)
         Recurring Nonsense Figures (Kimura, 1963)
         Non-verbal Sequential Memory Test (from Illinois Test of Psycholinguistic
             Abilities)
         Facial Recognition Tests

       * Amnesic Syndrome Tests (Lhermitte and Signoret, 1972)
         Maze Learning Task (Milner, 1965)

       * Auditory perceptual tasks:
         Seashore Rhythm Test (from Halstead-Reitan battery)
         Speech Sounds Perception Test (from Halstead-Reitan battery)
         Environmental Sounds Test (Faglioni et al, 1969)
         Austin Meaningless Sounds Test

   (c) Parietal
       * Constructional praxis:
         Benton, VRT (Copying)
         Rey Figure
         WAIS Block Design and Object Assembly
         Fairfield Substitution Test (Grassi, 1947)

Three dimensional Praxis Test (Benton and Fogel, 1962)
Halstead-Reitan Tactual Performance Test

* Quasi-spatial synthesis (Christensen, 1975)
  (i) logico-grammatical (ii) mathematical

* Cross-modal association tests
* Spatial tests:
  The following may supplement sundry 'spatial' tests shown above.
  Stick Test (Benson and Barton, 1970)
  Pool Reflection Test (Cattell, 1944)
  Money's Standardization Road Map Test (Butters et al, 1972)

(d) Occipital
Colour naming
Colour-form association (De Renzi et al, 1972)
Visual irreminiscence

3. NEUROLOGICAL TESTS
Finger-tapping test(Halstead-Reitan battery)
Motor Impersistence
Finger recognition (Benton, 1959)
Right-Left orientation (Benton, 1959)
Double simultaneous stimulation

4. MISCELLANEOUS
Symbol-Digit-Modalities Test (Smith, 1973)
Continuous Performance Test (Rosvold et al, 1956; Schein, 1962)
Reaction times tests (Pillon, 1973)
Queensland Test (McElwain and Kearney, 1970)

5. LANGUAGE
Comprehensive examination for aphasia (Spreen and Benton, 1969)

NOTE: The references after certain tests contain either original descriptions or key
articles.

---

undermined recovery is slow and unpredictable. The need for a warm, supportive social environment is crucial for the effective rehabilitation of the brain damaged. Too often this question has been overlooked in the study of recovery of function.

Aphasia

Perhaps the most devastating consequence of brain damage is the loss of communicative ability: aphasia. Previously fluent and articulate individuals can be reduced to making unintelligible noises, or producing a rapid stream of nonsensical phrases. This condition can be produced by a number of specific pathologies from CVA to ischaemia.

The study of aphasia is some 4,000 years old, but the first systematic investigations took place in the nineteenth century when anatomists first began to associate language

dysfunction with site of damage at post-mortem. This localizationist approach - attempting to relate specific function
with a specific cortical region - received a further boost
from the work of Pierre Broca (1861) who suggested that a
region in the posterior area of the left frontal lobe was
consistently damaged in cases of speechlessness. Wernicke
(1874) discovered a further region in the left temporal lobe
that was associated with the receptive language processes
but left speech undisturbed. These studies confirmed the
left hemisphere as dominant for language and began to map
surface regions which were concerned with different aspects
of communicative function.

Wernicke produced the first neuropsychological model of
aphasia when he postulated a specific process of interaction
between neural regions which accounted for communication
breakdown. The model emphasized the role of the first temporal gyrus (Wernicke's Area) in the comprehension of spoken
language. This area was seen as being a store of 'auditory
impressions' of words which were essential for the accurate
perception of words. Output from Wernicke's Area travelled
to Broca's motor speech area in the frontal lobe where the
'auditory impressions' were translated into motor speech
routines for expressive language. Lesions to different
points in this simple circuit would result in different
kinds of dysphasia. Damage to Broca's area would result in
a pure motor aphasia (expressive aphasia) with receptive
capacities left intact. Lesions to Wernicke's Area would
result in comprehension difficulties and if lesions occurred
in the pathway between Broca's and Wernicke's regions an
expressive deficit could occur in the absence of specific
damage to the motor speech area.

Running counter to this localizationist view of brain
functioning was the globalist school of neuropsychologists,
who argued that higher mental processes were the result of
integrated functioning taking place all over the brain
rather than localized activity. Amongst the advocates of
this view was Sigmund Freud, the father of psychoanalysis.
These holistic theorists maintained that aphasia could
result from many kinds of neural dysfunction. No specific
disturbances of language per se occurred; rather a number
of basic psychological processes, such as perceptual and
attentional systems, were disrupted by damage and resulted
in inefficient communication processes. This view was bol-
stered by the evidence from Gestalt psychology demonstrating
that perceptual processing does not obey the same principles
as the physiology of sensory reception. Although there are
no visual cells at the point in the retina where the optic
fibre departs we are not aware of a corresponding 'hole' in
our visual fields!

Weisenburg and McBride (1935) are credited with the
first systematic classification of the aphasias by quanti-
fying the behavioural and psychological deficits observed in
a large clinical population of brain-damaged patients. Four
major types of aphasia were found: expressive, receptive, a

mixed expressive-receptive and an amnesic form. Theorists such as Geschwind (1965, 1979) and Luria (1973) have tried to account for these types of aphasia by modified localization theories. Geschwind argues that in addition to the classic Broca and Wernicke areas there is a further region in the inferior parietal lobe (consisting of the angular and supramarginal gyri) which is not seen in other species and occupies a zone where the various sensory areas converge. This region is seen as a facilitator of cross-modal association (e.g. linking sound to sight, etc.) and particularly concerned with relating auditory stimuli (words) to their sensory representations. Thus symbolic auditory stimuli evoke memorized sensory properties such as visual appearance, smell, touch, etc. Geschwind argues that this species-specific area was an essential evolutionary development for the use of a complex, multi-modal, symbolic representation capacity (language).

Luria approaches aphasia from a more complex perspective. He contends that the brain functions at different hierarchical levels. The most primitive level (primary) consists of the deepest few millimetres of cortical tissue which extracts very general information from input and plays a basic role in output. The next two levels (secondary and tertiary) perform increasingly complex functions on input and output; damage to these levels of processing will result in different aphasic syndromes. A further point about Luria's approach involves his concept of variability in localization of function. Rather than seeing language functions localized in a particular anatomical region, he argues that such complex processes involve multiple cortical systems which are usually diffusely represented in the cortex. This position warns of the dangers in assuming that a particular function is invariably located in a given anatomical region. These models make a number of predictions about the consequences of particular types of brain damage and aphasic deficit.

Classification of aphasia

Receptive aphasia

In receptive aphasia spontaneous speech may be fluent or hyperfluent. Intonation and facial/gestural expression may be normal but the content of the utterance is incomprehensible. This is not due to unintelligibility for the motor speech processes are left intact. Rather the incorrect use of lexical items is observed (paraphasia) often without the patient's awareness. A pronounced word-finding difficulty exists which results in much circumlocution.

In this condition it is assumed damage has occurred to Wernicke's Area with consequent difficulties in comprehending incoming auditory information. Such damage may also result in the interruption of visual memory leading to difficulties describing what is seen. Reading is seriously affected as visual input no longer evokes auditory memory.

Expressive aphasia

PURE MOTOR APHASIA: this relatively rare condition presents intact comprehension, reading and writing abilities but a severe deficit in motor speech sequences. No words are produced although noises can be made. This condition is considered to be due to damage to the classical Broca's Area.

NON-FLUENT APHASIA: in addition to the complete loss of motor speech, a more common condition involves the production of only rudimentary speech sounds with a marked non-fluency. This effortful speech may be accompanied by object naming difficulties and impaired writing skills although copying capacities remain intact. Both spoken and written expression are therefore disturbed.

Conduction aphasia

In conduction aphasia receptive abilities are intact but there is an inability to repeat phrases that have been heard. The patient may be able to speak spontaneously, and often copiously, but the content of the speech may be inappropriate and incomprehensible. The inability to follow verbal instructions is a significant diagnostic feature of this form of aphasia. It is assumed that damage occurs in the major connecting pathways between Wernicke's comprehension area and Broca's expressive area. This pathway is known as the Arcuate Fasciculus and lesions in this region disconnect the Broca and Wernicke areas resulting in the characteristic expressive disturbance. This impaired ability to repeat utterances or read aloud may be accompanied by disorders of writing and spelling with preserved comprehension of both written and spoken language.

Transcortical aphasia

In some cases brain damage can be very diffuse over both hemispheres and thus interrupt several pathways to the Broca and Wernicke areas. This may result in a mixed pattern of expressive and receptive disability although the individual may be able to repeat what is said. Two sub-types have been distinguished: motor and sensory transcortical aphasia. In the motor sub-type impairment in the ability to initiate speech may be seen together with a severe non-fluency in spontaneous speech. Repetition can remain intact. In sensory cases there may be fluent, spontaneous speech with many paraphasias and severe comprehension impairment.

Amnesic aphasias (nominal aphasia)

A major general feature of aphasias is the inability to name objects and find the appropriate word. Within this dimension of disability there is a distinct group of patients who manifest a selective loss of lexical items yet have fluent, articulate and grammatical output with intact comprehension. This condition of anomia is termed amnesic aphasia or nominal aphasia. Nouns are most impaired, with verbs and adjectives also disrupted. There is still some controversy over the kind of damage which leads to this condition. Some favour a single lesion site whilst others argue for a multiple aetiology.

Pure alexia

Pure alexia is a disturbance of written language caused by a lesion in the left visual (occipital) cortex and damage to the posterior part of the corpus callosum: the splenium. This sequence of damage means the individual can still see in the left visual field (right visual cortex) but not in the right visual field (left visual cortex). Information reaching the right hemisphere cannot cross over the corpus callosum to the left language centres and consequently no understanding of written language is possible. Verbal comprehension and expressive speech are unaffected by such a pattern of damage.

This taxonomy of aphasias is only one of many that have been developed. Schuell (1965) combined a number of tests to form the Minnesota Test for the Differential Diagnosis of Aphasia, which yields seven categories of aphasic breakdown: simple aphasia; aphasia with visual involvement; mild aphasia with persisting dysfluency; aphasia with scattered findings compatible with generalized brain damage; aphasia with sensori-motor involvement; aphasia with intermittent auditory imperception; and irreversible aphasic syndrome. Powell, Clark and Bailey (1979) have subjected Schuell's categories of aphasia to the statistical technique of cluster analysis which resulted in four principal groups of scores: a severe, high moderate, low moderate and mild group emerged. Both sex and age were significant variables between these groups with men making up the largest proportion of the severe group and the mild group containing the youngest patients. This research demonstrates that there is little evidence for Schuell's clinical distinction of seven types of aphasic. A classification according to severity of defect rather than trying to pinpoint a specific type of language deficit, or organic site of lesioning, can have very practical implications for the treatment of the individual case.

A further move away from the investigation of cortical localization of damage through psychological assessment has resulted from recent evidence suggesting that a strict localization of function model cannot be sustained. In his early split brain work Sperry (1968) demonstrated how linguistic abilities were clearly localized in the left hemisphere whereas the processing of non-verbal, spatial stimuli was most efficiently performed by the right hemisphere. A marked superiority of the right hemisphere in a variety of visual-spatial tests (copying drawings, block design, etc.), together with evidence of very rudimentary expressive language, suggested a 'dumb' but efficient processor of non-verbal input. This view of the right hemisphere has been radically altered as more sophisticated test procedures have been developed. It now seems that the right hemisphere has a much greater capacity to comprehend both written and spoken language than was originally thought. It is also suggested that the apparent differences in verbal and non-verbal processing may be due to the different processing properties of the two hemispheres. The right hemisphere seems to be more efficient at processing information in a Gestalt (holistic) fashion and thus can readily grasp complex spatial relationships. The left hemisphere may specialize in sequential and articulated processing, thus demonstrating a superiority in verbal capacities.

This evidence, together with a growing awareness that there are very great individual differences in neuropsychological processing, has resulted in more cautious approaches to regional localization of functioning. A new form of neuropsychology has emerged in recent times which aims to describe highly abstract models of neuropsychological functioning without any direct reference to neuroanatomical sites. This approach draws heavily on the computer analogy of brain function and is often referred to as 'boxology' because of its unique flow diagrams.

Yet this abstract modelling is in the best tradition of experimental cognitive psychology and may have much more practical applications than the somewhat speculative localizationist position. The most important need of brain-damaged individuals is not to understand the anatomical extent of their neural damage but to attempt to recover physical and psychological functions that have been lost, or seriously impaired, as a consequence of damage. As Thompson (1978) concluded in a recent review of the status of neuropsychology:

> Neuropsychology has for the most part operated, until relatively recently, in isolation from academic psychology, even as it applies to cognitive processes. It is largely without practical consequences, despite the needs of brain-injured patients requiring rehabilitation. There has been too ready an acceptance of deficits as permanent facts about a person, rather than as difficulties which might possibly be overcome by an energetic application of psychological principles, a fact bemoaned by Meyer (1957) and little heeded in the subsequent twenty years. Stroke patients with speech disorders rarely have a psychologist to assist them, and still receive therapy for which it has proved difficult to find evidence of efficacy. Neuropsychologists have equally been too ready to rely on paper and pencil tests, rather than closely observing the patient under his normal working conditions.

Neuropsychology is becoming more concerned with the need to carry out further research on the effects of different kinds of therapy on recovery from brain injury and with making more natural and realistic assessments of handicap. The work of Farmer and O'Connell (1979) in applying neuropsychological models to the treatment of aphasia is a good example of this shift in emphasis.

Neuropsychological therapy Many textbooks of neuropsychology have depressingly little to say about therapy for the brain damaged. Powell (1981) has reviewed the various mechanisms which have been postulated to underlie recovery of function after damage. Typical recovery curves have been plotted for a range of brain-damaged patients which show a fairly substantial recovery a few months after damage and which then show rather steady improvement to a plateau stage which is usually short of 100 per cent recovery. These curves are, of course, averaged and thus mask the very considerable spread of individual difference in recovery. This period of good initial gains has often been referred to as 'spontaneous recovery' and was presumed to be due to several causes. Lesioning has rather general effects, such as oedema and raised intracranial pressure, which may recover within the first eight weeks resulting in improvements in function. Thus the extent of irreversible brain damage may be greatly exaggerated by these accompanying, but reversible, processes. Although this type of explanation covers initial recovery of function there is still a need to account for longer-term improvement given the fact that some individuals, with rather extensive damage, can make very remarkable recoveries.

Powell (1981) describes three types of explanation which have been advanced to account for recovery of function: physiological, structural and process models.

1. Physiological models

Four mechanisms have been postulated which attempt to account for recovery.

* DIASCHISIS: in diaschisis the threshold of cells surrounding an area of damage is raised and thus these cells are seldom fired. This is seen as a natural protective reaction to damage which gradually wears off, allowing the cells to fire once again. Although this explanation may account for the early surge of recovery it is doubtful whether it occurs long after the damage has stabilized.
* REGENERATION: it is an accepted fact that nerve regeneration is only found in the peripheral nervous system and never in the CNS. Some evidence exists which suggests a limited amount of regeneration may take place in the CNS, but whether this occurs to any great extent in Man is not known.
* COLLATERAL SPROUTING: it has been shown that neighbouring axons can take over the synaptic site vacated by a lesioned cell and thus complete a disrupted pathway.
* RELATIVELY INEFFECTIVE SYNAPSES: this position suggests that previously dormant connections are

activated following damage to a specific functional
system which then takes over the processing function.
This idea of built-in redundancy in neural connections
is often cited as the mechanism of 'neural plasticity'.

2. Structural models

Five mechanisms have been put forward under the heading of
structural models:

* REDUNDANCY: Laurence and Stein (1978) propose that
  more tissue and fibre is devoted to a particular neuropsychological function than is actually required. This
  built-in structural redundancy ensures resilience in the
  face of damage to some part of the system.
* EQUIPOTENTIALITY: this notion, of all brain tissue being
  capable of subserving any psychological function was
  popularized by Lashley in the 1930s to account for his
  fruitless search for the neural basis of learning and
  memory. Despite extensive surgical removal of brain
  tissue his experimental animals were still able to recall previously taught discriminations. This evidence
  boosted holistic theories of brain function, but in the
  light of recent split brain studies it would seem this
  mass action and equipotentiality is a difficult notion
  to substantiate.
* LEVELS OF REPRESENTATION: this idea is implicit in
  the neuropsychological model of Luria (1966) and has
  been advocated by Rosner (1974) as the mechanism of
  recovery of function. It is assumed that the brain
  operates in a hierarchical fashion with higher levels of
  representation controlling lower levels. When damage to
  higher levels occurs, lower levels can take over the
  damaged function as they are now freed from the higher
  'descending inhibition'. This explanation may account
  for the patterns of deficit that result from brain
  damage, but it would seem unlikely that functional
  representation would be identical at different levels.
* SUBSTITUTION: this rather vague idea referred to the
  existence of apparently extensive 'silent areas' in the
  brain. These areas were mapped through early stimulation
  work and were so called because nothing happened when
  they were directly stimulated. It was thought these
  'silent areas' could take over a disrupted function. The
  notion of 'silent areas' has been questioned by modern
  studies which demonstrate that these areas are
  extensively involved in everyday functioning.
* MULTIPLE CONTROL: this theory postulates a number
  of equivalent 'control centres' which can direct functioning in the event of damage to one of their number.
  It is difficult to see how any deficit would occur in
  this model.

3. Process models

Even given that some physiological and structural restitu-
tion occurs after brain damage we are still faced with the

problem of understanding the nature of the residual impairment. The steady recovery of function shown by some patients suggests that changes in neuropsychological processing may occur which assist in adaptation, coping and restoration of functioning. Three main forms of process explanations have been put forward:

* SIMPLE FUNCTIONAL SUBSTITUTION: Laurence and Stein (1978) argue that individuals cannot recover their lost functioning but rather develop the capacity to process the same input using a different (intact) functional system. A simple example would be if hearing were lost (auditory processing) and the patient subsequently learns to lip read (visual processing). Thus rather than any recovery of function there is further adaptation to handicap.

* RE-ORGANIZATION OR REROUTING OF THE PROCESSING FLOW: Luria (1963) has been in the forefront of describing the specific deficits found after brain damage. This detailed analysis has suggested that rather than whole functional systems being lost, a number of highly specific processes may be disrupted. These lost processes result in 'missing links' in a functional system. Rather than write off the entire system, Luria argues that these missing links can be filled in by therapy and full functioning restored. By teaching a number of subroutines designed to evoke additional contextual information, problems like loss of verbal memory can be offset by enhanced visual cuing. Information processing is therefore rerouted to become enhanced by additional information which modifies the effects of a missing link in the normal processing flow.

* NEURAL PLASTICITY: the notion of plasticity is close to the ideas of functional substitution. A damaged function can reappear in a new brain region because that region has in some way been 'primed' to take over that function in the event of damage. This model of recovery of function is supported by Searleman (1977) who reports stroke cases resulting in dysphasia with left-sided lesions. After a period of recovery these patients suffered further right-sided strokes which caused a further aphasia. These studies suggest the right hemisphere is capable of taking over language functions when lesions occur in the dominant hemisphere. Further dramatic examples of neural plasticity have been identified by Lorber (1980) where several cases are described of individuals suffering childhood hydrocephalus which results in only a few millimetres of brain tissue covering the inside of the skull with a central area of cerebrospinal fluid. Despite having 'virtually no brain' these individuals can have normal intelligence!

Brain function therapy   These models of brain functioning have generated several

different approaches to neuropsychological therapy. Physiological and structural models of recovery of function suggest that no special form of psychological input will have
much effect on the physical repair of damage. The recovery
curves of individual patients reflect the extent to which
physical reparation has proceeded. Intervention consists of
prescribing medication to control excessive affective behaviour. A number of prosthetic devices can be made available to assist the individual to cope with his handicap,
such as visual communication systems for aphasics.

The process models offer a more optimistic prognosis for
psychological therapy. Perhaps the earliest neuropsychological therapy was simple practice of the lost functions.
Through massive stimulation of these deficit areas it was
assumed that function would, sooner or later, recover. Both
physiotherapy and early speech therapy for aphasics was
based on this approach. A more structured neuropsychological
therapy has recently appeared in which the results of both
physical and psychological investigations are combined in a
form of therapy which is directed at a chosen region of the
brain in order to stimulate more efficient processing activity. An example would involve designing a variety of non-
verbal processing tasks in order to stimulate right hemisphere capacities. By making use of dichotic auditory,
visual and tactual processing tasks it is possible to
stimulate selectively a range of functions in each
hemisphere.

The status of therapies based on these approaches has
always proved elusive. Clinical reality seldom fits into
neat categorical classification systems. The individual case
may display a diffuse pattern of deficits which change over
time and are not indicative of a particular syndrome. This
reality has led clinicians to place their faith in whatever
forms of therapy seem to be doing the trick. Thus therapy
tends to be a highly individualized affair with specific
programmes being tailored to the individual case. In the
absence of any generally agreed classification system of
neuropsychological dysfunction it has been very difficult
for clinical researchers to compare their findings. This
problem, together with the individualized approach to therapy, has made hard evidence on the relative effectiveness
of different therapies difficult to come by. What evidence
there is involves single cases which have been intensively
investigated and followed up to estimate the effectiveness
of the treatment. Often these studies require careful design
to avoid the charge of being the 'exceptions rather than the
rule'.

Powell (1981) advocates a new approach to brain function therapy which treats each patient to a systematic,
scientific investigation to identify areas of deficit, both
physical and psychological. This information is utilized to
set up hypotheses about the nature and extent of dysfunction
which suggest direct stimulation of specific brain regions
and forms of processing. The target areas for such a directed stimulation approach are clearly defined at the outset

of therapy and continuously reviewed throughout therapy as a gauge of progress. Therapy is therefore designed to alter functioning towards a pre-set goal. However, this approach to therapy is not simply a technical process of selective stimulation of cognitive functioning. Deficit areas are described in terms of everyday problems in communication, memory and planning rather than as discrete neuropsychological processes. It further recognizes the social and emotional significance of brain damage and psychological dysfunction both for the patient and his relatives. Only by bringing the individual's total environment under therapeutic influence can any meaningful and consistent progress be achieved. Thus problem areas which are socially acknowledged (and are therefore the most emotionally significant ones) would require as much therapeutic attention as the patient's impaired reading and writing.

This need to enlarge our awareness of the full effects of neuropsychological dysfunction has become increasingly acknowledged amongst clinical workers. The importance of a positive, supportive, social and emotional environment for the patient is a clear therapeutic objective. Recently, techniques have been developed (Mulhall, 1978; Brumfitt and Clarke, 1982; Müller and Code, 1982) which allow detailed description of the social and emotional dimensions of brain damage. Often it is found that very great difficulties exist in coming to terms with handicap. Patients and relatives can become profoundly depressed and lose the will to persist with therapy. In such cases the clinician's task is to address these difficulties rather than specific dysfunctions.

There may well be a strong case to introduce multi-axial classification systems for brain damage which recognizes several dimensions of difficulties for each patient. Such a system would emphasize the need to analyse the psychosocial effects of handicap as well as specific neuropsychological functioning. By regarding each patient as a mini-experiment, treatment goals can be clearly set and progress towards these goals can be measured for different forms of therapy.

Conclusion

Modern clinical neuropsychology has evolved from earlier neuroanatomic studies of the brain which suggested the first localization theory of brain function. Although many of these early studies used single case methodology, the general notion of localization of function became accepted. The study of aphasia has been a particularly rich source of localization evidence, but recent split brain studies have seriously questioned these rather simple models of brain function. Clinicians have acknowledged the wide range of individual differences in brain damage which makes a categorical model of classification and diagnosis an unwieldy clinical tool. Given that there is still little more than informed speculation on the ways in which the brain processes complex psychological input, the clinical aim is to describe objectively the individual deficit and generate a series of goals for the individual patient. Therapy can be selectively aimed at different processes and progress towards the defined goals measured in order to evaluate the effectiveness of intervention. This scientific approach to neuropsychological dysfunction acknowledges the human dimension of handicap as well as testing hypotheses of recovery. A full description of modern brain function therapy can be found in Powell (1981).

Glossary

Afferent
Pathways conducting information into the brain.

Agnosia
Loss of ability to recognize familiar objects.

Alexia
Loss of ability to read.

Amygdala
Part of the limbic system involved in olfaction and motivation.

Anterograde
In amnesia, loss of memory for events prior to damage.

Aphasia
Loss of speech; a disorder of language (also dysphasia).

Apraxia
Inability to perform a familiar action.

ARAS
Ascending reticular activating system (see Reticular formation).

Arcuate fasciculus
Pathways connecting Broca's area with Wernicke's area.

Asomatognosia
Loss of knowledge of one's own body (body schema, body image).

Ataxia
Loss of ordered movements.

Autonomic
Acting independently. Refers to that part of the nervous system concerned with visceral (involuntary) processes.

Axon
Long slender part of a nerve cell.

Brain stem
First extension of the spinal cord. Many autonomic reflexes occur at the level of the brain stem.

Broca's Area
Third frontal gyrus of the left hemisphere.

Carotid
Main arteries supplying the brain with blood.

Catheter
Fine plastic tube which can be inserted in arteries and used to deliver fluids directly to specific areas without general contamination.

Cerebellum
Literally 'small brain'; refers to tissue beneath the cerebral mantles which regulates balance and motor activity.

Cerebral cortex
Literally 'brain bark'; outer crust of gray coloured tissue heavily convoluted and draped over the other parts of the brain.

Cerebral dominance
Refers to the specialization of one hemisphere (usually the left) for language. Contemporary literature refers to 'functional hemispheric asymmetry' recognizing specialization of each hemisphere in different psychological functions.

Cerebral hemispheres
Refers to two halves of the cerebral cortex separated by the longitudinal fissure.

Chiasma
A cross-over point. The optic chiasma refers to the point where retinal information is split and conveyed to each hemisphere.

Cingulate gyrus
Overlies the corpus callosum and forms part of the limbic lobe.

Collateral
A parallel structure.

Colliculus
Literally a 'mound'; a small rounded swelling.

Corpus callosum
Literally 'hard body'; main bundle of interconnecting fibres which conveys information between the two cerebral hemispheres.

Cortical blindness
Loss of vision due to damage in the cell columns of the visual cortices. The degree of visual impairment can be directly related to the extent of cortical dysfunction.

CSF (cerebro-spinal fluid)
Clear, colourless liquid which fills the ventricles of the brain and the subarachnoid space. Contains high concentrations of sodium, chloride and magnesium ions. Normally circulates at a pressure of 100-200 mm of water.

CVA (cerebro-vascular accident)
Refers to disruption of the brain's blood supply either through a thrombus (blood clot) or an embolus (a clot or group of cells/bacteria originating in another part of the body and travelling to the brain); such anomalies can result in rupture of the blood vessels causing bleeding into surrounding tissue.

Dendrite
Tree-like pathways which terminate close to the cell body of a neuron.

Diencephalon
Literally the 'between-brain'; term for the upper portion of the brain stem.

Dura mater
The tough, outer meningeal layer of membrane which protects the brain and anchors it within the skull.

Dysarthria
Defect of articulation manifesting as slurring of consonants.

Dysprosody
Defect of articulation where melodic intonation is disrupted.

Efferent
Pathways conducting information out of the brain.

Encephalitis
Inflammation of the brain.

Endocrine
Internal gland(s) which secrete hormones into the bloodstream.

Fasciculus
Literally 'little bundle'; refers to a slender bundle of nerve fibres.

Frontal
Of, or pertaining to, the forehead.

Geniculate
Literally 'little knee'; refers to bent or angled neural fibres.

Glial cells
Non-nervous cells which comprise half the bulk of the brain. These cells play an important supportive role to the nerve cells and are one of the major sources of primary tumours in the central nervous system (also called neuroglia).

Gyrus
Literally 'circle'; refers to a ridge in the convolutions of the cerebral cortex.

Hemiplegia
Paralysis or weakness of one side of the body.

Hippocampus
Brain structure next to the temporal horn of the lateral ventricle.

Hydrocephalus
Excessive production of cerebro-spinal fluid which leads to compression of the brain.

Hypothalamus
The brain structure immediately below the thalamus.

Infarct
Dead brain tissue caused by interruption of blood supply.

Inhibition
To restrain; refers to prevention of nerve cell firing.

Ischaemia
Refers to blood starvation of a region of neural tissue.

Lesion
Literally to 'hurt or injure'; refers to any morbid change in tissues due to disease or injury.

Limbic system
Literally 'a border'; the system forms a border around the upper end of the brain stem.

Macropsia
Refers to a disorder of perception where familiar objects appear enlarged.

Median longitudinal sulcus
The deep fissure that runs from the frontal to the occipital lobes and demarcates the two cerebral hemispheres (also longitudinal fissure).

Medulla oblongata
Situated between the pons and the spinal cord, this lowest
part of the brain stem contains the reticular formation,
cranial nerves and cells mediating cardio-vascular and
respiratory mechanisms.

Meninges
General term for any of the non-nervous membranes which
cover the brain.

Meningioma
A benign, slow-growing tumour emanating from the meninges.

Mesencephalon
Term for the midbrain.

Metastic
Unstable, fast growing; usually refers to secondary tumours
of the malignant variety found in tissue.

Micropsia
Refers to a disorder of perception where familiar objects
appear too small.

Neoplasm
New, abnormal growth of tissue.

Occipital
Of, or pertaining to, the back of the head.

Oedema
Swelling of tissue due to increase in fluid content.

Paradoxical sleep
Refers to a stage of sleep where brain wave activity is very
similar to the normal waking state. Behaviourally this can
be seen by rapid eye movements (REM) taking place although
the eyes remain closed. It is thought this stage coincides
with dreaming.

Paraphasia
Disorder of expressive language where an incorrect lexical
item is substituted for a correct one. Multiple paraphasias
result in the condition of Jargon-aphasia.

Parietal
Of, or pertaining to, the wall of the brain. The area
between the frontal and occipital lobes.

Perseveration
Refers to the tendency to repeat previously relevant actions
rather than solve current demands.

Plasticity
Tendency for psychological functions subserved by a
particular brain region to be transferred to a different
region when early damage occurs.

Pons
Literally 'a bridge'; consists of fibres which bridge across
the brain stem to the cerebellum on either side.

Posterior
At, or towards, the hind end of the brain.

Reticular formation
Literally 'a net'; the reticular formation is a lattice-like
arrangement of neurons which extent from the top of the
spinal cord through the brain stem and up into the thalamus
and hypothalamus. All incoming and outgoing transmissions of
the brain pass through the reticular formation.

Retrograde
In amnesia, loss of memory for events following damage.

Septal area
Part of the limbic system. It has widespread connections
with the brain stem and is involved in the central
processing of olfactory information.

Spike activity
Dramatic change in the amplitude of alpha waves recorded on
the electro-encephalogram. These variations in voltage
reflect changes in neuronal firing potentials which can
eventually culminate in a massive discharge producing a
seizure.

Splenium
Posterior area of the corpus callosum.

Split brain
Refers to the surgical procedure of commissurotomy where the
main bundle of interconnecting fibres between the cerebral
hemispheres (corpus callosum) is cut leaving only
subcortical interconnecting pathways intact.

Subarachnoid
Refers to the space between the second and third meningeal
membranes (the arachnoid and the pia mater). This space is
filled with cerebro-spinal fluid.

Sulcus
Literally 'a groove'; refers to the fissures in the cerebral
cortex.

Synapse
A conjunction or union; the space between an axon and the
body or dendrite of another cell.

Telencephalon
The far or endbrain.

Temporal
Of, or pertaining to, the temples of the head.

Thalamus
Literally 'inner chamber'; the thalamus receives the majority of sensory input and relays these transmissions to the cortex.

Ventral
Of, or on, the lower surface.

Ventricle
A chamber or cavity.

Vestibular
Literally 'passage or hall'; usually refers to specialized nuclei in the reticular formation which control muscular activity. These play a crucial role in balance and positional sense.

Wernicke's Area
First temporal gyrus of the left hemisphere.

References

Binet, A. and Simon, T. (1905)
Méthodes nouvelles pour le diagnostic du niveau intellectuel des anormaux. L'Année psychologique, 11, 191-244.

Benson, D.F. and Barton, M.I. (1970)
Disturbances in constructional ability. Cortex, 6, 19-46.

Benton, A.L. (1955)
The Visual Retention Test. New York: Psychological Corporation.

Benton, A.L. (1959)
Right-Left Discrimination and Finger Localization, Development and Pathology. New York: Hoeber-Harper.

Benton, A.L. (1967)
Problems of test construction in the field of aphasia. Cortex, 3, 32-58.

Benton, A.L. and Fogel, M.L. (1962)
Three dimensional constructional praxis. Archives of Neurology, 7, 347-354.

Broadbent, D.E. (1954)
The role of auditory localization in attention and memory span. Journal of Experimental Psychology, 47, 191-196.

Broca, P. (1861)
Nouvelle observation d'aphemie produite par une lésion de la moitié postérieure des deuxième et troisième circonvolutions frontales. Bulletin de la Societé Anatomique de Paris, 6, 398-407.

Brumfitt, S. and Clarke, P. (1982)

An application of psychotherapeutic techniques to the management of aphasia. In C. Code and D.J. Müller (eds), Aphasia Therapy. London: Arnold.

Butters, N., Soeloner, C. and Fedio, P. (1972)

Comparison of parietal and frontal lobe spatial deficits in man: extra-personal vs. personal (egocentric) space. Perceptual and Motor Skills, 34, 27-34.

Cattell, R.B. (1944)

A Culture Free Test. New York: Psychological Corporation.

Christensen, A.L. (1975)

Luria's Neuropsychological Investigation. Copenhagen: Munhogaard.

De Renzi, E., Faglioni, P., Savoiardo, M. and Vignolo, L.A. (1966)

The influence of aphasia and of hemispheric side of the cerebral lesion on abstract thinking. Cortex, 2, 399-420.

De Renzi, E., Faglioni, P., Scotti, G. and Spinnler, H. (1972)

Impairment in associating colour to form, concomitant with aphasia. Brain, 95, 293-304.

De Renzi, E., Vignolo, L.A. (1962)

The Token Test: a sensitive test to detect receptive disturbances in aphasics. Brain, 85, 665-678.

Duke, R. (1967)

Intellectual evaluation of brain damaged patients with a WAIS short form. Psychological Reports, 20, 185-206.

Faglioni, P., Spinnler, H. and Vignolo, L.A. (1969)

Contrasting behaviour of right and left hemisphere damaged patients on a discriminative and a semantic task of auditory recognition. Cortex, 5, 366-389.

Farmer, A. and O'Connell, P.F. (1979)

Neuropsychological processes in adult aphasia: rationale for treatment. British Journal of Disorders of Communication, 14, 39-49.

Gardener, E. (1975)

Fundamentals of Neurology. Philadelphia: Saunders.

Gazzaniga, M.S., Bogen, J.E. and Sperry, R.W. (1962)

Some functional effects of sectioning the cerebral commissures in man. Proceedings of the National Academy of Science, 48, 1765-1769.

Geschwind, N. (1965)

Disconnexion syndromes in animal and man. Brain, 88, 237-294.

Geschwind, N. (1979)

Some comments on the neurology of language. In D. Caplan (ed.), Biological studies of mental processes. Cambridge, Mass.: MIT Press.

Geschwind, N. and Levitsky, W. (1968)

Human brain: left-right asymmetries in temporal speech regions. Science, 161, 186-187.

Goldstein, K. and Scheerer, M. (1941)
Abstract and concrete behaviour: an experimental study with special tests. Psychological Monographs, 43, 1-151.

Grant, A.D. and Berg, E.A. (1948)
A behavioural analysis of degree of reinforcement and ease of shifting to new responses in a Weigl-type card sorting test. Journal of Experimental Psychology, 38, 404-411.

Grassi, J.R. (1947)
The Fairfield Block Substitution Test for measuring intellectual impairment. Psychiatric Quarterly, 21, 74-88.

Halstead, W.C. (1947)
Brain and Intelligence. Chicago: University of Chicago Press.

Hebb, D.O. (1949)
The Organization of Behavior. New York: Wiley.

Kimura, D. (1963)
Right temporal lobe damage: perception of unfamiliar stimuli after damage. Archives of Neurology, 8, 264-271.

Laurence, S. and Stein, D.G. (1978)
Recovery after brain damage and the concept of localization of function. In S. Finger (ed.), Recovery from Brain Damage. New York: Plenum Press.

Lezak, M.D. (1976)
Neuropsychological Assessment. New York: Oxford University Press.

Lhermitte, F. and Signoret, J.L. (1972)
Analysé neuropsychologique du syndrome frontal. Revue Neurologique, 126, 161-178.

Lorber, J. (1980)
Is your brain really necessary? Paper presented to the British Paediatric Association Annual Conference, York.

Luria, A.R. (1963)
Restoration of Brain Function after Brain Injury. New York: Macmillan.

Luria, A.R. (1966)
Higher Cortical Functions in Man. New York: Basic Books.

Luria, A.R. (1973)
The Working Brain. Harmondsworth: Penguin.

McElwain, D.W. and Kearney, G.E. (1970)
The Queensland Test. Melbourne: Australian Council for Educational Research.

MacKay, D. (1972)
The human brain. Reprinted from Science, special issue on the human brain, May, 1967. London: Paladin.

Meyer, V. (1957)
Critique of psychological approaches to brain damage. Journal of Mental Science, 103, 80-109.

Milner, B. (1965)
Visually guided maze learning in man: effects of bilateral frontal and unilateral cerebral lesions. Neuropsychologia, 3, 317-338.

Milner, B. (1974)
Functional recovery after lesions of the central nervous system. 3. Developmental processes in neural plasticity. Sparing of functions after early unilateral brain damage. Neurosciences Research Program Bulletin, 12, 213-217.

Milner, B., Branch, C. and Rasmussen, T. (1966)
Evidence for bilateral speech representation in some non-right handers. Transactions of the American Neurological Association, 91, 306-308.

Moniz, E. (1936)
Tentatives Operatoires, dans le Traitement de Certaines Psychoses. Paris: Masson et Cie.

Mulhall, D. (1978)
Dysphasic stroke patients and the influence of their relatives. British Journal of Disorders of Communication, 13, 127-134.

Müller, D.J. and Code, C. (1982)
Psychosocial Adjustment in Aphasia. In C. Code and D.J. Müller (eds), Aphasia Therapy. London: Arnold.

Osterreith, P.A. (1944)
Le test de copié d'une figure complexe. Archives de Psychologie, 30, 206-356.

Penfield, W. (1958)
The Excitable Cortex in Conscious Man. Springfield, Ill.: Thomas.

Penfield, W. and Perot, P. (1963)
The brain's record of auditory and visual experience. Brain, 86, 595-697.

Penfield, W. and Roberts, L. (1959)
Speech and Brain Mechanisms. Princeton, NJ: Princeton University Press.

Pillon, B. (1973)
L'apport de la méthode des temps de réaction dans l'étude des performances des malades atteints de lésions cérébrales. Anneé Psychologique, 73, 261-272.

Porteus, S.D. (1965)
Porteus Maze Test: Fifty years' application. Mountain View, Ca: Pacific Press.

Powell, G.E. (1981)
Brain Function Therapy. Farnborough, Hants.: Gower.

Powell, G.E., Clark, E. and Bailey, S. (1979)
Categories of aphasia: a cluster-analysis of Schuell test profiles. British Journal of Disorders of Communication, 14, 111-122.

Reitan, R.M. (1966)
A research programme on the psychological effects of brain lesions in human beings. In N.R. Ellis (ed.), International Review of Research in Mental Retardation. New York: Academic Press.

Rey, A. (1959)
Le test de copié de figure complexe. Paris: Editions Centre de Psychologie Appliquée.

Rosner, B.S. (1974)
Recovery of function and localization of function in

historical perspective. In D.G. Stein, J.J. Rosen and N. Butters (eds), Plasticity and Recovery of Function in the Central Nervous System. New York: Academic Press.

Rosvold, H.E., Mirsky, A.F. Sarason, I., Bransome, E.D. and Beck, L.H. (1956)
A continuous performance test of brain damage. Journal of Consulting Psychology, 20, 343–350.

Russell, E.W., Neuringer, C. and Goldstein, G. (1970)
Assessment of Brain Damage: A neuropsychological key approach. New York: Wiley.

Searleman, A. (1977)
A review of right hemisphere linguistic capabilities. Psychological Bulletin, 84, 503–528.

Schein, J.D. (1962)
Cross validation of the continuous performance test for brain damage. Journal of Consulting Psychology, 26, 115–118.

Schuell, H. (1965)
Differential Diagnosis of Aphasia. Minneapolis: University of Minnesota.

Smith, A. (1973)
Symbol Digit Modalities Test. Los Angeles, Ca: Western Psychological Services.

Sperry, R.W. (1968)
Hemisphere disconnection and unity in conscious awareness. American Psychologist, 23, 723–733.

Spreen, O. and Benton, A.L. (1969)
Neurosensory Centre Comprehensive Examination for Aphasia. Victoria, Canada: University of Victoria.

Thompson, J. (1978)
Cognitive effects of cortical lesions. In B.M. Foss (ed.), Psychology Survey No.1. London: Allen & Unwin.

Wada, J.A., Clarke, R. and Hann, A. (1975)
Cerebral hemispheric asymmetry in humans. Cortical speech zones in 100 adults and 100 infant brains. Archives of Neurology, 32, 239–246.

Walsh, K. (1978)
Neuropsychology - A clinical approach. Edinburgh: Churchill-Livingstone.

Wechsler, D. (1955)
The Wechsler Adult Intelligence Scale. New York: Psychological Corporation.

Weisenburg, T. and McBride, K.E. (1935)
Aphasia: A clinical and psychological study. New York: Commonwealth Fund.

Wernicke, C. (1874)
Der apasische symptomenkomplex. Breslau: Cohn and Weigert.

Questions

1. Describe the functioning of the major cortical lobes.
2. Outline the main neural pathologies which can result in physical and psychological dysfunction.
3. Discuss how you would set about investigating a case of suspected organic brain damage.

4. What factors should be kept in mind when assessing a recent stroke victim?
5. A patient is referred to you with temporal lobe epilepsy. This patient is being considered for a left temporal lobectomy to relieve the fits. How could you establish cerebral dominance for language function?
6. Compare the models of aphasia offered by Geschwind and Luria.
7. Discuss the models which have been put forward to account for recovery of function following brain damage.
8. Should neuropsychologists review their assessment procedures of psychological dysfunction?
9. Compare and contrast two treatment models in neuropsychology.
10. John is a 23-year-old accident victim. He has a right-sided hemiparesis and a pronounced non-fluent aphasia. Damage is diffuse to the left hemisphere which had to be subjected to emergency surgery after the accident. His parents wish to know what kind of prognosis can be expected. What assessments would you like to have carried out before making a statement?

Annotated reading

Benson, D.F. (1979) Aphasia, Alexia and Agraphia. New York: Churchill-Livingstone.
A modern review of disorders of language in clinical neuropsychology. This is a must for all clinicians.

Code, C. and Müller, D.J. (1982) Aphasia Therapy. London: Arnold.
A series of papers on different aspects of neuropsychological treatment.

Kolb, B. and Whishaw, I.Q. (1980) Fundamentals of Human Neuropsychology. San Francisco: Freeman.
A modern introductory text in human neuropsychology with useful illustrations.

Lezak, M.D. (1976) Neuropsychological Assessment. New York: Oxford University Press.
A very comprehensive and detailed text covering most clinical assessment methods.

Luria, A.R. (1973) The Working Brain. Harmondsworth: Penguin.
A classic introduction to Luria's unique approach to neuropsychology.

Powell, G.E. (1981) Brain Function Therapy. Farnborough, Hants.: Teakfield.
An important new book which reviews theories of neuropsychological treatment and offers a range of therapy strategies for different types of psychological dysfunction.

Walsh, K. (1978) Neuropsychology: A clinical approach. Edinburgh: Churchill-Livingstone.

This book provides a comprehensive statement of neuropsychology as well as discussion of assessment procedures.

Postscript
Harry Purser

Concluding remarks

In reflecting upon this book the reader may be struck by several aspects of psychology which deserve further reinforcement. There has been an emphasis throughout on the scientific basis of modern psychology. As Don Bannister pointed out in chapter 7 'definition is a social undertaking', and it should be clear that psychology does not lack definitions, nor does it tolerate dogma and the perpetuation of myths. Even our definition of what constitutes 'scientific psychology' is open to debate. However, sufficient agreement exists in psychology to maintain the momentum of development and generate both theoretical systems and practical explanations of human behaviour. Psychology does not claim these advances can only be appreciated and applied by psychologists; the relevance of psychological research to a whole range of professions is exemplified by the titles of other books in the series to which this book belongs. The relevance of methodical and critical enquiry to the practice of speech therapy should be clear.

Psychology also offers new ways of looking at old problems. The traditional medical approach to problems of personal health rests on certain fundamental assumptions of disease which are seriously questioned by recent research. A range of problems which were brought under the physiological umbrella are now seen as the result of complex interactions between mental and physical processes. We seem to be at the very beginning of a new era in health care. Psychology offers both the conceptual systems needed to view personal health in this way, and the techniques to investigate these complex interactions. The implications of this shift in emphasis are considerable. We may need to re-examine our classification systems to reflect changing knowledge; we will need constantly to review training in the health professions; we can look forward to the development of intervention strategies which improve their power by responding to the unique range of problems presented by each individual patient.

Psychology and speech therapy enjoy close relations because of their common interest in problems of human communication. This interest is not just academic, because speech therapists, together with educational and clinical psychologists, are the practitioners of psychological treatment. The demands of independent clinical status also ensure a common training between psychologists and speech therapists in relation to research design, intervention, evaluation and interaction. Such common concerns have been highlighted in the book and should lead to greater co-operation between the professions in the future.

Many professions now recognize the very considerable personal involvement that results from therapeutic transactions. No matter how objective and standardized our tools may be, they do not shield the clinician from the personal nature of therapy. Recognition of this fact of life makes for better therapists and better therapy. It provides opportunities for us to discuss honestly our difficulties in various situations. Psychology therefore has personal relevance for the professional and is not simply for application to 'patients'.

These considerations have formed the rationale for the book and have guided the selection of material. Within the limitations of one book only some aspects of a topic can be discussed. There are other areas of psychology of relevance to speech therapy which have either not been mentioned, or have been mentioned only briefly. Nevertheless, we hope the book has at least given a flavour of professional psychology which may whet the appetite of its readers to pursue their interests in psychology further.

Index